Batsford Chess Library

The Complete King's Indian

Raymond Keene and Byron Jacobs

An Owl Book
Henry Holt and Company
New York

To Sue

First published in the United States in 1992 by
Henry Holt and Company, Inc., 115 West 18th Street,
New York, New York 10011.
Originally published in Great Britain in 1992 by
B. T. Batsford Ltd.

Library of Congress Catalog Card Number: 92-54264

ISBN 0-8050-2429-8 (An Owl Book: pbk.)

Henry Holt books are available at special discounts for
bulk purchases for sales promotions, premiums,
fund-raising, or educational use. Special editions or
book excerpts can also be created to specification.

For details contact: Special Sales Director,
Henry Holt and Company, Inc., 115 West 18th Street,
New York, New York 10011.

First American Edition—1992

Printed in the United Kingdom
Recognizing the importance of preserving the written
word, Henry Holt and Company, Inc., by policy, prints
all of its first editions on acid-free paper. ∞

10 9 8 7 6 5 4 3 2 1

Advisor: R. D. Keene GM, OBE
Technical Editor: Andrew Kinsman

Contents

Symbols

+	Check	-+	Winning for Black
++	Double check	1-0	White wins
!	Good move	0-1	Black wins
!!	Excellent move	½-½	Draw
?	Bad move	=	The position is equal
??	Blunder	∞	Unclear positions
!?	Interesting move	⧜	With counterplay
?!	Dubious move	△	With the idea of
±	Small edge for White	Ch.	Championship
∓	Small edge for Black	Ol.	Olympiad
±	Clear edge for White	Corr.	Correspondence
∓	Clear edge for Black	Izt.	Interzonal
+-	Winning for White	Zt.	Zonal

Note on Evaluations

The trademark of the modern interpretation of the King's Indian Defence is that at the slightest excuse Black will make a sacrifice of a pawn, the exchange or even a piece to unsettle and disturb White's strategic manoeuvres. Black's king is so well protected in the King's Indian that if he can detonate the situation, even at material cost, White's king is liable to be drawn into the firing line. For this reason modern King's Indian positions are devilishly difficult to assess. The traditional textbook evaluations of "slightly better for White", "equal", "unclear" or "compensation for sacrificed material" virtually meld into one composite description which is germane to so many contemporary King's Indian situations.

Bibliography

A variety of sources were consulted in the preparation of this book. The following were particularly useful:

King's Indian Defence, Barden, Hartston & Keene (Batsford)
Encyclopaedia of Chess Openings, vol E, ed. Matanovic (Sahovski Informator)
Batsford Chess Openings, Kasparov & Keene (Batsford)
The Test of Time, Kasparov (Pergamon)
Winning with the King's Indian, Gufeld (Batsford)
Trends in the King's Indian 6 $\Diamond$e2, vol. 2, Gallagher (Trends Publications)
Informator, (Sahovski Informator)
New in Chess, (Interchess)

ChessBase has also been used as a source of opening material. For further information on *ChessBase*, please contact: Byron Jacobs, 23 Ditchling Rise, Brighton, Sussex BN1 4QL (Tel: 0273 – 686507, Fax: 0273 – 675486).

Introduction

The King's Indian Defence clearly belongs to the 'hyper-modern' group of responses to 1 d4 in that Black concedes his opponent the right to occupy the centre with pawns at the start of play. However, it was hardly used by the 'hypermodern' masters at all. A rudimentary form of the King's Indian is nascent in the games of Chigorin, but in the 1920s it was employed only by British masters, such as Yates and, sporadically, by Reti, Tartakower and Euwe.

Its dynamic potential was first recognised by the rising generation of Soviet players in the 1940s (notably Bronstein and Boleslavsky) and by the 1950s it was established as one of the most popular openings in tournament praxis. If we examine the games of the 1953 Candidates Tournament it transpires that one fifth of the games played opened with the King's Indian.

Up to the present day the King's Indian has occupied a prominent place in the repertoire of the world's leading masters. Perhaps its greatest exponent is the World Champion, Gary Kasparov, and references to his elegant victories with this defence will be found passim throughout this volume.

Kasparov's patronage of the King's Indian Defence at the very highest level, including games against Karpov, Ivanchuk, Yusupov, Timman and Korchnoi, has led to a massive explosion of interest in this defence. The emphasis of this book is very heavily directed towards recent material which has been generated as a result of the numerous enthusiastic followers of the World Champion's example. In many cases, it will be seen that the new material totally overturns long-established theoretical beliefs.

Our analysis also indicates that by far the two most popular systems employed against the King's Indian are the Classical with 6 ♗e2 and the Saemisch. We open this book with a sample of each system. Both of these games end in attractive victories for Black.

Krogius – Stein
Kiev 1960

1	d4	♘f6
2	c4	g6
3	♘c3	♗g7
4	e4	0-0
5	♗e2	d6
6	♘f3	e5

This is a major crossroads in this opening system: the main line, to which much of this book is devoted, is now 7 0-0 ♘c6 8 d5 ♘e7. After the follow-up 9 ♘d2 a5 10 a3 ♘d7 11 ♖b1 f5 12 b4 ♔h8 13 f3 ♘g8 14 ♕c2 ♘gf6, we come to what might be classed as a *tabiya* (or starting position) for the 1990s.

(see following diagram)

Vassily Ivanchuk recently produced an important novelty with 15 ♗d3!? in a crucial game against World Champion Gary Kasparov in

their game from Linares 1992. The game continued 15 ... f4 16 ♘b5 b6 17 c5 dxc5 18 bxa5 ♖xa5 19 ♘c4 ♖a8 20 a4 ♘e8 21 a5 ♗a6 22 ♗d2 ♗xb5 23 ♖xb5 ♘d6 24 ♖b2 ♕e7 25 ♘xd6 ♕xd6 26 ♗b5 and White held a clear advantage although Kasparov hung on for the draw.

Boris Gelfand was evidently impressed by Ivanchuk's innovation, as in the very next round at Linares, he sidestepped it with the relatively untested 14 ... ♗h6. However, in this instance, the cure turned out to be worse than the disease, and he went down horribly after 15 ♘b5 axb4 16 axb4 ♘df6 17 c5 fxe4 18 ♘xe4 ♘xd5 19 cxd6 c6 20 ♕c5 ♗d7 21 ♗xh6 ♘xh6 22 ♘c7 b6 23 ♕c1 ♘f4 24 ♕b2 ♘xe2+ 25 ♕xe2 ♖c8 26 ♕b2 ♘f7 27 f4 ♘xd6 28 ♕xe5+

♔g8 29 ♘e6 ♗xe6 30 ♕xe6+
♘f7 31 ♖bd1 ♕c7 32 ♖d7
♕b8 33 f5 1-0.

This gives some indica-
tion of the frightening rate
at which the theory of this
absorbing opening is developing. For the full theoretical background to these
fascinating encounters see
the game Epishin – van
Wely, Wijk aan Zee 1992,
analysed in chapter four.

7 d5 h6

The most straightfor-
ward method of preventing
White's pin with ♗g5. It is
not the best, though, since
it creates certain prema-
ture weaknesses in Black's
king's field.

8 0-0?!

Much too co-operative.
Better is the flexible 8 ♘d2
which gives White the op-
tion of 0-0-0, e.g. 8 ...
♘bd7 9 g4 a5 10 ♘f1 ♘c5 11
♘g3 c6 12 ♗e3 ♗d7 13 f3 a4
14 ♕d2 cxd5 15 cxd5 ♕a5 16
♘d1!± Keene – Westerinen,
Berlin 1971; or 8 ... a5 9
♘f1 ♘a6 10 g4 ♘h7 11 h4 f5
12 gxf5 gxf5 13 exf5 ♗xf5 14
♘g3 ♕d7 15 ♗e3 ♘b4 16 ♖c1
e4 17 ♖g1 Donner – Kavalek,
Skopje Ol. 1972. White later
decided the game by a di-
rect kingside assault.

	8	...	♘h7
	9	♘e1	♘d7
	10	♘d3	f5
	11	f3	

A passive decision which
permits Black a free hand
on the kingside. Gufeld recommends 11 f4, while 11
exf5 gxf5 12 f4 would also
lead to a safe position.

11 ... f4!

Black does not hesitate
to establish the kingside
pawn wedge which is so
characteristic of many variations of the King's Indian.

12 b4 ♖f7

An absolutely key move
which fulfils a number of
vital and typical King's Indian functions, viz.

a) The rook on f7 defends
c7, which, as the base of
Black's pawn chain, is the
principal target of White's
queenside ambitions.

b) By moving his rook,
Black vacates f8 for his
king's bishop, preparing the
possibility of ... ♖g7 and
then ... g5 - g4, assaulting
White's pawn chain at the
base on f3 and g2. In the
further course of this game,
the black king's bishop also

develops fierce activity from f8. This is an unusual bonus, since the lines of central pawns often remain fixed on d5, e4, f3 / d6, e5, f4, respectively, thus impeding any dramatic intervention by Black's king's bishop.

13 c5   ♘df6
14 c6

This advance was successful in broadly similar circumstances in other games around this time, but in this case, Stein has an amazing tactical counterstroke available, based on White's vulnerability on the a7 – g1 diagonal.

14 ...   bxc6

This could lead to positional disaster, since White is granted a threatening queenside pawn majority and a dream blockade square for the knight on d5; 14 ... b6 deprives White of these various advantages but then the pawn on c7 would be a horrible fixed weakness in any endgame and Black would not be able to generate any kind of dynamic counter-activity.

15 dxc6   ♗e6
16 b5   ♗f8
17 ♘b4

All now seems set for the successful implementation of White's blockade strategy, but Stein's next

move sprays napalm across the board.

17 ...   d5!!
18 ♘bxd5

Or 18 exd5 ♗f5 19 ♘d3 ♘h5 threatening the typical and ineluctable procedure ... ♗xd3 followed by ... ♗c5+, ♔h1, then ... ♘g3+. hxg3, ... ♕g5 and mate on the h-file.

18 ...   ♗c5+
19 ♔h1   ♘h5
20 ♕e1

Again, he has to stop 20 ... ♘g3+ 21 hxg3 fxg3 and ... ♕h4 mate.

20 ...   ♘g3+!

But Stein still plays it, apparently with the sole

motive of disorganising White's defensive wall. This sacrifice is barely credible, yet the ensuing justification looks even more of a fairy-tale.

  21 hxg3   ♕g5
  22 g4   h5
  23 g3

White can try to beat back Black's offensive king's bishop with 23 ♘a4 but then comes a fresh sacrifice: 23 ... hxg4 24 ♘xc5 g3 and White's king is entombed.

  23 ...   hxg4
  24 ♔g2   ♖af8
  25 ♗d2

A natural enough developing move, but Gufeld suggests that 25 ♖h1 might be better, preventing the following manoeuvre. But what Stein now plays is so arcane a method of pursuing his attack that it is not at all obvious what White should be preventing!

  25 ...   ♕h6
  26 ♖h1   ♕g7

Black's queen looks buried on g7, but the plan is to support ... g5 followed by ... gxf3+ and finally ... g4.

  27 gxf4

Apart from the concept mentioned in the previous note, Black was also threatening to open the f-file for the massed artillery of his rooks, with ... fxg3. Krogius', choice stops this, but invites the black queen to reappear along the a1-h8 diagonal.

  27 ...   exf4
  28 ♖d1   g5

Again ... gxf3+ and ... g4 looms.

  29 e5

Relying on one of two variations: 29 ... ♕xe5 30 fxg4 ♗xd5+ 31 ♘xd5 ♕xd5+ 32 ♗f3 ♕xa2 33 ♕e5; or 29 ... ♕xe5 30 fxg4 f3+ 31 ♗xf3 ♕xe1 32 ♖hxe1 ♖xf3 33 ♖xe6 ♖f2+ 34 ♔h1 ♖8f3 35 ♗e3! Both lines do credit to Krogius's powers of calculation and resourcefulness, but Stein has seen much more.

  29 ...   ♕xe5
  30 fxg4
  (see following diagram)
  30 ...   ♕xe2+!!

What a shock, a whole queen sacrificed, but it is totally sound: 31 ♘xe2 ♗xd5+ 32 ♔h2 ♘f6 and ... ♖h7 or 32 ♔f1 f3! followed

by ... ♗c4. White's choice survives longer but leaves him helpless.

31	♕xe2	f3+
32	♕xf3	♖xf3
33	♖hf1	♗xg4
34	♘e4	♗h3+
35	♔h2	♖xf1
36	♖xf1	♗xf1
37	♘xc5	♖f2+
38	♔g1	♖xd2
39	♘xc7	♗h3
40	a4	♖g2+
41	♔h1	♘f6
42	a5	♘g4
43	♘e4	♖e2
	0-1	

A game of mystical depth, which is certainly one of the most brilliant games ever played with the King's Indian.

**Gheorghiu – Kavalek
Amsterdam 1969**

1	d4	♘f6
2	c4	g6
3	♘c3	♗g7
4	e4	d6
5	f3	0-0
6	♗e3	♘c6
7	♘ge2	♖b8
8	♕d2	♖e8

This variation is dealt with in detail in chapter 12.

In the 1960s and early 1970s White almost invariably sought to maintain a space advantage in the centre in this variation of the Saemisch King's Indian. To that end manoeuvres such as ♘e2 - c1 - b3 combined with ♖d1 were common to shore up White's central bastions. Nowadays, all this is rightly regarded as an over-refinement. White players tend to prefer a blunt plan involving castling queenside followed by a vigorous advance of White's g- and h-pawns in order to come directly to grips with the black king.

| 9 | ♖d1 |

At the time, a state of the art concept introduced by Petrosian, the World Champion no less. In those days much analysis was also devoted to variations such as 9 ♘c1 e5 10 ♘b3 exd4 11 ♘xd4 d5 12 cxd5 ♘xd5 13 ♘xd5 ♘xd4 14 ♗xd4 ♕xd5 15 ♗xg7 ♕xd2+ 16 ♔xd2 ♔xg7 with equality. Alternatively 9 ♘c1 e5 10 d5 ♘d4 11 ♘b3 c5 12 dxc6 bxc6 13 ♘xd4 exd4 14 ♗xd4 d5 15 cxd5 cxd5 16 e5 ♘h5 17 ♗b5 ♖xe5+ 18 ♗xe5 ♗xe5 with immense compensation for Black for a trifling material investment.

	9	...	a6
	10	♘c1	e5
	11	dxe5	

If 11 d5 ♘d4 12 ♘ce2 c5 13 dxc6 bxc6 14 ♘xd4 exd4 15 ♗xd4 d5 16 cxd5 cxd5 17 e5 ♘h5 18 ♗e2 ♕h4+ 19 ♗f2 ♕b4 with active counterplay for Black.

	11	...	♘xe5
	12	♗e2	

After this game 12 b3 came into fashion!

| | 12 | ... | b5! |

This sacrifical thrust releases all of the energy stored in the Black position while White's development is still in its infancy.

	13	cxb5	axb5
	14	♗xb5	

Or 14 ♘xb5 ♘xf3+ 15 gxf3 ♘xe4 16 fxe4 ♕h4+ 17 ♗f2 ♕xe4 with a powerful attack.

| | 14 | ... | ♘xe4! |

So far Black has just sacrificed one pawn in the interests of liberating his pieces. The text move bombards White with a hail of piece sacrifices while his king is still stuck in the centre.

	15	fxe4	♖xb5
	16	♘xb5	♘c4
	17	♕f2	

17 ♕d3! was White's last chance to make a fight of it.

	17	...	♖xe4
	18	0-0	♘xe3
	19	♕xf7+	♔h8
	20	♕xc7	♕xc7
	21	♘xc7	♘xd1
	22	♖xd1	

After the storm has passed White is simply ground down by the power of Black's bishops. These pieces show up to superb advantage on an open board.

22	...	♗d4+
23	♔f1	♗g4
24	♖d2	♗e3
25	♖c2	♖d4
	0-1	

A wonderful display of imaginative pyrotechnics and a classic exposition of Black's dynamic resources in the King's Indian Defence

1) Classical 9 ♘e1 ♘d7 10 f3 f5 11 ♘d3

This chapter explores the complex variations arising from the above sequence. The material is split up as follows:

Game 1 examines the position after 11 ... ♘f6 12 ♗d2 f4 13 c5. This leads to the classical King's Indian horse race and whoever maintains stamina for the longest is liable to emerge victorious. These variations have fallen slightly into disfavour during the last few years, perhaps because the theory runs very deep and players have become bored with starting the real game on move 25. Nevertheless, these lines give an excellent flavour of how the respective flank attacks should be conducted.

Game 2 is similar to Game 1, but White plays to hold Black up on the kingside with 13 g4. This is obviously double-edged; if White succeeds in closing the kingside, Black will be almost lost as there will be no counterplay against the inevitable queenside breakthrough. Black must keep the situation fluid and be alert for chances to exploit the loosening of the white king.

Game 3 tidies up some odds and ends as well as examining Nunn's recent try 12 ... h5!?

Game 4 features the trendy 12 ... ♔h8. Following Kasparov's lead, this is the move that all the fashion-conscious King's Indian players are sporting. Black tucks the king away, maintains the tension and waits to see how White intends to set out his stall before responding.

Game 1
Ftacnik - Zsu Polgar
Trencianske Teplice 1985

1	d4	♘f6
2	c4	g6
3	♘c3	♗g7
4	e4	d6
5	♘f3	0-0
6	♗e2	e5

7	0-0	♘c6
8	d5	♘e7
9	♘e1	♘d7
10	♘d3	f5
11	f3	♘f6
12	♗d2	f4
13	c5 *(1)*	

13 ...   g5

13 ... c6 is a rather feeble move, not really in the spirit of the King's Indian. Black aims to equalise the position but remains slightly worse with few prospects for counterplay, e.g. 14 cxd6 ♕xd6 15 dxc6 ♘xc6 16 ♘b5 ♕e7 (16 ... ♕d8 17 ♘b4 ♗e6 18 ♗e1 ♖f7 19 ♕xd8+ ♖xd8 20 ♘xc6 bxc6 21 ♘a3 ♗f8 22 ♗c4 ♗c5+ 23 ♗f2 ♗xf2+ 24 ♖xf2± Cvetkovic - Pavlov, Trnava 1981. Black has no compensation for the weak queenside pawns) 17 ♘b4 ♗e6 18 ♘xc6 bxc6 19 ♘a3 ♕c5+ (19 ... ♘d7 20 ♕c2 ♖ab8 21 ♖fc1± Sosonko - Hübner, Wijk aan Zee 1982) 20 ♔h1 ♘h5 21 ♗c4! (A neat tactic to further White's positional aims

by exchanging the light-squared bishops) 21 ... ♗xc4 22 ♕c2 ♕e7 23 ♕xc4+ ♖f7 24 ♖fd1± Ftacnik - Gufeld, Tallinn 1981. Black has a miserable position.

14 cxd6

14 ♖c1 ♘g6 (14 ... h5 15 ♘b5 ♘e8 16 cxd6 cxd6 17 a4 ♖f6 18 ♘f2 ♖g6 19 h3 ♔h8 20 ♕b3± Neverov - Khalifman, USSR 1985) 15 ♘b5? (This loses White too much time and Black swiftly crashes through on the opposite wing) 15 ... a6! 16 ♘a3 (Larsen gives 16 cxd6 axb5 17 dxc7 ♕d7 18 ♕b3∞) 16 ... g4 17 cxd6 cxd6 18 ♘c4 g3 19 h3 ♗xh3! 20 gxh3 b5 21 ♖e1 bxc4 22 ♖xc4 ♘h4 23 ♗f1 h5 24 ♗g2 ♘h7 25 ♖f1 ♘g5 26 ♕a4 ♖c8 27 ♖b4 ♖c7 28 ♖b6 ♕c8 29 ♖c6 ♕xh3! (30 ♗xh3 ♘xh3+ 31 ♔h1 g2+ wins) 0-1 Hoeksema - Riemersma, Dutch Ch. 1987.

14 ...   cxd6
15 ♖c1

15 ♘f2 is a major alternative, usually indicating White's desire to leave c1 free for the king's rook. 15 ... ♘g6 (This is frequently an essential part of Black's plan, but attempts have been made to delay it or get by without it altogether, e.g. 15 ... h5 16 h3 *♖f7 (16 ... ♔h8 17 ♕c2 ♘eg8 18 ♘b5 ♘e8 19 a4 ♘h6 20 ♖fc1 ♗d7∞ Stone - Roeder,*

Gausdal 1991) 17 ♕c2 ♔h8
(17 ... ♗f8 18 ♖fc1 ♗d7 19 a4
♖g7 20 ♕d1 a6 21 a5 ♔h8 22
♘a4 ♘c8 23 ♖c4± Stean -
Sanz, Marbella 1982) 18 ♘b5
♘e8 19 ♖fc1 ♘g8 20 ♘xa7
♖c7 21 ♗a5 ♖xc2 22 ♗xd8
♖xe2 23 ♘xc8 ♖xb2 24
♗xg5 ♖axa2 25 ♖xa2 ♖xa2
and was soon drawn Kraut
- Hug, Zug 1989) 16 ♕c2 h5
17 h3 (This is almost a re-
flex action against ... h5,
but White doesn't neces-
sarily have to be so single-
minded, e.g. 17 ♘b5 ♖f7 18
♖fc1 ♘e8 19 a4 ♘h4 20 h3
♗f8 21 ♘xa7 ♗d7 22 ♘b5
g4∞ Kozul - Sznapik, Tbi-
lisi 1988).

After 17 h3 *(2)* Black's
possibilities are:

2
B

a) 17 ... a6 18 a4 ♖f7 19 a5
b5?!(Opening the queenside
for White seems a strange
way to play - it certainly
doesn't work well here) 20
axb6 ♕xb6 21 ♘a4 ♕d8 22
♖fc1 ♗f8 23 ♖a3± Sosonko
- Bouaziz, Hannover 1983.

b) 17 ... ♘e8!? (Black in-

tends to regroup his king's
bishop by means of the
manoeuvre ♗g7-f6-d8) 18
a4 ♗f6 19 ♖a3 ♕c7!? 20 ♖c1
♗d8 21 ♘b5 with a slight
edge for White, Karpov -
van der Wiel, Brussels 1987.

c) 17 ... g4!? 18 fxg4 hxg4
19 hxg4 ♘e8 20 a4 ♗f6 21
♘h3 ♗h4 22 ♘d1 ♖f7 23
♘df2 ♖h7 24 ♖a3 ♘f6 25 a5
♗d7 26 ♕d1 with unclear
play, Möhring - Uhlmann,
Halle 1981.

d) 17 ... ♖f7:

d1) 18 a4 ♗f8 (18 ... ♗h6 is
the wrong idea, e.g. 19 ♖a3
♘h4 20 ♖c1 g4 21 hxg4
hxg4 22 fxg4 f3 23 ♗xh6
♘xg4 24 ♘xg4 ♗xg4 25
♕d2 fxe2 26 ♘xe2± Hort -
Maier, West German Ch.
1987) 19 ♘b5 a6 20 ♘a3 ♖g7
21 ♖fc1 ♘h4 22 ♕d1 ♗d7 23
♘c4 g4 24 hxg4 hxg4 25
fxg4 ♘xg2! (Kasparov cra-
shes through in familiar
style) 26 ♔xg2 ♘xg4 27
♗xg4 ♗xg4 28 ♕xg4 ♖xg4+
29 ♘xg4 ♖c8 30 ♘h2 ♕h4 31
♖c3 ♖c7 32 ♖g1 ♖g7+ 33 ♔h1
♖xg1+ 34 ♔xg1 ♕h7! (This
terminates the struggle as
White cannot afford to
lose the e-pawn) 35 ♗xf4
exf4 36 ♘d2 ♕d7 37 ♖c4
♗g7 38 b3 ♗d4+ 39 ♔h1 ♗c5
40 ♘df3 b5 41 ♖c2 ♕e8 42
♖g2+ ♔f8 43 ♘g5 ♕h5 44
♘e6+ ♔e7 45 ♖g7+ ♔f6 46
♖g4 bxa4 47 bxa4 ♗e3 48
♘xf4 ♗xf4 49 ♖xf4+ ♔e7 50

♔g2 ♕d1 51 ♘g4 ♕xa4 52 ♘e3 a5 53 ♘f5+ ♔d7 54 ♖h4 ♕c2+ 55 ♔f3 a4 56 ♖h7+ ♔d8 57 ♖a1 ♕d3 58 ♘e3 a3 59 ♔f4 ♕b3 60 ♘f5 ♕b2 0-1 Yuferov - Kasparov, Minsk 1978.

In his youth, Kasparov was an avid King's Indian fan, but during the mid 80s he placed himself on a harsh regimen of QGDs to combat Karpov in their World Championship matches. Now, of course, he is back at the forefront of the theoretical debate and several of the main lines have undergone reassessments due to his efforts.

d2) 18 ♖fc1 g4 (This is the most thematic, but equally playable are 18 ... ♗f8 19 ♘b5 ♘e8 20 a4 ♗d7 21 ♕b3 ♘h4 22 ♖c3 a6 23 ♘a3 ♖g7± Neverov - Akopjan, Minsk 1990 or 18 ... a6 19 a4 ♗f8 20 a5 g4 21 fxg4 hxg4 22 hxg4 b5 23 axb6 ♕xb6 24 ♘a4 ♕a7 25 ♗a5 ♖b8 26 g5!± Rogers - Sznapik, Thessaloniki Ol. 1988) 19 hxg4 hxg4 20 fxg4 ♘e8 (20 ... ♘h7 21 ♘b5 ♘g5 22 a4 ½-½ Sosonko - Kavalek, Tilburg 1980 was not very revealing) 21 a4 ♗f6 22 ♖a3 ♗h4 23 ♘cd1 ♗g3 24 ♘h3 (not 24 ♖c3 ♗d7 25 ♗b5 ♗xb5 26 axb5 ♕h4 and Black had a powerful attack, Andruet - Spasov, Sofia 1990) 24 ...

♕h4 25 ♘df2 ♘f6 26 ♕d1 ♗d7 27 a5 ♖af8 28 ♗e1 ½-½ Sosonko - Hellers, Wijk aan Zee 1986.

15 ...   ♘g6
16 ♘b5 *(3)*

The most direct. This is not the moment for White to switch attention to the kingside, e.g. 16 ♘f2 h5 17 h3 ♖f7 18 a4 ♗f8 19 ♘b5 ♖g7 (less effective is 19 ... ♘h4 20 a5 ♖g7 21 ♗b4 g4 22 fxg4 hxg4 23 hxg4=) 20 ♖c3 ♘h4 21 ♗e1 a6 22 ♘a3 ♗d7 23 a5 ♖c8 24 ♘c4 ♗b5 25 ♘b6 ♖xc3 26 ♗xc3 ♕e8 and the threats are looming against the white king, Zaltsman - Evans, USA Ch. 1980.

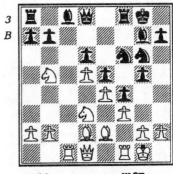

16 ...   ♖f7
17 ♕c2

17 ♘f2 a6! (this works out very well and the remainder of this game should serve as a warning to White not to hang around after ♘b5) 18 ♘a3 b5 19 ♕e1 h5 20 ♗a5 ♕f8 21 h3 g4 22 fxg4 hxg4 23

♘xg4 ♗xg4 24 ♗xg4 ♘xg4
25 hxg4 ♗f6 26 ♕e2 ♗h4 27
♖c3 ♗g3 28 g5 ♕e7 29 ♕h5
♕a7+ 0-1 Gligoric - Quinteros, Novi Sad 1982.

17 ...   ♘e8

Others:

a) 17 ... g4 18 ♘c7 gxf3 19
gxf3 ♗h3 20 ♘e6 ♕e7 21 ♖f2
♗h6 22 ♔h1 ♔h8 was unclear in Ftacnik - I Ivanov, Hastings 1984.

b) 17 ... ♕b6+ 18 ♘f2 g4!?
19 ♘c7 ♖b8 20 ♕b3 ♕xb3 21
axb3 g3 22 ♘d3 ♗d7 and White maintains an edge, Ftacnik - Babula, Czechoslovakia 1986.

18 a4   h5
19 ♘f2   ♗f8

Alternatively:

a) 19 ... a6 20 ♘a3 ♘h4 21
♘c4 g4 22 fxg4 b5 23 ♗a5
♕g5 24 ♘b6 hxg4 25 ♘xa8
g3 26 ♘g4 Ftacnik - Vokac, Czechoslovakia 1981 is a typical piece of King's Indian madness. Black jettisons his entire queenside in the interests of chasing the more substantial booty on the kingside.

b) 19 ... ♗d7 20 ♕b3 ♗f8
21 a5 ♖g7 22 h3 ♘h4 23 ♗e1
♔h8 24 ♘a3 ♘f6 25 ♖c3 ♗e7
26 ♕xb7 ♖b8 27 ♕xa7 g4 28
fxg4 ♖xb2 29 ♘c2 with a balanced position, Toth - Bouaziz, Reggio Emilia 1983.

20 h3 *(4)*

After 20 ♘xa7, Black can

either head for a marginally worse endgame or, more adventurously, play the position as a pawn sacrifice. For example:

a) 20 ... ♖c7 21 ♗a5 ♖xc2
22 ♗xd8 ♖xe2 23 ♘xc8
♖xa4 24 ♘d3 g4 25 ♖f2 ♖e3
26 ♘e1 ♖a8 27 ♖fc2 ♖b3 28
♔f2 ♖a2 29 ♖b1 ♔f7 30 ♔e2
♗g7 (30 ... ♗e7 31 ♘xe7
♘xe7 32 ♘d3 ♖a8 33 ♗xe7
♔xe7= Novikov - Glek, USSR 1985) 31 ♘d3 ♗f6 32
♗b6 ♖a8 33 ♗f2 ♗h4 34 ♗g1
♗d8 35 ♘c1± ♖b4 36 b3 ♖a3
37 ♖a2 ♖a6 38 ♖c2 ♘h4 39
♘a2 ♖xa2 40 ♖xa2 ♘xg2 41
♖a4 ♖xa4 42 bxa4 ♘h4 43
♖xb7+ ♔f8 44 fxg4 hxg4 45
♗b6 ♗xb6 46 ♘xb6 ♘f3 47
♘d7+ ♔g8 48 a5 ♘xh2 49 a6
1-0 Miles - Vukic, Bugojno 1978.

b) 20 ... ♗d7 (Black pretends nothing untoward has happened and proceeds with his kingside play) 21
♘b5 ♖g7 22 h3 ♘h4 23 ♕b3
(This is a standard move for White but here it has the extra point that 23 ... ♘f6?
can be met by 24 ♘c7 ♖c8
25 ♘e6 ♗xe6 26 dxe6 with a check coming up on the diagonal. Additionally, 23 ...
g4?! 24 fxg4 hxg4 25 hxg4
♘f6 26 ♘c7 ♘xg4 27 ♘e6
♘xf2 28 ♖xf2 ♗xe6 29 dxe6
♔h8 30 ♖c3 ♗e7 31 ♖h3
Ftacnik - Vokac, Czechoslovakia 1982, clearly fa-

vours White) 23 ... ♚h8 24 a5 g4 25 fxg4 hxg4 26 hxg4 ♘f6 27 ♘c7 ♘xg4! (Sax gets on with it. If now 28 ♘xa8 then 28 ... ♘e3 29 ♗xe3 ♖xg2+ 30 ♚h1 ♕g5 △ ... ♕g3 or ... ♖h2+ finishes White) 28 ♗xg4 ♗xg4 29 ♘xg4 ♖xg4 30 ♖f2 ♕g5 31 ♚h3 (The rook is still taboo, e.g. 31 ♘xa8 ♖xg2+ 32 ♚f1 ♖xf2+ 33 ♚xf2 ♕g2+ 34 ♚e1 ♘f3+) 31 ... ♖g3 32 ♕h1 ♖c8 33 ♗e1 ♗h6! 34 a6 bxa6 35 ♖c6 ♖g8 36 ♖xd6 (36 ♚f1 ♘xg2 37 ♖xd6 ♘e3+ 38 ♚e2 ♕g4+ 39 ♚d2 ♕d1+ 40 ♚c3 ♘g4+-+) 36 ... f3 37 ♖xa6 ♖xg2+ 38 ♖xg2 ♕e3+ 39 ♗f2 ♖xg2+ 40 ♕xg2 fxg2 0-1 Miles - Sax, London 1980. An impressive attacking performance by the aggressive Hungarian.

20 ... ♖g7
21 ♕b3

21 a5 ♗d7 (21 ... ♘h4 22 ♗e1 ♚h8 23 ♕c3 ♗d7 24 ♕b3 ♘f6 25 ♕d1 g4 26 hxg4 hxg4= Torre - Rodriguez, Toluca Izt. 1982) 22 ♕b3 ♘h4 23 ♗e1 ♗e7 24 ♖c3 ♗f8

25 ♖c2 ♚h7 26 ♖c3 ♚h8 27 ♕d1 a6 28 ♘a3 ♕xa5 (After much mysterious shadow-boxing, Black finally commits himself) 29 ♖c8 ♕xe1 30 ♖xa8 ♕b4 31 ♘c4 ♕c5 32 ♕d2 b5 33 b4 ♕c7 34 ♘a5 ♕b6 35 ♘c6 ♖g8 36 ♖a1 ♗xc6 37 dxc6 ♕xc6 38 ♖1xa6 ♕d7 39 ♖6a7 ♕c6 40 ♕d5 ♕c1+ 41 ♗f1 g4 1-0 Polugaevsky - Tal, Alma Ata 1980.

White can also play 21 ♘xa7 as in the note to White's 20th, but here the extra moves 20 h3 ♖g7 are thrown in. This would suggest that Black should avoid the endgame with 21 ... ♖c7 as he or she would then be a clear tempo down on Miles - Vukic. Nevertheless, Kasparov once tried this in his youth. Two examples of play after 21 ♘xa7 *(5)*:

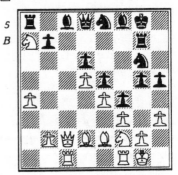

a) 21 ... ♖c7 22 ♗a5 ♖xc2 23 ♗xd8 ♖xe2 24 ♘xc8 ♖xa4 25 ♘d3 g4 26 ♖f2 ♖e3 27 ♘e1 g3 28 ♖fc2 ♖b3 29

♔f1 ♖a2 30 ♖b1 ♔f7 31 ♔e2
♖a8 32 ♘d3 ♗e7 33 ♗xe7
♘xe7 34 ♘xe7 ♔xe7 35 ♖bc1
♔f7∓ (½-½, 43) Averkin –
Kasparov, USSR 1979.

b) 21 ... ♗d7 22 ♘b5 ♘h4
23 ♕b3 and we have trans-
posed back into note 'b' to
White's 20th.

21 ... ♘h4
22 ♖c2 a6

As on virtually every
Black move, 22 ... g4 comes
into consideration. One
example is 23 fxg4 ♘f6 24
♗e1 ♔h8 25 ♕c4 hxg4 26
♘xg4 ♘xg4 27 ♗xg4 ♗xg4
28 hxg4 ♖xg4 29 ♕d3 ♕g5
Ftacnik – Pribyl, Bratislava
1983.

23 ♘a3 ♘f6
24 ♗e1 g4
25 hxg4 hxg4
26 ♘xg4

26 fxg4 ♘h5 (26 ... ♖b8
27 ♘c4 ♗xg4 28 ♗xg4 ♘xg4
29 ♘xg4 ♖xg4 30 ♕h3 ♕g5
31 ♗xh4 ♕xh4 32 ♕xh4
♖xh4 33 ♘b6± Barbero –
Helmers, Thessaloniki Ol.
1984) 27 ♘h1 ♗xg4 28 ♗xg4
♖xg4 29 ♕h3 ♕g5 30 ♗xh4
♖xh4 31 ♕e6+ ♔h8 32 ♖f3
♖g4 33 ♘c4 ♗e7 34 ♘xd6
♗xd6 35 ♕xd6 ♖g8 (Black
has methodically built up
the attack on the g-file and
now the pressure against
g2 has become intolerable)
36 ♘f2 (36 ♖ff2 f3! doesn't
help matters) 36 ... ♖xg2+
37 ♔f1 ♖h2 38 ♔e2 ♘g3+ 39

♔d3 ♖h6 40 ♕a3 ♕h5 41
♔d2 ♘f1+ 42 ♔c1 ♘e3 43
♖h3 ♖g1+ 44 ♔d2 ♘f1+ 0-1.
Anaya – Crespo, corr. 1985.

26 ... ♘h5
27 a5

27 ♘c4 ♘g3 28 ♗xg3 fxg3
29 ♕b6 ♕e7 30 ♘ce3 ♖h7 31
♖fc1± van Dyck – Chapman,
corr. 1989. The impending
invasion on c7 guarantees
White good play.

However, Black's play is
far from convincing. Nunn
suggests 29 ... ♗e7 as an
improvement, while 29 ...
♕g5 also appears highly
dangerous for White, e.g.
30 ♘xd6 ♗xg4 31 fxg4 ♗xd6
32 ♕xd6 ♕e3+ 33 ♔h1 ♘g6
with a vicious attack. If
instead 30 ♘ce3 (after 29 ...
♕g5) then 30 ... ♘g6 △ ...
♘f4 gives Black plenty of
play. In view of this, and
the poor position White
ends up with in the game,
potential Whites should
consider earlier improve-
ments, such as Polugaev-
sky's 21 a5.

27 ... ♘g3
28 ♗xg3 fxg3
29 ♕b6!

Not 29 ♕e3 ♖h7 30 f4
♘f5 31 exf5 ♕h4 and White
gets mated.

29 ... ♕e7!

Black has a big initiative
but must be careful, e.g.
29 ... ♕g5? 30 ♕e3 ♕g6 31
♕h6 and White forces the

exchange of queens.

30	♖fc1	♗xg4
31	fxg4	♘g6
32	♗f3	♕h4
33	♔f1	♘f4! *(6)*

Zsuzsa sees her way through a very murky position. 33 ... ♖f7 34 ♔e2 ♗h6 35 ♖c8+ would not be so good.

34 ♖c7!

34 ♔e1!? is an attempt to bail out, but Black would be clearly better after ♘d3+ 35 ♔d2 ♘xc1 36 ♖xc1∓.

34	...	♖xc7
35	♖xc7	♗h6
36	♘c4	♖f8

36 ... ♘xg2 looks very tempting as 37 ♔xg2 fails to 37 ... ♕h2+ and 37 ♗xg2 similarly goes down after 37 ... ♖f8+ 38 ♔e1 ♕h2 39 ♘e3 ♕g1+. However, as Polgar points out, the retreat 37 ♕g1! holds for White, e.g. 37 ... ♘f4 38 ♘e3 ♘h3 39 ♘f5=.

37	♘xd6	♘xg2
38	♘f5!	♕h1+

39 ♔e2

Not 39 ♕g1?, when 39 ... ♘e3+ would finish matters abruptly.

39 ... ♕e1+

39 ... ♘f4+ is a tempting possibility, but is far from clear after 40 ♔d2 ♘e6+ 41 ♔c2 ♕c1+ 42 ♔b3 ♘xc7 43 ♘xh6+ ♔h8 44 ♘f5.

40	♔d3	♕d2+
41	♔c4	♕c2+
42	♔b4	♕xb2+! *(7)*

43 ♔c4!

Ftacnik is hanging on grimly, continuously finding only moves. As Polgar points out, the other king moves lose immediately:

a) 43 ♔a4? ♕a2+ 44 ♔b4 ♗d2+ 45 ♖c3 (45 ♔c5 ♕a3+ 46 ♔c4 ♕c3+ mate) 45 ... ♗xc3+ 46 ♔xc3 ♖c8+-+.

b) 43 ♔c5? ♗e3+! 44 ♘xe3 ♕d4+ 45 ♔d6 ♖f6+ 46 ♔e7 ♖xb6 47 ♘f5 ♕b4+ 48 d6 ♖xd6 49 ♘xd6 ♘h4 50 ♗h1 ♕e1-+.

43	...	♕c2+
44	♔b4	♗d2+
45	♔a3	♗c1+

46	♔b4	♕b2+
47	♔c4	

47 ♔c5 ♗e3+–+.

47	...	♘e3+
48	♘xe3	♕xb6
49	axb6	♖xf3

It is not proving easy to put White away. 49 ... ♗xe3 looks good, but then 50 ♗g2 ♖f2 51 ♗h3 ♗xb6 52 ♖xb7 should hang on.

50	♘g2	♖f2 *(8)*

In spite of his tough defending, it looks as if White's efforts may have been in vain. The natural moves all lose, e.g. 51 ♘e1 ♗d2–+, 51 ♘h4 ♗g5–+ and 51 d6 ♖xg2 52 d7 ♖d2 53 ♖c8+ ♔g7 54 d8♕ ♖xd8 55 ♖xd8 g2 56 ♖d1 ♗e3–+. However, with the wolf at the door, Ftacnik finds a brilliant resource ...

51	♔b3!!	♖b2+
52	♔a3!	

The king voluntarily walks into a discovered check. 52 ♔a4? fails to 52 ... ♗g5.

52	...	♖xg2+

53	♖xc1	♖e2
54	♖g1	g2?

Black misses her last chance. She still had a chance to play for the full point with 54 ... ♖e3+. Ftacnik analyses the following continuation as winning for Black. 55 ♔b2 (55 ♔b4 ♖xe4+ 56 ♔c5 ♖xg4 57 ♔d6 ♖g7 58 ♔xe5 ♔f7 59 ♔d6 ♔e8 and White has nowhere further to go) 55 ... ♔f7 56 ♔c2 (56 g5 ♔g6 57 d6 ♖d3 58 d7 ♖xd7 59 ♖xg3 ♖d6–+) 56 ... ♔f6 57 ♔d2 ♖xe4 58 ♖xg3 ♖d4+ 59 ♖d3 ♖xd3+ 60 ♔xd3 a5 61 ♔e4 a4 62 g5+ ♔xg5 63 ♔xe5 a3–+.

After the text move Black can no longer win.

55	g5!	♔f7
56	♔b4	♔e7
57	♔c5	♖c2+
58	♔b4	♔d6
59	g6	♖e2
60	♔a5!!	♖a2+
61	♔b4	♖e2
62	♔a5	½–½

Game 2
Lautier – Nunn
Groningen 1988

1	d4	♘f6
2	c4	g6
3	♘c3	♗g7
4	e4	d6
5	♘f3	0-0
6	♗e2	e5
7	0-0	♘c6
8	d5	♘e7

9	♘e1	♘d7
10	♘d3	f5
11	f3	♘f6
12	♗d2	f4
13	g4 (9)	

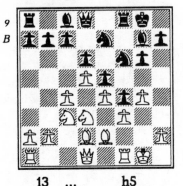

| 13 | ... | h5 |

Black has two other ways to approach this position:

a) 13 ... fxg3 14 hxg3 *(10)*. This has not worked out well in practice. It is difficult for Black to generate any kingside counterplay after this exchange. Witness the following material:

a1) 14 ... c6 15 ♗e3 (15 ♔g2 b5 16 b3 a5 {*It is a novelty to see Black attacking on the queenside in these var-*

iations of the King's Indian Defence, but it is hard to see how he can hope to profit from it. Wilder quietly strengthens his position} 17 ♖h1 bxc4 18 bxc4 ♗a6 19 ♘f2 ♖b8 20 ♖c1 ♕b6 21 ♖c2 ♖fc8 22 ♗g5 cxd5 23 ♗xf6 ♗xf6 24 ♘xd5 ♘xd5 25 ♕xd5+ ♔f8 26 c5 ♖xc5 27 ♖xc5 dxc5 28 ♗xa6 ♕xa6 29 ♖xh7 1-0 Wilder – Hellers, Haninge 1989) and now:

a11) 15 ... ♔h8 16 ♔g2 a5 17 ♘f2 ♘h5 18 ♖h1 cxd5 19 cxd5 ♘g8 20 ♕d2 a4 21 ♖h2 a3 22 b4 ♖f7 23 ♖ah1 h6 24 ♘h3 ♗xh3+ (This exchange is not one that Black wanted to make, but White was lining up g4 - g5) 25 ♖xh3 ♔h7 26 ♘b5 ♘gf6 27 g4 ♘f4+ 28 ♗xf4 exf4 29 ♕xf4 ♔g8 30 ♘xd6+- Schlosser – Paehtz, Altensteig 1990.

a12) 15 ... h6 16 ♔g2 g5 17 ♘f2 cxd5 18 cxd5 ♘g6 19 ♖h1 ♖f7 (In the previous two examples, Black got overrun on the kingside, so Fedorowicz is careful to strengthen his position there. Nevertheless, this doesn't deal with Black's fundamental problem here - lack of counterplay) 20 a4! ♗f8 21 a5 ♖h7 22 ♘b5 ♗d7 23 ♘xa7 ♘e8 24 a6 bxa6 25 ♖xa6 ♕f6 26 ♘c6 ♖xa6 27 ♗xa6 (White has taken the chequered flag on the queenside whereas on the kingside Black is still stuck in the pit lane) 27 ... h5 28 ♘b8 ♘c7 29 ♘xd7 ♖xd7 30 ♗c8 ♖g7 31 ♖xh5+- Lutz - Fedorowicz, Porz 1988.

a2) 14 ... h5 15 ♗e3 ♖f7 (15 ... ♘h7 16 c5 g5 17 ♖c1 ♘g6 18 cxd6 cxd6 19 ♘b5 ♖f7 20 ♘xa7 ♗h3 21 ♖f2 ♘f4 22 ♘b5 ♘xe2+ 23 ♕xe2 ♖c8 24 ♖xc8 ♗xc8 25 ♕c2 ♗f8 26 ♘c3 ♗d7 27 ♕e2± E Ragozin - S Ivanov, Leningrad 1989. Again White's queenside initiative has proved more successful than Black's play on the opposite wing) 16 ♕d2 ♔h7 17 ♖f2 ♘eg8 18 g4 (Black should not have allowed this - once again his counterplay on the kingside is completely stifled) 18 ... ♘e7 19 g5 ♘d7 20 ♖h2 ♔g8 21 ♔h1 c6 22 ♖d1 cxd5 23 cxd5 a6 24 a4 b6 25 b4 a5 26 ♘b5 ♘b8 27 ♖c1 axb4 28 ♕xb4 ♗a6 29 ♘xd6 ♘xd5 30 exd5 ♗f8 31 ♘xf7 1-0 Leveille - Puri, World Open 1989.

a3) 14 ... h6 15 ♔g2 g5 16 ♖c1 ♘g6 17 c5 (17 ♗e3 ♖f7 18 c5 ♗f8 19 cxd6 cxd6 20 a4 ♖h7 21 ♘f2 ♘e8 22 ♘b5 h5 23 ♕c1 ♗e7 24 ♗xa7 h4 25 ♕e3 ♘g7 26 g4 h3+ 27 ♔h2 ♘f4 28 ♗b6± Saether - Sowray, Gausdal 1991. It is beginning to look as if this line leads to a forced win

of the Black a-pawn!) 17 ... ♖f7 18 cxd6 cxd6 19 ♘f2 ♗f8 20 ♖h1 ♖h7 21 a4 ♘e8 22 ♘b5 h5 23 ♖c3 a6 24 ♘a3 ♗d7 25 ♘c4 b5 26 axb5 axb5 27 ♘e3 ♕f6 28 ♘f5 ♘g7 29 ♘xg7 ♕xg7 30 ♘h3± Tunik - Kaminski, Kecskemet 1989.

b) 13 ... g5 *(11)*

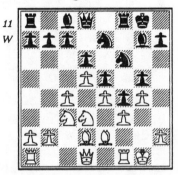

(Black wants to play ... h5 but doesn't wish to allow g5 in reply) 14 ♗e1 (White hurries to tidy up on the kingside. Ignoring this sector of the board can have unfortunate consequences - 14 c5 h5 15 h3 ♘g6 16 ♖c1 ♖f7 17 a4 ♗f8 18 ♘b5 a6 19 ♘a3 ♖h7 20 ♘c4 ♗e7 21 ♗a5 hxg4 22 hxg4 ♕f8 23 ♔f2 ♖h2+ 24 ♔e1 ♕h6∓ Daloz - Laclau, French League 1991; White managed somewhat better in Lobron - Renet, Novi Sad Ol. 1990: 14 ♖c1 h5 15 h3 ♖f7 16 ♗e1 ♗f8 17 c5 ♘g6 18 cxd6 cxd6 19 ♕b3 ♖h7 20 ♔g2 a6 21 a4 ♗d7 22 ♗f2 ♖c8 23 ♖h1 ♕e8 24 ♕b6 ♖g7 25 b3 ♘h4+ 26 ♗xh4 gxh4 27 ♘f2 ♘h7 28 ♘b1 ♘g5 29 ♘d2±. White has succeeded in keeping the kingside secure and is ready to cash in on his queenside gains) and now *(12)*:

12 B

b1) 14 ... c5 (An interesting idea - Black accepts a weakness in the hope of delaying White on the queenside) 15 ♗f2 h5 16 h3 ♘g6 17 b4 b6 18 bxc5 bxc5 19 ♕a4 hxg4 20 hxg4 ♘xg4 21 fxg4 f3 22 ♗d1 ♘f4 23 ♘xf4 exf4 24 ♗xf3 ♗xc3 25 ♖ab1 ♗e5 26 ♔g2 ♗d7 27 ♕d1 ½-½ Miladinovic - Todorovic, Belgrade GMA 1988.

b2) 14 ... ♘g6 15 c5 ♖f7 16 cxd6 cxd6 17 a4 ♗f8 (17 ... h5 18 h3 ♗f8 19 ♔g2 ♗e7 20 ♖c1 ♕f8 21 a5 ♗d8 22 b4 ♗d7 23 ♗f2 ♘h4+ 24 ♗xh4 gxh4 25 ♘f2 ♕e8 26 ♗d3 ♖g7 27 ♔h2 b6!∓ Bareev - Belotti, Aosta Open 1989. Black has played well, having kept White busy on the kingside without compromising his queenside position, and now with this

well-timed break he obtains the advantage) 18 a5 h5 19 h3 ♖h7 20 ♔g2 hxg4 21 hxg4 ♗e7 22 ♗f2 ♘h4+ 23 ♗xh4 gxh4 24 ♘f2 h3+ 25 ♔h1 (Taking the h-pawn would only help Black to open lines on the kingside. Shirov knows that it won't run away) 25 ... a6 26 b4 b5 27 axb6 ♕xb6 28 b5 ♗d8 29 bxa6 ♗xa6 30 ♗xa6 ♖xa6 31 ♕e2 ♖aa7 32 ♖ab1 ♕e3 33 ♕xe3 fxe3 34 ♖b8 ♖hd7 35 ♘xh3 ♖ab7 36 ♖b1 ♖xb1+ 37 ♖xb1+- Shirov - Hebden, London (Lloyds Bank) 1991.

b3) 14 ... h5 15 h3 ♘g6 (15 ... ♔f7 16 ♔g2 ♖h8 17 ♖h1 hxg4 18 hxg4 ♖xh1 19 ♔xh1 ♘g6 20 ♗f2 ♗d7 21 ♔g2 ♘h4+ 22 ♔f1 ♕e7 23 c5 ♖h8 24 cxd6 cxd6 25 ♗xa7 ♘xg4 26 fxg4 f3 27 ♘f2 fxe2+ 28 ♕xe2 ♕f6± Vuruna - Hebden, Vrnjacka Banja 1989. Once again Black has lost the a-pawn and although he does have counterplay on the kingside, it amounts to insufficient compensation) 16 ♔g2 (16 c5 ♖f7 17 ♔g2 ♗f8 18 b4 ♖h7 19 ♖h1 ♗d7 20 ♕b3 hxg4 21 hxg4 ♖xh1 22 ♔xh1 ♔g7 23 ♗f2 ♗e7 24 ♔g2 ♕c8 ½-½ Lazarev - Hazai, Hungarian League 1991) 16 ... ♖f7 17 a4 hxg4 18 hxg4 ♘h4+ 19 ♗xh4 gxh4 20 ♖h1 ♘h7 21 a5 ♘g5 22 ♘f2 a6 23 b4 ♗f8 24 ♕d3 ♖h7 25 ♘h3 ♘xh3 26 ♖xh3

(Black's kingside ambitions have been terminated and now he is reduced to sitting still and awaiting White's queenside breakthrough) 26 ... ♗d7 27 ♗d1 ♔h8 28 ♗a4 c6 29 ♖hh1 ♖c8 30 ♔h3 ♗e8 31 ♖hb1 ♕c7 32 ♕d2 ♗f7 33 ♗b3 c5 34 b5 ♖a8 35 ♘a4± Lutz – Timoshenko, Budapest 1989.

14 g5

Should the critical piece sacrifice in this line (see note to Black's 15th) prove to be good for Black, then exponents of the white side will have to fall back on the more restrained 14 h3. For example:

a) 14 ... ♘h7 15 ♔g2 ♔h8 16 ♖h1 ♘g8 17 ♗e1 ♘h6 18 c5 ♔g8 19 ♖c1 ♘g5 20 ♗h4 ♗f6 21 cxd6 cxd6∞ Bischoff – Rechel, Bad Wörishofen Open 1990.

b) 14 ... c6 15 ♔g2 ♗d7 16 ♗e1 ♘h7? 17 c5! (Sharply spotted) 17 ... cxd5 18 cxd6 ♘c8 19 ♘xe5 ♗e6 20 ♘xg6 d4 21 ♘xf8 ♘xf8 22 ♘b5+− Walker – Howell, British Ch. 1990.

14 ... ♘h7
15 h4 c6 *(13)*

This is much too slow and enables White to organise his forces on the kingside, after which Black can only sit and suffer. Similarly ineffective is 15 ... c5 16 ♖f2 ♗d7 17 b4 cxb4 (17 ...

13
W

b6 18 bxc5?! *{This looks unnecessarily committal and allows Black to successfully blockade the position}* 18 ... dxc5 19 ♕b3 ♘c8 20 ♘b5 a6 21 ♘c3 ♘d6 22 ♖b1± Hracek – Salai, Brno 1990) 18 ♘xb4 a6 19 ♗f1 ♕c7 20 ♗e1 ♖fb8 21 ♖c1 ♘c8 22 ♖b2 ♗f8 23 ♔h2 ♗e7 24 ♗f2 ♘f8 25 ♘d3 ♗e8 26 ♘a4 ♕a5 27 ♘b6 ♘xb6 28 ♗xb6 ♕a3 29 ♕d2 ♘d7 30 ♗c7 ♘c5 31 ♖c3 ♕xc3 32 ♕xc3 ♖c8 33 ♘xc5 ♖xc7 34 ♘e6 1−0 Züger – Haba, Prague 1989.

The experience of these games and of the text indicate that if Black is to get at the loose white kingside, it must be now. The only way to try to make 13 ... h5 work is to grab the bull by the horns with 15 ... ♘xg5, when the following sequence is forced: 16 hxg5 ♘f5 17 ♖f2 ♕xg5+ 18 ♖g2 ♘g3 19 ♘f2 ♕f6 reaching the critical position *(14)*.

In his notes to this game in *Informator*, Lautier re-

14
W

commends 20 ♖h2!, claiming an advantage for White following 20 ... g5 21 ♗f1; meeting 21 ... ♘xf1 with 22 ♔xf1! (see Djurhuus–Scholseth below) and 21 ... g4 with 22 fxg4 hxg4 23 ♘xg4! ♕g6 24 ♗h3. Nunn, meanwhile, recommends 20 ... ♕g5! when 21 ♖g2 ♕f6 leads to a repetition, while 21 ♗d3 ♘e2+ 22 ♔f1? ♕g1+∓ is not advisable.

Tournament play has witnessed the following examples:

a) 20 ♗d3 g5 21 ♗e1 g4 22 fxg4 hxg4 23 ♖xg3 fxg3 24 ♘h1 g2 25 ♔xg2 ♕h6 26 ♗f2 ♖f3 27 ♗e2 ♖f4 28 ♕d3 ♗d7 29 ♕g3 ♖af8 30 ♗e3 ♗f6 31 ♕h2 ♗h4 32 ♘g3 ♕f6 33 ♘f5 g3 34 ♕h3 ♗xf5 35 exf5 ♖xf5 36 ♘e4 ♕e7 37 ♕g4+ ♔h8 38 ♖h1 ♖f4 39 ♗xf4 ♖xf4 40 ♕g6 ♕f8 41 ♘f6 ♖f2+ 42 ♔g1 ♕xf6 43 ♕xf6+ 1-0 Steingrimsson – Dannevig, Gausdal 1991.

b) 20 ♗f1 g5 21 ♖h2 ♘xf1 (21 ... ♕g6 22 ♗h3 g4 23 fxg4

hxg4 24 ♗xg4 f3 25 ♗xf3 ♘xe4+ 26 ♖g2 1-0 Lukacs – Spiriev, Budapest 1991) 22 ♔xf1 ♕g6 23 ♖g2 ♗f6 24 ♔e2 g4 25 ♔d3 g3 26 ♘e2 h4 27 ♘g1 ♗d8 28 ♗a5 c5 29 ♗xd8 ♖xd8 30 a3 a5 31 b4 axb4 32 axb4 ♖xa1 33 ♕xa1 ♕h5 34 ♕a5 ♖f8 35 ♕c7 h3 36 ♘fxh3 ♗xh3 37 ♖b2 ♗f1+ 38 ♔c3 ♕h1 39 ♕xd6 ♕xg1 40 ♕g6+ ½-½ Djurhuus–Scholseth, Gjovik 1991.

16 ♗e1! ♖f7

16 ... ♘xg5? 17 hxg5 ♘f5 18 exf5 ♕xg5+ 19 ♔h2+- or 16 ... b5 17 ♘b4! c5 18 ♘c6 ♘xc6 19 dxc6 b4 20 ♘b5+-.

17 ♗f2 ♗h3
18 ♖e1 (15)

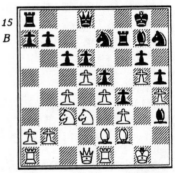

15
B

18 ... ♘xg5?

Compared to the earlier position where ... ♘xg5 should have been played, this is now unsound, but Black's position was without prospects anyway. After a normal move such as 18 ... ♘f8, White would prepare to open the queenside with 19 b4.

19 ♔h2!

Nunn must have either overlooked or underestimated this. 19 hxg5? ♘xd5! 20 ♔h2 ♘xc3 21 bxc3 ♗e6 gives Black reasonable compensation, but after the text move he loses a piece for very little.

19	...	♘h7
20	♔xh3	g5
21	♖g1	♗f6
22	♔h2	♖g7
23	♗f1	gxh4
24	♖xg7+	♔xg7
25	c5!	cxd5
26	cxd6	♕xd6
27	♗c5	♕d8
28	♗xe7	♕xe7
29	♘xd5	♕f7
30	♗h3	♔h6
31	♖c1 *(16)*	

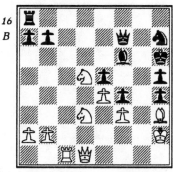

31	...	♖g8
32	♖c7	♕f8
33	♗f5	♖g7
34	♖c8	♕f7
35	♘c5!	h3
36	♘e6	♖g2+
37	♔h1	♗h4
38	♖c7	♗g3

It looks as if Black has

stirred up some trouble as 39 ♖xf7 allows a perpetual check along the second rank. However, Lautier's next move seals Black's fate.

39	♕g1!	♗f2
40	♖xf7	♖xg1+
41	♔h2	1-0

41 ... ♖g2+ 42 ♔xh3 ♖g3+ 43 ♔h2 ♗g1+ 44 ♔h1 and the game is up.

Game 3
Shirov - Nunn
Bundesliga 1991

1	d4	♘f6
2	c4	g6
3	♘c3	♗g7
4	e4	d6
5	♗e2	0-0
6	♘f3	e5
7	0-0	♘c6
8	d5	♘e7
9	♘e1	♘d7
10	♘d3	

Delaying ♘d3 in favour of a quick ♗d2 and ♖c1 is an idea that was given a whirl by Miles a few years ago, without any great success: 10 ♗d2 f5 11 ♖c1 ♘f6 (Also possible is 11 ... c5 12 f4 exf4 13 ♗xf4 ♘e5 14 ♕d2 fxe4 15 ♘xe4 ♗f5 16 ♘f2 ♕b6 17 g4 ♗d7 18 ♘ed3 ♘xd3 19 ♘xd3 ♖ae8∞ Miles - Sznapik, Malta Ol. 1980) 12 f3 c5 13 dxc6 (13 ♘d3 is preferable) 13 ... bxc6 14 ♘d3 ♗e6 15 c5 fxe4 16 fxe4 d5 17 exd5 ♘fxd5 18 ♖xf8+ ♕xf8 19 ♕a4 ♘f5 20 ♗g4 ♘xc3 21 ♗xc3 ♗d5 22 ♗xe5 ♗xe5 23 ♘xe5 ♕h6 24 ♖e1 ♕d2-+ Miles – Bukic, Bugojno 1978.

10 ... f5 *(17)*

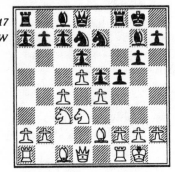

11 f3

In the early days of the development of the King's Indian, the move 11 exf5 was frequently played. Nevertheless, it creates no problems for Black and has more or less disappeared from contemporary practice. Black can happily recapture with either the pawn or the knight and play after either is well documented in other sources. We will content ourselves with two Hort efforts: 11 ... ♘xf5 12 f3 ♘d4 13 ♘f2 ♘f6 14 ♗d3 (14 ♗e3 ♘h5 15 ♘fe4 ♘f4 16 ♖f2 c5 17 ♗f1± Hort – Hellers, Wijk aan Zee 1986) 14 ... c5 15 ♗e3 ♘h5 16 ♗e4 ♖f7 17 ♖b1 b6 18 ♕d2 ♘f5 19 ♗g5 ♗f6 20 ♗xf6 ♘xf6 21 ♗xf5 ♗xf5 22 ♖be1

♕f8 23 ♘ce4 ♗xe4 24 ♘xe4 ♘xe4 25 fxe4 ♕e7 26 ♖xf7 ♔xf7 27 ♖f1+ ½-½ Hort – van der Wiel, Reykjavik 1985.

Assuming that White wishes to play the main line, then 11 ♗d2 is most frequently seen here, and superficially it may seem that it makes little difference whether White plays this or 11 f3, but there are some move order finesses which require examination.

White can try to avoid giving Black the chance to play 11 ... f4 (see note to Black's next move) with 11 ♗d2, but then Black can avoid the main lines with the following *(18)*:

a) 11 ... fxe4 12 ♘xe4 ♘f5 gives Black good chances to equalise. For example:

a1) 13 ♗c3 ♘f6 14 ♗f3 ♘h4 (14 ... ♗d7 15 a4 ♔h8 16 ♘xf6 ♕xf6 17 ♗e4 ♕h4 18 ♖e1 ♖ae8 19 c5 ♗c8 20 a5 ♘d4 21 cxd6 cxd6 22 ♖a4± Wells–Byrne, London {Wat-

son, Farley & Williams) 1991)
15 ♘xf6+ ♕xf6 16 ♗e4 ♗f5
17 ♕e2 ♗xe4 18 ♕xe4∞/=
Ftacnik - Mortensen, Esbjerg 1985.

a2) 13 ♗g4 ♘f6 14 ♗g5
♕d7 15 ♗xf6 ♗xf6 16 c5 ♗g7
17 ♖c1 ♕f7 and Black is
fine, Meduna - A Rodriguez, Prague 1980.

b) 11 ... ♖f7!? has been
the subject of some recent
experimentation, but received an awful pounding
in Khalifman - Watson,
London (Watson, Farley &
Williams) 1991, viz. 12 f3 f4
13 ♖c1 h5 14 c5! ♘xc5?! 15
♘xc5 dxc5 16 ♗c4 ♔f8
(Black's pieces are horribly
tangled and he soon gets
caught in the crossfire of
the white bishops) 17 ♗e1
b6 18 b4! cxb4 19 ♘b5 c5 20
d6 ♘c6 21 ♕d5 ♕d7 22 ♗h4
1-0 (There is no answer to
23 ♗e7).

c) 11 ... ♔h8. This semiwaiting move leads to similar play to the main line
of Gelfand - Kasparov, e.g.

c1) 12 b4 ♘g8 13 f3 f4 14
♖c1 ♘df6 15 c5 h5 16 ♘f2 g5
17 cxd6 cxd6 18 ♘b5 ♘e8 19
a4 ♘h6 20 ♖c3 ♗d7 21 h3
♗f6 22 ♕c2 ♕b8 23 ♖c1 ♗d8
24 a5 a6 25 ♘a3 b5 26 ♕d3
♗c7 27 ♘b1 ♕d8 28 ♗e1 ♗b8
29 ♔f1 ♖f7 30 ♘d2 ♘f6 31
♕c2 ♖g7 32 ♘b3 ♔g8 33
♘c5 dxc5 34 bxc5 ♗a7 35 d6
g4 36 hxg4 hxg4 37 c6 ♘h5

38 ♘d3 g3 39 cxd7 ♕h4 40
♖c8+ ♔h7 41 ♗d1 ♕h1+ 42
♔e2 ♕xg2+ 43 ♘f2 gxf2 44
♔d3 fxe1♕ 0-1 Farago - Hazai, Hungary 1991.

c2) 12 f3 f4 13 b4 g5 14 c5
♘f6 15 ♘f2 h5 16 h3 ♘eg8 17
♕c2 ♘h6 18 cxd6 cxd6 19
♘b5 ♘e8 20 ♖fc1 ♗d7 21 a4
a6 22 ♘a3 g4 23 fxg4 hxg4
24 hxg4 ♗f6 25 ♘c4 ♗h4 26
♗e1 ♗g3 27 ♖a3 ♖c8 28 ♕d2
♔g7 29 ♘h1 ♗xe1 30 ♕xe1
♘xg4 31 ♗xg4 ♗xg4 32 ♘f2
♕g5 33 ♘xg4 ♕xg4 34 ♖ac3
♖d8 35 ♖h3 ♘f6 36 ♘e3
fxe3 37 ♖g3 ♖c8 38 ♖xc8
♖xc8 39 ♕xe3 ♖c1+ 40 ♔h2
♔f7 41 ♕xc1 ♕h4+ 42 ♖h3
♕xe4 1-0 Neverov - Timoshenko, Tbilisi 1989.

11 ...   ♘f6

Black can try to exploit
the fact that White has
used the move order 11 f3
(instead of 11 ♗d2) with the
immediate 11 ... f4, leaving
f6 available for use by
pieces other than the
knight. (Meeting 11 ♗d2
with 11 ... f4 allows White
the possibility of 12 ♗g4).

After 11 ... f4 *(19)*, we
have the following material:

a) 12 g4 ♗f6 (An imaginative and positionally wellmotivated move; Gelfand
exploits the fact that he
has not yet returned his
knight to f6 in order to
exchange the dark squared
bishops) 13 ♗d2 h5 14 h3

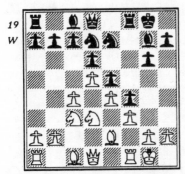

♔f7 15 ♗e1 ♖h8 16 ♔g2 ♘g8
17 ♖c1 ♗h4 18 ♖h1 ♔g7 19
♗xh4 ♕xh4 20 ♕e1 ♕d8 21
♕f2 b6 22 ♖cg1 a5 23 ♔f1
♘c5 24 ♔e1 ♘e7 ½-½ Dreev
- Gelfand, Kramatorsk 1989.

b) 12 ♗d2 g5 13 g4 (13 ♖c1
♖f6 14 b4 ♖g6 15 c5 ♘f6 16
♘f2 h5 17 h3 a6 18 a4 ♔h7 19
a5 ♘eg8 20 cxd6 ♕xd6!?
{*An instructive recapture;
Black doesn't wish to
weaken his b6 square, and
realises that it is not easy
for White to press against
the c7 pawn*} 21 ♘a4 g4 22
hxg4 hxg4 23 fxg4 ♘h6 24
♕c2 ♘e8 25 ♘c5 ♗f6 26 ♕a4
♘g7 27 ♖c3 ♗h4 28 ♖h3
♗xf2+ 29 ♔xf2 ♔g8 30 ♖fh1
b6 31 ♘d3 ♗xg4 32 ♗xg4
♘xg4+ 33 ♔f1 ♔f7∓ Karner
- Veingold, Tallinn 1981)
and now (20):

b1) 13 ... h5 14 h3 ♖f6 (14
... ♖f7 15 b4 ♘f6 16 c5 ♘g6
17 cxd6 cxd6 18 ♗e1 ♗f8 19
a4 ♖h7 20 a5 ♗d7 21 ♗f2
♖h6 22 ♔g2 ♕e7 23 ♖h1 ♕h7
24 ♖c1 ♗e7 25 ♘b2 ♖f8 26
♕f1 ♔g7 27 ♗b5 ♗c8 28 ♗d3

♖h8 29 ♕g1 hxg4 30 hxg4
♖h3 31 ♗e2 ♘xg4 32 fxg4
f3+ 33 ♗xf3 ♗xg4 34 ♗xg4
♘f4+ 35 ♔f1 ♖xh1 0-1 Hau-
gli - Badea, Haifa 1989.
White never got very far
with his queenside pawn
advance. Perhaps a plan
with ♖c1 and ♘b5 would
have been more to the
point) 15 b4 ♖h6 16 ♔g2
♘g6 17 ♖h1 ♘h4+ 18 ♔f2
♗f8 19 ♖c1 a5 20 a3 c6! 21
dxc6 bxc6 22 ♕b3 ♔g7 23
♘a4 axb4 24 axb4 ♘f6 25
c5 ♗e6 26 ♕c2 d5 27 exd5
♕xd5 28 ♗c3 hxg4 29 ♘xe5
♗f5 30 ♕d1 g3+ 31 ♔g1 ♔h7
32 ♘b2 ♕xd1+ 33 ♖xd1 ♘d5
34 ♗d4 ♘xb4 35 ♗c4 ♘c2
0-1 Shabtai - Komljenovic,
Biel 1989.

b2) 13 ... fxg3 14 ♗xg5!?
(This leads to a complex
position where the kings
suffer from a mutual lack
of pawn cover; the alternative was 14 hxg3 when
Black can continue 14 ...
♘g6 planning ... h5 - h4) 14
... gxh2+ 15 ♔h1 h6 16 ♗h4

♗f6 17 ♗xf6 ♖xf6 18 f4 exf4
19 ♘xf4 ♘e5 20 ♕d2 ♘7g6
21 ♘h5 ♖xf1+ 22 ♖xf1 ♕g5
23 ♕xg5 hxg5 24 ♔xh2 a6 25
♘f6+ ♔h8 26 ♔g3± Barlov -
Mortensen, Budapest 1987.
White has better develop-
ment and the pawn at g5 is
a weakness.

12 ♗d2 h5!? (21)

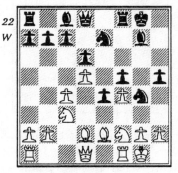

John Nunn is a constant
champion of the Black
cause in the King's Indian
and always willing to ex-
periment with new ideas.

12 ... h5 keeps open the
possibility of transposing
to a main line with ... f4
and ... g5, while trying to
sidestep variations where
White plays g4.

The more traditional 12
... ♔h8 is considered in the
next game.

13 exf5

13 c5 is a less critical test
of Black's idea; Hutchings -
Piket, Novi Sad Ol. 1990
continued 13 ... f4 14 cxd6
cxd6 15 ♖c1 g5 16 ♘f2?!
(Rather restrained; 16 ♘b5!

furthering the queenside
attack was more to the
point) 16 ... ♘g6 17 ♘b5 ♘e8
18 ♕c2 g4!∓ - Black has a
promising kingside initiative.

13 ... gxf5
14 f4 e4
15 ♘f2 ♘g4 (22)

22
W

16 ♘xg4

16 ♗xg4!? hxg4 17 ♗e3 ⌐
h3 is suggested by Piket.

16 ... fxg4

A vital decision which
leads to huge complications
in which both sides stand
on a precipice, Black's mobile pawn mass being an
important factor in his favour. However, this move
surrenders the passed e-
pawn and the quieter 16 ...
hxg4 might have been pre-
ferable.

17 ♘xe4 ♗xb2
18 ♖b1 ♗d4+
19 ♔h1 ♘f5
20 ♗d3 b6

Insufficiently energetic;
the immediate 20 ... ♘e3
deserved consideration.

21	♖e1	♗d7
22	♘g5	♖f6
23	♗b4	a5
24	♗a3	♗c3
25	♖e2	h4 (23)

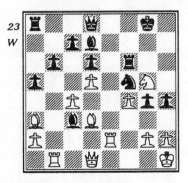

The moment of crisis has been reached. Black is operating with threats such as ... h3 or ... g3 or even ... ♘g3+, sacrificing a piece to come to grips with the white king. At this time, Shirov acts with the utmost resolution to wrench the initiative back into his own hands.

26 ♖e6!

Intending to meet 26 ... ♗xe6 with 27 ♘xe6 ♖xe6 28 dxe6 ♘h6 29 f5+-, or 27 ... ♕e7 28 ♗xf5 ♖xf5 29 ♕xg4+ winning.

26	...	♘h6
27	♗h7+	♔g7
28	♕d3	♗xe6
29	♕xc3	♗g8
30	♗b2	1-0

After 30 ... ♗xh7 31 ♘e6+ or 30 ... ♕e7 31 ♖e1 Black is utterly helpless.

Game 4
Gelfand - Kasparov
Linares 1990

1	d4	♘f6
2	c4	g6
3	♘c3	♗g7
4	e4	d6
5	♗e2	0-0
6	♘f3	e5
7	0-0	♘c6
8	d5	♘e7
9	♘e1	♘d7
10	♘d3	f5
11	f3	♘f6
12	♗d2	♔h8

A flexible move. Black refuses to commit himself immediately with ... f4 while at the same time clears the g8 square for the e7 knight. Black also keeps possibilities of ... c6, when the placing of the king on h8 will be useful.

13 ♖c1

White also keeps flexible, but various pawn moves are possible:

a) 13 b4 *(24)* and now:

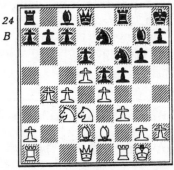

a1) 13 ... ♘eg8 14 g4 (14

♖c1 ♗h6 15 exf5 gxf5 16 f4
♘e4 17 ♗e1 ♘gf6 18 fxe5
dxe5 19 ♘xe4 ♘xe4 20
♘xe5 ♕e7 21 ♘f3 a5 22 ♖b1
♗e3+ 23 ♔h1 axb4 24 ♗xb4
♗c5 25 a3 ♖a6 26 ♕e1 ♖g8
27 ♗d3 ♕g7 28 g3 ♗xb4 29
axb4 ♖e8 30 ♗xe4 fxe4 31
♕e3 ♖f8 32 ♘g5 ♖xf1+ 33
♖xf1 ♖a1 34 ♖xa1 ♕xa1+ 35
♔g2 ♗f5 36 ♘xe4 ♕e5 37
♔f3 b5 38 cxb5 ♕xd5 39
♔f4 ♕xb5 40 ♕d4+ ♔g8 41
♕d8+ 1-0 Lutz - Paehtz,
Dortmund 1991. Black ge-
nerated some activity for
his pawn sacrifice, but it
never looked like enough)
14 ... ♘e8 15 ♔h1 ♗d7 16 ♖g1
♖f7 17 ♖c1 ♗h6? 18 gxf5±
♕f6 (If 18 ... gxf5 19 ♖xg8+
wins material) 19 fxg6 hxg6
20 ♗xh6 ♘xh6 21 ♕d2 and
White won, Kir. Georgiev -
Ree, Palma 1989.

a2) 13 ... c6 14 a4 f4 15 g4
h5 (As in the Lautier - Nunn
game, this commits Black
to an immediate sacrifice
of a piece, otherwise he
will have no play anywhere.
In this instance, White has
the possibility to take an
immediate draw if he wi-
shes) 16 g5 ♘h7 17 h4 ♘xg5
18 hxg5 ♘xd5 19 ♖f2 (Cap-
turing the knight allows
Black to deliver perpetual
check) 19 ... ♘c7 (19 ...
♘e3?! 20 ♗xe3 fxe3 21 ♖g2
Rashkovsky - Tsarev, USSR
1989) 20 ♖g2 ♗h3 21 ♖h2

♕xg5+ 22 ♔h1 ♗e6∞ Bareev
- Kuzmin, Moscow 1989.

b) 13 a4 *(25)* with the further branch:

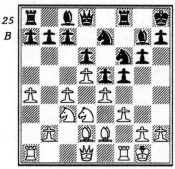

b1) 13 ... f4?! (A curious
decision - why play ... ♔h8
and then head for the standard kingside pawn storm
where the king move is
irrelevant?) 14 c5 g5 15 ♖c1
c6 16 cxd6 ♕xd6 17 dxc6
♘xc6 18 ♘b5 ♕e7 19 ♕e1 a6
20 ♖xc6 bxc6 21 ♗b4 ♕d8
22 ♘d6 ♗e6 23 ♕c3 a5 24
♗a3 ♘d7 25 ♕xc6 ♕b6+ 26
♕xb6 ♘xb6 27 ♘c5± Con-
quest - Botterill, British
Ch. 1984.

b2) 13 ... c6 14 a5 cxd5?!
(Doing White's work for
him; 14 ... ♘eg8 △ ... ♗h6
was better) 15 cxd5 ♘eg8 16
♘f2! ♗h6 17 ♗xh6 ♘xh6 18
♕d2 f4 19 ♖fc1 g5 20 h3
♘hg8 21 ♘b5 ♘e8 22 ♖c2
♘gf6 23 ♖ac1 h5 24 ♕b4
♗d7 25 ♘c7± Kozul - Pav-
lovic, Yugoslavia 1988.

b3) 13 ... a5 14 ♕c2 (14 g4
c5 15 ♖f2 b6 16 h4 ♖a7 17
♖h2 ♔g8 18 h5 fxg4 19 fxg4

gxh5 20 g5 ♘e8 21 ♗xh5
♘g6 22 ♘b5 ♖b7 23 ♗g4
♘f4 24 ♗xf4 exf4 25 ♗xc8
♕xc8 26 ♕h5 ♗e5 27 ♔h1±
Kozul - Gufeld, Tbilisi 1988)
14 ... c5 15 dxc6 ♘xc6 16 ♗e3
♘d4 17 ♕d1 ♗e6 18 b3 fxe4
19 fxe4 ♘xe2+ 20 ♕xe2 ♘g4
21 ♖xf8+ ♗xf8 22 ♖f1 ♗e7
23 ♘d5 ♘xe3 24 ♕xe3 ♗g5
25 ♕f2 ♗h4 26 g3 ♗g5 27 h4
♗xd5 28 exd5 ♗e7 29 ♔g2
♕d7 30 ♕e3 ♔g8 31 ♖f3± LB
Hansen - Berg, Graested
1990.

13 ... c5

Black has numerous alternatives here:

a) 13 ... ♘eg8 and now:

a1) 14 exf5? (This only helps Black by strengthening his centre; White now gets wiped out in the centre and on the kingside) 14 ... gxf5 15 f4 e4 16 ♘f2 c5 17 dxc6 bxc6 18 ♗e3 ♗e6 19 ♕a4 ♕c7 20 ♖fd1 ♖fd8 21 b4 ♘e7 22 ♖d2 d5 23 c5 d4 24 ♗xd4 ♕xf4 25 ♖cd1 ♖g8 26 g3 ♕h6 27 ♖c2 ♘fd5 28 ♘xd5 ♗xd5 29 b5 f4 30 ♘xe4 fxg3 31 ♘xg3 ♘f5 32 ♗xg7+ ♖xg7 33 ♗g4 0-1 Barbero - Gallagher, Bern Open 1989.

a2) 14 b4 ♖f7 15 c5 ♕f8 16 g4 ♕e7 17 ♔g2 ♘e8 18 g5 f4 19 h4 h6 20 ♖h1 ♗f8 (White's advanced g-pawn is about to be rounded up, but he conceives an ingenious plan to wipe out the

Black centre with the aid of a piece sacrifice) 21 ♘b5! ♖h7 22 ♘xc7! ♕xc7 (22 ... ♘xc7 runs into a similar tactic, e.g. 23 cxd6 ♕xd6 24 ♘xe5) 23 cxd6 ♕d8 24 ♘xe5 ♖g7 25 ♗xf4 h5 26 ♘c4 ♘xd6 27 ♗e5 ♘f7 28 ♗xg7+ ♗xg7 29 f4 ♘e7 30 d6 ♘c6 31 e5 ♘xb4 32 ♕d2 ♘a6 33 ♗d3 b5 34 ♗xg6 ♗b7+ 35 ♔h2 ♘h6 36 ♘e3 ♗xh1 37 ♖xh1 ♘g4+ 38 ♘xg4 hxg4 (It isn't every day you see five connected passed pawns!) 39 ♖e1 ♕b6 40 ♔g3 1-0 Hjartarson - Fedorowicz, Novi Sad Ol. 1990.

b) 13 ... c6 *(26)* and now:

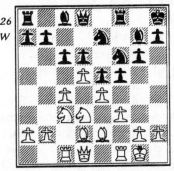

b1) 14 ♘f2 c5!? (Black is suggesting that the White knight is misplaced on f2) 15 g4 ♘eg8 16 ♔g2 ♖f7 17 h4 ♗f8 18 ♘h3 h6 19 exf5 gxf5 20 g5 f4 21 ♖h1 ♖g7 22 ♔f2 ♘h5 23 ♘e4 ♗f5 24 ♗d3± Ftacnik - Sznapik, Banja Luka 1983.

b2) 14 b4 b5 (Creating tension everywhere; the advantage of having the

king on h8 becomes clear)
15 dxc6 bxc4 16 ♘f2 ♘xc6 17
♗xc4 (17 b5 ♘d4 18 ♗xc4
♗b7 19 ♗g5 ♖c8 20 ♕d3
♕a5∓ Spassov – Zsu Polgar,
Bulgaria 1981) 17 ... ♘d4 18
♘d5 ♗b7 19 ♗e3 ♘xd5 20
♗xd5 ♗xd5 21 exd5 ♕b6 22
♗xd4 exd4 23 ♘d3 ♖ac8 24
♖xc8 ♖xc8 25 ♕a4 ♗h6 26
f4 ♕b7 27 ♖e1± Frias –
Sznapik, Thessaloniki Ol.
1984.

b3) 14 g4 b5 (Very logi-
cal. In comparison with b2
the extra weakening of the
White kingside with g4
should help Black. Unfor-
tunately, we don't see a
reasonable test of the idea
as, in this game, Malaniuk
simply proves too strong
for his opponent) 15 dxc6
bxc4 16 ♘f2 ♘xc6 17 ♗xc4
♘d4 18 ♔h1 ♗b7 19 g5 ♘h5
20 ♘d5 ♖c8 21 b3 ♘f4 22
♘xf4 exf4 23 ♗c3 ♕b6 24
♕d3 ♖fe8 25 ♖cd1 ♘xf3 26
♗xg7+ ♔xg7 27 ♕xf3 fxe4
28 ♕xf4 ♖f8 29 ♕h4 ♖xc4
30 bxc4 e3+ 31 ♘e4 ♖e8 32
♕h6+ ♔g8 33 ♖d5 ♗xd5 34
cxd5 1-0 Malaniuk – Griego,
Philadelphia Open 1990.

b4) 14 dxc6 (This doesn't
look right; Black now gains
very easy development for
his pieces) 14 ... ♘xc6 (The
alternative recapture 14 ...
dxc6 did not work out well
in Hübner – Nunn, Bunde-
sliga 1985 after 15 ♗e3 ♕e8

16 ♕a4 ♗e6 17 ♖fd1 fxe4 18
fxe4 ♘g4 19 ♗xg4 ♗xg4 20
♖d2 ♗e6 21 b3 ♖f7 22 ♘f2±)
15 ♗e3 ♗e6 16 ♕a4 (16 b3
♘d4 17 ♘f2 ♘h5 18 ♖e1 ♘f4
19 ♗f1 ♗g8 20 ♘e2 ♘fxe2+
21 ♗xe2 fxe4 22 ♘xe4=
Schacht – Schubert, Bun-
desliga 1985) 16 ... ♘d4 17
♖fe1 a6 18 c5 ♖c8 19 ♕a3
♗c4 20 cxd6 ♗xd3 21 ♗xd3
♖c6 22 exf5 gxf5∓ Lautier –
Wahls, Biel 1990.

14 g4 *(27)*

a) 14 a3 ♘eg8 15 b4 b6 16
bxc5 bxc5 17 ♖b1 h5 18 ♕a4
fxe4 19 fxe4 ♗h6 20 ♗xh6
♘xh6 21 ♕c6 ♗g4 22 ♗xg4
♘hxg4 23 ♖f3 ♕a5 24 ♖c1±
Titov – Kudriashov, USSR
1991.

b) 14 ♖b1 a5 15 a3 ♘eg8 16
b4 axb4 17 axb4 b6 18 ♕c1
(18 ♕c2 ♗h6 19 ♖a1 ♗d7 20
exf5 ♗xf5 21 ♖xa8 ♕xa8 22
♗xh6 ♘xh6 23 ♕b2 ♘h5 24
g3= Lobron – Neurohr, Bundesliga 1990) 18 ... f4 (Belov
doesn't like this and suggests instead 18 ... ♘h5, encouraging White to weaken
himself with g3) 19 ♕b2 g5
20 ♖a1 ♖xa1 21 ♖xa1 g4 22
bxc5 bxc5 23 ♕b8 ♘d7 24
♕b3 gxf3 25 ♗xf3 ♘h6 26
♘b5 ♘f6 27 ♖a7 ♘fg4 28 h3
♘e3 29 ♘f2 ♘f7 30 ♗xe3
fxe3 31 ♕xe3 ♗h6 32 ♕e2
♕g5 33 ♗g4 ♕c1+ 34 ♕f1
♗xg4 35 ♘xg4 ♕xf1+ 36
♔xf1 ♗f4 37 ♔e2 h5 38 ♘f6
h4 39 ♘xd6 ♘g5 40 ♘d7

♖d8 41 ♔d3 ♗g3 42 ♖b7 ♖a8 43 ♖b8+ ♖xb8 44 ⟳xb8 ♗f2 45 ⟳c6 1-0 Neverov - Belov, Voskresensk 1990.

c) 14 dxc6 transposes to b4 in the previous note.

14 ... a6

a) 14 ... ♗d7 15 ⟳f2 ⟳eg8 16 ♔h1 f4 17 b4 (This is based on a neat tactic, i.e. 17 ... cxb4 18 ⟳b5 ♕b6 19 ♗xb4 a6 20 c5!) 17 ... b6 18 ⟳b5 a6 19 ⟳a3 ⟳e8 20 ♖b1 ♕h4 21 ♗e1 h5 22 ⟳d3 ♕f6 23 h3 hxg4 24 hxg4 ⟳h6 25 bxc5 bxc5 26 ♖b6 ♕d8 27 ♖b2 ♗f6 28 ♔g2 ♗h4 29 ♖h1 ♗xe1 30 ♕xe1 ♔g7 31 ♕h4 ♕xh4 32 ♖xh4 ⟳f7 33 ♖h1 ⟳f6 34 ♖b6 ♖fb8 35 ♖hb1 ♖xb6 36 ♖xb6± Ftacnik - Geller, Sochi 1977.

b) 14 ... ⟳eg8 15 ♔g2 ⟳e8 (15 ... h6 16 h4 fxg4 17 fxg4 ⟳h7 18 ♖h1 ♗f6 19 ♔g3 {*Very brave!*} 19 ... a6 20 a3 b6 21 b4 ♖a7 22 ♗e3 h5 23 g5 ⟳xg5 24 hxg5 ♗xg5 25 ♕g1 ⟳h6 26 ♔h2 ⟳g4+ 27 ♗xg4 ♗xg4 28 ♗f2 ♗xc1 29 ♕xc1 ♖f3 30 ♕d2 ♕f6 31 ♗g3 h4

32 ♗e1 ♖f7 33 ♔g2 ♖g3+ 34 ♗xg3 ♕f3+ 35 ♔g1 ♕f1+ 36 ♔h2 ♕h3+ 37 ♔g1 ♖f1+ 0-1 Züger - Belotti, Mitropa Cup 1990) 16 g5 f4 17 h4 ♖f7 18 ♖h1 ⟳f8 19 ♕g1 ⟳g7 20 ♗d1 ⟳h5 21 ⟳e2 h6 22 ♔f1 ♗e7 23 ♗a4 hxg5 24 hxg5 ♗xg5 25 ♗e8! *(28)*

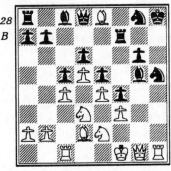

(It is interesting to compare this game to Hjartarson - Fedorowicz {*note a2 to Black's 13th*}. On both occasions White seems to have compromised his position by an ambitious advance of his g-pawn to g5 where it is, in the long run, indefensible. However, it is difficult for Black to undertake anything while this pawn is there, and the time and effort expended to capturing it leaves him exposed in other areas of the board) 25 ... ♖g7 26 ♗xg6 ♖xg6 27 ♖xh5+ ♔g7 28 ♗c3 ♕e7 29 ♖c2 ♗h6 30 ♕h2 ♔h7 31 ⟳exf4! exf4 32 ⟳xf4 ♕f7 33 ♖f2 ♖f6 34 ♗xf6 ♕xf6 35 ♖g2 ♕d4 36

♛g3 ♛d1+ 37 ♔f2 ♛d4+ 38 ♔e1 ♗f5 39 ♖xf5 ♛e3+ 40 ♖e2 1-0 Ftacnik - Nunn, Vienna 1986.

15 ♘f2   h6!?

Alternatively, 15 ... ♗d7:

a) 16 a3 ♘eg8 17 b4 b6 18 bxc5 bxc5 19 ♖b1± ♘e8 20 ♛c1 ♖a7 21 ♔g2 ♗f6 22 exf5 gxf5 23 g5 ♗g7 24 f4 ♘e7 25 ♗h5 e4 26 ♘e2 ♔g8 27 h4 ♘g6 28 ♖h1 ♛e7 29 ♗xg6 hxg6 30 h5 gxh5 31 ♖xh5 ♘c7 32 ♖h3 ♗e8 33 ♗c3 ♗g6 34 ♘d1 ♘e8 35 ♛b2 ♖f7 36 ♘e3 ♖b7 37 ♖bh1! ♖f8 38 ♛c2 ♗xc3 39 ♘xc3 ♘g7 40 ♖h8+ ♔f7 41 ♖xf8+ ♛xf8 42 ♖b1± Ftacnik - Ost-Hansen, Esbjerg 1982.

b) 16 ♖b1 b5?! (This is superficially attractive but, as is nearly always the case, the opening of the queenside favours White) 17 cxb5 axb5 18 ♘xb5 ♗xb5 19 ♗xb5 ♖xa2 20 b4 cxb4 21 ♖xb4 fxe4 22 fxe4 ♘exd5 (rather optimistic, but he had to attempt to create some play for his pieces) 23 exd5 ♘xd5 24 ♖b3 ♛a8 25 ♗c4 ♖xd2 26 ♛xd2 ♘f4 27 ♖g3 ♖c8 28 ♛a2 ♛c6 29 ♗d3 d5 30 ♘h3 ♘xh3+ 31 ♖xh3+- (although Black eventually managed to draw) Rosenberg - McDonald, British Ch. 1991.

16 h4   fxg4
17 fxg4   ♘eg8 *(29)*

Black's play looks

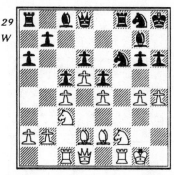

strange, but he has calculated that his attack is sufficiently quick to force a serious weakness to the white kingside pawns.

18 ♔g2   ♘h7
19 ♖h1   ♗f6
20 g5!

The main point of Black's play is revealed after 20 ♔g3 ♗xh4+! 21 ♖xh4 ♖xf2 regaining the sacrificed material. White can then try to exploit the awkward placing of the black pieces, but he will be ultimately unsuccessful, e.g. 22 ♛h1 (22 ♗xh6 g5! 23 ♗g7+ ♔xg7 24 ♖xh7+ ♔xh7 25 ♔xf2 ♘f6) 22 ... ♛f8! (22 ... ♛f6? 23 g5!) 23 ♗e3 ♖f4! 24 ♗xf4 exf4+ 25 ♔f2 g5∓.

With the text, White offers a sacrifice of his own. In return he cripples the 'King's Indian' bishop, obtains control over the critical blockading square g4 and opens the h-file to pursue his own kingside attack.

20	...	hxg5
21	h5	♕e8
22	b4!?	*(30)*

An amazing move typical of Kasparov himself. A more restrained positional approach would be 22 hxg6 ♕xg6 23 ♗h5 ♕g7 24 ♗g4 with compensation because of White's domination of the queenside light squares.

22	...	cxb4
23	♘a4	♗d8
24	♗xb4	♗d7
25	hxg6	♕xg6

The position is beginning to look very promising for Black, but Gelfand finds a way to stir up trouble.

26	c5!	g4

Kasparov plans to advance this pawn to g3 driving away the white knight at f2 from the defence of the e-pawn. Black will then be able to play ... ♕xe4+ when the white king will be wide open. However, White has sufficient resources against this plan and it might have been bet-

ter to activate one of his knights with 26 ... ♘f6.

27	c6	g3
28	♘d3	bxc6
29	dxc6	♖c8!
30	♗f3	*(31)*

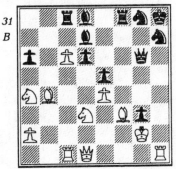

Not 30 cxd7, when Black's plan would come to fruition with 30 ... ♖xc1 31 ♘xc1 ♖f2+ 32 ♔g1 ♕xe4-+.

30	...	♖xf3!?

If 30 ... ♗xc6, White keeps his initiative alive with 31 ♘xe5! Therefore, Kasparov adds fuel to the fire with a sacrifice of the exchange.

31	♕xf3	♗g4
32	♕xg3	♕xe4+
33	♔g1	

White had a difficult decision to make between this and 33 ♔h2. After 33 ♔h2 play remains highly complex with one possible line: 33 ... ♖c7!? 34 ♘c3 ♕d4 35 ♗a5 ♘gf6 36 ♗xc7 ♗xc7∞.

33	...	♘gf6!
34	♗xd6!	♕d4+
35	♘f2	♕xd6

36	♘xg4	♕d4+
37	♘f2	♕xa4
38	♕xe5	♖c7

Kasparov tries a final attempt to win. An immediate draw resulted from 38 ... ♖xc6 39 ♖xh7+! ♔xh7 40 ♕h2+ ♘h5 (40 ... ♔g7? 41 ♕g2+) 41 ♕xh5+ ♔g7=.

39	♖h2	♖g7+
40	♖g2	♗c7
41	♕f5	♕xa2
42	♕c8+	♕g8
43	♕xg8+	♔xg8
44	♖xg7+	♔xg7
45	♘d3	½-½

Notes based on Kasparov's in *Informator*.

2) Classical 9 ♘e1 ♘d7 10 f3 f5 11 g4

This variation is named after the American grandmaster Pal Benko. Beginners must look at this move with astonishment, as it break a number of basic rules: don't make weakening pawn moves in front of your king; don't try to play actively where the opponent stands better; don't waste time in the opening and so on. Despite this, it is a perfectly playable move, which serves to emphasize what a difficult game chess is.

White plans to try to keep the kingside closed, and will often meet ... f4 with h4, when any further black pawn advance will allow White to achieve this objective. Black must be aware of this, avoid the potential blockade and look for opportunities (often with sacrifices) to break the position open.

Game 5
Pinter - Kr. Georgiev
Warsaw Zonal 1987

1	d4	♘f6
2	c4	g6
3	♘c3	♗g7
4	e4	d6
5	♗e2	0-0
6	♘f3	e5
7	0-0	♘c6
8	d5	♘e7
9	♘e1	♘d7
10	f3	f5
11	g4 *(32)*	

11 g4 looks like an attempt by White to punch Black in the face in the middle of his own attack and while Black is recovering from the shock White tries to blockade the entire kingside, so that he gets an absolutely free hand on the other wing.

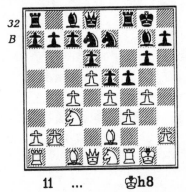

| 11 | ... | ♔h8 |

Black has tried numerous alternatives here:

a) 11 ... fxg4?! (This premature exchange gives White everything he wants; the remainder of this game is a good advertisement for maintaining the tension. We give the whole of this game as a warning for black players) 12 fxg4 ♖xf1+ 13 ♔xf1 a5 14 ♗e3 h6 15 h4 ♘f6 16 ♘d3 b6 17 ♘f2 ♘d7 18 g5 h5 19 b3 ♘c5 20 ♖b1 ♗d7 21 ♕d2 ♕f8 22 ♔g2 ♕f7 23 ♘b5± (White has a huge space advantage for which Black has no counterplay at all) 23 ... ♗xb5 24 cxb5 ♖f8 25 ♖f1 ♕e8 26 ♕c2 ♕a8 27 ♗c4 ♕c8 28 ♗e2 ♕a8 29 a3 ♕b7 30 b4 axb4 31 axb4 ♘d7 32 ♖c1 ♖c8 33 ♖a1 ♔f8 34 ♔g3 ♔e8 35 ♕a2 ♘b8 36 ♗f1 ♘d7 37 ♗h3 ♖b8 38 ♘d1 ♘f8 39 ♘c3 ♘d7 40 ♖f1 ♖a8 41 ♕f2 1-0 A Petrosian - Korenev, Belgorod 1991.

b) 11 ... h5?! 12 g5 h4 13 ♘d3 f4 14 ♔h1 ♔f7 15 c5 ♖h8 16 ♕b3 b6 17 cxd6 cxd6 18 ♕a3 ♘c5 19 ♘xc5 bxc5 20 b4± Larsen - Tal, Bled 1965.

c) 11 ... f4 12 h4 ♔h8 13 ♘g2 ♘g8 14 ♗d2 ♗f6 15 ♗e1 ♖f7 16 ♔h2 ♕f8 17 b4 ♗d8 18 ♖c1 a5 19 a3 axb4 20 axb4 g5 (It looks strange to block the kingside, but White's play has been very insipid and Black can take

the initiative with ... c6 or a piece sacrifice on g4) 21 h5 ♘gf6 22 ♖h1 c6 23 dxc6 bxc6∓ Lukacs - Zakic, Budapest 1991.

d) 11 ... ♘f6 12 ♘d3 (12 ♘g2 c6 13 ♖b1 cxd5 14 cxd5 ♗d7 15 ♗e3 f4 16 ♗f2 g5 17 ♕d3 h5 18 h3 hxg4 19 hxg4 ♔f7 20 ♘b5 ♗xb5 21 ♕xb5 ♖h8 22 ♗e1 ♕g8 23 ♖c1 ♕h7 24 ♖c7 ♕h2+ 25 ♔f2 ♕g3+ 26 ♔g1 ½-½ Halasz - Forgacs, Hungary 1991) and now *(33)*:

d1) 12 ... c5 13 ♖b1 f4 14 h4 h6 15 ♗d2 ♘h7 16 ♗e1 ♗f6 17 ♔g2 ♗d7 18 b4 b6 19 bxc5 dxc5 20 a4 ♘c8 21 a5 ♘d6 22 ♕b3= Ftacnik - Marjanovic, Bucharest 1978.

d2) 12 ... c6 13 ♗e3 (13 ♘f2 ♔h8 14 ♔g2 ♕c7 15 ♗e3 ♗d7 16 h4 ♖f7 17 ♖c1 ♖af8 18 ♗d2 fxg4 19 fxg4 cxd5 20 cxd5 ♕b6 21 ♘h3 h6 22 g5 ♗xh3+ 23 ♔xh3 hxg5 24 hxg5∞ Lukacs - Sznapik. Baile Herculane Zt. 1982) 13 ... ♔h8 (13 ... fxe4 14 fxe4 h6 15 h4 b5 16 ♘f2 b4 17 ♘b1

♕e8 18 ♕d2 g5 19 h5 {*19 hxg5? hxg5 20 ♗xg5 would be very bad value after 20 ... ♕g6, when Black can develop a powerful kingside attack*} 19 ... c5 20 a3 ♕a4 21 ♕d1 {*It looks as if Black has been forcing the pace, but the activity is only temporary and White holds all the positional trumps*} 21 ... ♕a6 22 ♘d2 ♕b7 23 axb4 ♕xb4 24 ♕a4 ♕b8 25 b4 cxb4 26 c5 ♔h8 27 cxd6 ♕xd6 28 ♘c4 ♕d8 29 d6+- 1-0 Lisik - Zaitsev, Voronez 1991) and now:

d21) 14 ♖c1 b5 15 c5 cxd5 16 cxd6 d4? (16 ... ♘c6, when the weakness of the pawn on g4 could be significant, looks better) 17 dxe7 ♕xe7 18 g5 ♘xe4 19 ♘d5 ♕d8 20 fxe4 dxe3 21 h4 h6 22 gxh6 ♗xh6 23 ♘xe5 ♕e8 24 ♘e7 ♖f6 25 ♖c7 ♗e6 26 ♘g4 1-0 Halasz - Riemersma, Porabka 1987.

d22) 14 h3 b5 15 ♘b4! (This innovation of Pinter's is a big improvement over 15 c5 cxd5 16 cxd6 ♘c6 17 exd5 ♘d4 18 f4 ♘xe2+ 19 ♕xe2 e4∓ Pinter - Mortensen, Helsinki 1983) 15 ... bxc4 (White has the advantage after 15 ♘b4 and 15 ... cxd5 also failed to solve Black's problems in Pinter - Sznapik, Prague Zt. 1985, viz. 16 ♘bxd5 ♘exd5 17 ♘xd5 ♗b7 18 ♘xf6 ♕xf6 19

cxb5±. Black has insufficient compensation for the missing pawn) 16 ♘xc6 ♘xc6 17 dxc6 ♗e6 18 ♕a4 fxe4 19 fxe4 d5 20 ♗c5± (White is better and Black's forthcoming exchange sacrifice proves inadequate) 20 ... d4 21 ♗xf8 ♗xf8 22 c7! ♕e7 23 ♕c6 ♖c8 24 ♘d5 ♘xd5 25 exd5 ♗d7 26 ♕xc4 ♗h6 27 ♔g2 ♗e3 28 b4 e4 29 ♕c5 ♕xc5 30 bxc5 d3 31 ♖f7 ♗b5 32 d6 ♗g5 33 h4 ♗xh4 34 g5 1-0 Pinter - Mortensen, Copenhagen 1985.

12 ♗e3

White can also manoeuvre the knight:

a) 12 ♘d3 ♘g8 13 ♔h1 c5 14 a3 ♘df6 15 ♖g1 b6 16 ♗d2 ♖b8 17 b4 ♖b7 18 ♖b1 ♖bf7 19 bxc5 bxc5 20 ♕e1 ♘d7 21 ♘c1 fxg4 22 fxg4 h6 23 ♘b3 a6 24 g5 hxg5 25 ♗xg5 ♕f6 26 ♗e3 ♗h4 27 ♕d2 ♔h7 28 ♖g2 ♘df6 29 ♖bg1 ♘e7 30 ♗g5 ♗xg5 31 ♖xg5 ♔h8 32 ♕e3 ♖h7 33 ♖5g3 ♘h5 34 ♗xh5 ♖xh5 35 ♘d2 ♕e8 36 ♘f3 ♕f7 37 ♘e2 ♕h7 38 ♖1g2 ♕f7 39 ♖f2 ♗d7 40 ♔g1 ♔g7= Dzevlan - P Popovic, Yugoslavian Ch. 1991.

b) 12 ♘g2 (34):

b1) 12 ... ♘g8 13 ♗d2 a5 14 h4 ♘c5 15 ♖b1 ♗d7 16 ♗e3 b6 17 b3 fxg4 18 fxg4 ♖xf1+ 19 ♔xf1 ♘f6 (With his pressure against e4 and g4, Black stands very comfortably) 20 ♗f3 ♕f8 21 ♔g1

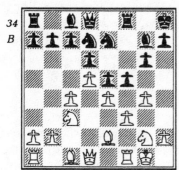

34
B

♕f7 22 ♕e2 h5 ½–½ Dridi – Campero, Novi Sad Ol. 1990

b2) 12 ... a5 13 h4 ♘c5 14 ♗e3 ♘g8 15 ♖b1 ♗d7 16 b3 (The weakness of the white pawns is evident by the fact that the natural 16 ♕d2? is unplayable on account of 16 ... fxe4 17 fxe4 ♘gf6, forking the two pawns and forcing the positionally awful capture on c5) 16 ... b6 17 a3 a4 18 b4 ♘b3 19 ♘b5 ♘f6 20 exf5 (If 20 g5 then 20 ... ♘h5 with two very typical themes from this variation in mind, i.e. 21 ... f4 followed by ... h6 and 21 ... ♘g3 followed by ... fxe4) 20 ... gxf5 21 ♘c3 e4! 22 g5 ♘h5 23 fxe4 f4 24 ♗d2 ♘xd2 25 ♕xd2 ♕e8 26 ♗f3 ♘g3 27 ♖fe1 ♗e5 (Black has a dream position from the King's Indian; a crushing dark square blockade and a weak white kingside to aim at. Nunn proceeds to methodically open lines against the white king) 28 ♘e2 ♘xe4!

29 ♗xe4 f3 30 ♘ef4 fxg2 31 ♘xg2 ♕h5 32 ♕d3 ♗g4 33 ♖e3 ♕f7 34 ♕d2 ♕g7 35 ♖d3 ♖f7 36 ♖e1 ♖af8 37 ♘e3 ♖f4 38 ♘g2 ♖4f7 39 ♘e3 ♗h5 40 ♖f1 ♖xf1+ 41 ♘xf1 ♖f4 42 ♕e1 ♗d4+ 43 ♖g2 ♕e5 44 ♘g3 ♗g4 45 b5 ♗f2 46 ♕xf2 ♗h3+ 0–1 Pinter – Nunn, Thessaloniki Ol. 1988.

12	...	♘g8
13	♕d2	♘df6

13 ... a6 14 ♘g2 f4 15 ♗f2 h5 16 gxh5 g5∓ 17 h4 ♗f6 18 ♕e1 ♖f7 19 ♔h2 ♖h7 20 ♖h1 ♕e8 21 hxg5 ♕xh5+ 22 ♗h4 ♗xg5 23 ♔g1 ♘f8 24 ♔f2 ♘g6 25 ♗xg5 ♕xg5 26 ♖xh7+ ♔xh7 27 ♕h1+ ♔g7 28 ♕h2 ♘f6 29 ♖g1 ♗g4 30 ♖h1 ♖h8 31 ♕g1 ♗h3 32 ♗f1 ♕g3+ 33 ♔e2 ♘g4 34 ♘d1 b6 35 b3 ♔f6 36 ♘f2 ♘xf2 37 ♕xf2 ♗xg2 38 ♕xg2 ♕xg2+ 39 ♗xg2 ♖xh1 40 ♗xh1 ♔g5 41 ♗g2 ♔h4 42 ♔f2 a5 43 a3 ♘f8 44 ♗f1 ♘d7 45 b4 ♘b8 46 ♔g2 axb4 47 axb4 ♘a6 48 b5 ½–½ Pinter – Nunn, Dubai Ol. 1986.

14	h3	h5
15	♔g2!	(35)

White finds a clever way to avoid the retrograde 15 ♕d1.

15	...	♘h7

The point of White's last move is revealed by the continuation 15 ... fxg4 16 fxg4 hxg4 17 hxg4 ♗xg4 18 ♗xg4 ♘xg4 19 ♖h1+ ♗h6 20 ♗xh6 ♘8xh6 21 ♖xh6+ ♔g7

22 ♖h3! ♖f2+ 23 ♕xf2 ②xf2 24 ♔xf2±. The pieces are much more effective than the queen.

Another try is 15 ... f4 16 ♗f2 ②h7 17 ②d3 ②g5 18 ♖h1 ②h6 19 ♖af1 ♔g8 20 ♗g1± Halasz-Shahal, Beer-Sheva 1991.

16	②d3	hxg4
17	hxg4	②gf6
18	♕d1!	♕d7 *(36)*

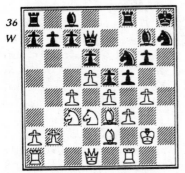

18 ... f4 19 ♗f2 ②h5 20 ♖h1 ②g3 21 ♗xg3 fxg3 22 ♕e1 ♗f6 23 ♕xg3 ♗g5 24 ♖h3 ♖f7 25 ♖ah1 ♕e7 26 c5 ♗d7 27 c6 bxc6 28 dxc6 ♗xc6 29 ②b4 ♗b7 30 ♗c4 ♖g7 31 ♗d5 ♖b8 32 ♕f2 ♗xd5 33 ②cxd5 ♕d7 34

♕xa7 ♕b5∞ Halasz - Borkowski, Porabka 1987.

19	②f2	f4?!
20	♗d2	②h6
21	♖h1	♔g7
22	b4	②g5
23	♔f1	♕e7
24	♖c1	♗d7

White's defensive moves on the kingside look horrible, but he has been careful not to allow any tactics based on sacrifices on g4 or e4 and Black's initiative on that wing has petered out. Now White takes his chance to pursue his queenside play with the aid of a dynamic pawn sacrifice.

25	c5!	dxc5
26	bxc5	♕xc5
27	②b5	♕b6
28	②a3!	

Not the obvious 28 ②xc7?, when 28 ... ♖ac8 traps the knight. White's target is the e-pawn which will come under intolerable pressure when White has regrouped with ②c4, ♗c3 and ②d3.

28	...	♖ae8
29	②c4	♕d4
30	♕c2	②f7 *(37)*
31	♗b4!?	

As this wins the exchange, it can hardly be called bad, but more consistent would have been 31 ♗c3! ♕c5 32 ♕b2 ♕e7 33 ②d3+-. The e-pawn drops

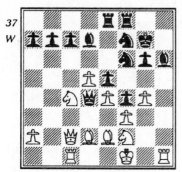

off and Black is left with weaknesses everywhere.

31	...	a6!

If the rook moves, the 32 ♖d1 traps the black queen.

32	♗xf8+	♖xf8
33	♘a5	♕b4
34	♕c3	♕xc3
35	♖xc3	b6
36	♘b3	♖c8
37	♔g2	

Not 37 ♗xa6 ♖a8 38 ♗d3 ♖xa2.

37	...	a5
38	♖hc1	♘e8
39	♘d2	♗g5
40	♘c4	♖b8
41	♘d3	♔f6
42	♖b1	♖a8
43	d6!	(38)

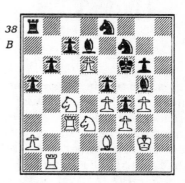

Being the exchange up, White forces open lines for the rooks. After this thrust, Black's positon falls apart.

43	...	b5
44	♘c5	♗c6
45	dxc7	♘xc7
46	♘b6	♖a7
47	♘b3	♘d8
48	♖bc1	1-0

3) Classical 9 ♘e1 ♘d7 10 f3 f5 11 ♗e3

As so often in chess, this move involves a straightforward trade of advantages. On the profit side of the balance sheet we find that White has acquired a much more active posting for the queen's bishop than the rather passive square of d2. The advance c5 will be supported, and the pressure against the vulnerable b6 and a7 squares can reap dividends. However, a search for the negative aspects of the move reveals that White will lose a tempo to ... f4, Black will find it easier to play ... g4 (no knight on f2) and when it drops back to f2, the bishop provides a further target for Black's kingside aspirations (... g3).

Following the natural sequence 11 ... f4 12 ♗f2 g5, White has two main ways of furthering the queenside play; 13 b4 which is the subject of game 6 (other 13th moves are also considered here), and 13 a4 (game 7). Kasparov dealt 13

b4 a hefty blow with his innovation against Piket (17 ... ♗f8!), and White needs an improvement here.

Game 6
Piket – Kasparov
Tilburg 1989

1	d4	♘f6
2	♘f3	g6
3	c4	♗g7
4	♘c3	0-0
5	e4	d6
6	♗e2	e5
7	0-0	♘c6
8	d5	♘e7
9	♘e1	♘d7
10	♗e3	f5
11	f3	f4
12	♗f2	g5 *(39)*

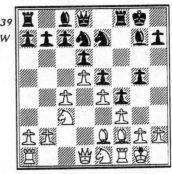

39
W

13 b4

White has various other possibilities here. For 13 a4 see the next game. Others are:

a) 13 ♖c1 ♘g6 (Black can also try the typical King's Indian strategem of swinging the king's rook over to h6: 13 ... ♖f6 14 b4 ♖h6 15 c5 a6 16 cxd6 cxd6 17 g4 fxg3 18 hxg3 ♘g6 19 ♘g2 ♘f4! {*A powerful sacrifice which gums up White's kingside and leaves Black with an enduring initiative*} 20 gxf4 gxf4 21 ♗h4 ♗f6 22 ♗xf6 ♘xf6 23 ♔f2 ♖h2 24 ♔g1 ♖h3 25 ♔f2 ♖g3 26 ♘xf4 exf4 27 ♕d4 ♘g4+ 28 ♔e1 ♘e5 29 ♔d2 ♗h3 30 ♖g1 ♗g2 31 ♘a4 ♗xf3 32 ♘b6 ♗xe2 33 ♔xe2 ♕g5 34 ♘xa8 f3+ 35 ♔f2 ♖g2+ 36 ♖xg2 ♕xg2+ 37 ♔e3 ♕g5+ 0-1 Speelman - Uhlmann, Leningrad 1984) 14 c5!? (The Yugoslav grandmaster Kozul has dabbled with this interesting sacrifice, but doesn't seem convinced of its worth and dismissed it with ?! in *Informator*. 14 b4 would transpose to normal lines) 14 ... ♘xc5 (Not 14 ... dxc5?! 15 b4! cxb4 16 ♘b5) 15 b4 ♘a6 (15 ... ♘d7? 16 ♘b5) 16 ♘b5 ♗d7 17 ♕a4 g4! (As so often in the King's Indian, counter-attack is the correct form of defence; 17 ... ♖f7 18 ♕a5 ♗xb5 19 ♗xb5 ♘b8 20 ♖c3

gives White excellent compensation) 18 fxg4 f3 19 gxf3 ♘f4 20 ♕d1 h5! (In Kozul - Cvitan, Yugoslavia 1990, Black mysteriously abandoned his kingside attack and after 20 ... ♘xb4?! 21 ♘c3! a5 22 ♔h1 ♘a6 23 ♗xa6 ♖xa6 24 ♘g2 ♖a8 25 ♘xf4 exf4 26 ♗d4 White had the advantage) 21 ♔h1 hxg4 22 ♘c3 ♘xe2 23 ♕xe2 gxf3 24 ♕d2 ♕f6 25 ♘d1 ♕g6∓ Kozul - Fedorowicz, Wijk aan Zee 1991.

b) 13 ♘b5!? *(40)*

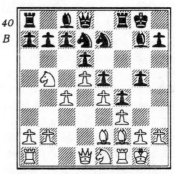

This is one of Korchnoi's numerous ideas to counter the King's Indian Defence. Black must either offer an exchange sacrifice, which seems to be dubious, or allow his queenside to be weakened. Black's possibilities are:

b1) 13 ... ♘f6!? (This is an interesting pawn sacrifice but, as it has only received one outing, it is difficult to form a conclusion) 14 ♘xa7 ♗d7 15 c5!? ♖xa7 16 cxd6

♘c8 17 dxc7 ♕xc7 18 ♗xa7 ♘xa7 19 ♕b3 ♘c5+ 20 ♔h1 ♘h5 21 ♘d3 ♕e3 22 ♘f2 ♕xe2 23 ♕xb7∞ Benjamin – Nunn, Hastings 1987/88.

b2) 13 ... a6?! (This was the original attempt to meet 13 ♘b5, but has now been rejected in favour of 13 ... b6) 14 ♘a7 ♖xa7 (Allowing the capture of the bishop on b8 would amount to positional suicide) 15 ♗xa7 b6 16 b4 ♗b7 17 c5 (17 ♕a4 is also promising, e.g. 17 ... ♘c8 18 c5 dxc5 19 ♗xa6 ♗xa6 20 ♕xa6 ♘d6 21 ♘d3 c4 22 ♘c5 bxc5 23 bxc5 ♘c8 24 c6 ♘db6 25 ♗xb6 ♘xb6 26 a4 ♕a8 27 ♕b5 ♕a7 28 ♔h1 ♖a8 29 a5 ♗f8 30 d6+– Zuger – Agnos, London {Lloyds Bank} 1987) 17 ... dxc5 18 ♖c1 ♘c8 (18 ... cxb4 19 d6 cxd6 20 ♕xd6 ♖f6 21 ♕c7 ♕c8 22 ♘d3 ♖c6 23 ♖xc6 ♘xc6 24 ♕xc8+ ♗xc8 25 ♖c1 ♘xa7 26 ♖c7± Honfi – Kupreichik, Budapest 1988) 19 bxc5 ♗a8 20 c6 ♘f6 21 ♗xb6 ♘xb6 22 ♗xa6 (White has more space and a strong pawn chain, whilst Black's bishop and knight are spectators) 22 ... g4 23 ♘d3 g3 24 h3 ♘e8 25 ♘c5 ♕b8 26 a4 ♘d6 27 a5 ♘bc8 28 ♔h1 ♕a7 29 ♕c2 ♘e7 30 ♖b1 ♘g6 31 ♖fc1 ♗f6 32 ♗f1 ♗xc6 33 dxc6 ♕xa5 34 ♖a1 ♕b4 35 ♘e6 1-0 Korchnoi – Hulak, Zagreb Izt.

1987.

b3) 13 ... b6 14 b4 (14 a4?! only seems to make White's task on the queenside more difficult, e.g. 14 ... a5 15 b4 axb4 16 ♘d3 ♘c5 17 ♘xb4 g4 18 a5 g3 19 hxg3 fxg3 20 ♗xg3 ♖xa5 21 ♖xa5 bxa5 22 ♘d3 ♘xd3 23 ♕xd3 ♘g6∓ Züger – Cvitan, Genf 1988) 14 ... a6 15 ♘c3 (15 ♘a3?! was tried in Huzman – Smirin, Sverdlovsk 1987. but it is difficult to see how the knight can be more useful here than on c3, as was indicated by the continuation: 15 ... h5 16 c5 b5 17 ♘ac2 ♘f6 18 a4 bxa4 19 ♖xa4 ♘g6 20 b5 g4 21 ♘b4 g3 22 hxg3 fxg3 23 ♗xg3 h4 24 ♘c6 ♕d7 25 ♗h2 ♗h6 26 f4 ♘xf4 27 bxa6 ♕g7 28 ♗xf4 ♗xf4 29 ♕d3 ♖xa6 30 ♖xa6 ♗xa6 31 ♕xa6 ♕g3 32 ♕d3 ♗e3+ 33 ♔h1 h3 34 ♖g1 ♔f7 0-1) and now we have a further branch *(41)*:

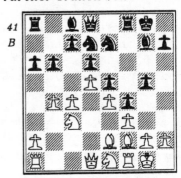

b31) 15 ... h5 16 ♔h1 ♘f6 17 c5 g4 18 cxb6 cxb6 19 ♖c1 g3 20 ♗g1 gxh2 21 ♗f2 (This body swerve by the bishop is a familiar means of dealing with the advance of the g-pawn) 21 ... h4 (Clearing the h5-square for the knight with the aid of a pawn sacrifice. Black cannot afford the luxury of 21 ... ♘g6?, when the response would be 22 ♘a4 ♖b8 23 ♖c6 and White piles in) 22 ♘a4 ♖b8 23 b5 axb5 24 ♗xb5 ♘h5 25 ♔xh2 ♘g3 26 ♖g1∞ Korchnoi - Ye Jiangchuan, Novi Sad Ol. 1990.

b32) 15 ... ♖f6 16 ♘d3 ♖h6 17 ♗e1 ♘f6 18 ♘f2 ♖g6 19 a4 h5 20 h3 ♔h8 21 a5 ♘eg8 22 b5 ♘h6 23 axb6 cxb6 24 bxa6 ♖xa6 25 ♖xa6 ♗xa6 26 ♕a4 ♗c8 27 ♕a8 g4∞ (Both sides have achieved their objectives and the position is dynamically equal) van der Sterren - Douven, Dutch Ch. 1987.

b33) 15 ... ♘g6 16 ♘d3 ♖f7 17 a4 ♗f8 18 a5 bxa5 (18 ... ♖b8 19 axb6 cxb6?! {*19 ... ♘xb6! 20 ♘c5 ♘d7*} 20 c5± Cebalo - Vukic, Yugoslavia 1987) 19 ♖xa5 (19 bxa5 may be an improvement notwithstanding the outcome of Thorhallsson - Jonsson, Reykjavik 1989: 19 ... ♖g7 20 c5 ♘f6 21 cxd6 ♗xd6 22 ♘c5 ♘f8 23 ♕b3 ♕e7 24 ♘e6 ♘xe6 25 dxe6 ♗xe6 26 ♕b7 ♕e8 27 ♖fd1 g4 28 ♗h4 ♗c5+ 29 ♔h1 ♖a7 30 ♕b2 ♕h5 31 ♗xf6 ♖g6 32 ♕b8+

♔f7 33 ♕d8 ♖xf6 34 ♖d7+ ♗xd7 35 ♕xd7+ ♔f8 36 ♕d8+ ♔g7 37 ♕d7+ ♔h8 38 ♕c8+ ♖f8-+) 19 ... ♖b8 20 c5 ♘f6 21 b5 axb5 22 ♘b4 ♗d7 23 c6 ♗c8 24 ♖a7 h5 25 ♘a6 ♗xa6 26 ♖xa6 b4 27 ♘b5 g4 28 ♕a4 g3 29 ♗a7 gxh2+ 30 ♔h1 ♖c8 31 ♗f2 h4 32 ♔xh2 ♘h5 33 ♕xb4 ♘g3 34 ♕e1 ♕g5 35 ♖g1 ♖h7 36 ♗f1 ♖e8 37 ♘c3 (White's pieces come scuttling back to defend the kingside) 37 ... ♖ee7 38 ♘e2 ♖h6 39 ♖a8 ♖eh7 40 ♔h3 ♘xe2 41 ♗xe2 *(42)* (Black now finishes off with a brilliant combination)

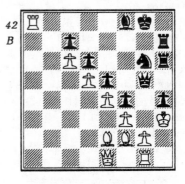

41 ... ♕g3+ 42 ♗xg3 hxg3+ 43 ♔g4 ♘e7 0-1 Piket - Douven, Dutch Ch. 1988.

13   ...   ♘f6

As is the case in numerous positions in the King's Indian, Black can also consider the immediate rook manoeuvre 13 ... ♖f6 14 c5 *(43)* and now:

a) 14 ... a6 15 c6 (Play now

43
B

becomes completely un-clear) 15 ... bxc6 16 dxc6 ♘f8 17 a4 ♖h6 18 b5 ♕e8 19 ♔h1 ♘e6 20 ♗c4 ♔h8 21 ♘d3 ♘d4 22 ♘b4 ♕h5 23 ♗g1 g4 24 ♘xa6 g3 25 ♘xc7 ♕g5 26 ♖f2 (The only way to defend against the threatened 26 ... ♖xh2+ and 27 ... ♕h4) 26 ... gxf2 27 ♘xa8 ♖g6 28 ♕f1 fxg1♕+ 29 ♕xg1 ♕h5 30 ♖f1 d5 31 ♘xd5 ♘xd5 32 ♗xd5 ♘e2 33 ♕b6 (44) (If your heart's desire is to finish off a game with a queen sacrifice, then this is clearly the variation to play! - see also G Burgess - Watson, note to Black's 17th)

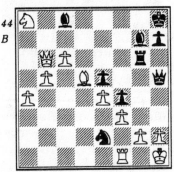

44
B

33 ... ♕xh2+! 0-1 Andruet -

van der Wiel, Montpellier Zt. 1985.

b) 14 ... ♖h6 (Watson has tried this twice, but allow-ing ♘b5 appears to give White the initiative) 15 cxd6 cxd6 16 ♘b5 ♘f6 (16 ... ♕e8 17 g4 fxg3 18 ♗xg3 ♕d8 19 ♕c1 ♘f8 20 ♕c7 ♕d7 21 ♖c1 a6 22 ♕xd7 ♗xd7 23 ♘c7± Korchnoi - Watson, Beer-Sheva 1987; with Black's rook stuck out of the game on h6, White has all the chances) 17 ♖c1 g4 18 fxg4 ♘xe4 19 ♘c7 ♘xf2 20 ♖xf2 ♖b8 21 ♗d3 ♖f6 22 h3 ♗d7 23 ♕b3 ♔h8 24 ♘f3 ♗c6 25 g5 ♖f8 26 ♗b1 ♕xc7 27 ♕d3 ♘f5 28 dxc6 ♖be8 29 ♕e4 bxc6 30 ♖xc6± D Gurevich - Watson, Beer-Sheva 1987.

14	c5	♘g6
15	cxd6	cxd6
16	♖c1	♖f7
17	a4 (45)	

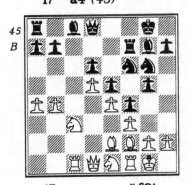

45
B

17 ... ♗f8!

17 ... h5 18 a5 ♗d7 (18 ... g4 19 ♘b5 b6 20 ♘xa7 ♖fxa7 21 ♗xb6 ♕e7 22 ♗xa7 ♕xa7+ 23 ♔h1 ♗d7 24 ♖c6

♗xc6 25 dxc6∞ Piket – Pieterse, Dutch Ch. 1988) 19 ♘b5 ♗xb5 20 ♗xb5 g4 21 ♔h1 (21 ♘d3 g3 22 ♗e1 gxh2+ 23 ♔h1 a6 24 ♗a4 h4 25 ♔xh2 ♘h5 26 ♖g1 ♘g3 27 ♘f2 ♘f8 28 ♘h3 ♘h7 29 ♗f2 ♗f6 30 ♗b6 ♕f8 31 ♖c4± D Gurevich – Weeramantry, US Open 1988) 21 ... g3 22 ♗g1 gxh2 23 ♗f2 h4 (23 ... a6 24 ♗b6 ♕f8 25 ♗e2 h4 26 ♔xh2 ♘h5 27 ♘d3 ♗f6 28 ♖g1 ♘g3 29 ♕d2 ♗d8 30 ♗xd8 ♖xd8 31 ♖c2 ♖h7 32 ♘f2 h3 33 gxh3 ♕h6 34 ♗f1 ♔h8 35 ♗g2 ♘h4 36 ♕c1 ♕g5 37 ♖c3 ♘e2 38 ♗h1 ♕g3+ 39 ♖xg3 fxg3+ 0-1 G Burgess – Watson, British Ch. 1989) 24 ♔xh2 ♘h5 25 ♖g1 ♘g3 26 a6! (an innovation at move 26(!); alternatively 26 ♘d3 ♗f8 27 ♗e1 ♖h7 28 ♘f2 h3! (*it is essential for Black to prevent the blockading ♘h3*) 29 gxh3 ♕h4 30 ♖c3 ♕h5 31 ♗f1 ♔h8∞ D Gurevich – Hellers, New York Open 1987) 26 ... bxa6 27 ♗xa6 (The point of White's manoeuvre is that he has weakened the light squares on the queenside and thus has possibilities to activate his king's bishop, the importance of which becomes clear in the game) 27 ... ♗f8 28 ♘d3 ♖h7 29 ♗e1 h3 30 gxh3 ♕h4 31 ♘f2 ♔h8 32 ♖c8 ♖xc8 33 ♗xc8 ♗e7 34 ♘h1 ♕h6 35

♗e6 ♘f8 36 ♗g4 ♗d8 37 ♘xg3 fxg3+ 38 ♗xg3 ♗b6 39 ♖g2 ♘g6 40 ♕a4 ♘f4 41 ♕e8+ ♔g7 42 ♗h4 ♕g6 43 ♕xg6+ ♘xg6 44 ♗f5 ♖xh4 45 ♖xg6++- Piket – Paneque, Adelaide 1988.

18 a5   ♗d7
19 ♘b5

The problem with the text move is that it weakens e4 and thus allows Black to get ... g4 in. There have been two games with the semi-waiting 19 ♔h1, but they have both confirmed that, in this position, Black's kingside play is more relevant than White's on the queenside, e.g. 19 ♔h1 ♖g7 *(46)* and now:

a) 20 ♘b5 g4 21 ♘xa7 g3 22 ♗b6 ♕e8 (Certainly not 22 ... ♕e7? 23 ♗b5, when the crucial Black light-squared bishop is exchanged and his counterplay is stillborn) 23 ♖c7 gxh2 24 ♖xb7 ♘h5 25 ♗f2 ♗e7 26 ♖xd7 ♕xd7 27 ♗b5 ♕c7 28

♘c6 ♗h4 29 ♘d3 ♕f7 30
♘dxe5 dxe5 31 ♘xe5 ♕f6 32
♘g4 ♕g5 33 ♗d4 ♘g3+ 34
♔xh2 ♘xf1+ 35 ♕xf1 ♖f7 36
♘f2 ♕h5 37 ♘h3 ♗f6 38
♗xf6 ♖xf6 39 ♗c6 ♖af8 40
a6 ♘e5 41 ♗b7?! ♕h4 42 ♕f2
♕xf2 43 ♘xf2 ♖b6 44 ♘h3
♖xb4 45 ♘xf4 ♖xf4 46 a7
♖f8 47 a8♕ ♖xa8 48 ♗xa8
♖b8 0-1 M Burgess – Badea,
Prestwich 1990.

b) 20 ♗b5 g4 21 ♗xd7
♕xd7 22 fxg4 ♘xg4 23 ♘f3
♗e7 24 ♗g1 ♘h4 25 ♕a4
♕d8 26 ♖c2 ♖c8 27 ♘xh4
♗xh4 28 ♘b5 ♖a8 29 h3 a6
30 ♘c3 ♕g5 31 ♖f3 ♘f6 32
b5 ♖c8 33 b6 ♔h8 34 ♘b5
♖xc2 35 ♕xc2 ♘xe4 36 ♘c7
♕g6 37 ♔h2 ♗g3+ 38 ♔h1
♗e1 39 ♘e6 ♘g3+ 40 ♖xg3
♗xg3 41 ♕c7 ♖xc7 42 bxc7
♕e8 43 ♘g5 ♗e1 44 ♘f7+
♕xf7 45 c8♕+ ♔g7 46 ♗b6
♗g3 47 ♕g4+ ♕g6 48 ♕d7+
♔h6 49 ♗g1 e4 50 ♕xb7 f3
51 gxf3 ♕f5 52 ♗e3+ ♔g6 53
♔g1 exf3 54 ♕b2 f2+ 55
♗xf2 ♕xf2+ 56 ♕xf2 ♗xf2+
57 ♔xf2 ♔f5 58 h4 ♔f4 0-1
D Gurevich – Gruenberg,
New York Open 1991.

> 19 ... g4!
> 20 ♘c7 g3! (47)
> 21 ♘xa8?

According to Kasparov,
this is the decisive mistake.
In a lengthy analysis in
New In Chess Yearbook 14,
he gives 21 hxg3 as the only
move, without reaching any

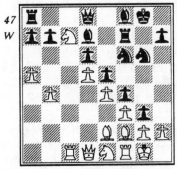

firm conclusion. The main
line of his analysis runs as
follows: 21 hxg3 fxg3 22
♗xg3 ♗h6 23 ♘xa8 ♘h5 24
♗f2 ♘gf4 25 ♘d3 ♖g7 26
♘xf4 ♗xf4 27 g4 ♗xc1 28
♕xc1 ♘f4 29 ♕e3 h5 30 ♖c1
hxg4 31 fxg4 ♘xe2+ 32
♕xe2 ♗xg4 33 ♕e3. Al-
though the outcome re-
mains in doubt, Black cannot possibly be worse, e.g.
33 ... ♕xa8 34 ♕xa7 ♕e8
and Black has counterplay
everywhere. White might
do better with 34 ♗g3 to
shield the king, but Black
still has the more secure
position.

> 21 ... ♘h5!

Highlighting the benefits
of keeping the h5-square
available for use by pieces.

> 22 ♔h1 gxf2
> 23 ♖xf2 ♘g3+
> 24 ♔g1 ♕xa8
> 25 ♗c4 a6

Kasparov finds an inge-
nious way to open up an-
other avenue to pursue his
dark square attack.

26	♕d3	♕a7!
27	b5	axb5
28	♗xb5 *(48)*	

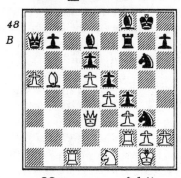

28	...	♘h1!

0-1

A brilliant finish from the World Champion.

Game 7
Korchnoi - Kasparov
Amsterdam 1991

1	♘f3	♘f6
2	c4	g6
3	♘c3	♗g7
4	e4	d6
5	d4	0-0
6	♗e2	e5
7	0-0	♘c6
8	d5	♘e7
9	♘e1 *(49)*	
9	...	♘d7

Black has two other 9th moves; 9 ... c5 is unimpressive, but 9 ... ♘e8 is worth a look. Thus:

a) 9 ... c5 10 f4 exf4 11 ♗xf4 ♘e8 12 ♘d3 f6 (Not really what Black wants to do, but e5 is looming, and he is hampered by the

self-inflicted weakness at d6) 13 h4 (Less direct, but not bad, was 13 ♕d2 ♗d7 14 ♖ab1 g5 15 ♗g3 ♘g6 16 ♘d1 ♕e7 17 ♘1f2 ♗h8 18 h3 ♘g7 19 b4 b6 20 bxc5 bxc5 21 ♗g4± Sosonko - Gunawan, Surakarta/Denpasar 1982) 13 ... a6 14 ♕e1 ♗d7 15 ♕g3 ♘c8 16 ♘f2 ♕e7 17 ♖ae1 ♖b8 18 h5 g5 19 ♗c1 b5 20 ♗g4 ♘b6 21 cxb5 axb5 22 ♕h3 h6 23 ♘cd1 ♖b7 24 ♘e3 ♗xg4 25 ♕xg4 ♕d7 26 ♘f5± Szygulski - Partos, Luzern Ol. 1982.

b) 9 ... ♘e8 (This can obviously transpose to other variations if Black quickly returns the knight to f6, but it can also have an independent existence) 10 f3 (10 ♘d3 has been played a few times, but doesn't cause Black problems, e.g. 10 ... f5 11 f4 exf4 12 ♗xf4 fxe4 13 ♘xe4 c6 14 dxc6 bxc6 15 ♕d2 ♘f5 16 ♖ae1 ♘f6 17 ♘c3 ♗e6= Pliester - Caessens, Groningen 1988. Black has free

and easy development) 10
... f5 11 g4 (11 ♗e3 is better,
e.g. 11 ... f4 12 ♗f2 g5 13 c5
♘g6 14 a4 ♖f7 15 cxd6 cxd6
16 ♖c1 h5 17 ♘b5 a6 18 ♘a3
♖b8 19 ♘c4± Farago –
Szekely, Hungary 1987) 11 ...
c5 12 ♘d3 ♗d7 13 ♖b1 ♔h8
14 b4 b6 15 ♗d2 ♘g8 (As a
result of White's kingside
play, he is weak on the dark
squares, so this is a very
logical plan) 16 ♘f2 ♗h6 17
♔g2 ♗xd2 18 ♕xd2 ♕h4 19
h3 ♘h6 20 ♘d3 ♘f7 21 ♕e1
♕e7 22 ♗d1 ♘f6 23 ♗a4
♗xa4 24 ♘xa4 h5∓ Tan –
Crawley, London (Chess for
Peace) 1987. White's kingside is vulnerable, and his
knight on a4 is very offside.

	10	♗e3	f5
	11	f3	f4
	12	♗f2	g5
	13	a4	*(50)*

The motivation behind 13
a4 is similar to that of 13
♘b5 - to force a weakening
of the black queenside.
White intends to follow up
with ♘b5, when ... b6 can

be met with a5, and ... a6
with ♘a7, harassing the vital dark-squared bishop. It
is yet another move that
was pioneered by Korchnoi
in his life-long quest to re-
fute the King's Indian.

	13	...	♘g6

The most usual, but
others are possible, e.g.

a) 13 ... ♖f7 14 a5 ♗f8 15
b4 (15 ♘b5 ♘f6 16 ♘xa7 ♗d7
would win a pawn at the
cost of some time. White
prefers to carry out the
assault with pawns, keep-
ing his piece placement
flexible) 15 ... ♘g6 16 c5
♘f6 17 ♘d3 ♖g7 18 b5 g4 19
fxg4 ♘h8 20 ♗h4± Ivanov –
Hebden, Hastings 1984.

b) 13 ... h5 14 ♘b5 ♘f6!?
is an interesting gambit
which led to the following
complex struggle in Korchnoi - Hellers, European
Club Cup 1987: 15 ♘xa7 ♗d7
16 ♘b5 g4 17 fxg4 (If 17 c5
Black can consider another
typical sacrifice, i.e. 17 ...
g3! 18 hxg3 fxg3 19 ♗xg3
♘g6∞) 17...hxg4 18 ♗h4
♘xe4 19 ♗xg4 ♘f6! 20 ♗xd7
♕xd7 21 ♖a3 ♘f5 22 ♗f2 e4
23 ♘c2 ♖ae8 24 ♗e1 f3 25
gxf3 e3 26 ♘cd4 ♘xd4 27
♘xd4 ♘h5 28 ♘e6? (28 ♔h1!
would have won) 28 ... ♖xe6
29 dxe6 ♕xe6 30 ♕d5 ♕xd5
31 cxd5 e2 32 ♖f2 ♗d4 ! 33
♔g2 ♘f4+ 34 ♔g3 ♘h5+ 35
♔g2 ♘f4+ ½-½.

c) 13 ... a5!? is a natural strategic counter which leads to a fascinating position. Classical theory says that you must play ... a5 when your opponent has gone a4 and c4. However, in this case the impending ♘b5 is a really annoying White response. Korchnoi's 13 a4 is actually a fantastic example of the way in which modern players are continually pushing forward the boundaries of strategic concepts. Play can continue 13 ... a5 14 ♘d3 *(51)* and now:

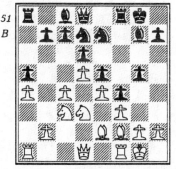

c1) 14 ... b6 15 b4 (Korchnoi later preferred 15 ♘b5, claiming it as a little better for White) 15 ... axb4 (15 ... h5 16 bxa5 ♖xa5 17 ♘b5 ♘f6 18 ♗e1 ♖a6 19 a5 g4 20 axb6 cxb6 21 ♗b4± Korchnoi - van der Wiel, Brussels Blitz 1987) 16 ♘xb4 ♘c5 17 ♘d3 ♘b7 18 ♘c1 ♖f6 19 ♘b3 ♗f8 20 ♘b5 ♗d7 21 ♕d2± Franco - Milos, Pamplona Open 1991. Black's manoeuvres

have only lost time and allowed White to build up on the queenside.

c2) 14 ... ♘g6 15 c5 ♘f6 16 ♖c1 ♖f7 17 cxd6 cxd6 18 ♕b3 (A double-edged move; White presses on with his queenside attack, but leaves his king dangerously short of defenders and permits the immediate ... g4) 18 ... g4 19 ♗b6 ♕e7 20 ♘b5 g3 21 ♖c7 (Not 21 h3? ♗xh3-+) 21 ... ♗d7 22 ♔h1 ♘h5 (Although this forces White to give up the exchange, it also enables him to secure the kingside, so maybe 22 ... hxg3 {△ ... ♘h5 - g3} was better) 23 h3 ♕h4 24 ♖xd7 ♖xd7 25 ♘c7 ♖c8 26 ♘e6 ♘f6 27 ♗xa5 ♕h5 28 ♕d1 ♘f8 29 ♗c3 ♖e7 30 ♘b4 ♕f7 31 ♘xf8 ♗xf8 32 a5 ♖ec7 33 a6 bxa6 34 ♗xa6 ♖xc3 35 bxc3 ♖xc3 36 ♘c6 ♕c7 37 ♕a1 ♖b3 38 ♗c4 ♖b6 39 ♖c1 ♘d7 40 ♕a2 ♗g7 41 ♖a1 ♗f6 42 ♗d3 ♘b8 43 ♕a8 ♕b7 ½-½, Franco - Reyes, Toledo 1991.

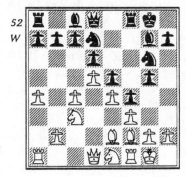

14 ♘d3

Or 14 a5 and:

a) 14 ... h5 15 ♔h1 ♖f7 16 ♘b5 a6 17 ♘a7 ♘f6 18 ♘xc8 ♕xc8 (It is highly unusual for Black to voluntarily relinquish his queen's bishop in these positions. Here, assisted by the weakness of the e4-pawn, he manages to generate some play on the kingside, but he ultimately lacks sufficient firepower to make it count) 19 ♘d3 g4 20 ♗g1 ♗f8 21 ♖e1 h4 22 ♘f2 h3 23 fxg4 hxg2+ 24 ♔xg2 f3+ 25 ♗xf3 ♘xd5 26 cxd5 ♘h4+ 27 ♔h1 ♘xf3 28 ♖e3 ♘xg1 29 ♔xg1 ♗h6 30 ♖f3 ♗f4 31 ♔g2 ♕d7 32 ♕e2 ♖af8 33 ♖f1 ♖g7 34 h3 ♖f6 35 ♖b3 ♗g5 36 ♘h1 ♖xf1 37 ♕xf1 c6 38 ♕c4 c5 39 ♘g3 ♗d8 40 ♘f5+- Ikonnikov - Mamadshoev, USSR 1991.

b) 14 ... ♖f7 15 b4 (If 15 ♘b5, the following variation, given by Nunn, is very instructive; 15 ... ♘f6 16 ♘xa7 g4! 17 ♘xc8 g3 18 hxg3 ♘h5 19 gxf4 exf4∓) 15 ... ♘f6 16 c5 ♗f8 17 cxd6 ♗xd6 (If 17 ... cxd6 18 ♘b5 and the b6-square will be weakened) 18 ♘d3 ♖g7 19 ♘c5 ♘f8 20 ♘b5 g4 21 ♗h4 (Much better than 21 ♕e1?, which allowed Black to develop a strong attack after 21 ... ♕e8 22 fxg4 ♘xg4 23 ♖a3 ♕g6 24 ♗f3 ♕h6! 25 h3 ♘xf2 26 ♔xf2 ♗e7 27 ♕c1 b6!∓ Korchnoi - Nunn, Amsterdam 1990) 21 ... h5 22 ♗c4 ♕e7 23 ♔h1 a6? (Better was 23 ... ♔h8, sidestepping the tactical trick that now arises) 24 ♘xc7 ♕xc7 25 ♗xf6 ♖f7 26 ♗g5 ♘d7 27 ♖c1 ♘xc5 28 bxc5 ♕xc5 29 ♕e1± Korchnoi - J Polgar, Pamplona 1990/91. White has pressure on the c-file and the black kingside is weak.

14	...	♘f6
15	c5	h5
16	h3	♖f7
17	c6	*(53)*

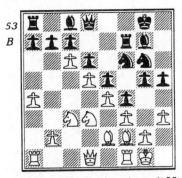

Setting Black the difficult problem of how to pursue his kingside attack without getting wiped out on the opposite wing. Plunging in with 17 ... g4? is unattractive after 18 fxg4 hxg4 19 cxb7 ♗xb7 20 ♗xg4, while waiting with 17 ... ♗f8? is similarly bad after 18 ♘b5 a6 19 ♘a7. Kasparov finds an ingenious solution.

17 ... a5!

This slows White down

on the queenside and guarantees the preservation of the light-squared bishop

18 cxb7

Black plans to meet 18 b4 with 18 ... b6! 19 bxa5 bxa5!

18	...	♗xb7
19	b4	♗c8
20	bxa5	♗h6!
21	♘b4?	

This ultimately loses too much time. Kasparov prefers 21 a6! ♗xa6 22 ♘b4 ♗c8 which he assesses as unclear. If Black gets carried away on the kingside, he can ultimately pay the penalty. The following remarkable variation is given by Kasparov: 21 a6! g4?! 22 fxg4 hxg4 23 hxg4 ♗g5? 24 a7 ♖h7 25 ♖e1 ♕f8 26 ♖b1! ♕h6 27 ♔f1 ♕h1+ 28 ♗g1 ♘h4 29 ♗f3 ♘xg4 30 ♖b8! ♘xf3 31 ♕xf3 ♘h2+ 32 ♔e2 ♘xf3 33 gxf3 ♕g2+ (Black has won the white queen and is still on the attack, but it is not enough) 34 ♔d1 ♕xf3+ 35 ♔c2 ♖h3 36 ♖d1 ♕g2+ 37 ♔b3 ♔f7 38 ♖xa8 ♗g4 39 ♖c1 ♖xd3 40 ♖b8! ♕d2 41 a8♕ ♕xc1 42 ♖f8+ ♔g7 43 ♖g8+ ♔h6 44 ♕f8+ ♔h5 45 ♖h8+ ♔g6 46 ♕e8+ *(54)* and White wins!

This is, of course, far from being forced, and may well be the fruit of a piece of extravagant post-mor-

tem analysis. Nevertheless, the variation is highly thematically instructive.

21	...	g4
22	♘c6	♕f8
23	fxg4	hxg4
24	hxg4	

If 24 ♗xg4 then 24 ... ♘xg4 25 hxg4 f3! is crushing.

24	...	♗g5
25	♗f3	♕h6
26	♖e1	♘h4 *(55)*

27 ♗xh4

Not what White would want to play, but there was no good way to deal with the threat of 27 ... ♘xf3+ 28 gxf3 ♗xg4! 29 fxg4 ♕h3 with a quick finish.

27 ...   ♗xh4!

Many players would have played 27 ... ♛xh4 here, which seems overpowering but actually allows White to put up resistance by heading for the hills with his king, i.e. 28 ♔f1 ♘xg4 29 ♔e2.

Having tracked down his prey, Black must be careful not to let it escape at the last moment.

28	g5	♛xg5
29	♖e2	♘g4
30	♖b1	♗g3
31	♛d3	♛h4
	0-1	

4) Classical 9 ♞d2

9 ♞d2 is a good choice for white players who want something that gets going quicker on the queenside than 9 ♞e1, but baulk at the outright aggression of 9 b4. The knight is heading for an ideal post on c4 (after c5) where it will pressurise the d6-pawn often in conjunction with ♗a3. White's play on the queenside comes very quickly and so although it is possible for Black to press ahead on the king-side, most players prefer to opt for some prophy-lactic action on the queen-side.

There are three app-roaches to to the problem which White's 9th presents Black:

a) 9 ... a5 (Games 8 and 9). This slows White down by a tempo or two, after which Black will join in the race, hoping to have impeded White down sufficiently to keep the balance.

b) 9 ... c5 (Game 10). This is rather less ambitious.

Black plays to block the position and to keep White under control on the queen-side.

c) 9 ... ♞e8 and others (Game 11). This commences a very ambitious strategy. Despite the warning signs on the queenside, Black plays the standard kingside plan.

Game 8
Kasparov – Smirin
USSR Ch. 1988

1	d4	♞f6
2	c4	g6
3	♞c3	♗g7
4	e4	d6
5	♞f3	0-0
6	♗e2	e5
7	0-0	♞c6
8	d5	♞e7
9	♞d2	a5 (56)

This is currently almost the main line of the King's Indian. All the top players are keen to have their say in the debate, the result of which is a host of fascina-ting encounters.

10 ♖b1

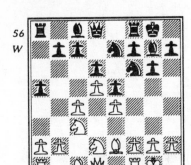

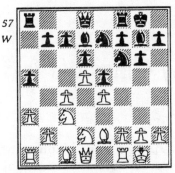

White must continue the queenside advance and so only the text, 10 a3 or 10 b3 come into consideration. Whichever one White opts for, the other two often occur on moves 11 and 12, but there are some possibilities for independent play:

a) 10 a3 ♗d7 (10 ... ♘d7 will usually emerge as a main line, but the extravagant rook manoeuvre 11 ♖a2 is also possible, e.g. 11 ... f5 12 b4 ♘f6 13 f3 c6 14 bxa5 fxe4 15 ♘dxe4 ♘f5 16 a6 ♖xa6 17 c5 ♖a5 18 ♗c4 b5 19 cxb6 ♕xb6+ 20 ♔h1 ♗a6 21 ♗xa6 ♕xa6 22 dxc6 ♘xe4 23 ♘xe4 d5∓ Nikolic - Nunn, Reykjavik 1988). The point of 10 ... ♗d7 is to play ... a4, but it is not clear if this is a threat or a bluff. The evidence suggests that White does best to treat it as a bluff *(57)*:

a1) 11 b3 c5 slows White down on the queenside, and Black should be fine, e.g. 12 ♖b1 ♘e8 13 b4 axb4 14 axb4 b6 15 bxc5 (15 ♘b3 cxb4 16 ♘b5 f5 17 f3 ♘f6 18 ♗d3 ♗xb5 19 cxb5 ♘d7 20 ♗d2 ♘c5 21 ♗xb4 ♗h6 22 ♖e1 fxe4 23 fxe4 ♔g7= Azmaiparashvili - Nunn, Amsterdam OHRA 1990) 15 ... bxc5 16 ♘b3 f5 17 f3 ♘f6 18 ♗d2 f4 19 ♘b5 ♘c8 20 ♖a1 ♖xa1 21 ♕xa1 g5 (White's queenside initiative is well balanced by Black's kingside play and the position is about equal) 22 ♕a6 ♕e7 23 ♘a5 g4 24 ♘c6 ♕f7 25 ♘b8 g3 26 ♘xd7 gxh2+ 27 ♔h1 ♕xd7 28 ♕c6 ♕d8 29 ♖a1 ♘h5 30 ♗e1 ♘g3+ 31 ♗xg3 fxg3∓ Vaganian - Gelfand, USSR Ch. 1989.

a2) 11 ♖b1 a4 12 b4 axb3 13 ♘xb3 (White's queenside has been slightly weakened, but he has more activity as compensation) 13 ... b6 (13 ... c5!? is well worth a look. Normally it is counter-productive for Black to force the play in the sector where White has the edge, but here things are not so clear, e.g. 14 dxc6 ♗xc6 15 ♕d3 ♘h5!? 16 g3?! f5 17 exf5 ♘xf5 18 ♗f3 ♗xf3 19 ♕xf3 e4∓ van der Sterren – Uhlmann, Novi Sad Ol. 1990) 14 ♖a1 h5 (14 ... ♕e8 is a consistent continuation of Black's plan, but it is difficult to believe that White can be permanently inhibited from advancing on the queenside; Chabanon – Kr. Georgiev, Sofia 1990 saw 15 ♕d3 ♗a4 16 ♗d1 ♔h8 17 ♗e3 ♘eg8 18 ♘xa4 ♖xa4 19 ♘d2 ♖a5 20 c5 bxc5 21 ♘c4 ♖a7 22 a4⩲) 15 a4 ♘h7 16 a5 f5 17 ♗a3!? bxa5 18 c5 ♗e8 19 ♖a2 ♘f6 20 f3 ♗h6 21 ♔h1 ♗e3 22 ♕d3∞ Blees – Piket, Dutch Ch. 1990.

b) 10 b3 *(58)* will again often transpose to the main line, but, given the chance, White might also consider a plan with ♗a3. Some possibilities:

b1) 10 ... c5 (Cutting across the ♗a3 plan and forcing White into more

normal positions) 11 a3 ♘e8 12 ♖b1 f5 13 b4 axb4 14 axb4 b6 15 ♕b3 ♘f6 16 ♗d3 ♗h6 (16 ... ♘h5!? is an alternative. White is essentially a tempo down on the variations with 9 ... c5, and so Black should be fine) 17 ♖b2 ♖a1 18 ♕c2 ♗f4 19 ♘f3 fxe4 20 ♘xe4 ♘xe4 21 ♗xe4 ♖xc1 22 ♖xc1 ♗xc1 23 ♕xc1 ♘f5 24 ♕g5 ♘d4 25 ♕xd8 ♘xf3+ 26 ♗xf3 ♖xd8 27 bxc5 bxc5 28 ♖b8± Karpov – Kasparov, Seville (17) 1987.

b2) 10 ... ♘d7 allows White to pursue his plan. i.e. 11 ♗a3 f5 12 b4 axb4 13 ♗xb4 ♔h8 14 a4 ♘g8 15 ♘b3 b6 16 a5 ♘c5 17 ♖a3 ♗d7 18 ♗xc5 bxc5 19 a6 ♘f6 20 a7 ♗h6 21 ♗f3 ♗f4 22 ♕e2 h5 23 g3± Lputian – Dorfman, Moscow 1986.

10	...	♘d7
11	a3	f5
12	b4 *(59)*	

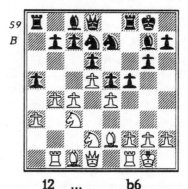

| 12 | ... | b6 |

12 ... ♔h8 is examined in the next game. Other alter-

natives here are:

a) 12 ... axb4 13 axb4 ♔h8 (13 ... ♘f6 allows White a free hand on the queenside, e.g. 14 c5 ♗h6 15 f3 ♘h5 16 ♘c4 ♗xc1 17 ♖xc1 ♘f4 18 g3 ♘xe2+ 19 ♕xe2 fxe4 20 fxe4 ♗h3 21 ♖xf8+ ♕xf8 22 ♕f2 ♕xf2+ 23 ♔xf2 ♘c8 24 ♘b5 ♖a2+ 25 ♔e3 dxc5 26 bxc5 c6 27 ♘c3 1-0 Dorfman – Balashov, USSR Ch. 1984) 14 ♕c2 (14 f3 ♘g8 15 ♕c2 f4 16 ♘b5 ♘df6 17 c5 ♘e8 18 ♘c4 g5 19 ♗d2 ♘gf6 20 ♖a1± de Boer – Odendahl, Dieren Open 1990) 14 ... ♘f6 15 f3 c6 16 dxc6 bxc6 17 b5 cxb5 18 ♘xb5 ♘h5 19 ♘b3 fxe4 20 fxe4 ♕b6+ 21 ♔h1 ♖xf1+ 22 ♗xf1 ♘f6 23 ♗a3± Shirov – Piket, Groningen 1990.

b) 12 ... ♘f6?! was given a going over in Shirov – Ivanovic, Manila Izt. 1990: 13 c5! (Of course!) 13 ... axb4 14 axb4 ♔h8 15 f3 ♘h5 16 g3 ♘g8 17 ♘c4 ♘gf6 18 ♗d2 fxe4 19 fxe4 ♗h3 20 ♖f2 ♕e7 21 c6 b6 22 ♗g5 ♕e8 23 ♕d2 ♕c8 24 ♗f1 ♗xf1 25 ♖bxf1 ♕g4 26 ♗xf6 ♖xf6 27 ♕e2+–. Black's pieces are horribly placed and c7 is very weak.

13 f3 (60)

Or 13 ♘b3 (On general principles, White doesn't want to do this – the knight should really be reserved for the c4-square) 13 ...

axb4 14 axb4 ♘f6 (Breaking the tension with 14 ... fxe4 is probably better, e.g. 15 ♘xe4 ♘f6 16 ♗d3 ♗d7 17 ♗b2 ♘xe4 18 ♗xe4 ♔h8 19 ♖a1 ♘g8 20 ♕d3 ♖xa1 21 ♖xa1 ♘f6= Vilela – A Rodriguez, Havana 1978) 15 ♗d3 f4 (Black goes for a typical King's Indian race, but the self-inflicted weakness on c6 has made White's task rather easier) 16 f3 g5 17 c5 ♘g6 18 cxd6 cxd6 19 ♗d2 h5 20 ♘b5 g4 21 ♖c1 ♘h7 22 ♘xd6 ♕xd6 23 ♖c6 ♕d8 24 ♖xg6 ♔f7 25 ♖c6 ♗d7 26 ♖c3 g3 27 h3 ♘g5 (White has won a pawn, but Black has awkward kingside counterplay) 28 ♕e2 ♗xh3 29 gxh3 ♘xh3+ 30 ♔g2 ♘f2 31 ♖xf2 gxf2 32 ♕xf2∞ and the game Conquest – Berg, Copenhagen Open 1987, was eventually drawn.

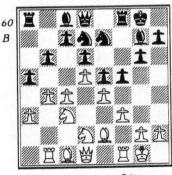

60
B

13 ... f4

Again closing the centre. but this seems illogical after ... b6. The rest of this game is a model demon-

stration for White. How-
ever, others have not fared
well either:

a) 13 ... ♗h6 is usually a
doubtful manoeuvre in
these positions. Black
achieves the exchange of
the theoretically 'bad' bishop, but loses time and
weakens the kingside.
Blees - Berg, Dieren Open
1987 saw 14 ♘b3 ♗xc1 15
♖xc1 axb4 16 axb4 ♘f6 17 c5
♔g7 18 cxb6 cxb6 19 ♖a1
♗d7 20 ♕d2 ♖xa1 21 ♖xa1±.

b) 13 ... ♔h8 is quite
playable, but if Black likes
this plan it would seem
better to execute it on
move 12. Play can now continue: 14 ♕c2 (14 bxa5 ♖xa5
15 ♘b3 ♖a8 16 a4 ♘g8 17
♖a1 ♘df6 18 a5 bxa5 19 ♖xa5
♖xa5 20 ♘xa5 ♗d7 21 ♗e3
♗h6 22 ♗xh6 ♘xh6= Wi-
nants - Riemersma, Am-
sterdam 1987) 14 ... ♘g8 15
♗d3 ♗h6?! (This gambit
turns out badly; 15 ... fxe4
∆ ... ♘gf6 looks better) 16
exf5 gxf5 17 ♗xf5 ♗e3+ 18
♔h1 ♕h4 19 ♗xd7 ♗xd7 20
♘de4 ♗xc1 21 ♕xc1 ♖f5 22
♕e1 ♕e7 23 c5± van der
Sterren - Peelen, Wijk aan
Zee 1990. Black has nothing
for the pawn.

14 ♘a4   axb4
15 axb4   g5 *(61)*

Black has set the tone
for the game - it will be
the familiar race on oppo-

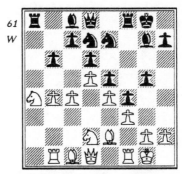

site wings. But White al-
ready has a head start.
since Black's pieces are
simply not aggressively
placed enough as yet to
pose a serious threat to the
white king.

16 c5   ♘f6
17 cxd6   cxd6
18 b5   ♗d7
19 ♘c4   ♘c8
20 ♗a3   ♘e8
21 g4±

Having established do-
minance on the left wing.
Kasparov seals up the kingside in order to reduce
possible black counter-
chances in that sector.
Smirin has little choice but
to capture, otherwise he
would be suffocated with-
out resistance.

21 ...   fxg3
22 hxg3   g4
23 ♗c1

A fine move. Kasparov
adapts to the changed situation and prepares to di-
vert his attention to the
king's wing. In particular.

he wishes to prevent Black from playing ... ♗h6.

23	...	gxf3
24	♗xf3	♘f6
25	♗g5	♖a7
26	♖f2	♖b7
27	♖b3	♖a7
28	♖b1	♖b7
29	♖b3	♖a7
30	♖b4!	*(62)*

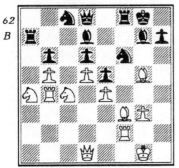

With this move Kasparov dashes any hopes Black might have harboured of achieving a draw by repetition. The text prepares a profound pawn sacrifice whereby White switches the decisive field of conflict towards the black king.

30	...	♔h8
31	♕f1	

Intensifying the pressure against the pinned knight on f6 and simultaneously offering a pawn which Black would have been best advised to decline.

31	...	♗xb5

Black snaps at the bait, perhaps in the erroneous belief that Kasparov had overlooked the possibility of this trick.

32	♖xb5	♖xa4
33	♗g2	h6
34	♗h4	♕e8

The only way to unpin, but now Kasparov unleashes a combinational storm which sweeps away Black's lines of defence.

35	♗xf6	♖xf6
36	♖xf6	♕xb5
37	♖e6	♔g8

If 37 ... ♕xc4 38 ♖e8+ wins or 37 ... ♖xc4 38 ♕f7 with a decisive attack.

38	♗h3	♖xc4 *(63)*

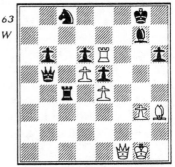

39 ♖xh6

Kasparov has sacrficed a knight and now a rook in most brilliant fashion. Black cannot avoid being checkmated.

39	...	♗xh6
40	♗e6+	♔h8
41	♕f6+	1-0

If 41 ... ♗g7 42 ♕h4+ or 41 ... ♔h7 42 ♕f7+ ♗g7 43 ♗f5+ ♔h8 44 ♕h5+ ♔g8 45 ♗e6+ with mate to follow. A wonderfully imaginative effort by the World Champion.

Game 9
Epishin – van Wely
Wijk aan Zee 1992

1	d4	♘f6
2	c4	g6
3	♘c3	♗g7
4	e4	d6
5	♘f3	0-0
6	♗e2	e5
7	0-0	♘c6
8	d5	♘e7
9	♘d2	a5
10	♖b1	♘d7
11	a3	f5
12	b4 *(64)*	

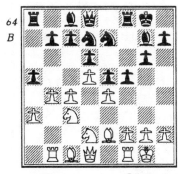

12 ... ♔h8

This is currently a highly fashionable continuation. Black tucks the king away and clears g8 for the knight. It has more or less superseded the alternatives.

13 f3

13 ♕c2 *(65)* is an important alternative:

a) 13 ... ♘f6 14 f3 axb4 15

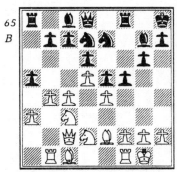

axb4 f4 16 c5 g5 17 ♘b5 (Naturally, White wants to pursue his queenside attack without delay, but this thrust runs into an unexpected counter. A better method would have been 17 ♘c4, avoiding the forthcoming tactic) 17 ... dxc5! (Horribly anti-positional. but Black intends a quick ... c6) 18 bxc5 c6 19 d6 cxb5 20 dxe7 ♕xe7 21 ♖xb5 g4 22 ♗b2 gxf3 23 ♗xf3 ♘g4 24 ♗xg4 ♗xg4 25 ♘f3 ♖fc8 ½-½ Ftacnik – Nunn, Groningen 1988.

b) 13 ... b6 14 ♘b3 (This allows Black to simplify, so 14 f3 would have been better) 14 ... axb4 15 axb4 fxe4 16 ♘xe4 ♘f6 17 ♗d3 ♘xe4 18 ♗xe4 ♘f5 19 ♕d3 ♕h4 20 g3 ♕f6 21 f3 ♗d7 22 ♗d2 ♘d4 23 ♘xd4 exd4 24 ♖a1 ♗h3 25 ♖xa8 ♖xa8 26 ♖d1 ♗f5 27 ♖e1± Gavrikov – Kasparov, USSR Ch. 1988.

c) 13 ... fxe4 14 ♘cxe4 ♘f5 (Black is hoping to exploit the position of the

white queen by hopping into d4 with a knight. It is
also possible to follow this
plan after throwing in 14 ...
axb4 15 axb4, e.g. 15 ... ♘f5
16 ♘f3 h6 17 ♗d2 ♘f6 18 ♗d3
♘h5 19 ♖a1 and now instead
of 19 ... ♖b8? 20 ♘g3±
Hertneck - J Polgar, Munich
1991, 19 ... ♖xa1 20 ♖xa1 ♘f4
gives good counterplay) 15
♘b3 (15 ♕d3 ♘f6 16 ♘xf6
♗xf6 17 ♗g4 ♗g5?! 18 ♗b2
♔g8 19 ♘e4 ♗h6 20 ♖be1±
Blees -- Carstens Krumba-
cher Open 1991; or 15 ♗d3
{*perhaps the best at this
juncture*} 15 ... ♘f6 16 ♗g5
h6 17 ♗d2 ♘h5 18 ♘e2 axb4
19 axb4 ♕h4 20 g3 ♕e7 21 f3
♘f6 22 ♖f2± Anapolsky -
Shchekachev, Jurmala 1991)
15 ... axb4 16 axb4 ♘f6 17
♗d3 ♘xe4 18 ♗xe4 ♕h4 19
♗d2 ♗d7 20 ♗c3 b6 21 ♖be1
♖a3 22 ♗b2 ♖a2 and now in
Stohl - Marin, Stara Zagora
Zt. 1990, White blundered
horribly with 23 ♖a1?? ♖xb2
24 ♕xb2 ♕xe4-+, but after
22 ... ♖a2 Black is doing
fine anyway.

d) 13 ... ♘g8 *(66)*. This
was Nigel Short's choice in
his solitary dabble with the
King's Indian. After his
adoption of it against Salov
in the Skelleftea World
Cup, it became extremely
popular. Some examples:

d1) 14 f3 ♘gf6 15 ♘b5
♘h5 16 g3 (Why not get on

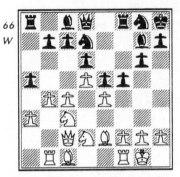

66
W

with it with the immediate
16 c5? - the extra tempo
wasted proves costly) 16 ...
♘df6 17 c5 fxe4 18 fxe4
axb4 19 axb4 ♗h3 20 ♖f2
♕d7= Ftacnik - Wang Zili,
Sydney 1991.

d2) 14 ♘b5 ♘df6 (Whe-
never White loosens con-
trol over the e4-square, it
is tempting to look at a
plan with ... fxe4 and ...
♘f6. Here, for example, 14
... fxe4 15 ♘xe4 ♘f6 looks
fine for Black) 15 f3 (15 ♗d3
axb4 16 axb4 ♘h5 17 ♘f3
♘gf6 18 ♗g5 {*18 exf5 e4! is
a cunning tactic*} 18 ... ♘f4
19 ♘d2 ♘xd3 20 ♕xd3 ♗d7
21 ♖a1 ♗xb5 22 cxb5 ♕d7=
Vaganian - Marin, Manila
Izt. 1990) 15 ... ♗d7 16 bxa5!?
♖xa5 17 c5 fxe4 (If 17 ...
dxc5 18 a4 △ ♘b3 or ♘c4
with compensation) 18 fxe4
♘g4 19 ♘f3 ♗xb5 20 ♖xb5
♖xb5 21 ♗xb5 ♗h6 22 ♕c3
♗xc1 23 ♕xc1 h6 24 a4 ♔g7
25 ♗d3 ♕b8 ½-½ Khalifman
- Torre, Manila Izt. 1990.

d3) 14 ♗b2. White hopes

this will prove a useful waiting move, but Khalifman shows the way to deal with it:

d31) 14 ... ♘gf6?! 15 ♖be1 f4 16 c5 dxc5 17 bxc5 ♘xc5 18 ♘b5 ♘fd7 19 ♘f3 b6 20 a4 ♗a6 21 ♗a3 ♗f6 22 ♖d1 g5 23 h3 ♖g8 24 ♘h2 ♗g7 25 ♗c4 ♗f8 26 d6 ♗xb5 27 dxc7 ♕xc7 28 ♗xb5 ♘f6 29 ♗b2 g4 30 hxg4± Salov – Short, Skelleftea World Cup 1989, although Black went on to win.

d32) 14 ... ♘df6! (This is much better. Black maintains the pressure on e4, and frees the queen's bishop. If now 15 c5, trying to exploit the knight move, then 15 ... fxe4 16 ♘cxe4 ♘xe4 17 ♘xe4 ♘f6 equalises comfortably) 15 ♖bd1 ♗d7 16 exf5 (This plays into Black's hands, but White is stuck for a plan as the natural 16 c5 fails to 16 ... axb4 17 axb4 fxe4 18 ♘dxe4 ♘xe4, and now White must play the awkward 19 ♕xe4 as 19 ♘xe4? loses to 19 ... ♗a4) 16 ... gxf5 17 f4 exf4 18 ♖xf4 axb4 19 axb4 ♘e7 20 ♖ff1 ♘g6 21 ♘b3 ♘g4 22 ♗xg4 fxg4 23 ♘e4 ♘e5 24 ♖xf8+ ♕xf8 25 ♖f1 ♕e7 26 ♘g3 ♕g5∓ Illescas – Khalifman, Manila Izt. 1990.

d4) 14 exf5 gxf5 15 f4 *(67)* This is the latest try for White, but it hasn't led

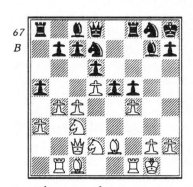

67
B

anywhere to date, e.g.

d41) 15 ... exf4 16 ♘f3 ♘e7 (16 ... ♘e5 also worked out fine after 17 ♗xf4 ♘xf3+ 18 ♗xf3 axb4 19 axb4 ♘h6 in Lputian – Torre, Manila Izt. 1990) 17 ♗xf4 ♘g6 18 ♗g5 ♘f6 19 ♖be1 axb4 20 axb4 h6 21 ♘h4 ♘e5 22 ♗f4 ♘h5 23 ♗xe5 ♕xh4 24 ♗xg7+ ♘xg7 25 ♕d2 ♗d7 26 ♖f4 ♕g5 27 ♖ef1 ♖ae8 28 ♕d4 ♖e5= Arlandi – J Polgar, Portoroz 1991.

d42) 15 ... axb4 16 axb4 e4 17 ♘b3 ♖f6 18 ♘d4 ♘f8 19 ♗e3 ♖g6 20 g3 ♘f6 21 ♖a1 ♖b8 22 ♔h1 h5 23 ♖g1 ♗d7 24 c5 dxc5 25 bxc5 c6= Browne – Fedorowicz, San Francisco 1991.

d43) 15 ... ♘e7 (This is more flexible than the pawn captures and so is perhaps the best) 16 ♘f3 e4 17 ♘g5 ♘f6 18 ♔h1 (18 ♗b2 axb4 19 axb4 c6 20 dxc6 bxc6 21 ♖fd1 ♕c7 22 ♕d2 h6 23 ♘h3 ♖d8 24 b5 ♗e6 25 ♕e3 c5 26 ♕g3 ♖g8 27 ♖d2 d5∓ Shirov - Fishbein, Kerteminde 1991) 18 ... axb4 19 axb4 h6 20 ♘h3 c6 21 dxc6 bxc6 22 ♖d1 d5 23 cxd5 cxd5 (As in the Shirov - Fishbein example, Black's centre becomes a powerful force) 24 ♘b5 ♗a6 25 ♘d4 ♗xe2 26 ♕xe2 ♕b6 27 ♘f2 ♘d7 28 ♗e3 ♕g6 29 ♖a1 ♖xa1 30 ♖xa1 ♘c6 31 ♕d2 ♘b6 32 ♖a6 ♘c4 33 ♖xc6 ♕xc6 34 ♘xc6 ♘xd2 35 ♗xd2 ♖a8 36 g3 ♖a2 37 ♗e3 ♖e2 38 ♗c5 e3 39 ♘h3 ♖c2 40 ♘d4 ♖xc5 41 bxc5 ♗xd4 42 ♘g1 ♗xc5 43 ♘e2 d4 44 ♘c1 ♗b4 45 ♔g2 e2 0-1 van der Sterren - Fishbein, Kerteminde 1991.

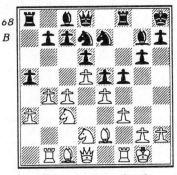

68
B

13 ... ♘g8

Over the last couple of years, following Kasparov's lead against Karpov from Skelleftea (see note 'c2' to White's 14th), this has become almost standard here. Others:

a) 13 ... b6?! is feeble. As so often in these positions this fails to hold up White on the queenside, wastes time, and creates a weakness. White oftens plays c5 as a pawn sacrifice and doesn't need this encouragement. Two examples:

a1) 14 ♘a4 axb4 15 axb4 ♗h6 16 c5 bxc5 17 bxc5 ♘xc5 18 ♘xc5 ♗e3+ 19 ♔h1 ♗xc5 20 f4 fxe4 21 ♗b2 ♘f5 22 fxe5 ♘e3 23 ♕b3 ♗xf1 24 e6+ ♔g8 25 ♗xf1 ♖f5 26 ♘xe4 ♗b6 27 g4 ♕h4 28 ♗g2 ♕xg4 29 ♕c3 1-0 Boensch - Gruenberg, East German Ch. 1989

a2) 14 ♕c2 f4 15 ♘b5 g5 16 c5 dxc5 17 bxc5 ♘xc5 18 ♘c4 ♗a6 19 ♖d1 ♗xb5 20 ♖xb5 ♘b7 21 d6 ♘xd6 22 ♖xe5 ♘g6 23 ♖ed5 ♕e7 24 ♘xd6 cxd6 Ostenstad - Kuzmin, Biel Open 1990. and now 25 ♕c6! keeps the advantage.

b) 13 ... f4 offers an invitation to the standard race. Now:

b1) 14 c5 (direct and dangerous) 14 ... axb4 15 axb4 dxc5 16 bxc5 ♘xc5 17 ♘c4 b6 18 ♗a3 ♗a6 19 ♗xc5 (19 ♘b5 ♘c8 20 ♗xc5 bxc5 21 ♘a5 ♘d6 22 ♘c6± Kanstler - Loginov, USSR Team Ch. 1991) 19 ... bxc5 20 ♕c2 c6 21 ♘b6 ♗xe2 22 ♘xe2 ♖b8 23 d6± van der Sterren - Gelfand, Amsterdam OHRA 1989.

b2) 14 ♘a4. Black should now take the opportunity to cut across White's plan with 14 ... axb4 15 axb4 c6!, planning ... b5, e.g. 16 ♗b2 (16 c5 cxd5 17 cxd6 ♘c6 18 exd5 ♘d4 19 ♘c3 ♘b6 20 ♘de4 ♗f5 21 ♗d3 ♖c8 22 ♗b2∞ Salov – Nunn, Rotterdam World Cup 1989) 16 ... ♘f6 (Curious, why not 16 ... b5?) 17 dxc6 ♘xc6 18 c5 dxc5 19 ♘xc5 ♘d4 20 ♘c4 ♘h5 21 ♖f2 b6 22 ♘d3± Polugaevsky – Hellers, Biel 1989.

b3) 14 ♘b3 is illogical, as this knight should be heading for c4. On b3 it does little to help the white effort. Dreev – Shirov, Borzomi 1988 was a good example: 14 ... axb4 15 axb4 g5 16 c5 ♘f6 17 ♗d2 ♘g6 (17 ... h5 18 ♖a1 ♖xa1 19 ♕xa1 g4 20 cxd6 cxd6 21 ♕a5 b6 22 ♕a7 ♘g6 23 ♘b5 ♘e8 24 fxg4 hxg4 25 g3 ♗d7∓ Dokhoian – Loginov, Pavlodar 1987. White will have serious problems confronting Black on the kingside) 18 c6 (White is hoping to get in round the back and attack the c7-pawn, but he will be mated long before) 18 ... b6 19 ♗e1 ♖g8 20 ♘d2 h5 21 ♘b5 g4 22 ♖a1 ♖xa1 23 ♕xa1 g3 24 ♕a8 ♘h7 25 hxg3 fxg3 26 f4 exf4 27 ♕b8 ♘e5 28 ♖xf4 ♕g5 29 ♖f3 ♘xf3+ 30 ♗xf3 ♕e3+ 31 ♔f1 ♗a6 0-1.

14 ♕c2
The theory here is still in a state of flux and there

are several other tries:

a) 14 c5 is a gambit that should be accepted, e.g. 14 ... axb4 15 axb4 dxc5 (not 15 ... ♘gf6? 16 ♘c4 ♘e8 17 c6 ♘df6 18 cxb7 ♗xb7 19 ♘a5 ♗c8 20 ♘c6 ♕d7 21 b5 ♕f7 22 b6± Lanka – Shirov, Riga Rapid Play 1988. Black's play was dreadfully passive) 16 bxc5 (16 ♘c4 cxb4 17 ♖xb4 is another way to pursue the initiative) 16 ... ♘xc5 17 ♘b3 ♘d7 18 ♗e3 c6 19 ♕d2 fxe4 20 dxc6 bxc6 21 ♘xe4 ♘gf6 22 ♘g5 ♕e7 23 ♘a5 ♘d5 24 ♘xc6 ♕a3 25 ♗f2 ♘c3 26 ♗c4 ♘xb1 27 ♖xb1 e4 28 fxe4∞ Ftacnik – Gruenberg, Stara Zagora Zt. 1990.

b) 14 ♘a4?! (Very suspicious – White puts the knight onto a tactically vulnerable square and weakens e4) 14 ... axb4 15 axb4 ♘df6 16 c5 ♘h5 17 g3 ♘hf6 18 b5 fxe4 19 fxe4 ♗h3 20 ♖f3 ♗h6 21 ♖b4 (A very clumsy move to have to play, but at least it defends the vulnerable spots a4 and e4) 21 ... ♘g4 22 ♘f1 ♘8f6 23 ♗xh6 ♘xh6 24 ♕c1 ♘fg4 25 b6 cxb6 26 cxd6 ♖xf3 27 ♗xf3 ♗xf1 28 ♕xf1 ♕g5 29 ♗xg4 ♘xg4 30 d7 ♕e3+ 31 ♔h1 ♘f2+ 32 ♔g2 ♖f8 0-1 Flear – Bibby, British Ch. 1990.

c) 14 ♘b3 is possible, but practice bears out the intuitive assumption that the knight doesn't belong here, e.g. 14 ... axb4 15 axb4 ♘df6 and now *(69)*:

c1) 16 c5 ♘h5 17 g3 ♘hf6 18 ♗d2 (18 g4 ♘e8 19 ♗d2 ♘h6 20 h3 ♘f7 21 ♔g2 ♗f6 22 cxd6 cxd6 23 ♘a5 h5 24 ♗e3 ♗g5 25 ♗f2 ♔g7 26 ♘a4 hxg4 27 hxg4 fxg4 28 fxg4 ♘h6∓ Amura - Dolmatov, Buenos Aires 1991) 18 ... fxe4 19 fxe4 ♗h3 20 ♖f2 ♕d7 21 ♗f1 ♗xf1 22 ♖xf1 ♗h6 23 ♗xh6 ♘xh6 24 ♖a1 ♖xa1 25 ♕xa1 ♕h3∓ Farago - Vogt, Tastrup 1990.

c2) 16 ♗d2 (Karpov continues more cautiously, but even he is unable to prevent Black from working up excellent kingside play) 16 ... ♘h5 17 g3 ♘hf6 18 ♖f2 ♘h6 19 ♖a1 ♖xa1 20 ♕xa1 ♘f7 (The unhurried way in which Kasparov has been massing his forces is deeply impressive. Next move he launches the attack proper by sacrificing a pawn which White dare not

accept) 21 ♕c1 f4 (If White accepts the sacrifice with 22 gxf4, then 22 ... exf4 23 ♗xf4 ♘h5 24 ♗e3 g5 grants Black all sorts of unpleasant counterplay around the weakened dark squares in the vicinity of the white king) 22 g4 h5 23 h3 ♘h7 24 ♗e1 ♗f6 25 ♔g2 ♔g7∓ 26 ♖f1 ♘hg5 27 ♖h1 ♘xh3! *(70)*

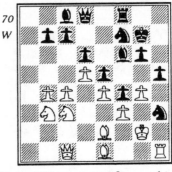

(A brilliant sacrifice which explodes the fortifications around White's king) 28 ♖xh3 ♘g5 29 ♖h2 (Despite his time trouble, Karpov noticed the clever tactical point, namely that 29 ♖h1 would fail to 29 ... f3+ 30 ♗xf3 ♘xf3 31 ♕h6+ ♔f7 32 ♔xf3 ♖h8, attacking White's queen and through it the undefended rook on h1. Now, however, after 29 ♖h2 White can safely go into this line, since 33 ♕d2 would protect the rook on h2) 29 ... hxg4 30 fxg4 ♖h8 31 ♗h4 f3+ (White's 31st move was forced in order to block the h-file, but now Kasparov regains his piece. Meanwhile, the situation of White's king remains precarious) 32 ♗xf3 ♘xf3 33 ♗xf6+ ♛xf6 34 ♖xh8 ♚xh8 35 ♚g3 *(71)*

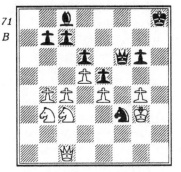

35 ... g5? (A much better chance for victory is offered by 35 ... ♚g7 or, as Kasparov himself later indicated, 35 ... ♚g8, to shield the black king from possible checks from the white queen. The way to win is, in fact, with 35 ... ♚g8, which Kasparov claimed deserved '!!'. The trouble with 35 ... ♚g7 is the problem-like defence 36 ♛e3 ♘d4 37 g5!! ♛f4+ 38 ♛xf4 exf4+ 39 ♚xf4 ♘xb3 40 ♘b5 and White can probably draw. The reason that 35 ... ♚g8!! is superior is that after 36 ♛e3 ♘d4 37 g5, Black has 37 ... ♛h8!!-+. The best defence to 35 ... ♚g8!! is 36 ♛e3 ♘d4 37 ♘d2 ♘c2 38 ♛f3 ♛xf3+ 39 ♘xf3 ♘xb4 40 ♘b5 ♘a6 when White is much worse) 36

♘e2 ♚g7 37 ♛h1 ♘d4 (The last chance to play for a win was 37 ... ♘h4 aiming for f4 via g6, e.g. 37 ... ♘h4 38 ♘d2 ♘g6 39 ♘f3 ♘f4 40 ♘c1 ♛g6 41 ♘e1 ♛e8 42 b5 ♛d7 43 ♛f3 ♘g6 and Black can continue to probe.) 38 ♘bxd4 exd4 39 ♛d1 ♛e5+ 40 ♚f3 ♛f6+ 41 ♚g3 ♛e5+ 42 ♚f3 ♛f6+ ½-½ Karpov - Kasparov, Skelleftea World Cup 1989.

14 ... ♘gf6
Or:
a) 14 ... ♗h6 15 c5 (15 exf5 axb4 16 axb4 gxf5 17 ♘b3 ♗g7 18 ♗d3 ♘df6 19 ♗g5 ♘e7 20 ♖a1 ♖xa1 21 ♖xa1 c6 22 dxc6 bxc6 23 ♖a8∞ Polugaevsky - Wahls, Biel 1990) 15 ... axb4 16 axb4 dxc5 17 bxc5 ♘xc5 18 ♘b5 b6 19 ♗b2 ♗g7 20 ♘c4 ♛e7 21 d6 cxd6 22 ♘xb6 ♖b8 23 ♘d5 ♛d7 24 ♘xd6 ♛xd6 25 ♗a3 ♖xb1 26 ♖xb1 ♗e6 27 ♖b6 ♛d7 28 ♗xc5 ♖a8 29 ♛d1= Illescas - Ivanovic, Manila Izt. 1990.
b) 14 ... axb4 15 axb4 ♘df6 16 c5 ♘h5 17 ♘c4?! (This game is a good example of why White usually prefers to be cajoled into playing the weakening g3 rather than allowing the black knight into f4) 17 ... ♘f4 18 cxd6 cxd6 19 ♘b5 ♖a6 20 ♖b3 fxe4 21 fxe4 ♗d7 22 ♘c3 ♖a1 23 ♗xf4 ♖xf1+ 24 ♗xf1 exf4 25 ♛f2 ♘h6∓ Khalifman - Kaspa-

rov, Paris (Immopar) 1991. Black has a fantastic position and proceeded to win easily.

15 ♘b5   axb4

15 ... b6 16 exf5 gxf5 17 f4 axb4 18 axb4 exf4 19 ♘f3 ♘e5 20 ♗xf4 ♘e4 21 ♘d2 ♗d7 22 ♖b3 ♖e8 23 ♘xe4 fxe4 24 ♖g3 ♗f5 25 ♕d2 ♕d7 26 ♘d4 ♗g6∞ Lerner - Smirin, USSR Ch. 1989.

16 axb4   ♘h5
17 g3   ♘df6 *(72)*

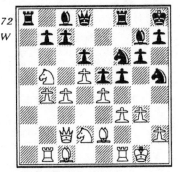

18 c5

18 ♖b3 fxe4 19 ♘xe4 ♗h3 20 ♖d1 ♘xe4 21 fxe4 ♕d7 22 ♖f3 (The more active 22 c5!? should also be considered) 22 ... ♘f6 23 ♘c3 ♖f7 24 ♖e1 h5∓ (Black has the chances here. The remainder of this game is a good demonstration of how to exploit an overextended position) 25 ♘d1 ♗g4 26 ♖ff1 ♖af8 27 ♘f2 ♗xe2 28 ♕xe2 h4 29 ♔g2 ♘h5 30 ♘h3 ♖xf1 31 ♖xf1 ♖xf1 32 ♕xf1 hxg3 33 hxg3 ♕a4 (Following the exchanges

White finds he has insufficient pieces on the board - if you want a large territory, you need a large army to defend it) 34 ♘g5 ♕c2+ 35 ♔h3 ♘f6 36 ♘f7+ ♔g8 37 ♘g5 ♗h8 38 ♗e3 ♕c3 39 ♗c1 ♕xb4 40 ♕d3 ♕e1 0-1 Lobron - Gelfand, Dortmund 1990.

18 ...   fxe4

The theory, in this complex and amazingly popular position, is developing at an alarming rate and so best play for both sides is far from being resolved. However, this move in conjunction with van Wely's improvement on move 20 is the latest word.

Much attention has also been given to 18 ... ♗d7, especially after Kasparov's bold knight sacrifice against Karpov at Tilburg in October 1991. White has always replied 19 ♖b3 *(73)*. invoking a lateral defence of the kingside, when practice has seen:

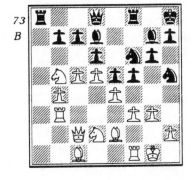

a) 19 ... fxe4 20 fxe4 ♗h3
21 ♖e1 ♗h6 22 ♘f3 ♗xc1 23
♖xc1 ♘g4 24 ♕d2 ♕e7 25
♖bc3 h6 26 ♗f1 ♗xf1 27 ♖xf1
g5 28 cxd6 cxd6 29 ♘c7
♘gf6 30 ♘xg5 hxg5 31 ♘xa8
♘xe4 32 ♖xf8+ ♕xf8 33 ♕e2
♘hf6 34 ♖a3 ♕c8 (The dust
has cleared, leaving White
with an extra exchange.
However, the horribly ex-
posed situation of his king
makes the practical task of
mounting a rescue opera-
tion for his stranded knight
on a8 very difficult to
achieve. Nevertheless, he
should not go down as
quickly as he does here) 35
♔g2 ♕c1 36 ♖f3 b5 37 ♘b6
♕c7 38 ♕xb5 ♕c2+ 39 ♔g1
♕d1+ 40 ♖f1 ♕d4+ 41 ♔h1
♘f2+ 42 ♔g2 ♘2g4 43 ♕e2
♕xb6-+ Gelfand - Kasparov,
Paris (Immopar) 1991.

b) 19 ... ♗h6 20 ♖c3 fxe4
21 fxe4 ♗h3 22 ♖e1 was
chosen as the battleground
for two games between Ep-
ishin and Judit Polgar:

b1) 22 ... dxc5 23 bxc5 c6
24 dxc6 ♗xd2 25 ♗xd2 bxc6
26 ♘d6 ♘g4 27 ♖f3 ♕e7 28
♖b1 ♖xf3 29 ♗xf3 ♖f8 30
♗xg4 ♗xg4 31 ♗h6 ♘g7=
Epishin - J Polgar, Brno
1991.

b2) 22 ... ♕d7 23 ♘f3 ♗xc1
24 ♖xc1 ♘f4 25 ♘g5 ♘xe2+
26 ♕xe2 ♗g4 27 ♕c4 ♘e8 28
♖f1± Epishin - J Polgar,
Vienna 1991. This position

is pretty unpleasant for
Black, although the re-
sourceful Judith broke out
and won in her opponent's
time trouble.

c) 19 ... ♘xg3!? (This is
highly speculative, but
Black may have generated
enough momentum in his
position to make it acceptable. However, Epishin's
recent antidote {see 'c23'}
may prove to be powerful
enough to banish this sacrifice from top-class tournament play) 20 hxg3 ♘h5
21 f4 *(74)* and now:

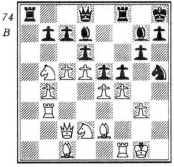

74
B

c1) 21 ... exf4 (This was
the move chosen by the
World Champion in Karpov
- Kasparov, Tilburg 1991,
the game which we now
follow) 22 c6 bxc6 23 dxc6
♘xg3 24 ♖xg3 fxg3 25 cxd7
g2 26 ♖f3 ♕xd7 27 ♗b2 fxe4
28 ♖xf8+ ♖xf8 29 ♗xg7+
♕xg7 30 ♕xe4 (This posi-
tion should only be dangerous for White, but here
Kasparov starts to drift) 30
... ♕f6 31 ♘f3 ♕f4 32 ♕e7

♖f7 33 ♕e6 ♖f6? (Kasparov later indicated 33 ... g5! as the correct way to play) 34 ♕e8+ ♖f8 35 ♕e7 ♖f7 36 ♕e6 ♖f6 37 ♕b3 g5 38 ♘xc7 g4 39 ♘d5 ♕c1+ 40 ♕d1 ♕xd1+ 41 ♗xd1 ♖f5 42 ♘e3 ♖f4 43 ♘e1 ♖xb4 44 ♗xg4 h5 45 ♗f3 d5 46 ♘3xg2 h4 47 ♘d3 ♖a4 48 ♘gf4 ♔g7 49 ♔g2 ♔f6 50 ♗xd5 reaching the highly unusual endgame of bishop and two knights against rook. Most experts suspected that the endgame should be a win for White, but Karpov couldn't make headway and eventually allowed a stalemate after 114 moves.

c2) 21 ... ♗xb5 22 ♗xb5 exf4 with the further division:

c21) 23 gxf4 ♘xf4 24 ♘f3 fxe4 25 ♕xe4 ♕c8 26 ♘h2 led to a draw in 33 moves in Khalifman - Kindermann, Germany 1991.

c22) 23 ♗b2 ♘xg3 24 ♗xg7+ ♔xg7 25 ♕c3+ ♔g8 26 ♖xf4 ♘h5 27 ♖f2 fxe4 28 ♖xf8+ ♕xf8 29 ♘xe4 ♕f5 30 ♕f3 ♕xd5 (Black has three solid pawns for the piece and the white king is completely devoid of shelter) 31 ♖d3 ♕e5 32 ♖d1 d5 33 ♘f2 c6 34 ♗f1 ♖f8∓ Beliavsky - Khalifman, Reggio Emilia 1991/92.

c23) 23 exf5! (The latest finesse, and one which

Black could find no answer to here) 23 ... ♘xg3 24 ♖xf4 ♘xf5 25 ♘f3 dxc5 26 bxc5 ♖a1 27 ♖d3 ♕e7 28 ♔h2± Epishin - Piket, Wijk aan Zee 1992.

19 fxe4 ♗h3 *(75)*

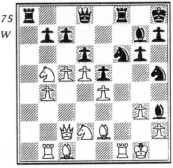

20 ♖f2

Boris Gelfand was evidently impressed by Black's idea in this game as, when he played White against van Wely later in the tournament, he diverged with 20 ♖e1 but this also accomplished little: 20 ... ♘g4 21 ♘f3 h6 22 cxd6 cxd6 23 ♕c7 (One would expect the exchange of queens to help White, but Black remains very active and has no problems holding the balance) 23 ... ♕xc7 24 ♘xc7 ♖a2 25 ♖b2 ♖a3 26 ♘h4 ♔h7 27 ♘b5 ♖a6 28 ♖c2 ♖f7 29 ♘f3 ♗f6 30 ♘d2 ♖d8 31 ♘c4 ♖f2 32 ♘e3 ♗b6 33 ♖c7+ ♗xc7 34 ♗xg4 ♗b6 35 ♗xh3 ♖c2 36 ♔h1 ♖xc1 ½-½.

20 ... ♕d7!

This is van Wely's important addition to the black armoury. Two other games saw Black rapidly getting into a tangle here:

a) 20 ... ♖c8 did not impress after 21 ♖b3 ♕d7 22 ♖c3 ♘g4 23 ♖xf8+ ♖xf8 24 ♘f3± in Browne – Root, USA 1990.

b) 20 ... ♘g4 21 ♖xf8+ ♗xf8 22 ♘f3 h6 23 ♘h4 ♕f6 24 ♗f3 ♘g7 25 ♕e2 h5 26 ♗g2 ♗xg2 27 ♔xg2± Polugaevsky – J Polgar, Aruba 1991.

21	c6	bxc6
22	dxc6	♕e7
23	♘c3	d5! *(76)*

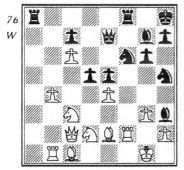

A tremendous pawn sacrifice, liberating all of Black's pieces which proceed to crawl over White's kingside. Van Wely plays the rest of this game with fantastic energy, never allowing the pressure to slacken for an instant.

Gary Kasparov's numerous successes with his dynamic handling of the King's Indian seems to have made other top grandmasters more inclined to have faith in such black set-ups – one did not see many games like this when Karpov was World Champion!

| 24 | exd5 | e4! |

The vulnerability of White on the b1 – h7 diagonal ensures the safety of this pawn.

25	♘c4	♘g4
26	♗xg4	♖xf2
27	♕xf2	♗xg4
28	♕e3	♖f8
29	♗d2	♕f7
30	h4	

An ugly weakening, but otherwise ... ♗h3 would have left White permanently crippled on the kingside.

30	...	♗f3
31	♗e1	♕f5
32	♖b2 *(77)*	

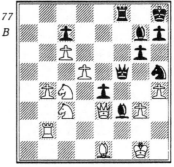

Now 32 ... ♕h3 gets nowhere after 33 ♖h2 but. hardly surprisingly, White's defences prove to be far from watertight.

| 32 | ... | ♘xg3! |
| 33 | ♗xg3 | ♕h3 |

34	♗xc7	♕h1+
35	♔f2	♗h5+
36	♗f4	♕xh4+
37	♔g1	♖xf4 (78)

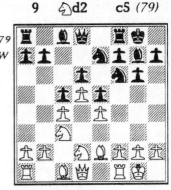

78
W

A highly satisfactory and thematic conclusion for Black who has abandoned his entire queenside, but won the ultimate prize on the other wing.

38	♖g2	♕f6
39	♘d2	♕d4
40	♕xd4	♗xd4+
41	♔h2	♗xc3
42	d6	♗e5!
43	d7	e3
44	♔h3	♗c7
	0-1	

Game 10
Farago - Watson
Beer-Sheva 1987

1	d4	♘f6
2	c4	g6
3	♘c3	♗g7
4	e4	0-0
5	♗e2	d6
6	♘f3	e5
7	0-0	♘c6
8	d5	♘e7

9	♘d2	c5 (79)

79
W

10 ♖b1

10 dxc6 used to be played here when, after 10 ... bxc6 11 b4 d5, White aimed to undermine the black centre. However, experience has shown that this hope is a forlorn one and white players have more or less abandoned the line. Some examples from before they did:

a) 12 ♗a3 ♗e6 13 ♖e1 a6 (13 ... h5!? appears adventurous, but worked well in Sinkovic - Uhlmann, Stary Smokovec 1985: 14 ♖b1 ♖e8 15 ♗f1 ♗g4 16 ♕b3 dxe4 17 ♘dxe4 ♘f5 18 ♘xf6+ ♗xf6 19 ♘e4 ♘d4∓) 14 ♗f1 ♖e8 15 ♗b2 ♕b8 16 a3 ♖a7 17 ♘a4 dxe4 18 ♘c5 ♗g4 19 ♕a4 a5 20 b5 cxb5 21 cxb5 e3∞ Marin - Vokac, Bucharest 1985.

b) 12 b5 d4 13 ♘a4 d3 14 ♗f3 cxb5 15 cxb5 ♗d7 16 ♖b1 (16 ♘c5 ♗xb5 17 a4 ♗c6 18 ♖a3 ♕d6 19 ♘xd3 ♖fd8 20 ♗b2 ♘d7 21 ♕a1 ♖ab8= Vilela - Vogt, Cienfuegos 1983) 16 ... ♖b8 17 ♘c3 ♕a5 18 ♗b2 ♗xb5 19 ♘b3 ♕b6 20 ♗a3 ♖fe8 21 ♘c5 a6 22 ♘xb5 axb5 23 ♘xd3 ♘c6 24 ♗c5 ♕a5 25 ♕b3 ♘d7∓ Gruen-feld - Enoshi, Tel-Aviv 1988.

10 ... ♘e8
An important alternative is 10 ... a5 (The careless 10 ... ♘d7? got bashed in fine style in Lputian - Khalif-man, USSR Ch. 1987 as fol-lows, 11 ♘b5 ♕b6 12 b4! cxb4 13 a3! bxa3 14 c5! ♘xc5 15 ♗xa3 ♕d8 16 ♘xd6 b6 17 ♘2c4 ♗a6 18 ♗xc5 bxc5 19 ♘b7 ♗xb7 20 ♖xb7±) 11 a3, leading to a position which can also arise from the move order 9 ♘d2 a5 10 a3 c5 11 ♖b1 *(80)*.

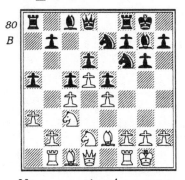

80
B

Here practice has seen:
a) 11 ... ♗h6!? (This has the usual pluses and mi-nuses - Black exchanges the bad king's bishop but loses time and weakens the kingside) 12 b4 axb4 13 axb4 b6 14 bxc5 bxc5 15 ♘b3 ♗xc1 16 ♕xc1 (If 16

♘xc1, Uhlmann gives 16 ... g5! 17 ♕d2 h6 18 h4 ♘h7∓) and now:
a1) 16 ... ♘e8 17 f4 exf4 18 ♕xf4 f6 and Black has a slightly constricted, but quite playable, position, e.g. 19 ♕g3 (or 19 ♖a1 ♖xa1 20 ♖xa1 ♕b6 21 ♘b5 ♗d7 22 ♔h1 g5 23 ♕d2 ♘g6 24 ♕a5 ♕xa5 25 ♘xa5 f5 26 exf5 ♖xf5 27 ♗g4 ♖f7 28 ♗xd7 ♖xd7= Lutz - Uhlmann. German Ch. 1991) 19 ... ♗d7 20 ♖a1 ♖xa1 21 ♖xa1 ♕b6 22 ♘d2 ♕b2 23 ♖a2 ♕c1+ 24 ♗f1 and now 24 ... f5? 25 ♘b3 ♕h6 26 e5!± was Shi-rov - Uhlmann, Stockholm 1989/90, but Uhlmann gives 24 ... ♘c8∞.
a2) 16 ... ♘d7 17 ♘b5! (Black's last keeps an eye on the e5-square, so the immediate 17 f4 exf4 18 ♕xf4 ♘e5= is less attrac-tive) 17 ... ♘f6 18 f4! ♘xe4 19 ♕e3 f5 20 fxe5 dxe5 21 ♗d3 ♘d6 22 ♕xc5± Her-nandez - Gonzalez, Mexico City 1991. The opening up of the position is greatly fa-vourable to White who is much the better developed.
b) 11 ... ♘e8 12 b4 axb4 13 axb4 b6 14 bxc5 bxc5 15 ♘b3 *(81)*.
Here, there are two schools of thought. The first says that if 15 ... f5 16 ♗g5 (with tactical threats based on ♘xc5) is an awk-

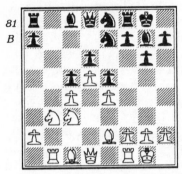

81
B

ward reply, and Black should prefer a slower build-up with, for example 15 ... ♔h8, and not play ... f5 until White has committed his bishop to d2. The second says that White's ♗g5 is no big deal and that Black should get on with it with 15 ... f5 instead of wasting time with potentially pointless waiting moves. Indeed, White has recently been declining the opportunity to meet 15 ... f5 with 16 ♗g5 and so it would seem that the latter argument has won the day. Some examples:

b1) 15 ... ♔h8 16 ♗d2 ♘g8 (This is slightly timid - the white bishop has moved so why not 16 ... f5?). Pekarek - Vokac, Kecskemet 1988 continued: 17 ♖a1 ♖xa1 18 ♕xa1 f5 19 ♕a8 ♘ef6 20 exf5 gxf5 21 ♕b8 ♕d7 22 ♕b6 ♘e4 23 ♘xe4 fxe4 24 ♗e3 ♘f6 25 ♘d2 ♖g8 26 ♖a1 ♗f8 27 g3± . The weak d6-pawn is more relevant than Black's kingside play.

b2) 15 ... f5:
b21) 16 ♗d2 ♔h8 (16 ... ♘f6 17 f3 ♘h5 {*Black intends to use the f4-square for his knight, but 17 ... f4 △ ... g5 etc. also came into consideration*} 18 ♖a1 ♖xa1 19 ♕xa1 ♘f4 20 ♗d1 fxe4 21 ♘xe4 ♗f5 22 ♕a5 ♕d7 23 ♘c1± Lputian - Shirov, Lvov Zt. 1990. A typical position - White's queenside play gives him the better of things, but he must also keep a wary eye on the kingside) 17 ♖a1 (17 f3 ♘g8 18 ♕c2 {*18 ♖a1 ♖xa1 19 ♕xa1 ♗h6 20 exf5 gxf5 21 ♗xh6 ♘xh6 22 f4 exf4 23 ♕c1 ♕f6 24 ♖xf4 ♘f7 25 ♘e4 ♕e7 26 ♘g3 ♘g7 27 ♖f1 ♗d7= Flear - Lewis, British Ch. 1990*} 18 ... ♗h6 19 exf5 ♗xd2 20 ♕xd2 gxf5 21 f4 exf4 22 ♗d3 ♘e7 23 ♘e2 ♘g6 24 ♘xf4 ♘e5 25 ♔h1 ♘g7 26 ♖a1 ♗d7 27 ♖xa8 ♕xa8 28 ♕c3 ♖e8 29 ♘d2 ♔g8 30 ♗e2 ♕d8= Ostenstad - Djurhuus, Oslo 1991) 17 ... ♖xa1 18 ♕xa1 ♘g8 (This, combined with Black's subsequent play, is rather slow. With the white queen out of the way, this looks like a good moment to consider 18 ... f4) 19 ♕a8 ♗h6 20 exf5 gxf5 21 ♘b5 ♗xd2 22 ♘xd2 ♘gf6 23 ♖a1 ♘e4 24 ♘xe4 fxe4 25 ♕a3 ♘g7 26 ♕e3 ♕f6 27 ♖a8 ♘f5 28

♕xe4 ♘h4 29 ♕e3 ♘f5 30 ♕f3 e4 31 ♕xe4 ♘d4 32 f3 ♖g8 33 ♘xd4 cxd4 34 ♗d3 1-0 Ftacnik - Hellers, Haninge 1990.

b22) 16 ♗g5 h6 17 ♗d2 (17 ♗xe7 ♕xe7 failed to create problems for Black in Beaumont - Howell, British Ch. 1988, viz. 18 ♖a1 ♖xa1 19 ♕xa1 ♘f6 20 ♗d3 f4 21 f3 g5 22 ♘b5 g4 ½-½) 17 ... ♘f6 18 f3 g5 19 ♖a1 ♖b8?! (Better, according to Shirov is 19 ... ♖xa1 20 ♕xa1 ♘g6 which he assesses as unlcear) 20 ♕c2 f4 21 ♘b5 ♘e8 22 ♖a7 ♗d7 23 ♖fa1 ♘g6 24 ♖1a6 ♖f6 25 ♘a5 g4 26 ♘c6 ♗xc6 27 ♗a5 gxf3 28 ♗xf3 ♘c7 29 ♗xc7 ♕e8 30 dxc6 ♘h4 31 ♗xb8 1-0 Shirov - Antonsen, Timisoara 1987.

11 b4 b6 (82)

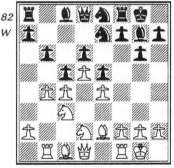

12 bxc5

This is not absolutely necessary; White can also maintain the tension on the queenside, e.g.

a) 12 a4 f5 13 a5 ♘f6 14 ♕a4 (14 axb6 axb6 15 ♕b3

♖a6!? 16 ♗d3 ♘h5 17 ♖e1 ♘f4 18 ♗f1 fxe4 19 ♘dxe4 ♘f5 20 ♘b5 ♘d4 21 ♕d1± Zarubin - Muratov, Moscow 1991) 14 ... ♗d7 15 ♕a3 ♗h6 16 bxc5 bxc5 17 a6 ♖b8 18 ♖xb8 ♕xb8 19 ♘f3 ♗xc1 20 ♖xc1 ♕b4? (Overlooking White's cunning retreat. Better is 20 ... ♕c7 21 ♖b1 ♖b8, when White has only a tiny advantage) 21 ♕a1! (Suddenly 22 ♖b1 is threatened and the black queen is in danger) 21 .. ♘xe4 22 ♘xe4 fxe4 23 ♖b1 ♕a4 24 ♕xa4 ♗xa4 25 ♘g5± Kristiansen - Hellers, Esbjerg 1988. With control of the b-file, weak black pawns at a7 and d6 and the vulnerable e6-square, White has an excellent endgame.

b) 12 ♘b3 f5 13 ♗d2 (13 ♗g5 h6 14 ♗xe7 ♕xe7 15 bxc5 dxc5 16 a4 ♗d7 17 a5 ♘d6 18 axb6 axb6 19 ♘d2 h5 20 ♗d3 ♗h6 21 ♘b3 h4 22 ♕e2 h3⩲ Stankovic - Bakic Yugoslav Ch. 1991) 13 ... ♘f6 14 f3 ♔h8 15 ♕c2 ♘eg8 16 exf5 ♗xf5 17 ♗d3 ♘h5 18 bxc5 bxc5 19 ♖ae1 ♗h6 20 ♘e2 ♖b8 21 ♗xf5 ♗xd2 22 ♘xd2 gxf5 23 f4 e4 24 ♕c3+ ♕f6 25 ♕xf6+ ♘gxf6 26 ♖b1 ♘d7 27 ♖fc1± Boensch - Wahls, Hannover 1991.

12 ... bxc5

12 ... dxc5 has been the subject of the occasional experiment, but it leaves

Black with a rather lifeless position. Most Whites have responded with a plan of a4 – a5 to weaken Black's queenside, but Pekarek's plan of f4 looks good. After all, 12 ... dxc5 leaves Black's centre a little weak, so why not try to undermine it further?

a) 13 ♕b3 ♘d6 14 a4 ♘d7 15 a5 ♘ec8 16 ♕a3 ♕c7 17 axb6 ♘xb6 18 ♕a2 a5 19 ♗a3 a4 20 ♖bc1 ♗h6 21 ♖c2 ♖fc8 22 ♖b1 ♕a7 23 ♘f3 f6 24 g3± Fedorowicz – Bastian, Bundesliga 1988/89.

b) 13 a4 a5 14 ♕b3 ♖a6 15 ♘b5 ♗d7 16 ♗b2 ♘c8 17 f4 ♕e7 18 fxe5 ♗xe5 19 ♗xe5 ♕xe5 20 ♕c3 ♕xc3 21 ♘xc3 f6 22 ♘f3 ♖a7 23 ♗d3 ♘ed6 24 ♖be1 ♘f7 25 e5±/= Umanskaya – Shashin, Moscow 1991.

c) 13 ♗b2 ♗d7 14 ♗d3 ♘d6 15 ♘e2 f6 16 f4 ♕c7 17 ♕e1 ♘f7 and now 18 ♕g3?! f5 19 fxe5 ♗xe5 20 ♗xe5 ♕xe5 21 ♘f3 ♕xg3 22 ♘xg3 fxe4 23 ♘xe4 left Black only very slightly worse in Pekarek – Kr Georgiev, Warsaw Zt. 1987 but, as Nunn points out, 18 f5 prevents Black's counter and leaves White well on top. Black may hang on to draw, but it is a pretty thankless task.

13   ♘b3 *(83)*
13   ...   f5
Others:

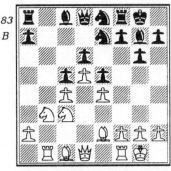

83
B

a) 13 ... a5 is an attempt to hold White up on the queenside, at the expense of obvious strategic concessions, e.g. 14 a4 ♘c7?! (14 ... f5±/∞) 15 ♘xc5 dxc5 16 d6 ♘e6 17 dxe7 ♕xe7 18 ♘d5 ♕a7 19 ♗e3 ♘d4 20 ♗xd4 exd4 21 f4 ♗e6 22 ♔h1 ♖ab8 23 ♕c2± Lerner – Renet, Geneva 1988.

b) 13 ... ♔h8. As is currently the case in numerous main line King's Indian positions, this quiet king move is the latest try. It is easy to understand why this should be the case. Much of the strategy in these positions revolves around a balance between attack and defence – White doesn't want to commit all the pieces to the queen's wing as this is liable to result in checkmate on the other side, while Black is similarly reluctant to abandon the queenside on the off-chance of generating a mating attack. In

these conditions, con-
structive waiting moves
become highly attractive,
as they allow the balance
to be kept while maintaining the ability to respond
quickly to changing cir-
cumstances. The move ...
♔h8 fits the bill very well
for Black as the king is
slightly safer here and the
g8-square is freed for the
knight or rook.

After 13 ... ♔h8, play
continues 14 ♗d2 (14 ♕c2!?
meeting 14 ... f5 with 15 f4
was successful in Baikov -
Krasenkov, Moscow 1989,
viz. 15 ... ♘g8 16 exf5 ♗xf5
17 ♗d3 ♖b8 18 ♗d2 exf4 19
♗xf4 ♖b7 20 ♗xf5 ♖xf5 21
♘e4±/± but has not, un-
fortunately, been given another test) 14 ... f5 (This
position might also arise
after 14 ♗g5 f6 15 ♗d2 f5)
and now *(84)*:

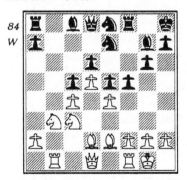

b1) 15 ♘b5 fxe4 16 ♗a5
♕d7 17 ♘d2 ♕f5 18 ♘c3
♘f6∞ Shirov - Lanka, Torcy
1990.

b2) 15 exf5 gxf5 16 f4
exf4 17 ♖xf4 ♘g6 18 ♖f1
♗d7 19 ♗d3 ♗e5 20 ♘e2±
Brunner - Frick, Bern Zt.
1990.

b3) 15 f3 ♘f6 (15 ... ♘g8
16 exf5 gxf5 17 f4 e4 18 ♕c1
♖f6 19 ♘d1 ♖h6 20 g3 a5 21
♗c3 a4 22 ♗xg7+ ♘xg7 23
♘a1 ♖g6 24 ♔f2 ♘f6∞
Dzhandzhgava - Fedoro-
wicz, New York Open 1990)
16 ♕c2 (16 ♗d3 a5 17 a4
♘eg8 18 ♕c1 ♘h5 19 g3
♘hf6 20 exf5 gxf5 21 ♕c2
♘h5 22 ♖be1 ♗h6 23 ♘b5
♗xd2 24 ♕xd2 ♖f7 25 ♔h1
♖g7 26 ♖g1 ♘gf6 ½-½ de
Boer - Nijboer, Dutch Ch.
1990. In the final position, it
is difficult for either side
to make progress) 16 ...
♘eg8 17 exf5 ♗xf5?! (17 ...
exf5 must be better) 18 ♗d3
♗xd3 19 ♕xd3 ♗h6 20 ♖b2
♖b8 21 ♖fb1 a6? 22 ♘e2
♗xd2 23 ♘xd2 ♖xb2 24
♖xb2± Bogdanovski - Bak-
ic, Yugoslav Ch. 1991. Black
has failed to generate any
counterplay and the re-
mainder of the game was a
dismal affair: 24 ... ♕a5 25
♕c3 ♕c7 26 ♕b3 ♕g7 27 ♘g3
♕h6 28 ♕c3 ♕f4 29 ♖b6 ♘e7
30 ♖xd6 ♘f5 31 ♘xf5 gxf5
32 ♖e6 1-0.

14 ♗g5 *(85)*
14 ...   ♔h8
Others:
a) 14 ... ♗f6 15 ♗d2 ♔h8 16
♗d3 ♗g7 17 f3 ♘g8 18 ♘e2

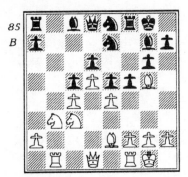

85
B

(According to Eingorn, White should preface this with 18 exf5 gxf5 and only now 19 ♘e2, which he assesses as slightly better for White) 18 ... f4 19 ♘a5 g5 20 ♘c6 ♕f6 21 ♕e1∞ Eingorn - Hebden, Moscow 1986.

b) 14 ... ♘f6 15 ♗d3 (This is a tame response. More testing is the familiar tactic 15 ♘xc5 dxc5 16 d6 when 16 ... ♗e6 17 dxe7 ♕xe7 18 f3! ♖ab8 19 ♘d5 ♕f7 20 ♗e3 ♖xb1 21 ♕xb1 ♖c8 22 ♕b5 ♗f8 23 ♕a6! was good for White in Shirov - Zarnicki, Timisoara 1988, but maybe 16 ... ♘c6 is better) 15 ... f4 16 f3 h6 17 ♗xf6 ♖xf6 18 ♗e2 h5 19 ♘c1 g5 20 ♘d3 and now instead of the peculiar 20 ... ♕a5?! 21 ♖b3 ♗a6 22 ♘f2 ♖ff8 23 ♕c1 ♖fb8 24 ♖a3 ♕b6 25 ♕c2 ♗b7 26 ♖b1± of Dokhoian - Cisneros, Pamplona 1991, Black should play the more thematic 20 ... ♖g6 21 ♘f2 ♔h8 22 h3 ♘g8, with counter-play.

c) 14 ... h6 15 ♗xe7 ♕xe7 16 ♘a5 ♘f6 17 ♘c6 ♕e8 (17 ... ♕d7 18 f3 {*Dokhoian suggests 18 ♗d3! f4 19 f3 _ ♖f1 - f2 - b2*} 18 ... h5 19 ♕e1 ♗h6 20 ♗d1 ♗a6 21 ♗a4 ♕h7 22 ♗b5 ♗c8 23 ♖b3 h4 24 exf5 gxf5 25 ♘e2∞ Hertneck - Wahls, Munich 1991) 18 ♗d3 f4 19 ♘b5 ♕d7 20 f3 g5 21 ♕e1 ♘e8 22 ♕a5 ♗f6 23 ♘bxa7 ♖f7 24 ♕b5 ♗b7 25 ♖b2 ♖g7 26 ♗e2 h5∞ Dokhoian - Wahls, Bundesliga 1991.

15 exf5

The play in these positions revolves, to a great extent, around whether White can make the tactical shot ♘xc5 work in his favour. Here for example. it would be premature, e.g. 15 ♘xc5 dxc5 16 d6 ♘xd6 17 ♘d5 ♖e8 18 ♘xe7 ♖xe7 19 ♕xd5 ♗e6! 20 ♗xe7 ♗xd5 21 ♗xd8 ♗xe4∓.

Another possibility is 15 ♗xe7 ♕xe7 16 ♘a5 ♘f6 17 ♘c6 ♕f7 18 ♗f3 g5 and now instead of 19 exf5?! ♗xf5 20 ♖b3 g4 21 ♗e2 ♗h6∓ Littlewood - Nunn, London 1987. White should play 19 ♘b5! g4 20 ♘xd6 ♕d7∞.

15 ... gxf5 (86)
16 ♘xc5

16 f4 has been tried recently, and may prove more dangerous than the text. Practice has seen 16 ... h6

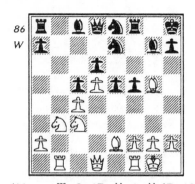

(16 ... ♖g8 17 ♕e1 ♕d7 18 ♗h5 ♗a6 19 ♕h4 e4 20 ♘xe4 fxe4 21 ♗xe7 ♗xc4 22 f5 ♗xf1 23 ♖xf1∞ Polugaevsky - Kr. Georgiev, European Team Ch. 1989) 17 ♗h4 exf4 (17 ... e4 looks suspicious as it robs the black position of its fluidity. In M Gurevich - Kuzmin, USSR 1988, White gained the advantage after 18 ♕c2 ♘f6 19 ♘d1 ♗d7 20 ♗e1 a5 21 ♗c3 a4 22 ♘a1 ♖b8 23 ♘e3 ♘g6 24 ♖xb8 ♕xb8 25 ♕d2) 18 ♕d2 ♘f6 19 ♗xf6 ♗xf6 20 ♗h5 ♗a6! (An improvement over 20 ... ♗g5 21 ♘e2 ♘g8 22 ♘xf4 ♘f6 23 ♕e2 ♗xf4 24 ♖xf4 ♘xh5 25 ♕xh5 ♕g5 26 ♕f3 ♗a6± Chernin-Kuzmin, USSR 1988) 21 ♘e2 ♗xc4 22 ♕xf4 ♗xd5 23 ♕xh6+ ♔g8 24 ♘f4 ♗g7 25 ♕g5 c4 26 ♖be1 ♘c6 27 ♕xd8 ♖axd8 28 ♘xd5 cxb3 29 axb3 ♔h7= Polugaevsky - Timoshenko, Moscow GMA 1990.

16	...	dxc5
17	d6	♘xd6
18	♘d5	♖e8

19	♘xe7	♖xe7
20	♕d5	♗b7

Not 20 ... ♗e6? 21 ♘xe7±.

21	♖xb7	♘xb7
22	♕xd8+	♖xd8
23	♗xe7	♖d2
24	♗h5?	*(87)*

In spite of having given the impression of forcing the pace over the past few moves, White should here content himself with equality after 24 ♖b1 ♖xe2 25 ♔f1 ♖xa2 26 ♖xb7 ♔g8 (Both back ranks are causing trouble!) 27 ♗xc5=.

24 ...   e4

All this had happened before in Flear - Nunn, Szirak Izt. 1987, but Nunn had played the inferior 24 ... ♖xa2? when after 25 g4 f4 26 ♖b1 f3 27 ♗f7 e4 28 ♗d5 ♗d4 White had a chance to win with 29 ♗h4!

25	♖b1	♖xa2
26	g4??	

A bad blunder. Nunn gives 26 ♗xc5! ♘xc5 27 ♖b8+ ♗f8 28 ♖xf8+ ♔g7 29 ♖f7+ ♔h6 30 g4 fxg4 31

♗xg4 and Black should have no trouble holding the draw.

26	...	♖a1
27	♖xa1	♗xa1
28	♗f7	

If 28 gxf5 then 28 ... ♔g7 △ ... ♗f6∓.

28	...	a5
29	♗e8	♔g7
30	g5?	

White's last chance was 30 gxf5 ♗f6 31 ♗c6! ♗xe7 32 ♗xb7 a4 when he may retain some drawing chances. Now Black wins by sacrificing the pride and joy of his position – the outside passed a-pawn.

| 30 | ... | a4! |
| 31 | ♗xa4 | ♔f7 |

White's bishop is trapped and he is left with a hopeless endgame.

32	♗f6	♗xf6
33	♗c6	♘d8
34	♗d5+	♘e6
35	gxf6	♔xf6
36	f3	e3
37	♔f1	♘f4
38	♗b7	♔e5
39	♗c8	h6
40	♔e1	♔d4
	0-1	

Game 11
Flear – Hebden
London (Watson, Farley & Williams) 1990

1	d4	♘f6
2	c4	g6
3	♘c3	♗g7
4	e4	0-0
5	♗e2	d6
6	♘f3	e5
7	0-0	♘c6
8	d5	♘e7
9	♘d2	(88)

| 9 | ... | ♘e8 |

This will transpose to the variation analysed in 'b' below (9 ... ♘d7) if the knight quickly returns to f6. Hebden, however, has an alternative strategy in mind.

Others that come into consideration here are:

a) 9 ... c6. This is a slightly odd move that has become quite popular recently. Black often uses the move ... c6, as a middlegame device, usually in response to White making a concession somewhere. There is a danger that playing it so early might merely assist White in opening queenside lines. Practical experience gives us the following: 10 b4 (10 a3

is more cautious; Boensch
- Lautier, Terrassa 1991
continued 10 ... cxd5 11 cxd5
♘e8 12 ♘c4 f5 13 exf5 gxf5
14 f4 ♘g6 15 fxe5 dxe5 16
♗e3 ♗d7 17 ♔h1 ♔h8 18 a4
b6 19 ♕d2 ♖c8 20 b3±; 10
♖b1 may well be the best
reply to 9 ... c6, e.g. 10 ... b5
11 dxc6 b4 12 ♘d5 ♘xc6 13
♘xf6+ ♗xf6 14 ♘f3 ♗g4 15
♘e1 ♗e6 16 ♘c2 ♖c8 17 b3±
Sher - Gallagher, Hastings
Challengers 1989/90. White
will always have a small
advantage with this pawn
structure) 10 ... a5 11 bxa5
♕xa5 *(89)* and now:

al) 12 ♕c2 c5 13 ♘b3 ♕d8
14 a4 ♘d7 15 ♗e3 (15 ♗d2 f5
16 f3 f4 17 a5 h5 18 ♘a4 ♖a6
(Preventing ♘b6) 19 ♖fb1 g5
20 ♘c1 ♘g6 21 ♖a3 ♗f6 22
♘d3 ♕e8 23 ♖b5 ♖f7 24 ♕b2
♖g7 25 ♘f2 ♘h4∓ Ftacnik -
Neurohr, Bundesliga 1991.
Black has excellent play) 15
... f5 16 f3 f4 17 ♗f2 g5 18 a5
h5 19 ♘a4 ♔h8 20 ♖fb1 ♖g8
21 ♕b2 ♘g6 22 h3 ♗f6∓ Shirov - Lanka, USSR 1989.

White is again struggling
to make progress on the
queenside.

a2) 12 ♗b2 c5 13 ♘b5 ♕d8
14 ♕c2 (14 a4 ♘e8 15 f4
proved to be an unsuccessful alternative strategy in
van der Sterren - Lautier,
Lyon Zt. 1990, i.e. 15 ...
exf4 16 ♗xg7 ♘xg7 17 ♖xf4
g5 18 ♖f2 ♘g6 19 ♗g4 f5 20
exf5 ♘xf5 21 ♕b3 ♘d4 22
♖xf8+ ♕xf8 23 ♘xd4 ♕g7
24 ♘c2 ♗xg4∓) 14 ... ♖a6
(This can be a useful move
for Black as was seen
earlier, but it looks premature here) 15 ♗c3 ♘d7 16
♕b2 ♘b6?! (Misplaces the
knight and provides a target for White - why not
simply 16 ... f5?) 17 ♗d1 f5
18 a4 ♗h6 19 a5 ♘d7 20 ♖e1
♘f6 21 f3± Stefansson -
Ioseliani, Gausdal 1991.

White has had the worse
of the play after 10 b4 a5.
so perhaps 10 ♖b1 should
be preferred.

b) 9 ... ♘d7 is an indication of Black's willingness
to play a race. It was
frowned upon for a long
time, as 9 ♘d2 allows
White to get going on the
queenside very quickly
compared to 9 ♘e1, but recent games by the young
grandmasters Shirov and
Akopian demonstrate that
life is not so easy for
White, e.g. 10 b4 f5 11 c5

♘f6 12 f3 f4 13 ♘c4 g5 *(90)* and now White can pursue the initiative with or without the a-pawn:

b1) 14 ♗a3 ♘g6 15 b5 ♘e8 16 b6 axb6 (16 ... cxb6 17 ♘xd6?! *{This is doubtful. Preferable is 17 cxb6 and if 17 ... a6 then White has the instructive manoeuvre ♘a5 - c6 - a7(!)}* 17 ... bxc5 18 ♘xe8 ♖xe8 19 ♗b5 ♗d7 20 d6 b6 21 ♕d5+ ♔h8∞/∓ Vaganian - Shirov, Manila Izt. 1990) 17 cxb6 cxb6 18 ♕b3 h5 19 ♖ab1 g4 20 ♘xb6 ♕h4?! (Black should keep this square free for the knight, e.g. 20 ... ♕g5! 21 ♘xc8 {*Not 21 ♘xa8? g3 22 h3 ♕h4∓}* 21 ... ♖xc8 22 ♔h1 ♘h4∞) 21 ♘xc8 ♖xc8 22 ♖fc1?! (22 ♘b5! is more to the point) 22 ... ♕g5 23 ♘b5 ♖d8 24 ♘c7 ♘xc7 25 ♖xc7 ♘h4 26 ♕d3 ♗h6 27 ♔h1 ♖f6∞ Shirov - Akopian, Daugavpils 1989.

b2) 14 a4 ♘g6 15 ♗a3 ♖f7 16 b5 ♗f8 17 b6 cxb6 18 ♘xd6?! (Curiously, White deviates from 18 cxd6 whch proved successful in a game between the same two players the previous year, viz. 18 ... ♘e8 19 ♖c1 ♗d7 20 ♕b3 h5 21 h3 ♖f6 22 a5 and White went on to win, Epishin - Akopian, Daugavpils 1989) 18 ... ♖g7! (Black's play looks antipositional, but the white pieces are very exposed tactically) 19 ♘xc8 ♖xc8 20 d6 bxc5 21 ♘b5 ♖c6 22 ♘c7 ♕xd6 23 ♗c4+ ♔h8 24 ♘e6 ♖d7 25 ♕xd6 ♖cxd6 26 ♘xg5 ♖d2∓ Epishin - Akopian, Minsk 1990.

b3) 14 ♗b2 (An interesting alternative set-up for White, which was unfortunately not seriously tested here) 14 ... ♔h8 15 ♖c1 ♘eg8 16 b5 b6 17 cxd6 cxd6 18 a4 h5 19 ♗a3 ♘e8 20 a5 ♘h6 21 axb6 axb6 22 ♘a4± Pein - Medina, Mexico City 1991. Black's play was very strange. The standard plan with ... ♘g6 and ... ♖f7 would have been better.

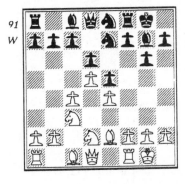

10	b4	f5
11	c5	♔h8
12	f3	f4
13	♘c4	h5

Hebden has previous experience of this variation, viz. 13 ... g5 14 g4 fxg3 15 hxg3 ♘g6 16 ♖f2 h5 17 ♖h2 h4 18 g4 ♘f4 19 ♗e3 ♕f6 20 ♗f1± Dzhandzhgava – Hebden, Hastings Masters 1990.

14	a4	g5
15	♗a3	♖f6
16	b5 *(92)*	

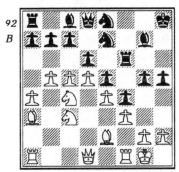

| 16 | ... | dxc5 |

This appears to be a major strategic concession which abandons the base of his pawn chain. Nevertheless, Black had to take some measure against the threat on b6.

17 ♗xc5

White avoids 17 ♘xe5 as this would ultimately open the diagonal for Black's king's bishop.

17	...	♖g6
18	h3	♘g8
19	♕d3	♘h6
20	♘d1	g4

After this, it is clear that Black has won the race. Although his centre looks exposed, White is unable to organise a breakthrough based on d6. Meanwhile Black has gained time to open up the g-file for his own purposes.

21	fxg4	hxg4
22	hxg4	♘xg4
23	♘f2	♘h6
24	♖fd1	♕g5
25	♗f3	b6
26	♗b4	♘g4
27	♘xg4	♗xg4
28	♔f2	♘f6
29	♖h1+	♔g8
30	♖ag1	♗f8 *(93)*

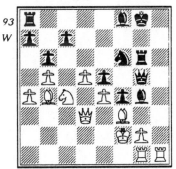

White has been driven into a thoroughly defensive posture. Black now siezes the opportunity to eliminate the less effective of his two bishops while simultaneously mobilising his last dormant piece.

31	♗xf8	♖xf8
32	♕c3	♖e8
33	♕d3	♗d7
34	♔f1	♕g3

35	d6	♘g4
36	♕c2	cxd6
37	♗xg4	♗xg4
38	♘xd6	

An ingenious last ditch defence but it is hardly surprising, given the overwhelming nature of Black's attack, that there is an elegant refutation.

38	...	♖xd6
39	♖h3 *(94)*	

The point of White's cunning defence. If now 39 ... ♗xh3 30 gxh3 winning the black queen for two rooks. However, Black has a vastly stronger continuation.

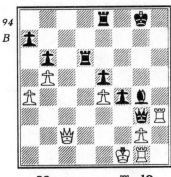

94
B

39	...	♖ed8
40	♕c4+	♗e6
41	♖xg3+	fxg3
42	♕c3	♗g4
	0-1	

Black's king is trapped and there is no good defence to ... ♖d1+.

5) Classical 9 b4 and others

This amounts to a blunt declaration of intent. Not wishing to expend time re-routing the king's knight, White commences the queenside advance. However, this impatience permits Black to move his own king's knight to h5, a much more active post than d7 or e8, and one from where it can hop into f4, a square irritatingly close the white king.

Nevertheless, it is not all plain sailing for Black. White will be very fast on the queenside and can sometimes consider meeting ... f5 with ♘g5 (△ ♘e6). All in all, this is an interesting method of meeting the King's Indian. It also has the advantage of being relatively unexplored (compared to some other lines of the classical) thus providing plenty of scope for investigation.

Game 12
Karpman - Frolov
USSR 1990

1	d4	♘f6
2	c4	g6
3	♘c3	♗g7
4	e4	d6
5	♗e2	0-0
6	♘f3	e5
7	0-0	♘c6
8	d5	♘e7 (95)

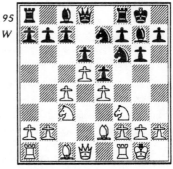

95
W

9   b4

White has four other moves here which merit consideration. The first three are essentially waiting moves; White wants to see the Black set-up before deciding how to lay out his own stall. A further point is that an early ... f5 can sometimes be met by ♘f3 - g5 - e6.

The fourth alternative, 9 ♗g5, has proved, for no

apparent reason, very po-
pular over the past two
years. Black has scored
well in these games, and
has several playable ways
to meet it.

a) 9 a4 a5 (Black should
probably avoid 9 ... ♘h5 10
a5! with a useful space
advantage on the queen-
side) 10 ♘e1 ♘d7 11 ♗e3 f5
12 f3 ♘c5! (it is best for
Black to challenge on the
queenside, as allowing
White a free hand there is
dangerous, e.g. 12 ... f4 13
♗f2 g5 {*Kasparov gives 13
... b6 14 ♘d3 ♘c5 15 b4! as
good for White*} 14 ♘d3
♘f6 15 c5 ♘g6 16 cxd6 cxd6
17 ♖c1 h5 18 h3 g4 19 hxg4
hxg4 20 fxg4 ♘e8 21 ♘b5
♗f6 22 ♖c3 with good play,
Peicheva – Ruxton, Oakham
1990) 13 ♘d3 b6 14 b4 ♘xd3
(14 ... axb4?! is not so good:
15 ♘xb4 ♗d7 16 ♘d3 ♗b7 17
♕b3 ♔h8 18 ♕b4 ♖b8 19
♖fb1 ♘g8 20 a5! bxa5 21
♕a3 ♗h6 22 ♗xh6 ♘xh6 23
c5 fxe4 24 ♘xe4± Peicheva
– Hennigan, Oakham 1990)
15 ♕xd3 axb4 16 ♘b5 ♔h8 17
♕b3 ♘g8 18 ♕xb4 ♘f6?!
(Kasparov prefers 18 ...
fxe4! 19 fxe4 ♖xf1+ 20 ♖xf1
♗h6!) 19 exf5 gxf5 20 ♗g5∞
Korchnoi – Kasparov, Bar-
celona 1989.

b) 9 ♔h1 ♔h8!? (a cheeky
move!; 9 ... ♘h5 10 g3 f5 is
playable, but White should
have an edge in the result-
ing structures, e.g. 11 exf5
♘xf5 12 ♘g5 ♘d4 13 ♗d3
♘f6 14 f3 c6 15 ♘ge4 ♗h3 16
♖f2 cxd5 17 ♘xf6+ ♗xf6 18
♘xd5 ♗g5 19 ♗e4 ♖c8 20 b3
♗xc1 21 ♖xc1± Larsen –
Nunn, Hastings 1987/88) 10
a4 (10 ♘g1?! {*very odd*} 10 ...
♘d7 11 g4 f5 12 f3 ♘g8 13
♗e3 ♗h6 14 ♗f2 a5 15 a3
♘c5∓ Kanko – Hazai, Hel-
sinki 1989) 10 ... a5 11 ♖a3
♘fg8 12 ♘e1 f5 13 ♘d3 ♘f6
14 f3 c5 15 dxc6 ♘xc6 16
exf5 gxf5 17 ♗g5 ♗e6 18 ♘e1
♖f7 19 ♘c2 ♕f8 20 ♘b5
♖d7∞ LB Hansen – Kotro-
nias, Bled 1991.

c) 9 ♗d2 (96).

This is a slightly more constructive waiting move
than 9 a4 and 9 ♔h1; White
intends a quick ♖c1 and
play can continue: 9 ... ♘h5
(9 ... ♘e8 10 ♘e1 f5 11 ♘d3
f4 12 ♖c1 ♖f7 13 c5 ♗f8 14
♗g4 ♗xg4 15 ♕xg4 h5 16
♕d1 ♖g7 17 f3 g5 18 cxd6
cxd6=/∓ Lechtynsky – Firt,
Brno 1990 was instructive.

White has achieved the highly desirable positional objective of exchanging the light-squared bishops, but at a cost of several tempi, and Black has a powerful kingside attack) 10 g3 (10 ♖c1 f5 11 ♘g5 ♘f4 12 ♗xf4 exf4 13 ♕f3 fxe4 14 ♗xe4 ♘f5 15 ♘e6 ♗xe6 16 dxe6 c6 17 ♖e1 ♕e7 18 ♕g4 ♔h8 19 ♖cd1 ♖ae8 20 ♗b1 ♘h6 21 ♕f3 ♖f6 22 ♗d3 ♖xe6 23 ♖xe6 ♕xe6 24 ♕xf4 ♖f8 25 ♕e4 ♕xe4 26 ♗xe4 ♖e8∓ Korchnoi - Spraggett, Montpellier Ct. 1985) 10 ... f5 11 exf5 (11 ♘g5 is perhaps more consistent: 11 ... ♘f6 12 f3 c6 13 ♕b3 ♔h8 14 ♗e3 f4 15 ♗f2 fxg3 16 hxg3 ♘h5 17 ♘e6 ♗xe6 18 dxe6 ♕c8 19 c5 d5 20 exd5 cxd5 21 ♘xd5 ♕xe6 22 ♘xe7 ♕xe7 23 ♔h2 ♕g5 24 ♖g1 and with the bishop pair and slightly more sound pawn structure, White stands better, Ree - Riemersma, Dutch Ch. 1987; whilst 11 ♘h4?! is a peculiar move: 11 ... ♘f6 12 f3 c6 13 ♔h1 f4 14 g4 h5 15 g5 ♘h7 16 ♖g1= Utemov - Timoshenko, Podolsk 1990) 11 ... ♘xf5 12 ♘e4 *(97)*.

Black has no problems here, e.g.

c1) 12 ... ♕e8 13 ♖e1 ♘f6 14 ♗d3 ♘xe4 15 ♗xe4 ♘h6 16 ♘g5 ♘g4 17 ♕f3 ♘f6 18 ♗e3 h6 19 ♘e4 ♗f5± Utemov - Shekachov, Moscow

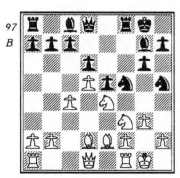

97
B

1991.

c2) 12 ... ♘f6 13 ♗g5 (13 ♗d3 ♗d7 14 ♖c1 ♔h8 15 ♗g5 b6 16 b4 a5 17 a3 axb4 18 axb4 ♖a4 19 ♕e1 ♕e8 20 ♗xf6 ♗xf6 21 ♖a1 ♖xa1 22 ♕xa1 ♕f7 23 ♕a2 ♗c8 24 ♖c1 ♗g7 25 ♖f1 ♗h6 26 ♕e2 ½-½ King - Davies, London (Watson, Farley & Williams) 1991) 13 ... h6 14 ♗xf6 ♗xf6 15 ♗d3 ♗g7 16 ♔g2 c6 17 ♕b3 ♔h8 18 h4 ♕d7! (a very sneaky move, threatening the h3-square) 19 ♖h1 ♕f7 20 ♗e2 b5 21 ♖ad1 ♗b7∓ Frias - Nijboer, Wijk aan Zee 1991. White has big problems in the centre and on the long diagonal.

d) 9 ♗g5 *(98)*:

d1) 9 ... ♘h5

d11) 10 g3 h6 (10 ... f6 11 ♗d2 f5 transposes to a line from 9 ♗d2(=), but Watson's method may be even better) 11 ♗d2 ♗h3 12 ♖e1 f5 13 ♘h4 ♘f6 14 exf5 g5 15 ♘g6 ♘xg6 16 fxg6 ♗f5 17 ♗e3 ♕e8 18 c5 a6 19 ♖c1 ♕xg6∓ Bern - Watson,

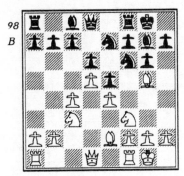

Gausdal 1991.

d12) 10 ♘e1 ♘f4 11 ♘d3 ♘xe2+ 12 ♕xe2 f6 (the immediate 12 ... f5 also worked okay for Black in Kern - Maeder, Dortmund 1991, i.e. 13 exf5 gxf5 14 ♘f4 ♗f6 15 ♗xf6 ♖xf6 16 ♘d3 f4 17 ♘e4 ♖g6 18 f3 ♘f5∓) 13 ♗e3 f5 14 f3 f4 15 ♗f2 g5 16 c5 h5 17 ♖ac1 ♗d7 18 b4 g4 19 b5 ♘g6 20 ♔h1 b6 21 cxd6 cxd6 22 a4 ♗f6 23 ♘a2 ♗h4 24 ♘ab4 ♖f7 25 ♖c6 (White is struggling to find counterplay) ♕f6 26 ♘b2 gxf3 27 gxf3 ♗xf2 28 ♕xf2 ♗xc6 29 dxc6 ♘e7∓ Ginsburg - Howell, London (Lloyds Bank) 1990.

d2) 9 ... h6 10 ♗xf6 ♗xf6 11 b4 *(99)*.

White has given up his good bishop but gained time for the queenside advance. Black now has two plans:

d21) 11 ... ♗g7 12 c5 f5 13 ♘d2 fxe4 14 ♘dxe4 ♘f5 15 ♗g4 ♗d7 16 ♕d3 ♗e8 17 a4 ♗f7 18 a5 ♘d4 19 a6 b6 20

cxd6 cxd6 21 ♕c4∞ Soffer - Nemet, Bern 1991.

d22) 11 ... ♔g7. This may be playable, but Black needs an improvement over the game Schmidt - Skalik, Polish Ch. 1991, which continued: 12 c5 ♘g8 13 a4! (both 13 cxd6?! cxd6 14 ♘d2 ♗g5 15 ♘c4 f5= Dussol - Shirov, Torcy 1990; and 13 ♘d2 ♗e7 14 c6 bxc6 15 dxc6 f5 16 ♘d5 ♗g5 17 ♗c4 ♗xd2 18 ♕xd2 fxe4 19 a4 ♗e6 20 ♕e2 ♗xd5 21 ♗xd5 ♘f6 22 ♗xe4 d5 23 ♗c2 ♕d6∓ D Gurevich - Mortensen, Reykjavik 1990 are less incisive than the text) 13 ... ♗e7 14 cxd6 cxd6 15 a5 f5 16 ♘d2 ♘f6 17 ♖c1 ♖f7 18 ♕b3 ♘g4 19 ♖c2 fxe4 20 ♘cxe4 ♗g5? (a blunder, but Black was struggling anyway) 21 ♖xc8! ♕xc8 22 ♘xd6 ♕d7 23 ♘xf7 ♗xd2 24 ♗xg4 ♕xg4 25 ♘xe5 ♕xb4 26 ♕d3 1-0.

d3) 9 ... ♘d7 10 ♘d2 f5 11 exf5 gxf5 12 f4 h6 (12 ... ♘f6 13 ♗h5? e4! Gelfand - Grivas, Haifa 1989) 13 ♗h4 ♘f6

(13 ... exf4?! looks very unnatural as, with hanging
pawns, Black usually wants
to keep the position fluid.
It certainly didn't work out
well in Pomes - Spraggett,
Terrassa 1990: 14 ♘f3 ♘f6
15 ♗xf6 ♖xf6 16 ♘d4 ♗d7 17
♗h5 c6 18 ♕b3 ♕b6 19 ♕xb6
axb6 20 ♖xf4±) 14 ♗h5?! c6
15 ♘b3 cxd5 16 ♗xf6 ♖xf6 17
♘xd5 ♖f8 18 ♕d2 ♗e6 19
♖ac1 ♖c8 20 ♔h1 ♔h8∓ Wi-
nants - Hellers, Wijk aan
Zee 1990. Black has good
central control and the two
bishops.

Returning to the position
after 9 b4 *(100)*:

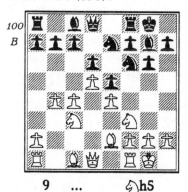

9 ... ♘h5

a) 9 ... ♘d7 and now:

a1) 10 ♗a3 f5 11 c5 ♘f6 12
cxd6 cxd6 13 ♘g5 fxe4 14
♘gxe4 ♘f5 15 ♘xf6+ ♖xf6
16 ♘e4 ♖f7 17 b5 ♗f8 18 ♗b2
♗d7 19 a4 ♕h4 20 ♕d3 ♖e8
21 ♗c1 ½-½ Karpman -
Akopian, Minsk 1990.

a2) 10 ♗d2 f5 11 ♘g5 ♘f6
12 f3 c6 13 c5 (this is very
odd, why not 13 ♕b3?) 13 ...

cxd5 14 exd5 h6 15 ♘h3
dxc5 16 ♗c4 ♔h8 17 bxc5
♘exd5 18 ♘xd5 ♘xd5 19 ♕c1
f4∓ Firt - Mrva, 1990.

a3) Nunn recommends 10
c5 f5 (10 ... dxc5 11 bxc5
♘xc5 12 ♗a3 b6 13 ♖c1 is
good for White) 11 ♘d2
dxc5 12 bxc5 ♘xc5 13 ♗a3±.

b) 9 ... a5 *(101)* and now:

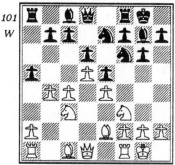

b1) 10 bxa5 c5 (10 ... ♖xa5
11 ♘d2 ♖a8 12 a4 b6 13 ♘b3
♘e8 14 a5 bxa5 15 ♘xa5 ♗d7
16 c5 dxc5 17 ♘b7 ♕c8 18
♖xa8 ♕xa8 19 ♘xc5 ♗c8 20
♘b5± Martin - McFarland,
British Ch. 1991. White has
made good progress on the
queenside, but Black seems
to have decided to re-
nounce his traditional
kingside counterplay) 11
dxc6 ♘xc6 12 ♗g5 ♕xa5 13
♗xf6 ♕xc3 14 ♕xd6 ♗e6 15
♗g5 ♖a6 16 c5 ♖xa2 17 ♖xa2
♗xa2 18 ♕d2 ♕xd2 19 ♘xd2
♘d4 20 ♗c4 ♗xc4 21 ♘xc4
♖c8= Bonin - Ree, New
York 1985.

b2) 10 ♗a3 axb4 11 ♗xb4
♘d7 12 a4 ♗h6 (The game

Berg – Nunn, Bundesliga 1985/86 reached the same position, but with both sides having taken a move more, White having captured on a5 and then played ♕b4. That game continued 13 ... ♘c5 14 ♘d2 ♘a6 15 ♕a3 f5 16 ♘b3 fxe4 17 ♘xe4 ♘f5 18 c5 ♕h4 19 ♕b1 ♘xc5 20 ♘bxc5 dxc5 21 ♗xc5 ♘d4 22 ♗c4 ♗f5 23 f3 ♗xe4 24 fxe4 ♖xf1+ 25 ♕xf1 ♕d8 ½-½) 13 ♕b3 ♔h8 14 ♖fd1 b6 15 a5 ♘c5 16 ♕b2 ♗a6 17 axb6 cxb6 18 ♖a3 f5 19 ♖da1 fxe4 20 ♗xc5 bxc5 21 ♘xe4 ♖b8 22 ♖b3 ♖xb3 23 ♕xb3 ♗c8 24 ♕b8± Tisdall – I Sokolov, Preston 1989.

10 c5

a) 10 ♘d2 is an interesting move. Play can continue 10 ... ♘f4 11 a4 f5 12 ♗f3 g5 13 exf5 ♘xf5 14 g3 ♘d4 (this is ingenious, but 14 ... ♘h3+ is better. Keene – Kavalek, Teesside 1975 continued 15 ♔g2 ♕d7! 16 ♘b3 ♘d4 17 ♘xd4 exd4 18 ♘b5 c6 19 ♘a3 ♖xf3! 20 ♕xf3 g4 21 ♕b3 ♕e7 with a strong attack) 15 gxf4 ♘xf3+ 16 ♘xf3! (16 ♕xf3? was played in a famous Petrosian – Gligoric game which Black won brilliantly, but the text is much stronger. Black should play this variation as Kavalek did in the above game) 16 ... exf4 (16 ... e4?? was less than successful in

Martin – Britton, British Ch. 1991; 17 ♘xg5 ♗xc3 18 ♖a3 ♗g7 19 ♖g3 1-0) 17 ♗b2 g4 18 ♔h1! and it will be difficult for Black to survive.

b) 10 g3 f5 (an alternative which deserves close consideration is 10 ... a5 11 bxa5 f5 12 ♘d2 {*This plays into Black's hands; 12 ♘g5 is much better*} 12 ... ♘f6 13 ♗a3 ♗h6 14 c5 ♗xd2 15 ♕xd2 ♘xe4 16 ♘xe4 fxe4 17 ♖ac1 ♗h3 18 ♖fd1 ♘f5 19 ♗b2 e3! 20 fxe3 ♘xg3 21 hxg3 ♕g5 22 g4 ♖f2! {*very attractive; if 23 ♔xf2 ♕h4+ mating*} 23 ♕e1 ♖af8 24 e4 ♕f4 0-1 Vanheste – Riemersma, Dutch Ch. 1987) 11 ♘g5 (11 c5 ♘f6 12 ♘d2 g5 13 exf5 ♘xf5 14 ♘de4 h6 15 cxd6 cxd6 16 ♘xf6+ ♗xf6 17 ♘e4= Ricardi – Schwanek, Buenos Aires 1990) 11 ... ♘f6 12 f3 *(102)* and now:

b1) 12 ... a5 13 bxa5 ♖xa5 14 ♕b3 b6 15 ♗d2 ♖e8 16 ♔g2 ♖a8 17 a4± van Wely – de Jong, Wijk aan Zee II

1990.

b2) 12 ... ♖e8!? (Black preempts the knight's arrival at e6) 13 c5? (this works out disastrously; 13 b5 looks much better) 13 ... h6 14 cxd6 ♕xd6 15 ♘e6 ♗xe6 16 dxe6 ♕xb4 17 ♕b3 ♕xb3 18 axb3 a6 19 ♗e3 ♘c6 20 exf5 gxf5 21 ♘d3 e4 22 fxe4 ♘g4 23 ♘d2 ♖ad8 24 ♘d5 ♗xa1 25 ♖xa1 ♘ce5 26 ♘e2 fxe4 27 ♘xc7 ♖xd2 28 ♗xg4 ♖e7 0-1 van Wely - Pieterse, Dutch Ch. 1991.

b3) 12 ... c6 13 b5 h6 14 ♘e6 ♗xe6 15 dxe6 ♘e8 16 bxc6 (16 ♗a3 allows Black to advantageously close the position: 16 ... c5 17 ♕d3 ♕c8 18 ♘d5 ♕xe6 19 exf5 gxf5 20 ♘xe7+ ♕xe7 21 ♖ad1 a6∓ Makarov - Cvitan, Belgrade GMA 1988) 16 ... bxc6 17 ♗a3 c5 18 ♕a4 ♘c7 19 ♕d7 ♕xd7 20 exd7 ♘c6 21 ♘d1 ♘d4 22 ♔g2 ♔f7 23 ♗a4 ♔e7 24 h4 h5 25 ♖ab1∞ van Wely - Reinderman, Dieren 1990.

b4) 12 ... f4 13 c5 (13 ♔g2 looks like an improvement over the text; it was certainly convincing in Ghitescu - Milu, Bucharest 1991: 13 ... fxg3 14 hxg3 ♘h5 15 ♖h1! h6 16 ♘e6 ♗xe6 17 dxe6 c6 18 ♗e3 ♕c7 19 ♕d2 ♔h7 20 ♖af1 ! ♘g8 21 f4 exf4 22 gxf4 ♘hf6 23 f5±) 13 ... dxc5 14 ♗c4 (White heads for great complications; 14 bxc5 would have led to an

unclear position after 14 ... h6 15 ♘e6 ♗xe6 16 dxe6 fxg3 17 hxg3 ♕d4+) 14 ... cxb4 15 d6+ ♔h8 16 ♘b5 (White cannot be greedy here; 16 dxe7 ♕xe7 17 ♘xa4 b5 18 ♗xb5 ♘h5, and although White has an extra piece, his position is a disaster) 16 ... h6 17 ♘f7+ ♖xf7 18 ♗xf7 cxd6 19 ♘xd6 ♗h3 20 ♗b3 ♔h7 21 ♖f2 ♘c6 (the dust settles and reveals a slight edge for Black, who has two pawns for the exchange and an active position) 22 ♘b2 ♕e7 23 ♖c1 ♘d4 24 gxf4 ♘h5 25 fxe5 ♗xe5 (Black has managed to loosen the white king a little more; if now 26 ♗xd4 ♗xd4 27 ♕xd4 ♕g5+ demonstrates the benefit of this. With his minor pieces playing such an active role. Black is not hampered by the material deficit of the exchange) 26 ♘f7 ♘xb3 27 ♘xe5 ♘xc1 28 ♕xc1 ♖c8 29 ♖c2 ♖xc2 30 ♕xc2 ♕g5+ 31 ♔h1 ♕e3 32 ♕c7+ ♘g7 33 ♕c1 ♕e2 34 ♕g1 g5 35 ♗d4 ♘e6 36 ♕g3 ♘f4 0-1 C Hansen - Nunn, Wijk aan Zee 1991.

10 ...   ♘f4 *(103)*

a) 10 ... h6. This is a sneaky waiting move; Black removes the ♘g5 possibility, and will meet 11 ♘d2 with 11 ... ♘f4. Meanwhile. White is lacking a con-

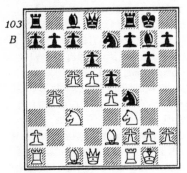

structive move. Some possibilities:

a1) 11 g3 f5 12 ♘d2 ♘f6 13 f3 fxe4 14 fxe4 ♗h3 15 ♖f2 ♕d7 16 ♘c4 ♘g4 17 ♖xf8+ ♖xf8 18 ♗f3 ♔h7= Lalic - Petrushin, Bosna v Trud 1985.

a2) 11 ♘d2 ♘f4 12 ♘c4 f5 13 f3 g5 14 ♗e3 (14 ♗a3 ♖f6 15 b5 ♖g6 16 b6∞ Ovchinikova - Gleizerov, Voronesh 1987; or 14 cxd6 cxd6 15 ♘b5 ♕f6 16 ♗e3 b6 17 ♖c1 ♗a6 18 a4 ♗xb5 19 axb5 ♕d7 20 ♘d2 ♖af8 21 ♖e1 ♖g6 22 ♘f1 h5 23 ♘g3 ♘xe2+ 24 ♘xe2 f4 25 ♗f2 g4∓ Law - Nielsen, Gausdal 1991) 14 ... ♘eg6 15 cxd6 cxd6 16 exf5 ♗xf5 17 ♘e4 ♘xe2+ 18 ♕xe2 ♘f4 19 ♕d2 ♗xe4 20 fxe4 ♕f6 21 g3 ♖ac8 22 ♘a5 ♘h3+ 23 ♔g2 ♕g6∓ Tisdall - Watson, London (Watson, Farley & Williams) 1990.

b) 10 ... a5 11 cxd6 cxd6 12 ♘b5 ♘f4 13 ♗xf4 exf4 14 ♖c1 axb4 15 ♕b3 ♗g4 16 ♖c7 ♘c8 17 ♖xb7 ♕a5 18 ♗c4 (18 ... ♗xf3 19 gxf3 ♘b6 20 ♖b1

♘xc4 21 ♕xc4= Grivas - Cooper, Novi Sad Ol. 1990) 18 ... ♘b6 19 ♖c7 ♘xc4 20 ♕xc4 ♖fc8 21 ♖c6 ♖xc6 22 ♕xc6 ♕xa2 23 ♘xd6 ♕a7 24 ♘b5 ♕a6∓ Grivas - Murey, Tel-Aviv 1991.

c) 10 ... f5 *(104)* and now:

c1) 11 ♕b3 h6 12 a4 (12 ♗d2 ♘f4 13 ♗xf4 exf4 14 e5 ♔h7 15 exd6 cxd6 16 ♖ad1 ♗d7 17 ♘b5 ♗xb5 18 ♗xb5 ♖c8 19 ♖fe1± Krasenkov - McDonald, Andorra 1991) 12 ... fxe4 13 ♘xe4 ♘f4 14 ♗xf4 ♖xf4 15 cxd6 cxd6 16 ♗d3 b6 17 ♖fe1 ♗b7 18 ♘c3 ♖c8 19 ♗e4 ♕f8 20 a5± Grivas - Nunn, Athens 1991.

c2) 11 ♘g5 ♘f4 12 ♗c4 fxe4 13 ♘gxe4 ♘f5 14 f3 a5 15 bxa5 ♖xa5 16 ♘b5 ♗d7 17 c6 bxc6 18 dxc6+ ♗e6 19 ♗xe6+ ♘xe6 20 ♕d5 ♘fd4 21 a4∞ Tisdall - M Gurevich, Reykjavik 1988.

c3) 11 exf5 gxf5 12 ♘g5 ♘f6 13 ♕b3 (this doesn't work; White should instead consider the immediate attack on Black's pawn

centre with 13 f4) 13 ... h6
14 cxd6 cxd6 15 ♘e6 ♗xe6 16
dxe6 d5 17 ♗b2 ♕b6 18 ♘a4
♕d6 19 ♘c5 b6 20 f4 bxc5 21
fxe5 ♕b6 22 exf6 c4+ 23 ♔h1
cxb3 and Black went on to
win, Djuric - Byrne, New
York 1990.

11   ♗xf4   exf4
12   ♖c1 *(105)*

12 ♕d2 f5 (Black falls a
long way behind in deve-
lopment after this; a plan
with ... h6, ... g5 and ... ♘g6
was preferable) 13 ♖ad1
fxe4 14 ♘xe4 h6 15 cxd6
cxd6 16 ♘d4 ♘f5 17 ♘xf5
♗xf5 18 ♕xf4 ♗e5 19 ♕e3
♗xh2+ 20 ♔xh2 ♕h4+ 21 ♔g1
♗xe4 22 ♖d4 ♖ae8 23 ♗f3±
Tisdall - Jonsson, Reykjavik
1989.

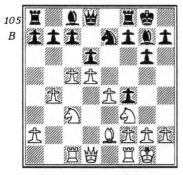

105
B

12   ...   h6

a) 12 ... a6 (this looks
slow, but it works out okay
in this game) 13 ♕d2 ♗h6 14
e5 dxe5 15 ♘xe5 f3 16 ♕xh6
fxe2 17 ♘xe2 ♕xd5 18 ♘c4
♘f5 19 ♕f4 ♕d3 20 ♘g3
♘xg3 21 hxg3 ♗e6= Halasz
- Segal, Beer-Sheva 1991.

b) 12 ... a5 13 ♘b5 (13 bxa5
♖xa5 14 cxd6 cxd6 15 ♕b3
♔h8 16 ♖fd1 ♖c5 17 ♘a4
½-½ Skembris - Ivanovic,
Novi Sad Ol 1990) 13 ... axb4
14 cxd6 cxd6 15 ♕b3 ♗g4 16
♖c7 ♖e8 17 ♖fc1 ♘f5 18
♕xb4 ♖xa2 19 exf5 ♖axe2
20 fxg6 hxg6 21 ♕xf4 ♗d7
22 ♘xd6 ♕xc7 23 ♕xf7+
♔h7 24 ♕xg7+ ♔xg7 25
♘xe8+ ♗xe8 26 ♖xc7+ ♔f6
27 ♖xb7 (White's last ten
moves have all been cap-
tures, so it is hardly surprisingly that Black has run
out of pieces!) 27 ... ♖a2 28
h4 1-0 Yrjola - Grivas,
Thessaloniki Ol. 1984.

13   ♘d4!?

a) 13 h3 g5 14 a4 ♘g6 15
♘b5 (a typical position for
this variation: Black has
the two bishops, the e5-
square and mobile pawns
on the kingside, while
White has the initiative and
a big lead in development)
15 ... a6 16 ♘bd4 ♖e8 17 ♖c4
♕f6 18 ♕c2 h5 19 ♘f5 (in
view of what happens in
the game, prefacing this
with the pawn exchange on
d6 might be better) 19 ...
♖xe4! 20 ♕xe4 ♗xf5 21 ♕d4
♕e7 22 ♕d1 g4 23 hxg4
hxg4 24 ♘h2 ♕g5∞ Suba -
Schmidt, Prague Zt. 1985.

b) 13 ♘d2 a6 (13 ... g5 14
♘c4 a6 15 a4 ♘g6 16 cxd6
cxd6 17 a5 ♖e8 18 ♘b6 ♖b8
19 ♗h5 ♘e5 20 h3 ♕f6 21 f3

♗d7∞ Skembris - Milos, Novi Sad Ol. 1990) 14 ♘c4 f5 (here we see Black's alternative plan to that of ... g5 and ... ♘g6: he tries to undermine the white centre) 15 ♗d3 fxe4 16 ♗xe4 ♘f5 17 ♖e1 ♘h4 18 ♗f3 ♗xc3 19 ♖xc3 ♕f6 20 ♖c2 ♗f5 21 ♗e4 ♖ae8 22 ♗xf5 ♕g5!∓ Hergott - Winants, Thessaloniki Ol. 1984.

13 ... g5

13 ... a6 14 h3 ♔h7 15 ♕d3 (15 ♗g4! ♗xg4 16 hxg4 ♘g8 17 ♘f3!) 15 ... ♘g8 16 cxd6?! cxd6 17 ♘f3?! ♖e8 18 a4 ♗d7 19 a5 ♖c8∓ Karpman - Kruppa, USSR 1990.

14 ♗h5

Preventing ... ♘g6 and forcing Black change plan.

14	...	a6
15	a3	♔h8
16	h3	♖b8
17	♖e1	♘g8
18	♗g4	♗e5
19	♗xc8	♖xc8
20	♘f5	♕f6
21	♘e2	♕g6 (106)

22 ♘ed4?!

White is slightly better, but starts to go astray. The right idea was 22 g4! fxg3 23 fxg3 ♖ce8 24 ♘ed4, consolidating the f5 outpost.

22	...	h5
23	♘f3	♖ce8
24	cxd6	cxd6
25	♖c7?!	

White should mount a damage limitation exercise with 25 ♘xe5 ♖xe5 26 g4 fxg3 27 fxg3 ♘h6!=.

25	...	g4
26	hxg4	hxg4
27	♘xe5	

White is getting carried away with his initiative and not paying attention to his own weaknesses, especially the e4-pawn.

27	...	♖xe5
28	♖d7?!	

28 ♕d4 ♕f6! (threatening 29 ... ♖xf5) 29 ♕c3 ♖fe8∓.

28	...	♘f6!
29	♖xd6	♖fe8
30	♕d2?	♕xf5! (107)

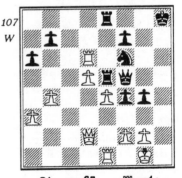

31	exf5	♖xe1+
32	♔h2	g3+!
	0-1	

6) Classical 8 ♗e3

With 8 ♗e3 White maintains the central tension by postponing the advance d5 and there often follows a period of shadow boxing, the main feature of which is Black's pursuit of the white queen bishop with moves such as ... ♘g4 and ... f6. Black will hope to gain time and further his kingside ambitions, whereas White presumes that these manoeuvres will only create weaknesses in his opponent's position.

Play can revert to familiar situations if White subsequently closes the centre with d5, and much of the tension in the ♗e3 lines revolve around whether White can play this advance in favourable circumstances.

This variation has much in common with 7 ♗e3, and they will often transpose into each other.

Game 13
Miles - Rogers
Manila Izt. 1990

1	c4	g6
2	e4	♗g7
3	d4	d6
4	♘c3	♘f6
5	♗e2	0-0
6	♘f3	e5
7	0-0	♘c6
8	♗e3	(108)

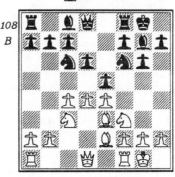

108
B

8 ... ♘g4

An important alternative is 8 ... ♖e8 9 dxe5 (9 d5 leads to dead equality, e.g. 9 ... ♘d4 10 ♘xd4 exd4 11 ♗xd4 ♘xe4 12 ♗xg7 ♔xg7 13 ♘xe4 ♖xe4 14 ♗d3 ♖d4 15 ♕c2 ♕f6 16 ♖ae1 ♗d7 17 h3 b6 18 ♖e3 ♖e8 19 ♕c3 a5 ½-½ Rajkovic - Wahls, Bundesliga 1991) 9 ... dxe5 (9 ... ♘xe5 is playable, but Black will always be slightly worse, e.g. 10 ♘xe5

♖xe5 {*10 ... dxe5 led to the following drastic conclusion in Gschnitzer - von Gleich, Bad Wörishofen 1991: 11 ♕xd8 ♖xd8 12 ♘b5 ♖d7 13 ♖fd1 ♘xe4 14 ♘xc7 1-0*} 11 f3 ♖e8 12 ♕d2 ♗e6 13 ♖fd1 ♘d7 14 ♖ac1 f5 15 exf5 ♗xf5 16 ♗f1 ♘e5 17 ♘d5 ♕d7 18 ♗g5± Nogueiras - Timoshenko, Bayamo 1981) and now *(109)*:

109
W

a) 10 h3 ♗e6 11 c5 ♕e7 12 ♕c2 ♖ad8 13 ♖ad1 and now instead of 13 ... ♖xd1?! 14 ♖xd1 ♖d8 15 ♗b5± Speelman - Nunn, Hastings 1987/88, 13 ... a6 is okay for Black.

b) 10 c5!? has been tried recently. White plans ♕b3 with uncomfortable pressure against b7 and f7. Some examples:

b1) 10 ... ♘g4?! (This gets Black into a tangle) 11 ♗g5 f6 12 ♗d2 ♘h6 (12 ... f5 13 ♘g5 is bad for Black, but maybe 12 ... ♔h8 is playable, e.g. 13 ♕c1 f5 14 ♗g5 ♕d7 15 ♗b5 f4 16 h3 ♘f6 17 ♗xf6 ♗xf6 18 ♘d5 ♕g7 19 ♘b4± Gschnitzer - Brunner, Bundesliga 1991) 13 ♕b3+ (White can win a pawn with 13 ♗xh6!? ♗xh6 14 ♕xd8 ♖xd8 15 ♘d5, but after 15 ... f5 Black will obtain counterplay) 13 ... ♔h8 14 ♖ad1 ♘g8 15 ♗e1 ♕e7 16 ♘d5 ♕f7 17 ♗c4 ♖b8 18 ♗c3 ♗e6 19 ♘e1 ♘d4! (Otherwise Black will have great difficulty in freeing his position) 20 ♗xd4 exd4 21 ♖xd4 f5 22 exf5 ♗xd4 23 fxe6 ♕g7, Miles - Wahls, Biel 1990, and now 24 ♘d3! is very good for White.

b2) 10 ... ♕e7!? 11 ♕b3 (11 h3!?) 11 ... ♖b8 12 ♗b5? (White over-estimates the power of this pin, missing a clever black tactic) 12 ... ♗g4 13 ♘d5 ♘xd5 14 exd5 ♗xf3 15 gxf3 ♖ed8!∓ Martynov - Shchekachev, Malmo 1991.

b3) 10 ... h6 11 h3 (This is rather slow; 11 ♕b3 is an alternative, and if 11 ... ♘g4 12 ♖ad1 ♕e7 13 ♘d5) 11 ... ♗e6 12 ♕a4 ♕c8 13 ♖fd1 a6 14 ♘d5 ♘h5 15 ♘h2 ♔h7 16 ♗g4 ♗xg4 17 hxg4 ♘f4 18 ♘xf4 exf4 19 ♗xf4 ♗xb2 20 ♖ab1 ♗g7 21 ♘f3 ♕xg4 22 ♖xb7 ♘d4= Boensch - Volke, German Ch. 1991.

c) 10 ♕xd8 and now the recapture with the rook gives White a slight edge, but taking with the knight is fine for Black, e.g.:

c1) 10 ... ♖xd8 11 ♖fd1 ♗g4 12 ♘d5! (More troublesome than 12 ♘b5 ♖xd1+ 13 ♖xd1 ♘e8 14 c5 a6 15 ♘c3 ♖d8 16 ♖xd8 ♘xd8 17 ♘d2 ♗xe2 18 ♘xe2 ♔f8 19 ♘c4 ♔e7 20 ♘c3 c6 21 ♘a4, although even here, White retains a nagging edge, Suba - Zuckerman, New York Open 1987) 12 ... ♘xe4 13 ♘xc7 ♖xd1+ 14 ♖xd1 ♖c8 15 ♘d5 ♘f6 16 ♘xf6+ ♗xf6 17 h3 ♗e6 18 b3 a5 19 ♘g5! ♗d4 20 ♗d3 ♗d7 21 ♗e4± Dlugy - Fishbein, New York Open 1991. White has pressure against the weak queenside pawns.

c2) 10 ... ♘xd8 11 ♘b5 ♘e6 12 ♗g5 ♖e7 13 ♖fd1 b6 14 a4 (14 c5 ♘xc5 15 ♖d8+ ♗f8 16 ♘xa7 ♖xa7 17 ♖xc8 ♖e8 18 ♖xe8 ♘xe8 19 ♘f3 f6 20 ♗c4+ ½-½ Piket - Nunn, Wijk aan Zee 1991) 14 ... c6 15 ♘xe6 ♗xe6 16 ♘c3 ♖b7 17 b4 (White must play this or Black will prevent it with ... ♗f8 and then the plan of ... ♘d7 and ... ♗c5 will give him the edge) 17 ... ♗f8 18 b5 (18 ♖ab1?! left White struggling to hold the balance in Portisch - Nunn, Amsterdam OHRA 1990: 18 ... ♘d7 19 b5 ♖c8 20 ♘d5 ♘c5 21 bxc6 ♖xc6 22 a5 bxa5 23 ♘f6+ ♔h8 24 ♖xb7 ♘xb7 25 ♘d7 ♗d6 26 c5 ♖c7 27 cxd6 ♖xd7 28 ♗g5 ♖xd6

29 ♗f6+ ♔g8 30 ♗xe5 ♖xd1+ ½-½) 18 ... ♖c8 19 ♗g5 ♔g7 20 bxc6 ♖xc6 21 ♗xf6+ ♔xf6 22 ♖d8 ♗c5 23 ♖g8 ♖c8 24 ♘d5+ ♔g5 25 ♖xc8 ♗xc8 26 g3 f5= Gausel - Hellers. Oslo 1991.

9   ♗g5 *(110)*

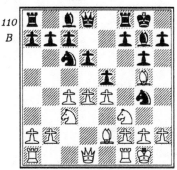

110
B

9   ...   f6

After 9 ... ♗f6 White must play accurately to keep the advantage, i.e. 10 ♗xf6 ♘xf6 11 h3! (Not 11 dxe5 dxe5 12 ♕xd8 ♖xd8 13 ♘d5 ♘e8! △ ... ♗g4=) 11 ... exd4 12 ♘xd4 ♖e8 13 ♘xc6 bxc6 14 ♕c2 ♕e7 15 ♖fe1 ♖b8 16 ♖ad1 ♕e5 17 ♕d2 a5 18 ♗f1± Vodinovic - Mollov, Plovdiv 1988.

10   ♗c1

10 ♗h4, preventing ... f5 is an important alternative. which gives rise to the following *(111)*:

a) 10 ... g5 11 ♗g3 ♘h6 12 dxe5 fxe5 (This is a very double-edged position: Black has a strong central position, but some weaknesses on the kingside) 13

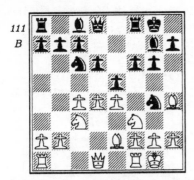

h3 (13 c5 g4 14 ♘d2 dxc5 15 ♘b3 ♘d4 16 ♘xc5 c6 17 ♗c4+ ♔h8 18 ♘e2 ♕e7 19 ♘b3 ♗e6 20 ♗xe6 ♘xe6 21 ♕c2 ♘f7 22 f3 gxf3 23 ♖xf3 ♘fg5 24 ♖f5± Chekhov - Paehtz, Berlin 1990) 13 ... ♘f7 14 c5 (14 ♘d2 ♗e6 15 ♗g4 ♘d4 16 ♘d5 ♘h8 17 ♘b3 ♘g6 18 ♖c1 ♗f7 19 ♘e3 ♘f4 20 ♘xd4 exd4 21 ♘f5∞ Zsu Polgar - Hellers, Wijk aan Zee II 1990) 14 ... ♗e6 15 cxd6 ♕xd6 16 ♕a4 ♕b4 17 ♕xb4 ♘xb4 18 a3 ♘c6 19 ♘d5 ♗xd5 20 exd5 ♘e7 21 ♖fd1 ♘f5∞ Gruenberg - Vogt, Leipzig 1988.

b) 10 ... ♔h8 (A more solid continuation than 10 ... g5, but lacking in dynamism) 11 dxe5 (11 ♖c1 ♘h6 12 dxe5 dxe5 13 c5 ♗g4 14 ♘d2 ♗xe2 15 ♕xe2 ♘d4 16 ♕d1 ♘g8 17 ♘c4 ♕d7 18 ♕d3 ♖ae8 19 f3 ♘e7 20 ♗f2 ♘ec6 21 ♘d5± Rajkovic - Pavlovic, Yugoslavia 1987) 11 ... dxe5 12 c5 ♘h6 13 h3 ♗e6 14 ♕a4 ♕e8 15 ♖ad1 f5 (Black gets into trouble after this, so

maybe 15 ... a6!? is better) 16 ♘b5 a6 17 ♘xc6 bxc6 18 exf5 gxf5 19 ♖fe1± Suba - Watson, New York Open 1987.

c) 10 ... ♘h6 (Also solid) 11 dxe5 dxe5 12 c5 ♗e6 13 ♕a4 g5 (13 ... ♕e8 14 ♗c4 g5 15 ♗g3 g4 16 ♘h4? (*This knight takes little further part in the game. 16 ♘d2, as in Gruenberg - Fernandez, is much better*) 16 ... ♘d4 17 ♗xe6+ ♕xe6 18 ♘b5 ♘xb5 19 ♕xb5 c6 20 ♕a4 ♖fd8 21 ♖ad1 ♖xd1 22 ♖xd1 ♗f8 23 b4 ♕c4∓ Simic - Hazai, Smederavska Palanka 1987) 14 ♗g3 g4 15 ♗c4 ♕e7 16 ♘d2 ♔h8 17 ♘b3 ♕f7 18 ♗xe6 ♕xe6 19 ♖ad1 ♖f7 20 ♘d5± Gruenberg - Fernandez, New York Open 1991.

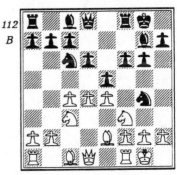

10 ... f5

Black has two important alternatives:

a) 10 ... ♘h6 11 dxe5 (This is more testing than 11 d5, when 11 ... ♘e7 12 b4 ♘f7 13 c5 f5 14 ♘g5 ♘xg5 15 ♗xg5 h6 16 ♗d2 fxe4 17 ♗c4 ♗f5

18 g4!? ♗c8 19 ♘xe4 ♔h7 20
cxd6 cxd6 21 ♖c1 was not
worse for Black in Agde-
stein - Cvitan, Novi Sad Ol.
1990) 11 ... dxe5 (In some
previous variations, with 10
♗h4, the recapture with the
f-pawn was fine for Black,
but here it is dangerous, as
the white queen's bishop
can play an active role, e.g.
11 ... fxe5 12 ♗g5 ♕d7 13
♘d5! *{13 ♕d2 ♘f7 14 ♗e3
b6= let Black off the hook
in Wells - Vukic, Graz 1991}*
13 ... ♔h8 14 ♖c1 ♘f7 15 ♗e3
*{c5 is coming and Black has
big problems}* 15 ... ♘cd8 16
c5 ♘e6 17 cxd6 ♕xd6 18
♘xc7 ♘xc7 19 ♕xd6 ♘xd6
20 ♖xc7+- Thorsteins -
Yedidia, Paris 1991) 12 ♕d5+
(This activates the queen,
but White can also station
it on a4, e.g. 12 c5 ♗e6 13
♕a4 ♔h8 14 ♗b5 ♗d7 15 ♖d1
♕c8 16 ♕a3 ♗g4 17 ♗xc6
bxc6 18 ♘e2 ♘f7 19 h3 ♗e6
20 ♕a4 ♕b7 21 b3± D Gure-
vich - Fedorowicz, USA Ch.
1989) 12 ... ♘f7 (12 ... ♔h8 13
♗e3 ♕e8 14 ♖ad1 ♗e6 15 ♕b5
♖b8 16 ♕a4 a6 17 ♗c5 ♖f7 18
♘d5 ♘g8, and now 19 ♔h1!
dealt with Black's threat of
... ♘d4 and left White with
the advantage in Portisch -
Spraggett, Moscow GMA
1990) 13 ♗e3 ♗g4 14 ♖ad1 (14
♖fd1 ♕c8 15 ♘e1 ♗e6 16 ♕b5
♘d6 17 ♕a4 ♘d4 18 c5
♘xe2+ 19 ♘xe2 ♘c4 20 ♗c1

♖d8 21 ♘d3 ♕d7 22 ♕c2 ♕f7
23 b3 ♘a5 24 ♗d2 ♘c6 25
♘b4 ♘xb4 26 ♗xb4 ♗f8=
Fauland - Vukic, Graz 1991)
14 ... ♕c8 15 c5 ♗e6 16 ♕d3
♘e7 17 ♘d5 ♖e8 18 ♕b3 c6
19 ♗c4 cxd5 20 exd5 ♘xd5
21 ♗xd5 ♗xd5 22 ♖xd5 ♖e7
23 ♖fd1± Barbero - Vukic,
Graz 1991.

b) 10 ... ♔h8 *(113)* and
now:

113
W

b1) 11 d5 ♘e7. If this position is compared to the
main line (8 d5 ♘e7) it
would, at first sight,
appear to be a bad deal for
White. Black has played the
useful ... ♔h8 and has also
cleared the way for the
advance of the f-pawn.
However, Black's knight on
g4 is a greater handicap
than one would expect. If it
is defended with ... h5, then
a subsequent ... f5 may
allow White to play exf5
gxf5 and then h3, possibly
winning the exposed h-
pawn. If it retreats to h6,
then Black has lost time

and placed the knight on a poor square. Let's see how this works out in practice:

b11) 12 ♘e1 h5 (12 ... f5 worked well in Z Polgar - Xie Jun, Novi Sad Women's Ol. 1990: 13 ♗xg4 fxg4 14 ♗e3 c5 15 dxc6? {*Opening up the position for the bishops cannot be right. White should simply play 15 ♘d3 ⌓ b4 with a small plus*} 15 ... bxc6 16 ♗g5 ♕c7 17 ♗xe7 ♕xe7 18 ♘c2 h5 19 ♘e3 ♗e6 20 ♕e2 ♗h6∓) 13 ♘d3 f5 14 exf5 ♘xf5 15 h3 ♘f6 16 ♗g5 c6 17 ♗f3 ♘d4 18 ♗e4 ♕e8 19 f3 cxd5 20 cxd5 ♘f5 21 ♔h2 ♗d7 22 ♕b3± Brenninkmeijer - Shirov, Groningen 1990.

b12) 12 ♘d2 ♘h6 (After 12 ... h5, it is difficult for Black to get going on the kingside, e.g. 13 b4 ♘h6 14 c5 f5 15 cxd6 cxd6 16 exf5 ♘exf5 17 ♘ce4 ♘d4 18 ♘c4 ♘xe2+ 19 ♕xe2 ♘f5 20 ♗g5 ♕d7 21 a4 b6 22 b5± Djurhuus - Lanka, Peer Gynt International 1991) 13 b4 f5 14 c5 ♘eg8 15 ♘c4 f4 16 a4 ♘f6 17 f3 g5 18 h3 (Black has opted for the traditional race, but the knight on h6 is horrible - by blocking the h-pawn and preventing the use of h6 by a bishop or rook, several of Black's thematic ideas have been taken away) 18 ... ♘f7 19 ♗a3 ♖g8 20 b5± Djurhuus -

Watson, Gausdal 1991. White is way ahead in the race.

b13) 12 ♘g5!? alters the structure and leaves White with a small edge, e.g. 12 ... ♘xh2 13 ♔xh2 fxg5 14 ♗xg5 h6 15 ♗e3 ♘g8 16 ♖h1 ♗f6 17 ♕d2 ♗g5 18 ♗xg5 hxg5 19 g3± Miles - Ye, Beijing Open 1991.

b2) 11 h3 exd4 (This initiates a forcing sequence which leaves Black with a perfectly satisfactory position. Less good is 11 ... ♘h6 12 dxe5 dxe5 13 ♗e3 ♗e6 14 ♕xd8 ♖axd8 15 ♘b5 ♖d7 16 ♖fd1 when White retains an edge) 12 ♘xd4 ♘xd4 13 ♕xd4 f5 14 ♕d1 ♘e5 15 exf5 ♗xf5 16 f4 (16 ♗e3 ♗e6 17 c5 ♘c4 18 ♗xc4 ♗xc4 19 ♖e1= Cebalo - Belotti, Reggio Emilia 1991) 16 ... ♘c6 17 ♗e3 ♕d7 (17 ... ♕f6 18 ♕d2 ♖ae8= as in van der Sterren - Arakhamia, Aosta 1990, is also fine) 18 ♕d2 ♖ae8 19 ♔h2 ♕f7 20 ♘d5 ♗e4 21 ♖ac1 ♘d8 22 ♘c3 ♗c6 23 ♗d4 ♘e6 24 ♗xg7+ ♕xg7 25 ♗g4 ♘c5 26 ♖ce1 a5= A Maric - Xie Jun, Novi Sad Women's Ol. 1990.

11 d5 *(114)*

11 ♗g5 is, rather unusually for the opening, a fourth consecutive bishop move. Play can go:

a) 11 ... ♗f6 12 ♗xf6 ♘xf6 13 exf5 (Less good is 13

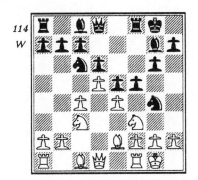

dxe5?! dxe5 14 ♕xd8 ♖xd8
15 ♘d5 ♘xe4! 16 ♘xc7 ♖b8
and now in Portisch - Ka-
sparov, Linares 1990, White
played 17 ♖fd1?! and was a
little worse after 17 ... ♗d7
18 ♗d3 ♖bc8. 17 ♖ad1 would
have been better, but only
equal) 13 ... ♗xf5 (13 ...
gxf5?! 14 dxe5 dxe5 15 ♕xd8
♖xd8 16 ♘d5 ♘e8 17 ♖fd1
♗e6 18 ♔f1± Cebalo - Iva-
novic, Yugoslavia 1990. The
Black e- and f-pawns are
vulnerable) 14 d5! (This
causes Black some trouble.
Kasparov also mentions 14
♕d2 ♕e7 15 ♖ae1±) 14 ...
♘e7 15 ♘g5 c6 16 ♗d3 ♗g4
17 ♕d2 ♕b6 18 h3 ♗d7 19
dxc6 bxc6 20 ♖ae1 (Black is
struggling. His centre is
exposed to attack, and
there are no weaknesses in
the white position to provide a source of counter-
play) 20 ... ♖ad8 21 ♘a4 ♕c7
22 f4 ♘f5 23 c5 exf4 24
♕xf4 ♘d5 25 cxd6 ♘xd6 26
♕h4 ♗f5 27 ♗xf5 ♘xf5 28
♖xf5 ♖xf5 29 ♘e6 g5 30

♕g4 ♕a5 31 b4 ♘xb4 32
♘xd8 h5 33 ♖e8+ 1-0 Raj-
kovic - Nunn, Bundesliga
1990/91.

b) 11 ... ♕e8(!) *(115).*

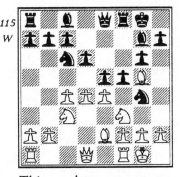

This makes more sense
than exchanging the king's
bishop. White must now be
careful or Black can be very
fast with the kingside
attack, e.g. 12 d5 (In Lputian - Bologan, USSR Teams
1991, White tried to stir up
trouble with the unlikely
combination 12 ♘d5 ♕f7 13
♗e7!? but after 13 ... ♘xe7
14 ♘g5 ♕e8 15 ♘xc7 ♕d8 16
♘ce6 ♗xe6 17 ♘xe6 ♕d7 18
exf5 gxf5 19 ♘xf8 ♖xf8,
Black was certainly not
worse) 12 ... ♘e7 (12 ... ♘b8
is an unusual retreat for
the black knight, but is not
necessarily bad, e.g. 13 ♘e1
♘f6 14 exf5 ♗xf5 15 ♘c2 a5
16 ♘e3 ♗d7 17 ♘g4 ♘a6 18
♘xf6+ ♗xf6 19 ♗e3 e4 20
♗d4 ♘c5 21 ♗xf6 ♖xf6 22
♕d4 ♖f5 23 ♘d1 ♖e5 24 ♘e3
♕e7 25 b3 ♖f8 26 ♖ab1 ♖f4
27 a3 ♖h4 28 b4 ♘d3= Mu-

rugan - Bologan, Peer Gynt International 1991) 13 ♞e1 (13 ♞d2 cuts off the retreat of the queen's bishop which was immediately exploited in Deak - Hazai, Debrecen 1991, viz. 13 ... h6! 14 ♝xe7 ♛xe7 15 ♝xg4 fxg4 16 ♛e2 h5 17 ♞d1 ♝h6 18 ♞e3 h4 19 g3 ♛g5 20 ♜ac1 hxg3 21 hxg3 ♛h5!∓) 13 ... ♞f6 (I like the look of the zwischenzug 13 ... h6, as then if 14 ♝xe7 Black can continue as in Deak - Hazai, while if 14 ♝d2, then he can play as in the main game, but the white bishop is on a much less active square) 14 f3 h6 15 ♝e3 b6 16 b4 g5 17 c5 ♞g6 18 ♞b5 ♛d8 19 cxd6 cxd6 20 ♜c1 fxe4 21 fxe4 ♞f4 22 ♝d3 ♞g4 23 ♛d2 ♜f7 24 ♜c6 ♝f8 25 ♝xf4 exf4 26 ♞f3 ♞e3 27 ♜fc1 g4 28 ♞fd4 g3∞ Schlosser - Hazai, Budapest 1991. The game has degenerated into a total mess, but the verdict is that 11 ... ♛e8 is the way to deal with 11 ♝g5.

| 11 | ... | ♞e7 *(116)* |
| 12 | ♞g5! | |

12 b4 ♞f6 leads to an amusing situation. It is as if White has played the main line with 9 b4 (i.e. 8 d5 ♞e7 9 b4) and Black has replied with the illegal 9 ... f5! Since Black often expends two tempi to play this move, it is clear that

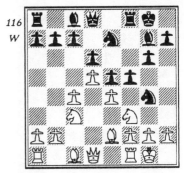

116
W

White must try to exploit it immediately, or be much worse. Therefore 13 ♞g5 is logical, but nevertheless did not get White very far after 13 ... h6 14 ♞e6 ♝xe6 15 dxe6 fxe4 16 b5 ♞f5 17 ♝g4 c6 18 ♝xf5 gxf5 19 ♝a3 ♜e8 20 bxc6 bxc6= in Gonzales - Hazai, Camaguey 1987.

12	...	♞f6
13	exf5	gxf5
14	f4	e4

As a general principle in the King's Indian, Black prefers to keep the tension in such a position. Thus 14 ... ♞g6 comes into consideration, and although White can then pursue the initiative with 15 fxe5 dxe5 16 c5!, this may be the better choice.

After the text, Black's centre is robbed of all its fluidity and White can prepare an undermining operation.

| 15 | ♝e3 | h6 *(117)* |
| 16 | ♞e6 | |

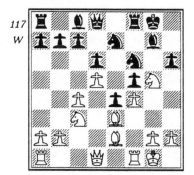

117
W

The simple 16 ♘h3 also keeps the advantage, but this is more dynamic.

16 ...   ♗xe6
17 dxe6   c6

17 ... ♕c8 would be met by 18 ♘d5 ♘fxd5 19 cxd5 ♗xb2 20 ♖b1 ♗g7 21 ♗h5!, when White plans ♗f7+ and ♖b3 with a monstrous attack.

18 ♔h1!

Preparing the undermining g4, which has the additional benefit of opening the g-file against the black king.

18 ...   ♘g6
19 g4   ♕e7
20 ♖g1 *(118)*

118
B

Methodically continuing the build-up.

20 ...   ♘h4?

Now Black loses by force. The only chance was 20 ... ♕xe6 21 gxf5 ♕xf5 22 ♕xd6, although with an open g-file, two white bishops and a weak pawn at e4 to cope with, Black's task is far from enviable.

21 ♗f2   ♘xg4
22 ♗xg4   fxg4
23 ♗xh4   ♕xh4
24 ♕xg4!

The exchange of queens removes any possibilities for counterplay. Hampered by his problems on the g-file, Black now has no chance to deal with the white e- and f-pawns.

24 ...   ♕xg4
25 ♖xg4   ♔h7
26 ♘xe4   ♖ae8
27 ♖e1

Equally decisive was 27 ♖ag1 intending ♖h4. The only trap to avoid was 27 f5? ♗e5 (27 ... ♖xf5? 28 ♘xd6) 28 ♖f1 ♖xe6.

27 ...   ♗xb2
28 ♖b1   d5
29 ♖xb2   dxe4
30 ♖xb7+   ♔h8
31 ♖gg7   ♖xf4
32 ♖h7+   ♔g8
33 ♖bg7+   ♔f8
34 e7+   1-0

Annotations based on Miles's notes from *Informator 49*.

7) Classical 7 ... ♘bd7

Many players like to play the King's Indian, but harbour reservations about the positional simplicity of the main lines with 7 ... ♘c6. In these variations, Black is often obliged to burn his boats early on, and if checkmate isn't forthcoming on the kingside, the result can be a demoralising defeat. Players priding themselves on the subtle, strategic nature of their game often resent reducing the complexity of the struggle to a simple equation of 'give checkmate or lose'.

If you come into this category, then 7 ... ♘bd7, maintaining the tension, is a perfectly reasonable choice. Black reserves the possibility of playing in all sectors of the board, and leaving the centre open means that it is not so easy for White to formulate a plan.

Here we consider the replies 8 ♕c2, 8 ♖e1 (game 14) and the currently highly popular 8 ♗e3 (game 15). 8 d5 transposes to the Petrosian System, which is considered elsewhere.

Game 14
Ftacnik – Nunn
Gjovik 1983

1	♘f3	g6
2	d4	♗g7
3	c4	♘f6
4	♘c3	0-0
5	e4	d6
6	♗e2	♘bd7
7	0-0	e5
8	♕c2	(119)

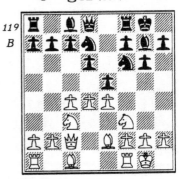

8 ♖e1 c6 (Various others are playable here for Black, e.g. 8 ... ♖e8 9 ♗f1 a5 10 ♖b1 h6 11 b3 ♘g4 12 d5 f5 13 ♗d3 f4 14 a3 h5 15 b4 b6 16 ♘b5

g5 17 ♘d2 ♘gf6 18 ♗b2 g4=
Murugan - Ubilava, Alma-
Ata 1989; 8 ... h6 9 ♕c2 ♘h7
10 dxe5 dxe5 11 ♗e3 ♖e8 12
♖ad1 ♘hf8 {12 ... c6, preventing the advance of the
white c-pawn, is more cir-
cumspect, e.g. 13 c5 ♕e7 14
♖d6 ♘df8 15 h3 ♘e6 16 ♗c4
♔h8 17 ♖ed1 ♖f8 18 b4 ½-½
Serrer - Poldauf, German
Ch. 1991. Typically, Kasparov prefers to create a
mess} 13 c5 ♘e6 14 c6 bxc6
15 ♘a4 g5 16 ♕xc6 ♖b8 17
h3 h5 18 ♕c1 g4 19 hxg4
hxg4 20 ♘h2 g3 21 fxg3
♘d4 22 ♗c4∞ Andersson -
Kasparov, Moscow Izt. 1982;
8 ... exd4 9 ♘xd4 ♘c5 10 f3
c6 11 ♗e3 ♖e8 12 ♕d2 a5 13
♖ad1 ♘fd7 14 ♘b3 ♘xb3 15
axb3 ♖e6 16 ♘a4± Neverov
- Timoshenko, USSR Team
Ch. 1988) 9 ♗f1 (9 ♖b1 a6 10
b4 exd4 11 ♘xd4 ♖e8 12 f3
b5 13 ♗e3 ♘e5 14 cxb5 axb5
15 ♗f2 d5 16 exd5 ♘xd5 and
now, instead of 17 ♘xd5?!∞,
Gligoric - Ivkov, Yugoslavia
1987, 17 ♘xc6! would have
caused problems as 17 ...
♘xc3 18 ♘xd8 ♘xd1 19
♖bxd1 ♗d7 20 ♘b7 ♖xa2? 21
f4 wins) and now (120):

a) 9 ... a6 10 a3 (10 d5 c5
11 a3 ♘b6 12 ♘d2 a5! {Black
demonstrates that it pos-
sible to successfully challenge White on the queen-
side} 13 b3 ♘e8 14 ♖b1 ♘c7
15 b4 axb4 16 axb4 cxb4 17

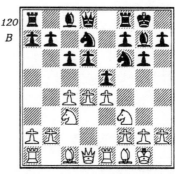

120
B

♖xb4 ♘a6 18 ♖b1 ♘c5 19
♘b3 ♘ba4 20 ♘xa4 ♘xa4 21
♗d2 f5= Sosonko - Rome-
ro, Novi Sad Ol. 1990) 10 ...
exd4 (It makes sense to
open the centre after White
has expended a tempo on
a3. Black can also try to
take the initiative with 10
... b5 11 h3 ♗b7 12 dxe5 dxe5
13 ♗e3 ♕e7 14 ♕c2 ♘h5 15
♖ad1 ♘f4 16 b4 ♘e6 17 ♕b3
♔h8 18 c5 ♖ad8∞ Gomez -
Romero, Pamplona 1991) 11
♘xd4 ♖e8 12 ♘b3 ♕c7 13 h3
♘e5 14 ♗e3 ♗e6 15 c5 ♖ad8
16 cxd6 ♖xd6 17 ♕c2 ♘h5 18
♗e2 ♘d3!∓ Lev - Soltis.
London (Lloyds Bank) 1990.
White can ruin Black's
pawns by capturing on h5,
but he has correctly ass-
essed that his central control and two bishops are
more than sufficient com-
pensation.

b) 9 ... a5 10 dxe5 (10 ♖b1
♖e8 11 d5 ♕c7 12 a3 a4 13 b4
axb3 14 ♖xb3 ♘c5 15 ♖b4
♖f8 16 ♕c2 ♘e8 17 ♘a4
♘xa4 18 ♖xa4 ♖xa4 19 ♕xa4

c5 20 ♘d2 f5= Elsness - Djurhuus, Gjovik 1991) 10 ... dxe5 11 ♘a4 ♕e7 (11 ... ♖e8 12 ♕c2 ♗f8 13 c5 ♕e7 14 ♗e3 ♘g4 15 ♗g5 f6 16 ♗d2 ♘xc5 17 ♘b6 ♖b8 18 ♗xa5 ♘d7 19 ♘xc8 ♖exc8 20 ♖ed1 b5 21 ♖d2± Hölzl - Rantanen, Randers Zt. 1982) 12 ♕c2 ♖e8 13 h3 ♘c5 14 ♘xc5 ♕xc5 15 ♗e3 ♕e7 16 ♖ad1 ♗e6 17 c5 a4 18 ♗c4 ♗xc4 19 ♕xc4 h6 20 ♖d6 b5 21 ♕c2 ♖ec8 22 ♖ed1± Malich - Vogt, Halle 1978.

c) 9 ... exd4 10 ♘xd4 ♘g4 *(121)* and:

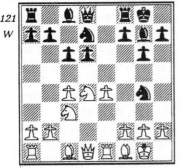

c1) 11 ♕xg4 ♗xd4 12 ♗e3 (12 ♕d1 ♕f6 13 ♗e3 ♗xe3 14 ♖xe3 ♘e5 15 ♕d2 ♗e6 16 b3 ♖ad8 17 ♖g3 ♕h4= Karolyi - Bosboom, Amsterdam II 1988. Black has successfully simplified the position and has no problems) 12 ... ♘c5 13 ♕d1 ♗e5 14 ♕d2 ♖e8 (14 ... ♕h4 15 g3 ♕h5 16 ♗g2 ♗h3 17 ♗h1 ♗g4 18 f4 ♗g7 19 e5 ♖fd8 20 exd6 ♗f8= Pinter - Knaak, Szirak 1985) 15 f3 a5 16 ♖ad1 ♕f6 17 ♗g5

♕h8!= Lalev - Ivanchuk, Lvov 1988. Black's unusual queen manoeuvre has exacerbated his central control.

c2) 11 h3 ♕b6 12 hxg4 (12 ♕xg4!? ♗xd4 13 ♕e2 ♘c5 14 ♗h6 ♖e8 15 ♕d2 ♗e5 16 ♔h1 f5 17 ♖ad1 ♘xe4 18 ♘xe4 fxe4 19 ♖xe4 ♗f5 20 ♖e2± Lerner - Vogt, Berlin 1989) 12 ... ♕xd4 13 ♗e3 ♕e5 14 ♕d2 ♕e7 15 ♖ad1 ♘e5 16 f3 ♗e6 17 b3 ♖fd8 18 ♘e2 a6 19 ♘f4 ♗h6 20 ♘d5 ♗xe3+ 21 ♘xe3 b5 22 ♕f2 bxc4 23 ♗xc4 ♗xc4 24 ♘xc4 ♘xc4 25 bxc4 ♖ab8 26 ♕d4= Petran - Marin, Berlin Open 1988.

8 ... c6 *(122)*

Now 9 ♗e3 will transpose into note 'c' to 9 d5 in the next game. Others are:

a) 8 ... exd4 9 ♘xd4 ♖e8 10 ♖d1 (or 10 ♗e3 ♘c5 11 f3 ♘h5 12 ♕d2 f5 13 exf5 gxf5 14 f4 ♘f6 15 ♗f3 ♘fe4 16 ♗xe4 ♘xe4 17 ♘xe4 ♖xe4 18 ♖ad1 ♕e7 19 ♖f3 ♗d7= Garcia Palermo - Knaak, Camaguey 1987) 10 ... c6 11 ♗g5 a5 12 ♗f1 ♕b6 13 ♘f3 ♘c5 14 ♗e3 ♕b4 15 ♖ab1 ♘g4 16 ♗d4 ♘e5±/∞ Boensch - Marin, Dresden 1988. Black is actively placed but his exposed pieces also act as targets for White.

b) 8 ... h6, intending ... ♘h7 followed by kingside

counterplay with ... f5 or even g5 - g6, is a common plan in this type of position. An example here is Lputian - Yudasin, Podolsk 1990: 9 ♖d1 ♘h7 10 dxe5 dxe5 11 c5 c6 12 b4 ♕e7 13 a4 ♖e8 14 a5 a6 15 ♘a4 ♘hf8 16 ♗c4 ♖b8 17 ♗b2 ♘e6 18 ♕b3 ♘f4 19 g3 ♘h3+ 20 ♔g2 ♘f8 21 ♖d6±.

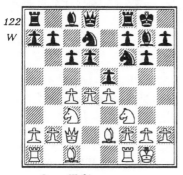

9   ♖d1
Others:

a) 9 ♗g5 is always a double-edged move. White hopes to lure the black kingside pawns forward in the hope of creating weaknesses, but will look pretty silly if these advances give Black a dangerous kingside attack. Play can continue: 9 ... h6 10 ♗h4 g5 11 dxe5 dxe5 12 ♗g3 ♘h5 13 ♘d1 ♘f4 14 ♘e3 ♘f6 15 ♖fe1± Ftacnik - Vogt, Trnava 1983.

b) Closing the centre with 9 d5 *(123)* has been popular recently. It is a logical move - White assumes that with Black having played ... c6, the queenside attack will be speeded up. Some examples:

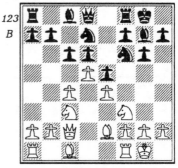

b1) 9 ... ♕c7 10 ♗e3 a6 (10 ... ♘g4 11 ♗d2 f6 {*This is a very slow way to generate counterplay, the immediate 11 ... f5 being preferable. One possibility is then 12 exf5 gxf5 13 ♘h4 ♘c5 14 b4 ♘a6∞*} 12 b4 ♘h6 13 ♖fd1 ♘f7 14 ♖ab1 ♔h8 15 ♘e1 a5 16 a3 axb4 17 axb4 ♖g8 18 ♗e3± van der Sterren - Piket, Dutch Ch. 1989) 11 ♘d2 ♘e8 12 b4 f5 13 f3 c5 14 ♖ab1 b6 15 ♖b2 ♘df6? (Piket indicates the superior 15 ... f4 16 ♗f2 g5 17 ♖fb1 h5⩲. It is striking how often Black's strongest continuation in the King's Indian is the one that involves using a blunt instrument against the white kingside. Often Black seems to opt for some subtle positional regrouping when simply getting on with it would be better) 16 bxc5 bxc5 17 ♖fb1 f4 18 ♗f2 g5 19 ♘a4 g4 20 ♘b6 ♖a7 21 ♘xc8 ♕xc8 22 ♗e1± Piket - Damljanovic, Novi Sad Ol. 1990.

b2) 9 ... c5 10 a3 ♘e8 11 b4 b6 (11 ... h6 12 g3 b6 13 ♖b1 ♘df6 14 bxc5 bxc5 15 ♘h4 ♗h3 16 ♖e1 ♘h7 17 ♗d2 h5 18 ♖b2 ♗f6 19 ♘f3± Lukacs - Werner, Budapest 1991) 12 ♖b1 h6 13 ♗d3 (13 ♗d1 is an odd move. Perhaps White was hoping to use this 'bad' bishop effectively on a4, but this idea never comes to fruition: 13 ... f5 14 ♘d2 ♘df6 15 ♕d3 ♘h5!? 16 ♗xh5 gxh5 17 exf5 ♗xf5 18 ♘de4 ♔h8 19 bxc5 dxc5 20 ♕e2 ♘f6 21 ♖b3 h4 22 h3 ♕d7 23 ♔h2 ♖f7 24 ♘xf6 ♖xf6 25 ♘e4=/∞ Ostenstad - Remlinger, Gausdal 1991) 13 ... ♕e7 14 ♗d2 ♘df6 15 bxc5 dxc5!? 16 g3 (A slight weakening, but if 16 ♖fe1 then 16 ... ♗g4 causes problems) 16 ... ♘d6 17 ♖fe1 ♘fe8 18 a4 ♗g4 19 ♘h4 ♘c7 20 ♘b5 ♘cxb5 21 axb5 a6 22 bxa6 ♖xa6 23 ♖b2 ♖fa8 24 ♖eb1 ♕d8 25 ♗c3± Cebalo-Damljanovic, Yugoslavia 1988.

9 ... exd4

9 ... ♕e7 10 d5 (10 ♖b1 a5 {10 ... exd4 11 ♘xd4 ♘c5 12 f3 ♘h5 13 ♕d2 ♖d8 14 ♗f1 a5 15 ♕f2 ♖e8 16 g4 ♘f6 17 ♗f4 ♘fd7 18 ♖d2 ♘e5 19 ♖bd1 ♕f6 20 ♕g3± Azmaiparashvili - Vogt, Berlin 1989} 11 b3 ♘h5 12 g3 ♖e8 {Open-

ing the centre with 12 ... exd4 would be preferable. Now White changes plan and gets an edge} 13 d5 c5 14 ♘e1 ♘hf6 15 a3 ♘b8 16 b4 axb4 17 axb4 b6 18 bxc5 bxc5 19 ♗d2 ♘a6 20 ♘b5 ♖f8 21 ♘g2 ♘e8 22 ♗d3 f5 {Loosening, but White was planning ♗d3, ♖e1 and f4} 23 exf5 ♗xf5 24 ♖e1 ♗xd3 25 ♕xd3 ♘f6 26 ♘f4!± Lautier - Hort, Novi Sad Ol. 1990) 10 ... c5 (10 ... a5 11 b3 ♘c5? {This merely provides White with a target. 11 ... h6 was advisable} 12 ♗g5 ♖d8 13 ♘d2 h6 14 ♗e3 ♘g4 15 ♗xg4 ♗xg4 16 f3 ♗d7 17 a3 ♗e8 18 b4 ♘d7 19 ♘b3 axb4 20 axb4 ♖xa1 21 ♖xa1± LB Hansen - Piket, Munich 1989) and now Black's main problem is to find a useful role for the queen's knight which, at the moment, is merely getting in the way. Some examples of play (124):

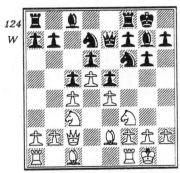

a) 11 ♖b1 ♘h5 12 g3 ♘df6 13 b4 b6 14 bxc5 bxc5 15

♕a4 a6 16 ♗d2 ♖a7 17 ♘h4
♘g4 18 ♖b8 ♗d7 19 ♕b3±
Lputian - Soltis, New York
Open 1990.

b) 11 h3 ♘e8?! 12 g4! (A
strange-looking, but re-
markably effective move.
However, the negative side
of 11 h3 would have been
shown up better by 11 ...
♘h5, as the f4-square has
been weakened) 12 ... ♔h8
13 ♗g5 f6 14 ♗e3 f5?! 15 exf5
gxf5 16 gxf5 ♘b6 17 ♗d3±
Stefansson - Schlueter, Vienna Open 1991.

c) 11 ♗g5 h6 12 ♗h4 g5 13
♗g3 ♘h5 14 ♘d2 ♘f4 15 ♗g4
(15 ♘f1 ♘f6 16 ♘e3 ♘xe4 {*A
familiar King's Indian combination, but there is
always a danger that it will
lead to Black losing con-
trol of the light squares*} 17
♘xe4 f5 18 ♘c3 ♘xe2+ 19
♕xe2 f4 20 ♘f1 fxg3 21
♘xg3 ♗d7 22 ♘ge4± Sma-
gin - Kochiev, Voronezh
1987) 15 ... h5! (Sharply
spotted! Black gets tre-
mendous compensation for
this pawn sacrifice) 16
♗xf4 exf4 17 ♗xh5 ♗d4 (17
... ♘e5!?) 18 ♘b5 ♘e5 19 ♗e2
g4 20 ♘xd4 cxd4 21 f3 f5!
with excellent chances,
Lputian - Pavlovic, Erevan
1988.

d) 11 g3 is a reasonable
waiting move. White often
has to play this anyway, so
it makes sense to see what

Black wants to do before
forming a plan:
d1) 11 ... ♘e8 12 ♘h4 ♘b6?
(Black is obviously unaware
of Tarrasch's dictum that a
knight is always badly
placed on b6) 13 ♗e3 f5?
(Compounding the error by
opening up the position for
White. Black now loses
more or less by force) 14
exf5 gxf5 15 f4! exf4 16
♗xf4 ♗e5 17 ♖f1 ♗xf4 18
♖xf4 ♘g7 19 ♖af1 ♗d7 20
♗d3 ♕g5 21 b3+- Olafsson -
Lautier, Wijk aan Zee 1991.

d2) 11 ... ♔h8 12 ♗g5 a6 13
♘h4 ♕e8 14 ♖e1 ♘g8 15 ♗d2
♕e7 16 ♘g2 f5 17 exf5 gxf5
18 f4 e4 19 g4± Korchnoi -
Romanishin, Brussels 1986.

d3) 11 ... ♘b8?! (This is
one way of dealing with the
awkward queen's knight,
but it loses a lot of time)
12 ♘h4 ♘e8 13 ♗d3 ♘a6 14
a3 ♗d7 15 ♖b1 f6 16 ♖e1 ♖f7
17 ♘d1? (After this, White
loses control. 17 f4! looks
very strong, the tactical
point being 17 ... exf4 18
♗xf4 g5 19 ♘f5±) 17 ... ♕f8
18 ♘e3 ♗h6∞ Sher - Gerber,
Genf Open 1991.

10 ♘xd4 ♕e7 *(125)*
11 ♗g5
a) 11 ♗f1 a5 (11 ... ♘c5 12
f3 a5 13 ♗f4 ♘fd7 14 ♕f2
♘e5 15 ♖d2 ♘e6 16 ♗e3
♘xd4 17 ♗xd4 ♖e8 18 ♖ad1
a4 19 c5± Nikcevic - Na-
randzic, Yugoslav Ch. 1991)

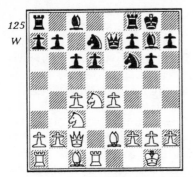

125
W

12 b3 ♘c5 13 f3 ♗d7 14 ♖b1 ♘h5∞ Gouret – Lautier, French Ch. 1989.

b) 11 ♗f4 ♘e8?! (This is very passive) 12 b4 a5 13 b5 ♘c5 14 ♗g3 ♘e6 15 ♘f3 ♘c5 16 bxc6 bxc6 17 ♘d4 ♗d7 18 ♖ab1 f5 19 f3 ♘e6 20 ♘xe6 ♗xe6 21 ♔h1± Garcia Ilun-dain – Nunez, Andorra 1991.

c) 11 f3 ♘h5 12 g4!? ♘hf6 13 ♗g5 a6 14 ♕d2 (White's play is very ambitious. He is trying to completely re-strict Black's counterplay, but is creating weaknesses in his own position) 14 ... ♘e5 15 ♘c2 ♗e6 16 ♘e3 h6 17 ♗h4 g5 18 ♗g3 ♖fd8 19 h4 b5 20 hxg5 hxg5 21 cxb5 axb5 22 a3 ♘fd7 23 ♕xd6 ♕xd6 24 ♖xd6 b4 25 ♘cd1 bxa3 26 ♖xa3 ♖xa3 27 bxa3 ♖a8 28 ♘c2 ♗f8 29 ♖d2 ♗xa3= Flear – Chiburda-nidze, Biel 1991.

11 ... ♘c5

11 ... h6 12 ♗h4 ♘c5 13 f3 ♕c7 14 ♖d2 ♘h5 15 ♗f2 a5 16 ♖ad1 a4 17 ♗f1 ♕a5 18 a3 ♖e8∞ Danieljan – Shcheka-

chev, Sochi 1990.

12 f3 ♖e8

An interesting try, which stops 13 ♕d2 because of 13 ... ♘fxe4 14 ♘xe4 ♘xe4 15 fxe4 ♗xd4+. In some lines, the rook on e8 can take a white bishop arriving on e7. One other idea is to play 12 ... a5, answering 13 ♕d2 with 13 ... ♖d8. In an earlier game at Esbjerg in 1982, Mortensen tried the un-pinning 12 ... ♕c7 against Ftacnik. That game conti-nued 13 b4 ♘e6 14 ♘xe6 ♗xe6 15 ♗f4 ♘e8 16 c5 ♗e5 17 ♗xe5 dxe5 18 a4 a5 19 b5 ♕e7 20 ♘b1 ♘f6 21 ♘a3 and White stood better, as Black will have some trouble completing his de-velopment because of the potentially loose a-pawn.

13 b4

Perhaps White might also try 13 ♔h1 to prepare 14 ♕d2 and play against the backward d-pawn.

13 ... ♘e6
14 ♘xe6 ♗xe6 (126)

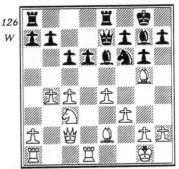

126
W

15 ♕d2

15 c5 dxc5 16 e5 does not work because Black can flick in 16 ... ♗f5 winning material after 17 exf6 ♗xc2 18 fxe7 ♗xd1.

15 ...   ♕c7
16 ♖ab1?

Having opened up the a1-h8 diagonal it is natural that Ftacnik would want to move his rook out of danger. Immediately taking the d-pawn peters out to a drawn ending: 16 ♕xd6 ♕xd6 17 ♖xd6 ♘xe4 18 ♘xe4 ♗xa1 19 ♗f6 ♗xf6 20 ♘xf6+ ♔f8 21 ♘xe8 ♔xe8. Instead Nunn suggests the excellent try 16 ♖ac1! as White's best, where the rook is logically placed to prepare a future ♘d5. Nunn points out the tactical justification of the move – the white b-pawn, as so often early in the game, is poisoned: 16 ... ♕b6+ 17 ♔h1 ♕xb4 18 ♗xf6 ♗xf6 19 ♘d5 ♕b2 20 ♖c2 ♕e5 21 f4 and Black loses a whole rook, as after 21 ... ♕d4 White has 22 ♕c1. Black's alternative is 16 ... ♘d7 when Nunn gives 17 ♘d5 cxd5 18 cxd5 ♕b6+ 19 ♗e3 ♗h6 20 ♗xb6 ♗xd2 21 ♖xd2±. However, we feel that Black will be very hard pressed to draw this position, e.g. 21 ... ♘xb6 22 dxe6 ♖xe6 23 ♗d1 ♖c8 24 ♖xc8 ♘xc8 25 ♗b3 ♖e7 26 ♖c2 ♘b6 27 a4. White has all the chances and they are quite good. Therefore the conclusion is that 21 ♖xd2 is more like ± than ±. So unless Black has an improvement here he may be forced to consider the solid 12 ... a5.

16 ...   ♘d7

Now Black is threatening to pressure c4 with ... ♘e5.

17 ♘d5   cxd5
18 cxd5   ♗g4! *(127)*

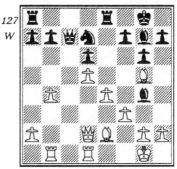

127
W

A spectacular sortie which must have come as a shock to White. The point is to avoid the unpleasant consequences of White's playing dxe6, opening up on the d-pawn.

19 h3

If 19 fxg4 ♖xe4 and Black's knight still jumps in to e5.

19 ...   ♗xf3
20 gxf3   ♘e5
21 ♔g2

Black's plan is now to weaken White's e-pawn with a timely ... f5 and then to exchange the dark-squared bishops. This would simultaneously reduce any chances Ftacnik has of using the two bishops, while increasing Black's positional hold. 21 ♖bc1 would be met by 21 ... ♕b6+ 22 ♗e3 ♕d8, but not 21 ... ♕d7? 22 f4 ♕xh3 23 ♖c3!

| | 21 | ... | f5 |
| | 22 | ♖bc1 | ♕f7 *(128)* |

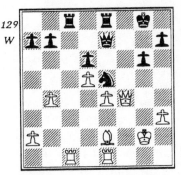

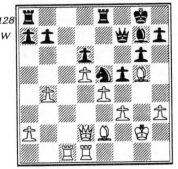

23 ♗e3?

Ftacnik had to try 23 f4 ♘f7 24 exf5 ♕xf5 25 ♗g4, trying to get into e6.

| 23 | ... | fxe4 |
| 24 | fxe4 | ♕e7 |

Eyeing h4.

25	♗g5	♗f6
26	♗f4	♘f7
27	♗d3	♗g5
28	♖e1	♗xf4
29	♕xf4	♘e5
30	♗e2	♖ac8 *(129)*

This is the kind of position which strong players regard as a technical win for Black. White's king is open and his bishop lacks mobility, in a typical bad bishop vs good knight structure. In addition, in any ending, Black can create an outside passed pawn on the kingside, whilst White's central majority is completely immobilised. In fact, it is sheer torture for White, who has no way of putting together a constructive plan before he is squashed.

31 ♖xc8

31 ♗g4 loses after 31 ... ♖xc1 32 ♖xc1 ♘d3 33 ♗e6+ ♕xe6.

31	...	♖xc8
32	♖c1	♖xc1
33	♕xc1	♔g7
34	♕e3	♕h4
35	a4	

In reply to 35 ♗f1, which has the advantage of stopping ... ♕e1, Black could creep forward with 35 ... ♔f6, threatening ... ♕g5+, and after 36 ♕e2 centralise with 36 ... ♕f4 followed by ... h5 - h4 and ... ♕g3+.

| 35 | ... | ♕e1 |
| 36 | b5 | ♔g8 |

Black must be careful. 36 ... b6 allows 37 a5! ♕xa5 38 ♕g5 activating the queen.

| 37 | ♔h2 | b6 |
| 38 | ♔g2 | |

If 38 a5 then simply 38 ... bxa5 and 39 ♕xa7 is not with check.

38	...	h6
39	♔h2	g5
40	♔g2	♘g6
41	e5	♘f4+
42	♔f3	♕xe2+
43	♕xe2	♘xe2
44	exd6	♘d4+
	0-1	

After 45 ♔e4 Black has ... ♘b3 - c5.

Game 15
Gelfand - Ivanchuk
USSR Junior Ch.
Kramatorsk 1989

1	d4	♘f6
2	c4	g6
3	♘c3	♗g7
4	e4	d6
5	♗e2	0-0
6	♘f3	♘bd7
7	0-0	e5
8	♗e3	*(130)*
8	...	c6

Many other moves are possible here:

a) 8 ... a6 9 dxe5 dxe5 10 b4 ♘g4 11 ♗g5 f6 12 ♗d2 ♘h6 13 c5 c6 14 ♕b3+ ♔h8 15 ♖ad1 ♕e7 16 ♗xh6 (Unusual, but it gains White several

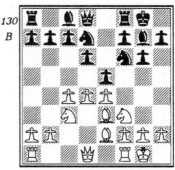

130 B

tempi) 16 ... ♗xh6 17 ♖d6 a5 18 a3 axb4 19 axb4 ♖e8 20 ♖fd1 ♘f8 21 b5± Dzhandzghava - Todorcevic, Genf Open 1991.

b) 8 ... ♖e8 9 d5! (Closing the centre is a very logical way to meet ... ♖e8. If Black now plays a plan with ... f5, then the rook belongs on f8) 9 ... ♘g4 10 ♗g5 f6 11 ♗d2 f5?! (This is much too early. Black should go solid with 11 ... f6 and ... ♘f7) 12 ♘g5! ♘f8 13 exf5 gxf5 14 ♗xg4 fxg4 15 ♘ge4 ♗f5 16 f3 ♕d7 17 ♗h6 ♔h8 18 ♕d2± LB Hansen - McNab, Novi Sad Ol. 1990.

c) 8 ... exd4 9 ♘xd4 c6 10 ♕d2?! (This allows Black to equalise easily. 10 ♕c2 would have defended the e-pawn.) 10 ... ♖e8 11 f3 d5! 12 exd5 (*ECO* offers 12 cxd5 cxd5 13 ♘db5 dxe4 14 ♘d6 ♖f8 15 fxe4 ♘e5 16 ♔h1 ♗e6 17 ♖ad1, Naumkin - Perelstein, Budapest 1989, and now assesses the continuation 17 ... ♕e7?! 18 ♗c5 as ±)

12 ... cxd5 13 ♖ad1 a6 14 cxd5 ♘b6 15 ♘c2 ♗f5 16 ♗d3 ♘fxd5 17 ♘xd5 ♘xd5 18 ♗xf5 ♘xe3 19 ♘xe3 ♕xd2 20 ♖xd2 ♗h6= Gruenberg – Bosboom, Lippstadter 1991.

d) 8 ... h6 9 dxe5 (9 d5 ♘g4 10 ♗d2 a5 {*10 ... f5!?*} 11 ♘e1 ♘gf6 12 ♘d3 ♘e8 13 a3 f5 14 b4 axb4 15 axb4 ♖xa1 16 ♕xa1 fxe4 17 ♘xe4 ♘ef6 18 f3± Sinkovics – Farago, Hungarian League 1991) 9 ... dxe5 (9 ... ♘g4?! is imaginative, but insufficient, e.g. 10 exd6 ♘xe3 11 dxc7 ♕xc7 12 fxe3 and if 12 ... ♘b6 13 ♘d5±) 10 ♘d2 ♘h7 11 b4 (11 c5 ♘g5 12 ♗c4 ♘f6 13 f3 c6 14 ♘b3 ♕e7 15 ♕c2 ♘e6 16 ♖ad1 ♖e8 17 ♖f2 ♘h5 18 ♖fd2 ♔h7 19 ♘e2 ♗f6 20 ♔h1 ♗g5 21 ♕c3± Browne – Yermolinsky, Philadelphia Open 1990) 11 ... f5 12 exf5 gxf5 13 ♘b3 ♘g5 14 ♕d5+ ♔h8 15 ♖ad1 ♕f6 16 f3 ♕g6 17 ♔h1 ♖g8 18 ♕d2 ♗f8= D Gurevich – Nunn, Helsinki 1983.

e) 8 ... a5 (This is suspicious, as it can easily just turn out to be a weakness, especially after ... c6, and will never really hold up White's b4. Nevertheless, it is a popular choice here, e.g. 9 ♕c2 (9 dxe5! is a more direct attempt to treat 8 ... a5 as a queenside weakening, e.g. 9 ... dxe5 10 ♘d2 b6 {*Otherwise c5 was coming*}

11 ♕a4 ♗b7 12 ♖fd1 ♕e7 13 ♘d5 ♘xd5 14 cxd5 f5 15 f3 ♔h8 16 ♖ac1± Shirov – Djurhuus, Gausdal 1991) 9 ... ♘g4 (Black wisely takes the opportunity to clear the centre. In Wells – Durao, Dublin 1991, White was allowed to achieve a favourable set-up after 9 ... c6 10 ♖fd1 ♕e7 11 dxe5 dxe5 12 ♘a4 ♘g4 13 ♗g5 f6 14 ♗d2 ♘c5 15 ♘b6 ♖a6 16 ♘xc8 ♖xc8 17 h3 ♘h6 18 ♗e3 ♖aa8 19 a3±) 10 ♗g5 f6 11 ♗d2 exd4 12 ♘xd4 ♘c5 13 ♘b3 ♘xb3 14 ♕xb3 f5 15 ♗xg4 fxg4 16 ♗e3 ♗e6 17 ♖ad1 ♖f7 18 ♘d5 b6 19 ♕c2 ♕f8 20 b3 ♗h6 21 ♕c3= Gelfand – McNab, Novi Sad Ol. 1990.

f) 8 ... ♘g4 9 ♗g5 f6 *(131)* and now:

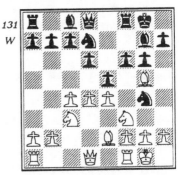

f1) 10 ♗c1 c6 (10 ... ♘h6 11 dxe5 dxe5 12 b3 c6 13 a4?! {*This careless advance severely limits White's subsequent queenside options*} 13 ... a5! 14 ♗a3 ♖e8 15 ♕c1 ♘f7 16 ♖d1 ♗f8 17 c5 ♕e7 18 ♘e1 ♘xc5 19 ♕e3 b6 20 ♘d3

♗e6 21 ♘xc5 bxc5 22 ♘a2 ♖ed8∓ Miralles - Strikovic, Novi Sad Ol. 1990) 11 h3 ♘h6 12 ♗e3 ♕e7 13 ♕c2 ♘f7 14 ♖ad1 ♖e8 (Black is clearly a believer in the theory of over-protection. He has seven (!) pieces covering the e5-square – Nimzowitsch would have been proud!) 15 ♖fe1 ♗h6 16 ♗xh6 ♘xh6 17 b4 ♘f7 18 a3 ♘f8 19 ♗f1 g5!? (There is obviously a danger that White may be able to exploit the weak light squares after this move, but it is worth remembering that weaknesses are only relevant if the opponent is in a position to exploit them, and here White is not sufficiently actively placed to do so) 20 ♖d2 ♘g6 21 d5 c5 22 ♘h2 ♘f4 23 ♗e2 ♔g7 24 ♕d1 b6 25 ♗g4∞/= Miles - Zapata, Manila Izt. 1990.

f2) 10 ♗d2 c6 11 d5 f5 12 ♘g5 ♘df6 13 b4 a5?! 14 bxa5 ♖xa5 15 ♕b3 c5 16 f3 ♘h6 17 ♘e6 ♗xe6 18 dxe6 ♖a7 19 ♘d5± Gelfand - Marin, Tallinn 1989.

f3) 10 ♗h4 ♘h6 11 ♕d2 (11 dxe5 dxe5 12 ♖b1 ♘f7 13 b4 h5 14 h3 a5 15 a3 axb4 16 axb4 c6 17 ♕c2 ♗h6 18 ♖fd1 ♕e7 19 c5 ♖e8 20 ♗c4 ♘f8= Hjartarson - Zapata, Thessaloniki Ol. 1988) 11 ... ♘f7 12 ♖ad1 c6 (12 ... a5 13 dxe5 dxe5 14 ♕c2 b6 15 c5 bxc5 16

♗c4 g5 17 ♗g3 ♔h8 18 ♘a4 ♕e7 19 ♘d2 ♘b6 20 ♗b5 ♘xa4 21 ♕xa4 ♖b8 22 b3∞ Kandiba - Sadriev, Voronez 1991) 13 h3 a5 14 ♕c2 ♕e7 15 c5!? (A typical strategem when Black has moved the queen to e7, as 15 ... exd4 can be met by 16 cxd6. Nevertheless, it is not clear that the text continuation is favourable for White) 15 ... dxc5 16 dxe5 b5! 17 exf6 ♗xf6 18 ♗g3 a4 19 ♖fe1 ♘fe5 20 ♘h2 ♗h4 21 ♗xh4 ♕xh4 22 ♗g4∞ Farago - Conquest, Hastings Masters 1990.

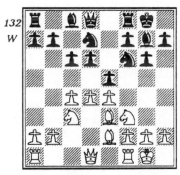

9   d5

a) 9 dxe5 is an insipid continuation, e.g. 9 ... dxe5 10 h3 ♕e7 11 ♕c2 ♘h5 12 ♖fe1 ♘f4 13 ♗f1 ♘e6 14 ♖ad1 f5 15 exf5 gxf5 16 a3 ♔h8 17 b4 e4 18 ♘d4 ♘e5 19 ♘xe6 ♕xe6∓ Fyllingen - Djurhuus, Gausdal 1991.

b) 9 ♘e1 exd4 10 ♗xd4 ♖e8 11 f3 ♗h6 12 ♘c2 ♘h5 13 g3 ♘c5 14 ♗xc5 dxc5 15 ♕xd8 ♖xd8 16 ♖fd1 ♗e6 17 f4∞ Zlatilov - Calvo, Andorra 1991.

c) 9 ♕c2 and now:

c1) 9 ... ♕e7 10 ♖fe1 exd4 11 ♗xd4 ♖e8 12 ♖ad1 ♘c5 13 b4 ♘e6 14 ♗e3 ♘g4 15 ♗c1 a5 16 a3 axb4 17 axb4± Sadler - Calvo, Andorra 1991.

c2) 9 ... h6 10 h3 ♕e7 11 ♖fe1 ♘h5 12 ♗f1 f5 13 dxe5 dxe5 14 exf5 gxf5 15 ♖ad1 ♕f7 16 c5 ♖e8 17 ♖d6 ♘df6 18 ♕a4 ♔h8 19 ♗c4 ♕c7 20 ♕b3± Uhlmann - Chiburdanidze, Graz 1991.

c3) 9 ... exd4 10 ♗xd4 ♖e8 11 ♖ad1 ♕e7 12 ♖fe1 ♘c5 13 ♘d2 a5 (Tal once found a more imaginative plan here, e.g. 13 ... h5!? 14 h3 ♗h6 15 ♗f1 ♗f4 16 ♘f3 ♘fd7∞ Pinter - Tal, Taxco Izt. 1985) 14 f3 ♘e6 15 ♗f2 ♘d7 16 ♘b3 a4 17 ♘d4 ♘dc5 18 ♘xe6 ♗xe6 19 ♕d4± Barle - Neverov, Voskresensk 1990.

c4) 9 ... ♘g4 10 ♗g5 f6 *(133)*

and now White has the familiar choice of bishop retreats:

c41) 11 ♗h4 ♘h6 12 dxe5 dxe5 13 b4 ♕e7 14 c5 ♖e8 15 ♘d2 ♘f8 16 ♖fd1 ♘e6 17 ♘b3 ♘f4 18 ♗f1 ♕e6= Sadler - Soltis, London (Lloyds Bank) 1990.

c42) 11 ♗d2 f5 (11 ... a5 12 h3 ♘h6 13 ♖ad1 ♘f7 14 ♗e3 ♕e7 15 c5!? dxc5 16 d5! ♗h6 {*16 ... cxd5 17 ♘xd5 ♕d6 18 ♗xb5 leaves White well on top*} 17 ♗xh6 ♘xh6 18 dxc6 bxc6 19 ♖d2 ♘f7 20 ♘a4 ♖d8 21 ♖c1± Garcia Palermo - Zapata, Camaguey 1987) 12 exf5 gxf5 (12 ... exd4? is tempting, but very bad after 13 ♗g5! ♗f6? {*13 ... ♕c7 was forced but 14 ♘xd4 ♗xd4 15 ♗xg4 ♘e5 16 ♗e2 ♘f7 17 ♗f4 ♗xf5 18 ♕d2, Uhlmann - Knaak, East German Ch. 1986, is much better for White*} 14 ♗xf6 ♘dxf6 15 ♘xd4 gxf5 16 ♘xf5+- Tisdall - Djurhuus, Gjovik 1991) 13 dxe5 dxe5 14 ♘g5 ♘df6 15 ♔h1 h6 (15 .. e4 16 f3 exf3 17 gxf3 ♘e5 18 ♖g1 ♕c7 19 ♖g2 ♖e8 20 ♖ag1± Adamski - Romero, Debrecen 1987) 16 ♘h3 ♘h5 17 f3 ♘gf6 18 ♗d3 ♘e8 19 ♖ad1 ♕e7 20 ♗e3 ♘c7 21 a3 ♔h8 22 f4 e4 23 ♗e2 ♘f6 24 b4 ♘e6 25 ♖d2 ♖g8 26 ♘f2 h5∞ Uhlmann - Knaak, Dortmund 1991.

9   ...   c5 *(134)*

a) 9 ... ♕e7 10 b4 (10 ♘e1 ♘e8 11 f3 f5 12 g4!?, Condie - Mestel, Bath Zt. 1987, is

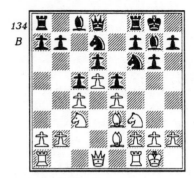

an ambitious attempt to contain the black position) 10 ... ♘g4 11 ♗g5 f6 12 ♗c1 c5 13 ♘b5 cxb4 14 a3!± Groszpeter-Plachetka, Belgrade 1988.

b) 9 ... ♘g4 10 ♗g5 f6 11 dxc6 (11 ♗d2 c5 12 ♕c1 f5 13 ♘g5 ♘df6 14 exf5 gxf5 15 h3 ♘h6 16 ♘e6 ♗xe6 17 ♗xh6 ♗d7 18 ♗xg7 ♔xg7 19 f4 ♕e7 20 ♕d2 ♔h8 21 ♖ae1 ♖g8= Carlhammar - Vogt, Saltsjobaden Open 1988. Black is well advanced on the kingside) 11 ... bxc6 12 ♗c1?! (12 ♕xd6! wins a pawn, e.g. 12 ... fxg5 13 ♕e6+ ♔h8 14 ♕xg4, and now, in Adamski - Jadoul, Thessaloniki Ol. 1988, Black continued 14 ... ♗f6 and White promptly got his queen trapped by 15 ♕e6?? ♘b8!. 14 ... ♗f6 threatens ... h5 and places White in a slightly awkward situation, but 15 ♘e1 should solve the problems. This implies that Black should meet 11 dxc6 with 11 ... ♘c5 when White

is a little better after 12 c7) 12 ... ♕e7 13 b4 ♗b7 14 ♘d2 ♘h6 15 ♘b3 ♖ad8 16 ♗e3 f5 17 f3 ♘f6 18 ♕c1± Bonin - Popovych, New York Open 1990.

10 ♘e1
Two alternatives here:
a) 10 ♘d2 ♘e8 11 a3 f5 12 f3 ♗f6 13 b4 ♗g5 14 ♗f2 b6 15 ♖a2 ♘df6 16 bxc5 bxc5 17 ♕a4 ♘h5 18 ♖b1 ♘f4 19 ♘f1 ♖f7 20 ♖ab2 ♗d7 21 ♕a6 ♗h4 22 ♗g3∞ Mohr - Khalifman, Bled 1991.

b) 10 g3 signals White's intention to renounce immediate queenside play in favour of central and kingside expansion. Barbero - Alber, Frankfurt 1990 was equal after 10 ... ♔h8 11 ♕c2 ♘g8 12 ♘h4 ♘df6 13 f3 ♘h5 14 ♘g2 ♗h3 15 ♖f2 ♕e7 16 ♕d2 ♖ae8 17 ♗f1 f5 18 ♗g5 ♗f6 19 ♗xf6+ ♘gxf6=.

10 ... ♘e8 *(135)*

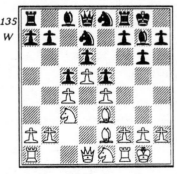

11 g4!?
An ambitious plan from Gelfand. When Black now plays ... f5, both kings will

be weakened. More modest alternatives are:

a) 11 a3 f5!? (The preparatory 11 ... ♕e7 would inhibit White's coming manoeuvre, albeit at the cost of some time) 12 exf5 gxf5 13 f4 exf4 14 ♗xf4 ♘e5 15 ♕d2 ♘f6 16 ♘f3 ♘g6 17 ♗g5?! (Better was 17 ♗h6, when the tactical line 17 ... ♘e4 18 ♘xe4 fxe4 19 ♗xg7 exf3 20 ♗xf8 fxe2 21 ♕xe2 ♘xf8 22 ♖ae1 ♘g6 23 ♕e3 favours White) 17 ... ♕b6 18 ♗d3 ♘g4 19 ♖ae1 ♗d7 20 h3 ♘4e5 21 ♘xe5 dxe5 22 ♗e3 e4∓ Naumkin – Gelfand, Vilnius 1988.

b) 11 ♘d3:

b1) 11 ... ♘b6!? misplaces the black knight, but also forces the white queen to an inferior outpost, e.g. 12 ♕b3 f5 13 f4 exf4 14 ♘xf4 ♕e7 15 a4 ♘c7 16 a5 ♘d7 17 ♘e6 ♘xe6 18 dxe6 ♕xe6 19 ♘d5∞ Olafsson – Lautier, Novi Sad Ol. 1990.

b2) 11 ... ♕e7 12 ♕d2 f5 13 exf5 gxf5 14 f4 e4 15 ♘f2 ♘ef6 16 ♖ab1 ♖e8 17 ♘b5 ♘b8 18 b4 b6 19 bxc5 bxc5 20 ♖b3 ♘a6 21 ♖fb1± Groszpeter – Ginting, Novi Sad Ol. 1990.

b3) 11 ... ♔h8 12 f4 exf4 13 ♗xf4 ♕e7 14 ♕d2 a6 15 ♗g5 f6 16 ♗f4 ♘e5 17 ♘xe5 fxe5 18 ♗g5 ♖xf1+ 19 ♖xf1 ♗f6 20 ♗h6 ♗d7 21 h3 ♗g7= Clara – Gruenberg, Bundesliga 1991.

11 ... ♕h4?

It is tempting to place the queen in on the vulnerable dark squares, but this sortie turns out to be unsustainable. Playable alternatives were 11 ... f5!? or the restrained 11 ... ♔h8.

12 ♔h1!

If White cuts off the queen's retreat with 12 g5 then 12 ... ♘b6 13 ♘g2 ♕h3 generates counterplay.

12 ... ♔h8
13 ♖g1 ♕e7

An admission of the error of his 11th, but White now really was threatening g5, when the black queen would be highly vulnerable.

14 a3 (136)

14 ... ♘df6

If 14 ... f5, then 15 g5! makes it very difficult for Black to get going on the kingside.

15	b4	b6
16	♘d3	♘g8
17	a4	f5
18	g5?!	

For tactical reasons, this

move is now misguided. White should content himself with 18 a5 ♖b8 19 axb6 axb6 20 f3 with a sizeable advantage.

| 18 | ... | ♕f7? |

Black returns the favour. He should make use of his regrouping of the g8-knight with 18 ... h6!, e.g. 19 a5 ♖b8 20 axb6 axb6 and now if White tries to keep the kingside closed with 21 h4?! he runs into 21 ... f4 22 ♗d2 hxg5 23 hxg5 ♗f6!. Therefore, he has to reconcile himself to the anti-positional 21 gxh6 ♗xh6 22 ♗xh6 ♘xh6 23 f3, when he is still sightly better, but the opening of the kingside means that Black is very much in the game.

19	a5	♖b8
20	f3	h6
21	axb6	axb6 *(137)*

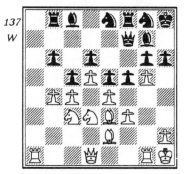

| 22 | h4! | |

Now the tactics on the kingside favour White, and he can keep the g-file firmly locked shut.

22	...	f4
23	♗f2	hxg5
24	hxg5	♗f6
25	♖g2!	

This is the crucial difference - the g-pawn is not under attack, so White has time for this regrouping move.

25	...	♗d8
26	♘b5	♘e7
27	♖h2+	♔g8
28	♗f1	*(138)*

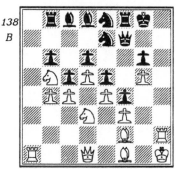

White is now in control of the entire board and has a winning position.

| 28 | ... | ♕g7 |
| 29 | ♘a7 | ♗d7 |

Gelfand now finishes off with a powerful stroke which energises his entire position.

30	bxc5	bxc5
31	♗xc5!	dxc5
32	♘xc5	♘c8
33	♘xd7	♕xd7
34	♗h3	♕c7
35	♗e6+	♔g7
36	♘xc8	♖xc8 *(139)*

White now finds a crisp manoeuvre to end the game.

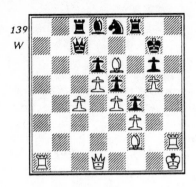

37 ♕g1!   1–0

A beautiful geometric move of the type much favoured by problemists. White threatens both 38 ♖a7 and 38 ♖h7+!. Black's only defence is 37 ... ♖f7. but this goes down after 38 ♕g4 ♘d6 39 ♗xc8 ♘xc8 40 c5! ♕xc5 41 ♕h4 ♔f8 42 ♕h8+ and 43 ♕xe5+.

8) Classical 7 ... ♞a6 and others

The last two years have witnessed a tremendous surge of interest in this move. The idea is to play in similar style to the 7 ... ♞bd7 variations and there are clearly possibilties for transposition after a sequence with ... exd4 and ... ♞c5. The main advantage of placing the knight on a6 as opposed to d7 is that the queen's bishop is not blocked in. This means that Black does not have to rush into capturing on d4 in order to free the queenside, but can wait to see where the white pieces go.

The classical players of the 1920s, such as Tarrasch, would probably pronounce Black's game to be lost after 7 ... ♞a6, but the move has been played at the highest levels and is clearly a viable interpretation of the King's Indian.

Game 16
Karpov - Kasparov
World Championship (7)
New York 1990

1	d4	♞f6
2	c4	g6
3	♞c3	♝g7
4	e4	d6
5	♞f3	0-0
6	♝e2	e5
7	0-0	*(140)*

7 ... ♞a6!?

a) 7 ... ♝g4 is a rarity. Black has an understandable desire to simplify the position, but this exchanges off his good bishop. White should have little difficulty maintaining an edge, e.g. 8 d5 c5 9 ♖b1 ♝xf3 10 ♝xf3 ♞bd7 11 ♝g5 a6 12 ♛e2 ♛c7 13 a3 ♖ac8 14 h4 h5 15 g3 ♚h7 16 ♞d1 ♝h6 17 ♞e3± Krasenkov - Yanvarjov, Moscow 1991.

b) 7 ... ♛e7 8 dxe5 dxe5

9 ♘d5 ♕d8 10 ♗g5 ♘bd7 11 ♘xe5!? (This appears promising, but Black is eventually able to reach equality) 11 ... ♘xe5 12 f4 ♘ed7 13 e5 h6 14 exf6 ♘xf6 15 ♘xf6+ ♗xf6 16 ♕xd8 ♗xd8 17 ♗xh6 ♖e8 18 ♗d3 ♗f6 19 ♖ae1 ♗f5 20 ♗xf5 gxf5 21 b3 ♗d4+ 22 ♔h1 f6 23 g4 fxg4 24 f5= van der Sterren - Damljanovic, Wijk aan Zee II 1990.

c) 7 ... ♕e8 8 dxe5 (8 d5 ♘h5 9 g3 f5 10 exf5 ♗xf5 11 ♘g5 ♘f6 12 ♗d3 ♗d7?! {12 ... ♘a6± is better, as the text wastes time} 13 ♕e2 ♘a6 14 ♗e3 ♘g4 15 ♘ge4± Flear - Kupreichik, Torcy 1989) 8 ... dxe5 9 ♗e3 b6 (9 ... ♘a6 10 c5 {10 ♘d2 c6 11 a3 h5 12 f3 h4 13 c5 ♘h5 14 ♘c4 ♘f4∞ D Gurevich - Mark Tseitlin, Moscow 1989} 10 ... b6 11 ♘d2 ♘xc5 12 ♗xc5 bxc5 13 ♘a4 ♕e7 14 ♕c2 ♘d7 15 ♘b3 ♕g5 16 ♘axc5 ♘f6 17 ♖ad1± {White holds all the trumps} 18 ♕d2 ♕h4 19 g3 ♕h3 20 f3 ♗e6 21 ♘a5 ♘h7 22 ♖fe1 ♗h6 23 ♕c3 1-0 Shirov - Yunieyv, Daugavpils 1989. The queen will be trapped with ♗f1) 10 ♘d5 ♘a6 11 ♘d2 ♘d7 (Keeping the tension. 11 ... c6 12 ♘xf6+ ♗xf6 13 c5!± was the alternative) 12 ♕a4 ♗b7 13 ♕a3 f5!? (Loosening, but it gains Black counterplay) 14 c5 ♗xd5 15 ♕xa6 f4 16 exd5 fxe3 17 fxe3 ♘xc5 18 ♕c4 ♗h6 19 ♕c3 a5 20 ♗c4 ♔h8 21 ♖xf8+ ♗xf8= Dreev - Gelfand, Arnhem 1988/89.

d) 7 ... c6 8 d5 (8 ♕c2!? looks risky as it weakens d4. However, in Suba - Watson, London (Watson, Farley & Williams) 1989, it encouraged Black to get carried away: 8 ... exd4 9 ♘xd4 ♖e8 10 ♗g5 ♕a5 11 ♗h4 ♘xe4? {Opening the position for the better developed player} 12 ♘xe4 ♕e5 13 ♗f3 ♕xd4 14 ♖ad1 ♕xb2 15 ♕xb2 ♗xb2 16 ♘xd6 ♖f8 17 ♗e7 ♗e6 18 ♗xf8 ♔xf8 19 ♘xb7 ♗xc4 20 ♖d8+ ♔e7 21 ♖e1+ ♔f6 22 ♘c5 1-0) 8 ... ♘a6 9 ♖b1 ♘c5 10 ♗g5 a5 11 ♘d2 h6 12 ♗e3 ♕e7 13 a3 cxd5 14 cxd5 ♗d7 15 ♗xc5 dxc5 16 a4 ♘e8 17 ♗b5 ♘d6 18 ♗xd7 ♕xd7 19 ♕e2 ♖a6 20 ♘c4± Ostenstad - Manninen, Gausdal 1991.

e) 7 ... exd4 8 ♘xd4 ♖e8 9 f3 (141) has been much tested recently. Black now has two main ideas - either to break in the centre with ... d5, or to play on the dark squares. Practice has seen:

e1) 9 ... ♘h5 and now:

e11) 10 g4!? ♘f6 (10 ... c5!? 11 ♘c2 ♗e5!? 12 ♕e1 {If 12 gxh5 Black has at least a draw with 12 ... ♗xh2+} 12 ... ♘f4 13 ♘d5 g5 14 ♘xf4 gxf4 15 ♔h1 ♔h8 16 ♖g1 ♖g8 17 ♗d2 ♕f6 18 ♗c3 ♘c6 19 ♗xe5 dxe5 20 b4∞/= Gia-

141
B

comazzi - Chevallier, Paris 1991) 11 ♗e3 ♘c6 (11 ... h5?! 12 g5 ♘h7 13 f4 a6 14 ♗f3 ♗h3 15 ♖f2± Legky - Martinovic, Fourmies 1991. White has a powerful kingside grip) 12 ♕d2 ♘d7 13 ♘c2 ♘de5 14 ♘d5 f6 15 ♖ad1 ♘f7 16 ♔h1 ♘ce5 17 ♖g1 ♘g5 18 ♘e1 ♘ef7 19 ♕c1 b6± A Maric - Chiburdanidze, Novi Sad Women's Ol. 1990.

e12) 10 f4 c5 11 ♘c2 ♘f6 12 ♗f3 ♘c6 13 ♖e1 a6 14 ♗e3 (Smirin recommends instead 14 ♖b1!, planning b3 and ♗b2) 14 ... ♗e6 15 ♘d5 ♘a5! and the attack on c4 is awkward to meet, Pira - Smirin, Paris 1991.

e2) 9 ... c6 10 ♔h1 (10 ♘c2 d5!? {*The text is an ambitious gambit. More solid is 10 ... ♘a6 11 ♔h1 ♘c7 12 ♗f4 d5 13 exd5 cxd5 14 c5 ♘e6 15 ♗d6∞ Dzevlan - Cvitan, Yugoslav Ch. 1991*} 11 cxd5 cxd5 12 exd5 ♗f5 13 ♘e3 ♗d7 14 ♔h1 ♘a6 15 ♗d2 {*Black obtains reasonable counterplay after 15 ♗xa6* bxa6 16 ♕d3 ♘h5 17 g3 ♖b8 18 ♖b1 ♖b4 19 ♕d2 ♖d4 20 ♕c2 ♕c7 21 ♖g1 f5∞* Dzevlan - Mukic, Yugoslav Ch. 1991*} 15 ... ♕b6 16 ♘c4 ♕c5 17 ♗g5 b5 18 ♗xf6 ♗xf6 19 ♘e4 ♕d4 20 ♘cd6 ♖eb8 21 a4± Ribli - Gheorghiu, Baden Baden 1981) 10 ... ♘bd7 (10 ... ♘a6 11 ♘c2 ♘c7 12 ♗e3 d5 13 exd5 cxd5 14 c5 ♘h5 15 ♕d2 d4! 16 ♗xd4 ♗f5 17 ♘e4 ♘e6 18 ♖ad1 ♘xd4 19 ♘xd4 ♕h4 20 ♕e1∞ LB Hansen - Epishin, Warsaw 1990; 10 ... d5?! 11 cxd5 cxd5 12 ♗g5 dxe4 13 fxe4 h6 {*Not even Boris Spassky's ingenuity could cope with the white initiative here, e.g. 13 ... ♘bd7 14 ♘db5 ♖e5 15 ♗f4 ♘xe4 16 ♗xe5 ♗xe5 17 ♘xe4 ♕h4 18 h3± Tal - Spassky, Montreal 1979*} 14 ♗h4 g5 15 ♗g3 ♘c6 16 ♘db5 ♘xe4 17 ♘xe4 ♖xe4 18 ♕xd8+ ♘xd8 19 ♗f3 ♖a4 20 ♘c7 ♖b8 21 ♖ad1 ♗g4 22 ♗xg4 ♖xg4 23 ♘d5+- Plachetka - Ac, Capelle la Grande 1991) 11 ♗g5 (11 ♘c2 ♘b6 12 ♗g5 h6 13 ♗h4 g5 14 ♗g3 d5 15 cxd5 cxd5 16 ♘b5 ♘h5 17 ♗c7 ♕d7 18 ♘cd4 ♘c4∓ Vuruna - Reyes, Vrnjacka Banja 1989; 11 ♗f4?! ♘h5! 12 ♗e3 {12 ♗xd6 ♕f6 13 ♘c2 ♘f4∓} 12 ... f5 13 ♕d2 f4 14 ♗f2 ♗e5 15 ♖fe1 ♘f8 16 ♖ad1 ♕f6 17 ♘b3 ♗e6 18 c5 ♘g3+ 19 ♔g1 ♘xe2+ 20 ♕xe2 ♗xb3 21 axb3 dxc5= Lautier - Piket, Adelaide 1988) and now *(142)*:

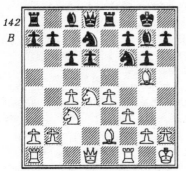

e21) 11 ... h6 12 ♗f4 ♘h5? (Black gets very little for this pawn sacrifice) 13 ♗xd6 ♕f6 14 ♘b3 ♘f4 15 c5 b6 16 ♖e1 ♘e5 17 ♗f1 bxc5 18 ♘xc5 ♖d8 19 ♗xe5 ♕e7 20 ♕xd8+ ♕xd8 21 ♗xf4+- Ostenstad - Remlinger, Gausdal 1991.

e22) 11 ... a5 12 ♕d2 a4 13 ♖fd1 ♕a5 14 ♖ab1 ♘h5 15 ♗e3 ♘e5 16 b4 axb3 17 axb3 f5 18 ♗f1 fxe4 19 b4 ♕c7 20 ♘xe4∞ Belov - Kuzmin, Leningrad 1991.

e23) 11 ... ♕b6 12 ♘b3 a5 13 ♕d2 (13 ♘a4 ♕b4 14 ♘d4 {*Better is 14 ♘d2 which also sets a nasty trap, viz. 14 ... b5? 15 a3! ♕xa4 16 b3+-*} 14 ... ♘c5 15 ♘xc5 dxc5 16 ♘b3 a4 17 ♘c1 ♕xb2 18 ♘d3 ♕d4 19 e5 ♘d7∓ Blees - Brendel, Krumbacher Open 1991) 13 ... a4 14 ♗e3 ♕d8?! (Black must be looking for ideas to stay active in such positions and here there is one: 14 ... ♘c5!

when 15 ♕xd6 runs into 15 ... ♘cxe4! 16 ♕d3 ♘g3+!∓. The text sacrifices precious time) 15 ♘d4 ♘b6 16 ♖ad1 d5 17 exd5 cxd5 18 ♘db5 ♗e6 19 ♗f4± Ftacnik - Paunovic, Belgrade Open 1987.

e24) 11 ... ♕a5 12 ♗e3 (This looks odd, but the black queen is misplaced on a5) 12 ... ♘e5 13 ♕d2 a6 (13 ... ♕c7 led to a fine mess in van der Sterren - Piket, Wijk aan Zee 1988, i.e. 14 ♖ad1 a6 15 ♗h6 b5 16 ♗xg7 ♔xg7 17 f4 ♘ed7 18 cxb5 axb5 19 ♗xb5!? cxb5 20 ♘dxb5 ♕c6 21 ♘xd6 ♖xe4! 22 ♘cxe4 ♘xe4 23 ♘xe4 ♕xe4 24 ♖fe1 ♕f5 and although White is ahead on material, Black's minor pieces generated tremendous activity and he went on to win) 14 ♖ad1 (Better is 14 ♘b3 ♕c7 15 ♖ac1 ♗e6 16 ♘d5 ♗xd5 17 cxd5 c5± *ECO*) 14 ... ♗e6?! (Black wants to get active with ... b5, but this is the wrong way. Correct is 14 ... ♕c7 15 ♘b3 ♗e6 16 c5 d5=) 15 ♘xe6 ♖xe6 16 a3 b5 17 c5 dxc5 18 ♗xc5± Lautier - Schlosser, Adelaide 1988.

7 ... ♘a6 was Kasparov's surprise weapon for his 1990 world title match, though there had been the occasional obscure reference beforehand.

8   ♗e3 *(143)*

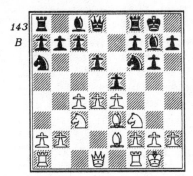

This position often arises via the move order 7 ♗e3 ♘a6 8 0-0. The move ... ♘a6 is currently all the rage in the King's Indian and so there is a wealth of recent material here:

a) 8 ♖b1 exd4 9 ♘xd4 ♖e8 10 f3 c6 11 b4 ♘xb4 (More incisive than 11 ... ♘h5 12 ♗e3 ♘c7 13 ♕d2 f5 14 exf5 gxf5 15 ♗d3 ♕f6 16 ♘de2 f4 17 ♗d4 ♕h6 18 ♗xg7 ♕xg7 19 ♘e4± Guseinov - Glek, USSR Team Ch. 1991) 12 ♖xb4 c5 13 ♖b3 cxd4 14 ♘b5 ♗d7 15 ♗b2 ♗xb5 16 ♖xb5 ♘d7 17 ♗xd4 ♘c5 18 ♖b2 ♗e5∓ Simonenko - Sokolin, USSR Team Ch. 1991.

b) 8 ♖e1 and now:

b1) 8 ... exd4 9 ♘xd4 ♖e8 10 f3 ♘h5 11 g4? ♗e5! (This is a very important tactic, the point of which is that 12 gxh5? loses to 12 ... ♕h4 13 f4 ♗xd4+, when the rook on e1 hangs) 12 ♗f1 ♕h4 13 ♖e2 ♘f4 14 ♖f2 ♘c5 15 ♗xf4 ♗xf4 16 ♘d5 ♗h6 17 ♖g2 ♕d8∞ Blees - Bosboom,

Dutch Ch. 1990.

b2) 8 ... ♕e8 9 ♗f1 (9 dxe5 dxe5 10 b3 ♘d7 11 ♗a3 ♘dc5 12 ♕c2 ♗g4 13 ♖ad1 ♕c8 14 ♘g5 ♗xe2 15 ♕xe2 h6 16 ♘f3 ♖e8 17 g3 c6 18 ♕e3± LB Hansen - Douven, Lugano Open 1989) 9 ... ♗g4 10 d5 (10 ♗e3 ♗xf3 11 ♕xf3 ♘g4!? 12 d5 ♘xe3 13 ♕xe3∞ Neverov - Asanov, USSR Team Ch. 1991. Superficially, this position appears attractive for Black, but the knight on a6 is badly offside) 10 ... ♘b4 11 ♕b3 a5 12 ♘d2 ♘d7 13 ♘a4 ♘a6 14 ♕c2 ♘f6 15 ♘b1 ♗d7 16 ♘bc3 ♘h5 17 ♗d2 f5= Eingorn - Asanov, Beijing Open 1991.

b3) 8 ... c6 *(144)*. Black creates the possibility of the central break with ... exd4 and ... d5, and reaches what is currently a highly fashionable position. Practice has seen:

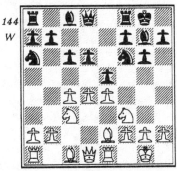

b31) 9 h3 ♖e8 10 d5 ♘h5 11 ♗g5 ♕d7 12 ♕d2 c5 13 ♘h2± C Hansen - I Sokolov, Wijk aan Zee 1991.

b32) 9 ♖b1 exd4 (9 ... ♕e7 10 ♗f1 ♗g4 11 d5 c5 12 a3 h6 13 h3 ♗d7 14 g3 ♔h7 15 ♘h4 ♘g8 16 ♔h2 b6 17 ♗d2 ♖ab8 18 b4± Pinter - Dufrenoy, French League 1991; 9 ... ♘g4 is an interesting attempt by Black to free his position with exchanges, but after 10 h3 exd4 11 ♘xd4 ♕f6 12 hxg4 ♕xd4 13 ♗f4 ♕xd1 14 ♖exd1 ♗e5 15 ♗h6 ♖e8 16 ♘a4 c5 17 ♗e3 the exchanges had favoured White in Huseinov - Nikitin, USSR Team Ch. 1991) 10 ♘xd4 ♖e8 11 ♗f3 (11 f3 {*Rather passive*} 11 ... ♘c7 12 ♗f1 d5 13 cxd5 ♘fxd5!? 14 ♘ce2 ♘b6 15 ♘b3 ♕xd1 16 ♖xd1 ♘b5 17 ♘f4 a6= Pinter - Szekely, Hungarian League 1991) 11 ... h6!? (This plan looks good. Black is intending to play on the kingside and central dark squares in classical King's Indian fashion. White's response is slightly feeble and gives Black what he wants. More testing is 12 ♗f3) 12 h3?! ♘h7! 13 ♘c2 ♕h4!? 14 ♕xd6 ♗e5 15 ♕d1 ♘c5 16 ♗e3 ♖d8 17 ♕e2 ♘d3 18 ♖ed1 ♘xb2 19 ♖xd8+ ♕xd8 20 ♖xb2 ♗xc3= Piket - Khalifman, Wijk aan Zee 1991. Another way for Black to excecute his plan was 13 ... ♘g5.

b33) 9 ♗f1 ♗g4 (9 ... exd4 10 ♘xd4 ♘g4 11 h3 ♕b6

{*With the black knight on d7 instead of a6, this is a well-tested position*} 12 hxg4 ♕xd4 13 ♕e2 ♕e5 14 ♗e3 ♘c5 15 f3 ♕e7 16 ♕d2 ♗e5 17 ♗g5 ♕c7 18 b4 ♘e6 19 ♗e3 f5 20 gxf5 gxf5 21 f4 ♗f6∞ W Schmidt - P Cramling, Novi Sad Ol. 1990) 10 d5 (10 ♗e3 ♘d7 11 d5 c5 12 h3 ♗xf3 13 ♕xf3 f5 14 a3 ♘c7 15 ♕d1 ♘e8 16 exf5 gxf5 17 g4? {*This crude attempt to gain control of the e4-square might have worked against a weak opponent, but here Black immediately exploits the dark side of this advance - the weakening of the kingside*} 17 ... e4! 18 gxf5 ♗xc3 19 bxc3 ♘e5 20 ♗g2 ♕h4 21 ♗d2 ♖xf5 22 ♖xe4 ♕xf2+ 23 ♔h1 ♘f6 0-1 Karolyi - Timoshenko, London {Lloyds Bank} 1991) 10 ... ♘b4 (Using a tactic {*11 a3? ♗xf3*} to gain space on the queenside. 10 ... c5 is a solid alternative, after which White could make no headway in Shirov - Epishin, Tbilisi 1989, i.e. 11 ♗g5 ♕d7 12 ♗e2 ♗xf3 13 ♗xf3 ♔h8 14 a3 ♘g8 15 ♗g4 f5 16 exf5 gxf5 17 ♗h3 ♕f7 18 f4 ♘e7 19 fxe5 ♗xe5 20 ♕d2 ♖ae8 21 ♖f1 ♕g6 22 ♖f3 ♗g7 23 ♖af1 ♘c7 24 ♗h4 ♗h6 25 ♕c2 f4 26 ♕b3 ½-½) 11 ♗e2 a5 12 ♗g5 (12 h3 ♗d7 13 dxc6 ♗xc6 14 ♗f1 ♘a6 15 ♗g5 h6 16 ♗h4 g5 17 ♗g3

♘h5 18 ♘d5 ♘c5 19 ♘d2 ♘xg3 20 fxg3 ♗xd5 21 cxd5 f5= Aseev - Glek, Krumbacher Open 1991; 12 ♗e3 c5 13 g3 ♘e8 14 a3 ♘a6 15 ♕d2 ♖b8 16 ♘h4 {*Black has placed a large clamp on the queenside so White switches his attention to the opposite sector*} 16 ... ♗d7 17 ♘g2 ♘ac7 18 a4 f5 19 f4 b6 20 fxe5 dxe5 21 exf5 gxf5 22 ♗g5 ♗f6∞ Bareev - Glek, Moscow 1989) 12 ... h6 13 ♗e3 ♘h5 14 a3 ♘a6 15 g3 ♘f6 16 ♕d2 h5 17 ♖ad1 cxd5 18 cxd5 ♗d7 19 ♗h6 ♘c5 20 ♗xg7 ♔xg7 21 ♘g5 ♕e7 22 ♗c4 h4∓ Eingorn - Christiansen, Reykjavik 1990.

8 ... ♘g4

Alternatives are:

a) 8 ... ♕e8 with:

a1) 9 dxe5 dxe5 10 ♘d2 ♘d7 (10 ... b6 11 a3 ♘c5 12 b4 ♘e6 13 ♘b3 ♗b7 14 ♕c2 ♖d8 15 ♖ad1 ♘d4!= Browne - Tal, San Francisco 1991) 11 a3 (11 ♘b5 ♕e7 12 a3 b6 13 b4 c6 14 ♘c3 ♘c7 15 ♘b3 ♗b7 16 ♕c2 ♖ac8 17 ♖fd1 ♘e6 18 ♗g4 ♖c7 19 ♗xe6 ♕xe6 20 c5± Winants - Bosboom, Wijk aan Zee 1991) 11 ... f5 12 f3 f4 13 ♗f2 ♘ac5 14 b4 ♘e6 15 c5 g5 (Black adopts a more direct strategy than in the previous two examples) 16 ♖a2 ♖f6 17 ♗c4 ♘df8 18 ♘d5 ♖f7 19 b5 ♔h8 20 ♘b3 c6 21 ♘c3 ♖f6 22 bxc6 bxc6 23 ♖d2∞

Piket - Kozul, Wijk aan Zee 1991.

a2) 9 h3 *(145)* and now:

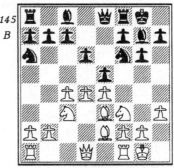

a21) 9 ... exd4 10 ♗xd4 ♘xe4? (One of the points of 9 h3 is that this tactic fails miserably, as Anand discovers to his cost) 11 ♗xg7 ♔xg7 12 ♕d4+ ♘f6 13 ♘d5 ♕d8 14 ♘g5 ♖e8 15 ♘xh7 ♖e4 16 ♕c3 ♖xe2 17 ♘hxf6 ♕h8 18 ♘e4+ 1-0 Miles - Anand, Rome Open 1990. Anand used to produce games like this on a fairly regular basis. Now that he has elimated such disasters his rating has advanced from being around 2530 to nearly 2700!

a22) 9 ... ♘d7 10 ♖e1 f5 11 exf5 gxf5 12 dxe5 dxe5 13 c5 c6 14 ♗xa6 bxa6 15 ♗f4 ♕e7 16 ♕b3+ ♔h8 17 ♕c4 ♖g8 18 ♖e2 ♗f6 19 ♗h2 e4= Fishbein - Tseitlin, Beer-Sheva 1991.

a23) 9 ... c6 10 ♖e1 h6 11 ♖b1 ♕e7 12 c5! ♘d7 13 cxd6 ♕xd6 14 ♗xa6 (It is unusual for this capture to benefit

White as the open b-file and two bishops compensate Black for the smashed pawns. Here, however, White has seen a way to make it work) 14 ... bxa6 15 dxe5 ♕xd1 16 ♖exd1 ♖e8 17 ♖bc1 g5 18 ♖d6 ♘xe5 19 ♘xe5 ♗xe5 20 ♖xc6± Bareev - Mohr, Bled 1991.

b) 8 ... c6 9 dxe5 (9 a3 looks suspiciously slow and in Wells - Timoshenko, Hastings Challengers 1990, Black swiftly obtained a comfortable position: 9 ... exd4 10 ♗xd4 ♖e8 11 ♕c2 ♘c5 12 e5 ♘g4 13 exd6 ♗xd4 14 ♘xd4 ♕xd6 15 ♘f3 ♗f5 16 ♖ad1 ♕f6 17 ♕d2 ♖ad8=/∓) 9 ... dxe5 10 ♕xd8 ♖xd8 11 ♖fd1 ♖e8 12 h3 ♗f8 13 ♘d2 b6 14 a3 ♘c5 15 b4 ♘e6 16 ♘b3 ♗a6 17 f3 ♘h5 18 ♗f2 ♖ed8= Karpov - Kasparov, World Ch. (5) 1990.

9   ♗g5 *(146)*

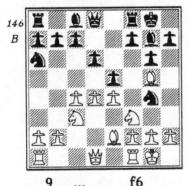

146
B

9   ...   f6

9 ... ♕e8 leaves Black in danger of drifting into a passive position, e.g. 10

dxe5 dxe5 11 h3 (This is the most frequently used, but 11 ♘d2 may create more serious problems for Black, e.g. 11 ♘d2 h6 {11 ... ♘f6 12 ♘d5 ♕d8 13 f4 ♘xd5!? 14 ♗xd8 ♘e3 15 ♕c1 ♘xf1∞/± *Zilberman - Har-Zvi, Tel-Aviv 1991*} 12 ♗h4 ♘f6 13 ♘d5 g5 {*This is unpleasantly weakening, but the alternative 13 ... ♕d8 14 f4 exf4 15 e5 ♘xd5 16 ♗xd8 ♘e3 17 ♕c1 ♘xf1 18 ♗f6 Wells - Brunner, Graz 1991, leaves Black struggling*} 14 ♗g3 c6 15 ♘xf6+ ♗xf6 16 ♗g4 ♗e6 17 ♕f3 ♔g7 18 ♖fd1 ♖d8 19 ♘f1 ♗xg4 20 ♕xg4± *LB Hansen - Schandorff, Kerteminde 1991*) 11 ... h6 12 ♗d2 ♘f6 13 ♗e3 and now:

a) 13 ... ♘d7 14 a3 ♘ac5 (14 ... c6 15 b4 f5 16 c5 f4 17 ♗c1 g5 18 ♘d2 ♘c7 19 ♘c4 ♘f6 20 ♗b2± van Wely - Piket, Amsterdam 1990) 15 b4 ♘e6 16 c5 c6 17 ♗c4 ♕e7 18 ♕d2 ♔h7 19 ♖fd1± Zsu Polgar - Kindermann, Munich 1991.

b) 13 ... ♘h5 14 c5 ♘f4 15 ♗xa6 bxa6 16 ♘d5 ♗xd5 17 ♕xd5 ♖b8 (17 ... ♗e6 18 ♕d2 ♖d8 19 ♕c3 ♕c6 20 ♖fe1 f6 21 ♘d2 ♖f7 22 ♘b3 ♕xe4 23 ♗xh6 ♕c4 24 ♕xc4 ♗xc4 25 ♗xg7 ♔xg7= Miles - Timoshenko, Moscow GMA 1989) 18 b3 (18 ♕d2?! is much weaker, e.g. 18 ... ♗b7 19 ♕c4 ♕b5 20 ♕xb5 axb5 21

♘d2 f5 22 c6 ♗xc6 23 ♖fc1
♖f6 24 ♗xa7 ♖d8 25 ♖c2
♖fd6∓ Timoshenko - Gall-
agher, Hastings Challen-
gers 1990) 18 ... ♔h7 19 ♕c3
♕b5 20 b3 ♗b7 21 ♘xe5
♗xe4 (21 ... ♕e8 22 ♗d4 ♖d8
23 f4 ♗xe4=) 22 ♗d4 ♖bd8
23 ♖fe1 f5 24 ♖ad1 ♖fe8 25
a4 ♕b8 26 c6 ♖xd4 27 ♖xd4
♗xe5 28 ♖d7+ ♔h8 29 ♕c4
♖f8 30 ♕c5 1-0 Novikov -
Glek, Odessa 1989.

10 ♗c1 *(147)*

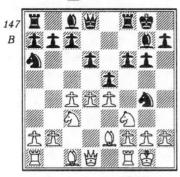

147
B

10 ... ♔h8

Kasparov is planning ac-
tive play, but the position
does not really justify it.
The following are prefer-
able, when White's advan-
tage should be kept to a
minimum:

a) 10 ... ♘h6 11 ♖b1 (11 a3
♕e8 12 b4 c6 13 h3 ♘f7 14 d5
c5 15 ♖b1 f5 16 ♘e1± Sokolin
- Asanov, USSR Team Ch.
1991) 11 ... ♘f7 12 dxe5 dxe5
13 b4 c6 14 b5 ♘c7 15 ♗a3
♖e8 16 bxc6 bxc6 17 ♕a4
♗d7 18 ♖fd1± Benjamin -
Kindermann, Novi Sad Ol.

1990.

b) 10 ... c6 11 h3 ♘h6 12
♗e3 ♘f7 13 dxe5 dxe5 14 c5
♘c7 (14 ... ♗e6 15 ♕a4 ♕c8
16 ♖ad1 ♖d8 17 ♖xd8+ ♘xd8
18 ♖d1 ♘f7 19 ♘d2± Boensch
- Fecht, Bundesliga 1991) 15
♗c4 ♗e6 16 ♕e2 ♕e7 17 b4
♗h6 18 ♗xh6 ♘xh6 19 ♘d2
♘f7= Khalifman - P Cram-
ling, Hamburg 1991.

11 h3 ♘h6
12 dxe5 fxe5? *(148)*

148
W

Black should prefer 12 ...
dxe5 in this position, but
Kasparov was possibly de-
terred by the memory of
game 5 where, although he
was in little danger, the
position was without chances for him. However, with
Black against Karpov it is
almost impossible to avoid
this kind of situation and
the desire to tear Karpov
apart with bare hands as it
were, is quite unrealistic.
After the text recapture,
Black has no real prospects
of attack along the f-file
while his central pawn

structure becomes curiously inflexible.

13 ♗e3 ♘f7
14 ♕d2 ♘c5
15 ♘g5

A fine move which removes one of Black's useful defensive pieces.

15 ... ♘xg5
16 ♗xg5 ♗f6
17 ♗e3 ♘e6
18 ♗g4

A move in the same vein as his 15th. Karpov expertly perceives that his bishop is worth less than the black knight which has future perspectives on both d4 and f4. If now 18 ... ♘d4 19 ♗xc8, and whichever way Black chooses to recapture White will win a pawn with 20 ♗xd4 exd4 21 ♘b5.

18 ... h5

The first sign of impatience. Perhaps 18 ... ♗g5 is best, playing to eliminate White's dangerous queen's bishop.

19 ♗xe6 ♗xe6
20 ♘d5 ♗h4 *(149)*

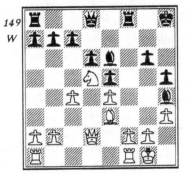

21 ♖ac1

An alarming idea here is 21 ♘xa7 ♖xa7 22 ♕h6+ ♔g8 23 ♕xg6+, but this fails to 21 ... ♗xd5 when White can do no more than force a draw. It is interesting, though, that Kasparov immediately takes measures to eliminate such possibilities in the future.

21 ... ♔h7
22 ♖c3 ♖f7
23 b3 c6

We do not like this move at all since it gratuitously weakens Black's pawn formation in the centre. Black should simply tolerate the presence of the knight on d5 and seek to develop his remaining pieces.

24 ♘b4 ♖d7

This also looks suspect since Black weakens his presence on the f-file. Surely 24 ... ♗e7 is superior.

25 ♖cc1

A typically Karpovian move. He has no memory of previous positions, his earlier moves are like footprints in the sand which vanish, and now he feels the rook is better placed on c1 in the current position. I can think of no other player who, having played ♖c1 - c3 four moves earlier, would patiently put the rook back on the square it had just come from.

25	...	♗f6
26	f4	exf4
27	♗xf4	*(150)*

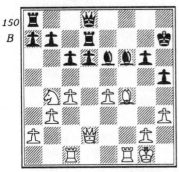

| 27 | ... | ♕a5?? |

This move is a blunder, highly reminiscent of Spassky's in the catastrophic eighth game of his match against Bobby Fischer in 1972. Everyone now saw exactly what was coming, except, perhaps, Kasparov.

"The instant I took my hand off the queen I wanted to resign, but then I went back to my room off-stage and said okay let's see what he plays. I had already resigned in my soul." (Kasparov in *The European*). For the record, both 27 ... ♕e7 and 27 ... ♕h8 are still quite playable.

28 ♘d5

Now 28 ... ♕xd2 fails to 29 ♘xf6+ while 28 ... cxd5 fails to 29 ♕xa5. Meanwhile, 28 ... ♕d8 would be disastrous after 29 ♘xf6+ ♕xf6 30 ♗g5 ♕e5 31 ♗f6 ♕xe4 32 ♖ce1. Black there-

fore has no choice.

28	...	♕c5+
29	♔h1	

Although this wins easily, 29 ♗e3! is considerably more murderous according to Kasparov.

Kasparov in *The European* gives the variation 29 ♗e3 ♗g5 30 ♘f4! ♕e5 31 ♗d4 ♕xe4 32 ♖ce1 ♕f5 33 ♗e3! and White wins, since Black has no defence to a knight discovery on h5 or d5, while 33 ... ♗xf4 34 ♖xf4 ♕e5 35 ♗d4 ♕g5 36 ♖f7+ ♔h6 37 ♗g7+ wins Black's queen. Nevertheless, on showing this line to the Mephisto Computer, the metal mind came up with the defence 33 ... ♗h4! 34 ♖e2 ♖f8 or 34 ♗f2 ♗g5! which, annoyingly, seems to hold for Black. The shape of things to come? So, Karpov's 29th move was justified after all.

29	...	♗xd5
30	cxd5	♕d4 *(151)*

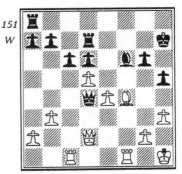

After this Black is com-

pletely lost in a simple
technical fashion, but if 30
... ♕b5 31 a4 ♕xb3 32 dxc6
bxc6 33 e5 ♗g7 34 exd6
and White emerges with a
completely overwhelming
position.

"I made a second blun-
der, 30 ... ♕d4. I gave up
the pawn. 30 ... ♕b5 was
necessary. I don't know
why I didn't play it. A black
hole. I was in a black hole.
I don't know why. A mental
block. Unbelievable." (Kasparov in *The European*)

31	dxc6	bxc6
32	♖xc6	♖e8
33	♖c4	♕xd2
34	♘xd2	♗e5
35	♗e3	♗g3
36	♖f3	h4
37	♗f2	♗xf2
38	♖xf2	♖de7
39	♖f4	g5
40	♖f6	♖xe4
41	♖xe4	♖xe4
42	♖xd6	♖e7
43	♖a6	♔g7
44	♔g1	1-0

9) Classical 7 ♗e3

7 ♗e3 gives rise to the variation named after the Yugoslav grandmaster Svetozar Gligoric. White avoids being immediately coerced into the advance d5 and, by keeping the situation temporarily fluid, makes it more difficult for Black to formulate a clear-cut plan.

The drawback is that the bishop is something of a target on e3 and Black can exploit this by gaining time with ... ♘g4, simultaneously freeing the way for the f-pawn to advance. White hopes that such play will prove premature, and that a chance will arise to exploit the awkward placing of the knight on g4. If Black does not grasp the metal early with ... ♘g4, then White may sacrifice a tempo with h3 to eliminate the possibility altogether.

The play in this chapter is obviously similar to that in chapter 6 (Classical with 8 ♗e3), and the two should be studied together. There are transpositional possib-

ilities between the two, but here White is usually looking to make use of the fact that he has not yet castled.

Game 17 investigates 7 ... exd4 and other, less popular, alternatives, while in game 18 we examine the favoured choice 7 ... ♘g4.

Game 17
Karpov – Kasparov
World Championship (11)
New York 1990

1	d4	♘f6
2	c4	g6
3	♘c3	♗g7
4	e4	d6
5	♘f3	0-0
6	♗e2	e5
7	♗e3	(152)

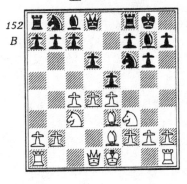

152
B

7 ... exd4

a) 7 ... c6 generated some interest following its adoption by Kasparov in the last World Championship encounter: 8 d5 (8 dxe5 is pretty tame, e.g. 8 ... dxe5 9 ♘d2 {9 ♕xd8 ♖xd8 10 ♘xe5 *is rarely a favourable tactic for White and that is certainly the case here, as Black quickly hits back with 10 ... ♖e8 11 f4 ♘bd7 12 ♘xd7 ♘xe4!*} 9 ... ♕e7 10 c5 ♘bd7 11 ♕a4 ♖d8 12 ♘b3 ♘f8 13 0-0 ♘e6 14 ♖ad1 ♖xd1 15 ♖xd1 ♘f4 16 f3 h5 17 ♗c4 h4 18 ♕a5 ♗e6= Portisch - Ivanchuk, Reykjavik 1991; 8 ♕d2 ♖e8 9 d5 ♘g4 10 ♗g5 f6 11 ♗h4 ♘h6 12 0-0 ♘f7 13 ♕c2 ♘a6 14 a3 c5 15 ♖ab1 h5 16 h3 ♗d7 17 b4 ♖f8 18 ♘d2 ♘h6 19 ♖fe1 ♖f7= A Maric-Xie Jun, Beijing 1991. The errant white bishop provides a handy target for Black's kingside advance) 8 ... ♘g4 9 ♗g5 (9 ♗d2 f5 10 ♗g5?! {*We don't understand what White is trying to do here. Whatever it is, it certainly doesn't work!*} 10 ... ♘f6 11 dxc6 bxc6 12 ♕d2 fxe4 13 ♗xf6 ♗xf6 14 ♘xe4 ♗f5 15 ♘xf6+ ♕xf6 16 ♖d1 ♖d8 17 ♕g5 ♔g7 18 0-0 ♘a6∓ Fishbein - Dolmatov, Beer-Sheva 1991) 9 ... f6 10 ♗h4 ♘a6 11 ♘d2 ♘h6 12 a3 ♘f7 13 f3 ♗h6 14 ♗f2 f5 15 ♕c2 ♗d7 16 b4 c5 17 ♖b1 b6

18 ♘f1 ♗f4!= Karpov - Kasparov, World Ch. (19) 1990. The point of Black's last move is to hold up ♘e3 (19 ♘e3? ♕g5 20 ♘cd1 ♗xe3 21 ♘xe3 f4). White can only drive this bishop away with g3, weakening his kingside.

b) 7 ... ♘c6 used to be popular, but is rarely seen these days. Play can continue 8 d5 ♘e7 9 ♘d2 and now:

b1) 9 ... ♘d7 10 b4 f5 11 f3 a5 12 bxa5 ♖xa5 13 ♘b3 ♖a8 14 c5 ♘f6 15 cxd6 cxd6 16 a4 ♗d7 17 0-0 ♖c8= Magerramov - Lechtynsky, Baku 1980.

b2) 9 ... ♘e8 10 f3 f5 11 c5 ♘f6 12 ♘c4 ♔h8 13 a4 ♘eg8 14 cxd6 cxd6 15 0-0± Lalic - Gunawan, Sarajevo 1988.

b3) 9 ... c5 10 g4 ♗d7 11 h4 ♕c8 12 ♖g1 ♘e8 13 g5 f5 14 gxf6 ♘xf6 15 h5 a6 16 a4 ♕e8 17 hxg6 ♘xg6 18 ♕b3± but Black's play left a lot to be desired, Andruet - Gouret, French League 1991.

c) 7 ... ♕e7 was for a long time considered, due to variation c11, to be simply an inferior move, where the best Black can get is a slightly worse position with no prospects. However, Kasparov changed all that with his amazing gambit against Karpov in New York. The variation may still be inferior for Black, but the positions are razor-sharp.

c1) 8 dxe5 dxe5 9 ♘d5 *(153)*:

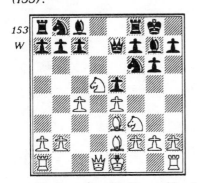

c11) 9 ... ♘xd5 10 cxd5 c6 11 d6 ♕e6 12 h4! (12 ♘g5 is perfectly okay, but not as incisive as the text, e.g. 12 ... ♕e8 13 ♕d2 f6 14 ♘f3 ♗e6 15 0-0± Bukic - Ivanovic, Yugoslavia 1978) 12 ... h6?! (This is too slow and Black now gets mated while trying to deal with the giant passed d-pawn. However, 12 ... ♖d8 also allows White a big attack after 13 ♘g5! ♕xd6 14 ♕b3) 13 ♕d2 ♖d8 14 ♖d1 ♗f8 15 ♗xh6 ♖xd6 16 ♕c1 ♖xd1+ 17 ♗xd1 ♘d7 18 ♗b3 ♕e7 19 h5 ♘c5 20 ♗xf8 ♕xf8 21 ♕g5 ♘xb3 22 axb3 ♕b4+ 23 ♔f1 ♗e6 24 hxg6 ♕xe4 25 gxf7+ 1-0 I Sokolov - Djuric, San Bernardino 1988.

c12) 9 ... ♕d8 (This is Kasparov's new ingredient. The move had actually been played before, in the game Marin - Khait, Budapest

Open 1990, a game which was published with annotations in *New in Chess Yearbook 17*. However, no-one except the eagle-eyed World Champion had paid any attention. Nevertheless, although highly effective as a one-game weapon, the move is objectively doubtful due to the note to White's 13th) 10 ♗c5 ♘xe4! (This is the point, as 10 ... ♖e8?? loses immediately to 11 ♗e7) 11 ♗e7 ♕d7 12 ♗xf8 ♔xf8 *(154)*

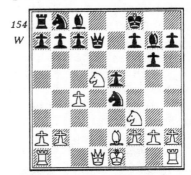

13 ♕c2 (The refutation, as pointed out by no less an authority than Bobby Fischer in his first contribution to chess theory for many years, is 13 ♕d3! ♘d6 14 ♕a3! and Black is unable to organise a defence against the various threats such as ♖d1 and c5. 13 ♕d3 was also given by Azmaiparashvili in his notes in *Informator*, but he mysteriously assesses 13 ♕d3 ♘d6 as only ±) 13 ... ♘c5 14 ♖d1 ♘c6!

(Kasparov adds further fuel to the flames with a queen sacrifice. Karpov accurately judges that there is no immediate need to accept, and waits for a move) 15 0-0! ♘e6 16 ♘b6 axb6 17 ♖xd7 ♗xd7 18 ♕d2 ♗e8 19 b3 e4 20 ♘e1 and after further adventures, the game was eventually drawn, Karpov - Kasparov, World Ch. (3) 1990.

c2) 8 d5 avoids getting involved in the above complications, but has little else to recommend it: 8 ... ♘g4 9 ♗g5 f6 10 ♗h4 ♘h6 11 ♘d2 a5 12 f3 (12 a3 is rather slow, e.g. 12 ... ♗d7 13 b4 g5 14 ♗g3 f5 15 exf5 axb4 16 f6 ♗xf6 17 axb4 ♖xa1 18 ♕xa1 e4∓ Ivanchuk - Ehlvest, USSR Ch. 1988) 12 ... ♗d7 13 g4 ♘f7 14 ♗d3 ♘g5 15 h3 ♘a6 16 ♕e2 ♘c5 17 ♗c2 c6= Conquest - Kozul, Tbilisi 1988.

d) 7 ... h6 *(155)*, favoured by Kng's Indian afficionado John Nunn, is an important alternative here. Of the following material, only 'd3' presents any challenge to Black.

d1) 8 dxe5 ♘g4 9 ♗f4 (9 ♗d2?! is rather feeble, e.g. 9 ... ♘xe5 10 ♗e3 ♘g4 11 ♗d4 ♘f6 12 ♘d2 c5 13 ♗e3 ♘c6 14 0-0 ♖e8 15 f3 ♗e6 16 ♖c1 a6∓ Fedorowicz - Nunn, Reykjavik 1990) 9 ... ♘xe5 10

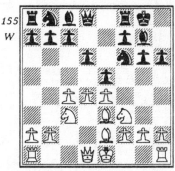

155
W

♕d2 ♔h7 11 0-0 ♘bc6 (11 ... ♗e6 12 b3 ♘bd7 13 ♘d4 ♘c5 14 ♗e3 ♗d7 15 f4 ♘c6 16 ♗f3 ♖e8 17 ♖ad1 a5 18 e5 ♘xd4 19 ♗xd4 ♘e6 20 ♗e3 ♗c6= Kozlov - Timoshenko, Frunze 1988) 12 ♖ac1 a6 13 ♖fd1 ♗e6 14 b3 ♖b8 15 ♗e3 (The - white position is completely lacking in dynamism) 15 ... ♘g4 16 ♗f4 ♘ge5 17 ♗e3 ♘xf3+ (Black avoids the immediate repetition, but is unable to achieve more) 18 ♗xf3 ♗e5 19 ♗e2 g5 20 ♘d5 ♘e7 21 ♘xe7 ♕xe7 22 c5 ♖fd8 23 ♕c2 dxc5 24 ♗xc5 ♕f6 25 ♗e3 ♖xd1+ 26 ♖xd1 ♖d8 27 ♖xd8 ♕xd8 28 ♕d1 ♕xd1+ 29 ♗xd1 f5= G Horvath - Kindermann, Berlin Open 1988.

d2) 8 h3?! is doubtful. White is speculating that Black's loss of time with ... h6 allows this luxury, but the problem is that White will now be reluctant to play f3, as this will seriously weaken the dark squares. Consequently, White is forced into contortions to defend the e-pawn. Two examples: 8 ... exd4 9 ♘xd4 ♖e8 10 ♕c2 ♕e7 11 ♗f3 c5 12 ♘b3 (12 ♘de2 ♘c6 13 ♕d2 ♗e6 14 b3 ♔h7 15 ♖d1 ♖ad8 16 g3 a6∓ Hort – Nunn, Krefeld Open 1986) 12 ... ♘c6 13 0-0 ♗e6 14 ♘d5 ♗xd5 15 exd5 ♘e5 16 ♗e2 b5 17 ♖ad1 ♘xc4 18 ♗xc4 bxc4 19 ♘a5 c3 20 bxc3 ♕e4∓ A Sokolov – Shchekachev, Jurmala 1991.

d3) 8 0-0 ♘g4 9 ♗c1 ♘c6 (9 ... ♘d7 is unambitious and will transpose to familiar ♗e3 positions where the insertion of h3 and h6 favours White, e.g. 10 h3 ♘gf6 11 ♗e3 c6 12 ♕c2 ♕e7 13 ♖fe1 a6 14 a3 exd4 15 ♗xd4 ♖e8 16 ♗f1 ♘e5 17 ♘d2 ♘h5 18 ♗e3 ♕h4 19 ♘e2 f5 20 g3± Suba – Davies, Blackpool Zt. 1990) 10 d5 ♘e7 11 ♘e1 (11 ♘d2 is an alternative, but practice indicates that the knight is not well placed here, e.g. 11 ... f5 12 ♗xg4 fxg4 13 b4 b6 14 ♘b3 *{14 c5 bxc5 15 bxc5 g5 16 a4 ♘g6 17 ♗a3 ♖f6 18 ♖c1 ♗f8 19 ♘b5 a6= Zaichik – Edelman, New York Open 1990}* 14 ... g5 15 a4 ♘g6 16 a5 ♗d7 17 c5 bxc5 18 bxc5 a6 *{Not 18 ... ♘f4?, when 19 c6 ♗c8 20 a6! leaves the a7-pawn doomed}* 19 ♘d2∞ Kasparov – Nunn, Reykjavik World Cup 1988) 11 ... f5 (11 ... h5!? has not been seen much

but it looks attractive. Black avoids the rigid pawn structure that he is saddled with in the main lines, e.g. 12 ♘d3 *{12 ♘c2 c5! 13 f3 ♘h6 14 f4 exf4 15 ♗xf4 f6 16 ♖b1 h4 17 ♕e1 g5 18 ♗d2 a5! Wells – Uhlmann, Graz 1991. White is locked out on the queenside}* 12 ... f5 13 exf5 ♘xf5 14 h3 ♘f6 15 ♗g5 ♕e8 16 ♗f3 ♘d4 17 ♗e4 ♗f5 18 ♗xf5 gxf5 19 ♗e3 c5= Przewoznik – Sznapik, Polish Ch. 1990) 12 ♗xg4 fxg4 *(156)* reaching the following position:

156
W

Black can no longer undermine the white centre, but in compensation has a solid clamp on the kingside and chances to develop the initiative there. Practice has seen:

d31) 13 ♗e3 b6!? (Clearly weakening the queenside, but also creating the possibility of ... ♗a6; one alternative is 13 ... ♖f7 14 ♘d3 ♗f8 15 c5 ♔g7 16 f4 gxf3 17 ♖xf3 ♘g8 18 ♖xf7+ ♔xf7 19

♕f3+ ♘f6 20 ♖f1+- but Black's play was incomprehensible, Damljanovic - Tosic, Yugoslav Ch 1991) 14 ♘d3 g5 15 b4 ♘g6 16 a4 ♘f4 17 a5± Korchnoi - Nunn, Wijk aan Zee 1990.

d32) 13 ♘c2 g5 14 ♘e3 ♖f4 15 ♗d2 (15 f3 gxf3 16 ♖xf3 ♕f8= Geschnitzer - Nunn, Bundesliga 1990) 15 ... ♗d7 16 b4 ♘g6 (16 ... ♕f8 17 ♕c2 ♕f7 18 ♖ac1 ♖f8 19 ♘b5 ♖xf2 20 ♘xc7 ♕f4 21 ♘f5 ♗xf5 22 ♖xf2 ♕xf2+ 23 ♔xf2 ♗xe4+ 24 ♔e2 ♗xc2 25 ♖xc2= Kasparov - Nunn, Skelleftea World Cup 1989) 17 ♖c1 ♘h4 18 ♔h1?! ♕e8 19 f3?! (This is really asking for it, but White must have been concerned that after ... ♕h5 a move such as ... ♘f3 could be immediate mate) 19 ... gxf3 20 g3 ♕h5! (Nunn relishes positions such as this) 21 gxh4 (One brilliant point of Black's play is revealed if White accepts the more substantial offer, e.g. 21 gxf4? exf4 22 ♘f5 ♗xf5 23 exf5 ♕g4! 24 ♖g1 *(157)*
24 ... ♕g2+! mating) 21 ... ♖xh4 22 ♖f2 g4 23 ♘f1 (Despite the extra material, White is lost as he has no way to improve his position before Black sits on it) 23 ... ♖h3 24 ♔g1 ♕g6 25 ♘g3 ♖f8 26 ♘f5 ♖xf5! 27 exf5 ♗xf5 28 ♘e2 fxe2 29 ♕xe2

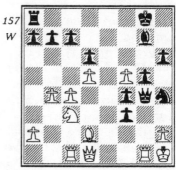

♗d3 30 ♕d1 0-1 Portisch - Nunn, Skelleftea World Cup 1989. Games like this make playing the King's Indian worthwhile!

d33) 13 ♘d3 c5!? 14 ♖b1 a5 15 a3 ♔h7 16 b4 axb4 17 axb4 b6 18 ♗d2 h5 19 ♘b5 ♗a6 20 bxc5 bxc5 21 ♘b2 ♕d7 22 ♘a4 ♖fb8 23 ♘ac3 ♘c8 24 f3± Ivanchuk - Uhlmann, Debrecen 1988.

8   ♘xd4   ♖e8
9   f3

9 ♕c2?! ♕e7 10 f3 c6 11 g4 a6 12 g5 ♘fd7 13 h4 b5 14 h5 led to an impressive win for White in Kamsky - Tal, New York Open 1990. However, Kamsky himself suggests the antidote of 9 ... c6 10 0-0 ♕e7 11 f3 d5 12 cxd5 cxd5 13 ♗g5 ♕e5 with no problems for Black.

9   ...   c6 *(158)*
10   ♕d2

Others are not testing for Black, e.g.

a) 10 ♗f2. In order to keep the balance, Black should respond actively to

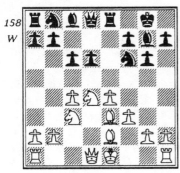

this:

a1) 10 ... ♘bd7?! 11 0-0 a5 12 ♕d2 ♘c5 13 ♖ad1 ♕b6 14 b3 ♘fd7 15 ♘c2 ♕c7 16 ♗d4 ♗e5 17 f4± Azmaiparashvili - Sorin, San Sebastian 1991.

a2) 10 ... ♘h5 11 ♕d2 ♗e5 12 g3 a6 13 0-0 c5 14 ♘c2 ♘c6 15 ♖fe1 ♘f6 16 ♗d3 ♕a5 17 ♖ad1 ♖b8 18 f4 ♗xc3 19 bxc3 ♗g4 20 ♖c1 ♗f3∓ Nickoloff - Kozul, Mississauga 1990.

b) 10 ♘c2 d5 11 cxd5 cxd5 12 exd5 ♗f5 13 ♗f2 ♘h5 (Black has excellent play for a pawn. Instead, the spectacularly unambitious 13 ... ♗xc2?! 14 ♕xc2 ♘xd5 15 ♘xd5 ♕xd5 left Black with a dreary position in Tisdall - Remlinger, Gausdal 1991, and after 16 0-0 ♘c6 17 ♗c4 ♘d4 18 ♗xd5 ♘xc2 19 ♖ac1 ♘e3 20 ♗xe3 ♖xe3 21 ♖c7 ♗xb2 22 ♖xf7 ♔h8 23 ♖xb7, he eventually went down) 14 0-0 ♕g5 15 ♗b5 ♘d7 16 ♘e4 ♖xe4! 17 fxe4 ♗xe4 18 ♗g3 ♘xg3 19 hxg3 ♗xc2 20 ♕xc2 ♘d4+ 21 ♔f2 ♘f6∓ Dannevig - Vladimirov, Gausdal 1991.

10 ...   d5
11 exd5   cxd5
12 0-0   ♘c6

12 ... dxc4 clears the centre, but the loss of time leaves White with a niggling initiative, and after 13 ♘db5 it is difficult for Black to equalise:

a) 13 ... ♕e7 14 ♗f4 ♘a6 15 ♗d6 ♕d8 16 ♗xc4 ♗e6 17 ♗xe6 ♖xe6 18 ♖ad1 ♕b6+ 19 ♕f2 ♕c6 20 ♗f4 ♘h5 21 ♗e3 ♕c4 22 ♗d4 ♗h6 23 ♖fe1 ♖xe1+ 24 ♕xe1 ♘b4 25 ♘d6 and Black never managed to escape from the bunker, Dzhandzhava - Ballesteros, San Sebastian 1991.

b) 13 ... ♘c6 14 ♕xd8 ♖xd8 15 ♖ad1 ♗f5 16 ♗xc4 ♘e5 (16 ... ♘d7? is considerably worse, e.g. 17 ♗g5 ♖f8 18 ♘d6 ♗c2 19 ♖d2 ♘d4 20 ♘cb5 h6 21 ♗e7+- Parker - Bibby, British Ch. 1990) 17 ♗b3 ♗d3 18 ♖fe1 ♘c6 19 ♘xa7! ♘xa7 20 ♗xa7 ♖xa7 21 ♖e3± Tunik - Belov, Podolsk 1989.

13 c5 *(159)*

The white alternatives quickly burn out to equality, e.g.:

a) 13 ♖ad1 ♘xd4 14 ♗xd4 dxc4 15 ♗xc4 ♗e6 (15 ... a6 16 ♖fe1 ♗f5 17 g4 ♖xe1+ 18 ♕xe1 ♕c7!= Polugaevsky - M Gurevich, Reggio Emilia 1991) 16 ♗b5 ♖f8 17 ♕f2 ♕a5

18 ♕h4 ♘h5 19 ♗xg7 ♘xg7 20 ♕a4 ½-½ Sofrevski - Mukic, Yugoslav Ch 1991.

b) 13 ♘xc6 bxc6 14 ♖ad1 ♗a6 15 cxd5 ♗xe2 16 ♕xe2 ♘xd5 17 ♘xd5 cxd5 18 ♕f2 ♗xb2 19 ♗xa7 ♕d7 ½-½ Portisch - Bouaziz, Szirak Izt. 1987.

159
B

A well-known position, played many times before, where White was considered to have a small advantage, e.g. 13 ... ♘h5 14 ♗f2 ♗e5 15 g3 ♘g7 16 ♖fe1 ♘e6 17 ♘db5± Lev - G Burgess, London (Lloyds Bank) 1990. Kasparov's 13th move sacrifice may upset this verdict.

13 ... ♖xe3!?
14 ♕xe3 ♕f8!!

An amazing idea which nobody had predicted. Black speculates on the weakness of White's pawn on c5. I had been looking at 14 ... ♘xd4 15 ♕xd4 ♘g4 16 ♕d2 (16 ♕xd5 ♗d4+) 16 ... ♘xh2 17 ♖d1 (17 ♔xh2 ♕h4+ 18 ♔g1 ♗d4+) 17 ... ♕h4 18

♘xd5 ♗e6 19 ♘c7 ♗e5 20 ♘xa8 ♘xf3+ 21 ♗xf3 ♗h2+ 22 ♔f1 ♗c4+ 23 ♗e2 ♕f6+ but somewhere in all this I feel there must be a refutation. Kasparov's move is much deeper and stronger.

15 ♘xc6

The attempt 15 ♘cb5 ♕xc5 16 ♖ac1 ♕b6 17 ♕f2 failed after 17 ... ♗d7 18 ♘b3 ♗h6 19 ♖c3 ♖e8 20 ♕xb6 axb6 21 ♔f2 d4 22 ♘3xd4 ♘d5 23 ♖b3 ♘a5 24 ♖a3 ♗f8 25 ♖a4 ♗c5 26 ♖c1 ♘c6 27 ♖ac4 ♘f4 28 ♖xc5 bxc5 29 ♖xc5 ♖xe2+ 30 ♘xe2 0-1 Fishbein - Schandorff, Kerteminde 1991.

15 ... bxc6
16 ♔h1 ♖b8
17 ♘a4 ♖b4

A tremendous way to activate the rook, which now operates on both flanks.

18 b3 ♗e6 *(160)*

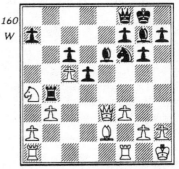

160
W

A very useful developing move which in some cases could prepare ... d4 and ... ♗d5. A further point of the move is to introduce the extra threat of ... ♕b8 allied with ... ♖h4. The New York grandmasters were all for the immediate 18 ... ♘h5. Jon Speelman, writing in the now sadly defunct *Sunday Correspondent* had this to say about their exuberant ideas: "The New York press room castigated Kasparov for wimpishness when he played 18 ... ♗e6, but it is far easier to play an unclear line like 18 ... ♘h5 19 ♖ad1 ♖h4 20 ♕f2 ♖xh2+ 21 ♔xh2 ♗e5+ with someone else's pieces rather than one's own."

19	♘b2	♘h5
20	♘d3	♖h4
21	♕f2	♕e7
22	g4	*(161)*

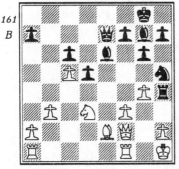

161
B

22 f4? ♗d4 23 ♕xd4 ♘g3+ 24 ♔g1 ♘xe2+ wins for Black.

It now looks as if Black must retreat or supinely capture on a1, when his pieces on the king's wing remain stranded. Instead,

comes a superbly sparkling way to force a perpetual.

22	...	♗d4!
23	♕xd4	

If 23 ♕g2 ♗xa1 24 ♖xa1 ♗xg4 (Black can also play 24 ... ♘g7 or 24 ... ♕f6 25 ♖g1 ♘f4 26 ♘xf4 ♕xf4 27 ♕g3 ♕xg3 28 ♖xg3 g5) 25 fxg4 ♕xe2 26 ♕xe2 ♘g3+ 27 ♔g2 ♘xe2 when Black has won a pawn, although the weakness of the c6-pawn combined with the presence of the advanced white pawn cancels this out.

23	...	♖xh2+
24	♔xh2	♕h4+
½–½		

Game 18
Speelman – Kasparov
Madrid (Rapid) 1988

1	c4	g6
2	e4	♗g7
3	d4	d6
4	♘c3	♘f6
5	♘f3	0-0
6	♗e2	e5
7	♗e3	*(162)*

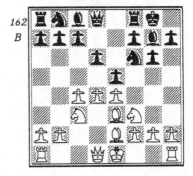

162
B

7 ... ♘g4
8 ♗g5 f6
9 ♗h4 *(163)*

9 ♗c1 obviously loses time, but White hopes that the black pieces will prove to be misplaced; 9 ... ♘c6 and now:

a) 10 d5 ♘e7 11 h3 (11 0-0?! *{This is very odd. After Black's reply he has effect- ively achieved a position where he has managed to meet the main line 9 ♘e1 with 9 ... f5, not having needed to waste time with ... ♘d7}* 11 ... f5 12 ♘e1 ♘f6 13 f3 c6?! (Surely 13 ... f4, and Black would be very quick on the kingside) 14 ♗e3 ♔h8 15 g4 b5 16 dxc6 bxc4 17 h3 ♘xc6 18 ♗xc4 h5= Barbero - Fedorowicz, Buenos Aires 1991) 11 ... ♘h6 12 b4 a5 13 bxa5 ♖xa5 14 ♘d2 f5 15 ♘b3 ♖a8 16 g4 fxe4 17 ♘xe4 ♘f7 18 h4 c6∞ Korchnoi - Nijboer, Wijk aan Zee 1990. Korchnoi has played in typically ambi- tious style, but Black has counterplay.

b) 10 h3 ♘h6 11 ♗e3?! (White has an understand- able desire to keep the ten- sion, but the bishop proves to be very vulnerable here) 11 ... f5 12 exf5 ♘xf5 13 ♗g5 ♕e8 14 dxe5 dxe5 15 0-0 h6 16 ♗c1 ♗e6∓ Nickoloff - Damljanovic, St. John Open 1988.

163
B

9 ... g5

a) 9 ... ♕e8 10 0-0 ♔h8 (Black should consider a more combative response, e.g. 10 ... h5!? 11 h3 ♘h6 12 dxe5 dxe5 13 c5 ♗e6 14 ♘d5 ♕f7 15 ♕c2 ♘c6 16 ♖ad1 ♔h8 17 b3∞ Timoshenko - Gazik, Douai 1991) 11 dxe5 dxe5 12 ♘d5 ♖f7 13 h3 ♘h6 14 c5 ♗e6 15 ♕d2 ♕f8 16 ♖ac1 ♘c6 17 b4± van Wely - Kr Geor- giev, Belfort Open 1989.

b) 9 ... ♘d7 10 c5!? dxc5 11 dxe5 ♘gxe5 12 ♘xe5 ♘xe5 13 f4 ♘f7 14 ♕xd8 ♖xd8 15 ♘d5 ♖xd5! (White had pro- mising threats, but this timely exchange sacrifice enables Black to hold the balance) 16 exd5 b6 17 0-0 f5 18 ♗f3 ♘d6 19 ♗d8 ♗a6 20 ♗xc7 ♗xf1 21 ♗xd6 ♗c4 22 ♗e5 ♖d8= Mohr - Daml- janovic, Bled 1991.

c) 9 ... ♘c6 *(164)* is an important alternative to the main line:

c1) 10 h3 ♘h6 11 dxe5 dxe5 12 c5 (12 ♕b3 ♔h8 13 ♖d1

164
W

♕e8 14 ♘d5 ♕f7 15 0-0 ♘d8
16 ♕a3 ♘e6 17 ♖fe1 ♖e8 18
♗g3 ♗d7 19 c5 c6 20 ♘e3
♕e7= Azmaiparashvili -
Reyes, Toledo 1991) 12 ...
♕e7 13 b4 ♗e6 14 ♘d5? (This
is a good idea, but the tim-
ing is completely wrong;
White lacks the develop-
ment to support this ad-
vance) 14 ... ♗xd5 15 exd5
e4! 16 dxc6 exf3 17 gxf3 ♘f5
18 ♗g3 ♖ad8 19 ♕b3+ ♔h8
20 ♖d1 ♖fe8-+ Tisdall -
Hebden, London (Watson,
Farley & Williams) 1990.

c2) 10 d5 ♘e7 11 ♘d2:

c21) 11 ... f5?! leads to
structures familiar from
the 7 ... h6 variation, but
here Black is unable to
generate serious counter-
play, e.g. 12 ♗xg4 fxg4 13
♗g5 h6 (13 ... ♔h8 14 0-0
♗f6 15 ♗e3 ♘g8 16 c5 ♗g5 17
♗xg5 ♕xg5 18 cxd6 cxd6 19
♘c4 ♕e7 20 ♕b3 ♖d8 21 f4±
Damljanovic - Matkovic,
Yugoslav Ch. 1991) 14 ♗e3 b6
15 0-0 g5 16 b4 ♘g6 17 c5

♘h4 18 ♘c4 ♖f4 (Black tries
to lure White into complications, but White sensibly
ignores the bait) 19 ♖c1 ♗f8
20 a4 ♖b8 21 ♘b5± Brenn-
inkmeijer - van Wely, Wijk
aan Zee 1990.

c22) 11 ... ♘h6 12 f3 (12
g4!? c6 13 f3 ♘f7 14 ♕c2 a6
15 a4 ♕c7 16 a5 f5 17 ♗f2
♘h6 18 ♗b6 ♕b8 19 ♖g1 fxg4
20 fxg4 ♗f4 21 h4 ♗d7 22
b4∞ Ivanchuk - Yermolin-
sky, Frunze 1988) 12 ... g5
(12 ... f5 13 b4?! {This is
careless and allows imme-
diate equality. Correct was
13 ♗f2} 13 ... fxe4 14 fxe4
♖f4 15 ♗f2 ♘g4 16 ♗xg4
½-½ Marin - Kr Georgiev.
Stara Zagora 1990) 13 ♗f2 f5
14 c5 (14 h4!? g4 15 fxg4
♘xg4 16 ♗xg4 fxg4 17 ♗e3
c5 18 g3 a6 19 a4 ♔h8 20 ♖f1
b6 21 ♖b1 ♘g8 22 ♖xf8 ♕xf8
23 b4± Magerramov - Bolo-
gan, USSR Team Ch. 1991)
14 ... ♘g6 15 cxd6 cxd6 16
♘c4 ♘f4 17 0-0 g4 18 fxg4
♘xe2+ 19 ♕xe2 ♘xg4 20
exf5 ♘xf2 21 ♖xf2 ♗xf5 22
♖af1 ♗g6 23 ♘e4 ♖xf2 24
♖xf2± I Sokolov - P Cram-
ling, Haninge 1989.

10   ♗g3   ♘h6 *(165)*
11   h3

11 dxe5 dxe5 (11 ... fxe5?!
is nearly always a doubtful
recapture: 12 h4 g4 13 ♘h2
♗e6 14 ♘d5 ♕d7 15 ♘e3 ♘c6
16 ♘hxg4 ♘xg4 17 ♗xg4
♘d4 18 0-0 ♔h8 19 ♔h2 ♗h6

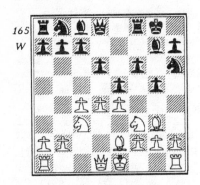

165 W

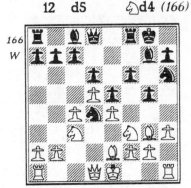

12 d5 ♘d4 (166)

166 W

20 ♗xe6 ♕xe6 21 ♘d5± Magerramov - Shirov, Klaipeda 1988. White has an extra pawn, but untangling the kingside will not be an easy task) and now White can probably get a small advantage, but nothing serious, e.g.

a) 12 ♕d5+ ♔h8 (12 ... ♘f7 13 h4 ♕e7 14 hxg5 fxg5 15 0-0-0 c6 16 ♕a5 ♘a6 17 ♘e1 ♘c5 18 ♕a3 ♖e8∞ Granda - Fedorowicz, Buenos Aires 1991) 13 c5 c6 14 ♕xd8 ♖xd8 15 ♘d2 ♗f8 16 ♘a4 ♗e6 17 b3 ♘d7 18 ♖c1 ♖ac8 19 f3 b5 20 cxb6± Korchnoi - Fedorowicz, Lucerne 1989.

b) 12 ♕b3 c6 13 c5+ ♔h8 14 ♘d2 ♘d7 15 ♕c4 ♕e7 16 ♘a4 ♖d8 17 ♕c3 f5 18 f3 ½-½ Georgadze - Zsu Polgar, San Sebastian 1991.

c) 12 0-0 ♕e7 13 h4 ♘c6 14 ♘d5 ♕d8 15 b4 g4 16 ♘h2 ♕d7 17 c5 ♖d8 18 ♕b3 ♔h8 19 ♖ad1± Azmaiparashvili - J Polgar, San Sebastian 1991.

11 ... ♘c6

An enterprising sacrifice, but not necessarily sound. Safe is 12 ... ♘e7, e.g. 13 ♕d2 ♘g6 14 0-0-0 a6 15 ♔b1 ♗d7 16 ♖c1 ♕e7 17 ♘e1 f5 18 f3 ♘f4 19 ♗f1 ♘f7 20 ♗f2 c5 21 g3 ♘g6 22 exf5 ♗xf5+ 23 ♘e4 ♖ab8 24 ♗d3∞ A Maric - Xie Jun, Belgrade 1991. This looks more like a position from the Saemisch: White has solid control over e4, but her king is not happily placed.

13	♘xd4	exd4
14	♕xd4	f5
15	♕d2	f4
16	♗h2	♘f7
17	h4?!	

17 0-0-0 ♘e5 18 f3 is perhaps the critical test of Kasparov's gambit. It was certainly found wanting for Black in Arlandi - Cvitan, Reggio Emilia 1991, which continued 18 ... c5 19 dxc6! (This looks dangerous, but White is calculating that he can grab more material and take control before the

threats against b2 become serious) 19 ... bxc6 20 h4! ♛a5 (The problem is that 20 ... h6 21 hxg5 hxg5 leaves Black terribly vulnerable to a check on the a2-g8 diagonal. Now however, his position falls apart before he can generate any play) 21 hxg5 ♖b8 22 ♛xd6 ♖b4 23 ♗g1 ♖b7 24 ♛c5 ♛a6 25 ♘d4+-.

17	...	h6
18	hxg5	hxg5

White's next move is too belligerent. He should instead play 19 f3 in order to reintroduce his queen's bishop into the game via g1. Speelman's choice permits Kasparov to offer a second pawn, in the interests of permanently locking the white bishop out of play.

19 g3 *(167)*

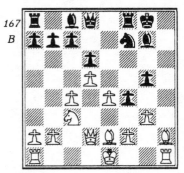

| 19 | ... | f3! |

Kasparov is never afraid to sacrifice material for the initiative. Indeed, he soon offers a third pawn to clear lines of attack against the white king.

20	♗xf3	♘e5
21	♗e2	g4
22	♗g1	c5
23	dxc6	bxc6
24	0-0-0	♗e6
25	♛xd6	♛g5+
26	♔b1	♛g6
27	♔a1	♖ab8 *(168)*

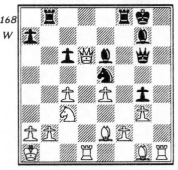

Speelman's next move is amazingly ingenious but ultimately fails to solve the problem of the incarcerated queen's bishop. The inventive Korchnoi suggested afterwards that 28 f4! is correct, e.g. 28 ... gxf3 29 ♗f1 and now if 29 ... f2 30 ♗xf2 ♖xf2 31 ♛xb8+. Although 28 f4 commits White to returning some material, the threat of liberating the bishop by ♗c5 or ♘d4 would still render the situation unclear.

28	♖h5	♛xh5
29	♛xe6+	♔h8
30	♛e7	♘f3
31	♗xf3	♖xf3
32	♘a4	♖e8
33	♛xa7	♛e5

34	♕b6	♕xe4
35	♕b4	♕c2

Now Black's forces converge on the white king for the final attack.

36	♖b1	♖d3
37	♕c5	♖e2
38	♕h5+	♔g8
39	♕xg4	*(169)*

169
B

39	...	♕xb1+
	0-1	

10) Classical 7 d5 and others

The immediate closing of the centre with 7 d5 is known as the Petrosian system, after the Armenian World Champion who did much to develop and popularise the move, especially in conjunction with 8 ♗g5, pinning the black knight.

However, the passage of time and numerous grandmaster games have demonstrated adequate methods for Black to deal with White's plan, and the variation has become something of a rare guest at a high level.

Game 19
Yusupov - Kasparov
Barcelona World Cup 1989

1	♘f3	♘f6
2	c4	g6
3	♘c3	♗g7
4	e4	d6
5	d4	0-0
6	♗e2	e5 *(170)*
7	d5	

7 dxe5 dxe5 8 ♕xd8 ♖xd8 9 ♗g5 has always been a favourite of those spoil-

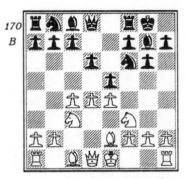

170
B

sports who want to dampen the ardour of the King's Indian player, but it has never caused any theoretical problems. In fact, the opposite is the case - it is usually Black who is discovering some new and interesting way to complicate the game. The current state of play is that 'a' is the old reliable method for Black, 'b' is a relatively new idea involving a pawn sacrifice, while 'c', the odd-looking 9 ... ♖f8, favoured by Alexei Shirov, the brilliant young Latvian and first teenager ever to break the 2700 barrier, is the latest model. All three are perfectly acceptable:

a) 9 ... ♖e8 10 ♘d5 ♘xd5 11 cxd5 c6 12 ♗c4 cxd5 13 ♗xd5 ♘d7 14 ♘d2 ♘c5 15 0-0-0 ♘e6 16 ♗e3 ♘f4 17 ♗xf4 exf4 18 f3 ♗e6= P Cramling – Gallagher, Biel 1991.

b) 9 ... c6 10 ♘xe5 ♖e8 11 0-0-0 ♘a6 *(171)*

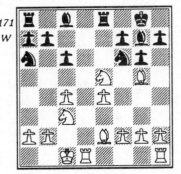

12 ♖d6 (12 ♘f3 ♗g4 13 ♗d3 ♘c5 14 ♖he1 ♘fd7! 15 ♗f4 ♘b6 {*Thanks to this rerouting of the knight, Black will recover his pawn and obtain a small edge*} 16 ♔c2 ♗xf3 17 gxf3 ♘xd3 18 ♖xd3 ♘xc4 19 ♗g3 ♖ad8 20 ♖ed1 ♖xd3 21 ♖xd3 ♘e5 22 ♖e3 ♘c4 23 ♖d3 ♘e5 24 ♖e3 ♘d7 25 e5 ♔f8 26 f4 f5∓ Barlov – Watson, Bor 1986) and now:

b1) 12 ... ♗e6 13 f4 h6 14 ♗xf6 ♗xf6 15 ♖hd1 ♗xe5 16 fxe5 ♖ac8 17 ♔d2 ♖e7 18 ♔e3 ♖ce8 19 ♖d8 ♔f8 20 h4 ♘c5 21 ♖xe8+ ♖xe8 22 b4 ♘d7 23 ♔f4 ♔e7 24 ♘d5+ (A neat trick, but it fails to disturb the balance) 24 ... cxd5 25 cxd5 ♖c8 26 dxe6

fxe6 27 ♖d2 ♖f8+ ½-½ Korchnoi – Kasparov, Tilburg 1991.

b2) 12 ... ♘xe4 13 ♘xe4 ♗xe5 14 ♘f6+ ♗xf6 15 ♗xf6 ♘c5 16 ♗f3 ♗f5 17 ♖hd1 (White has a modest initiative but with careful defence Black holds the balance) 17 ... ♘e4 18 ♗xe4 ♖xe4 19 b3 h6 20 f3 ♖e6 21 ♖d8+ ♖e8 22 ♖xa8 ♖xa8 23 g4 ♗e6 24 h4 b5 25 cxb5 cxb5 26 ♖d6 a5 27 ♖b6 ♗d7 28 ♖d6 ♗e6 29 ♔d2 a4= Olafsson – Remlinger, New York Open 1991.

c) 9 ... ♖f8 (This tucks the rook out of harm's way. The continuation that White adopts here leads nowhere, but it is hard to envisage how the first player could ever gain the initiative here) 10 ♘d5 ♘xd5 11 cxd5 c6 12 ♗c4 b5 (12 ... cxd5 is slightly more cautious but perfectly acceptable: 13 ♗xd5 ♘c6 14 0-0-0 h6 15 ♗e3 ♗d7 16 ♔b1 ♖fd8 17 ♖d2 ♗e8 18 ♖hd1 ♖d7 19 ♘e1 ♖c7 20 ♘d3 ♘e7 21 ♗b3 a5 22 ♗b6 ♖d7 23 ♘c5 ♖xd2 24 ♖xd2 a4 25 ♗d5 ♘xd5 26 exd5 ♗f6 27 f3 ♗b5 28 ♗c7 ♗g5= H Olafsson – Fedorowicz, Wijk aan Zee 1991) 13 ♗b3 ♗b7 14 ♖c1 a5 15 a3 a4 16 ♗a2 ♖c8 17 ♗e3 b4 18 axb4 ♘a6 19 dxc6 ♖xc6 20 ♖xc6 ♗xc6 *(172)* 21 ♗c4 (Black had been

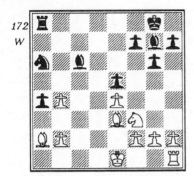

172
W

down this path before, viz.
21 0-0 ♘xb4 22 ♗b1 f6 23
♖c1 ♗f8 24 ♗d2 ♖d8 25 h4
♗e8 26 ♗xb4 ♗xb4 27 ♗a2+
♔f8 28 ♗d5 ♖b8∓ P Cram-
ling - Shirov, Stockholm
1990) 21 ... ♘xb4 22 ♗c5 ♗f8
23 ♗xf8 ♔xf8 24 ♘xe5 ♗xe4
25 f3 ♗d5 26 0-0 ♖e8 27
♘d7+♔g7 28 ♗xd5 ♘xd5 29
♘c5= Wegner - Shirov,
Gausdal 1991.

Returning to the position
after 7 d5 (173):

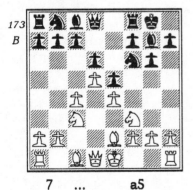

173
B

7 ... a5
By far the most popular
move. Others are:
a) 7 ... ♘a6 8 ♘d2 ♘e8?!
(Black should beware of
moving this knight before

White has committed him-
self to kingside castling.
A more flexible, and soun-
der approach, was seen in
Alekssandrov - Neverov.
USSR Ch. 1991: 8 ... c6 9 a3
cxd5 10 cxd5 ♗d7 11 ♘c4
♘e8 12 b4 f5 13 0-0 ♘ac7∞)
9 a3 c5 10 h4! (Speelman
takes his chance) 10 ... f5 11
h5 f4 12 hxg6 hxg6 13 ♗g4
♘f6 14 ♗xc8 ♕xc8 15 ♘f3
♘c7 16 ♗d2 ♔f7 17 b4±
Speelman - Ivanchuk, Li-
nares 1991. Black has a miserable position without
hope of counterplay.
although he hung on to
draw.
  b) 7 ... ♘bd7 8 ♗g5 h6 9
♗h4 g5 10 ♗g3 ♘h5 (174)

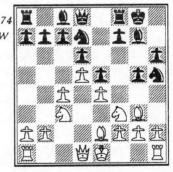

174
W

For a long time, this was
the main line of the Petrosian system and there have
been numerous encounters
starting from this position.
The lesson that has been
learnt is that the position
is absolutely fine for Black
and nowadays it is a *rara
avis* at international stan-

dard. A couple of recent exceptions, which did not buck the trend are:

b1) 11 ♘d2 ♘f4 12 0-0 ♘c5 13 ♗g4 ♘xe4 14 ♘dxe4 f5 15 c5 fxg4 16 cxd6 cxd6 17 ♘b5 ♗f5 18 ♘bxd6 ♗xe4 19 ♘xe4 ♛xd5 20 ♛xd5+ ♘xd5∓ Kouatly - Ree, Cannes 1990.

b2) 11 h4 (More aggressive than 11 ♘d2, but Black's resources are completely adequate) 11 ... ♘f4 (11 ... ♘xg3 12 fxg3 gxh4 13 ♘xh4 ♛g5 14 ♗g4 ♘c5 15 ♗xc8 ♛xg3+ 16 ♔f1 △ ♘f5+- Balashov - Penrose, Hastings 1966) 12 hxg5 hxg5 13 ♛c2 ♘xe2 (In the old days, a few players snatched the g-pawn with 13 ... ♘xg2+, but then after 14 ♔d2! △ ♖ag1, they all lost in less than 30 moves) 14 ♔xe2 (This might look strange, but White connects his rooks and keeps e4 under control) 14 ... ♘b6 15 ♘d2 f5 16 f3 fxe4 17 ♘cxe4 c6 18 ♘xd6!? ♛xd6 19 ♛h7+ ♔f7 20 ♘e4 ♛g6 21 ♗xe5 ♛xh7 22 ♖xh7 ♖g8 23 ♗xg7 ♖xg7 24 ♘xg5+ ♔g6 25 ♖xg7+ ♔xg7 26 dxc6∞/= Ivkov - Lautier, Dortmund 1989.

8   ♗g5 *(175)*

The full-blooded Petrosian continuation. White develops the queen's bishop rather extravagantly in an attempt to hamper

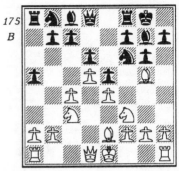

175
B

Black on the king's wing. The great strategist Tigran Petrosian won many games with this move, usually because his opponents would make one of two basic mistakes: They would chase the bishop with ... h6 and ... g5, but then fail to follow up sufficiently energetically and thus remain with horrendous light square weaknesses; or they would make no attempt to deal with the pin, when White would continue ♘d2 (preventing an eventual ... ♘h5) and it became very hard for Black to free the position. Nowadays, however, all King's Indian players know about these problems and the seamier side of the bishop move (i.e. loss of time, target for Black's kingside advance) is more often shown up.

There have been attempts recently to approach this position in a different manner:

8 ♗e3 (This has been very popular recently, but Kasparov's treatment here is rather convincing) 8 ... ♘g4 9 ♗g5 f6 10 ♗h4 ♘a6 11 ♘d2 h5 (This position resembles those emerging from 7 ♗e3, but it looks like a favourable version for Black) 12 a3 ♗d7 13 h3 ♘h6 14 ♖b1 ♘c5 15 b4 axb4 16 axb4 ♘a4 17 ♕c2 ♘xc3 18 ♕xc3 g5 19 ♗g3 h4 20 ♗h2 f5∓ Bareev - Kasparov, Tilburg 1991.

8 h4!? was a pet favourite of the French grandmaster Bachar Kouatly for a while and should not be underestimated. From the following material Black's best approach is not clear: 8 ... ♘a6 (8 ... h5 is timid: 9 ♗g5 ♘a6 10 ♘h2 ♕e8 11 ♕d2 ♘h7 12 ♗h6± Kouatly - Gunawan, Thessalonika Ol. 1988) 9 ♘d2 ♘c5 10 g4! (Kouatly had previously played 10 h5 but after the cunning 10 ... ♕d7! {*Preventing g4*}, Kouatly - Cvitan, Geneva 1988, White was rather stuck for a good move) 10 ... a4 11 h5 gxh5 12 g5 ♘g4?! (This commits Black to a highly speculative piece sacrifice) 13 ♘f1 f5 14 f3 ♘f2 15 ♔xf2 fxe4 16 ♔g2 a3 17 ♖xh5 exf3+ 18 ♗xf3 e4 Kouatly - Kasparov, Evry Simul 1989. The World Champion proved too hot to handle in this game and

he eventually won, but it is difficult to believe that Black has sufficient compensation here.

8 ... h6
9 ♗h4 ♘a6 *(176)*

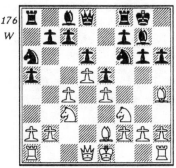

176 W

10 ♘d2

10 0-0 ♕e8 11 ♘d2 ♘h7 12 a3 f5? (The correct way for Black is 12 ... ♗d7 13 ♖b1 a4 14 ♘b5 h5 15 f3 ♗h6∞ Agamaliev - Sukhorukov, Moscow 1991) 13 exf5 ♗xf5 14 g4! (The problem is that White has not yet moved the b-pawn and so the counter-stroke ... e4 is unavailable to Black. Consequently White gains solid control over the vital e4-square) 14 ... ♗d7 15 ♘de4 a4 16 f3 b6 17 ♗d3± Veingold - Kasparov, USSR 1979.

10 ... ♕e8
10 ... h5!? (This is certainly worthy of further attention. The point of this move is to meet 11 0-0 with 11 ... ♗h6 12 f3 ♗e3+ 13 ♔h1 g5 with good counterplay)

11 ♗g5 ♕e8 12 a3 ♗d7 13 b3 ♘h7 14 ♗e3 h4 15 ♕c2 f5 16 f3 ♗f6∞ Lerner - Uhlmann, Berlin 1989.

11 0-0

An alternative strategy for White is to delay castling, e.g. 11 a3 ♗d7 12 b3 ♘h7 13 f3 h5 14 ♖b1 ♗h6 15 ♗f2 ♕e7 *(177)* and now:

a) 16 b4 axb4 17 axb4 h4 18 ♕c2 ♕g5 (This is a standard attacking ploy - White cannot castle as the knight on d2 would hang) 19 ♖g1 c6 20 c5 ♘f6 21 dxc6 bxc6 22 ♘c4 dxc5 23 bxc5 ♖fe8 24 g3 hxg3 25 hxg3 ♗f8 26 ♘a4 ♘c7 27 ♘ab6 ♖ad8∞ Rossiter - Gallagher, British Ch. 1987.

b) 16 h4 (White prevents ... h4 and ... ♕g5, but at a cost) 16 ... ♘c5 17 ♕c2 f5 18 b4 axb4 19 axb4 ♘a4 20 ♘b5? (White's knight is sent behind enemy lines on a suicide mission. 20 ♘d1 ♘f6 21 ♗d3 ♗f4?! 22 ♘e3∞/± was Speelman - J Polgar, Holland 1991. Black should

have played 21 ... ♗xd2=) 20 ... c6 21 dxc6 bxc6 22 ♘c7 ♖ac8 23 ♘a6 c5 24 bxc5 dxc5 0-1 Damljanovic - Fedorowicz, Wijk aan Zee 1990.

11	...	♘h7
12	a3	♗d7
13	b3	f5!?! *(178)*

In the style of his hero, the great champion Alexander Alekhine, Kasparov sometimes hurls himself on the foe without any regard for the material sacrifices being offered. Such was the case here, where Kasparov makes a sacrifice of rook for bishop, which would have been considered a blunder had it been perpetrated by a lesser mortal.

The normal line is 13 ... h5 (threatening ... g5 and ... h4 to trap White's bishop) 14 f3 ♗h6 15 ♖b1 (15 ♔h1 ♗e3 16 ♖b1 ♗c5 17 ♕c1 ♔h8 18 ♘a2 f5 19 b4 axb4 20 axb4 ♗e3 21 ♘c3 c5 22 dxc6 bxc6 23 ♕d1 ♗d4 24 ♘a2 ♘c7 25 ♘c1 ♘e6 26 exf5 gxf5 27

♘db3± Naumkin - Fedorowicz, London {*Lloyds Bank*} 1990) 15 ... ♗e3+ 16 ♗f2 ♗c5 17 ♗xc5 (17 ♕c1 c6 18 ♘a4 ♗d4 19 ♗f2 ♗xf2 20 ♖xf2 ♕d8 21 dxc6 ♗xc6 22 ♘c3 ♘c5 23 b4 axb4 24 axb4 ♘e6 25 b5 ♗d7 26 ♘b3= Yusupov - Damljanovic, St. John 1988) 17 ... dxc5:

a) 18 ♕e1 ♕e7 19 h4? (White cannot hope to get away with this when he has already castled) 19 ... f5 20 exf5 gxf5 21 ♗d3 ♖f7 22 ♖b2 ♔h8 23 ♘db1 ♖g8 24 ♖e2 ♖fg7 25 ♗c2 ♖g3∓ J Cooper - Hebden, British Ch. 1988.

b) 18 ♕c2 ♘f6?! (This is very odd. Why not simply ... h4?) 19 ♘d1 ♕e7 20 ♕c3 ♕d6 21 ♘f2 ♖ae8 22 ♕xa5 b6 23 ♕c3 ♗c8 24 ♘d3± Zlotnik - Kr Georgiev, Belgrade GMA 1988.

14 exf5 gxf5

14 ... ♗xf5 15 g4 and if Black retreats the bishop he will be saddled with a positionally inferior game, so 15 ... e4 16 ♖c1 e3 is obligatory and now (*179*):

a) 17 fxe3 ♕xe3+ 18 ♗f2 ♕g5 19 ♔h1 ♗d7 20 ♘de4 ♕e7 21 ♕d3 ♖ae8= Khenkin - Shirov, USSR 1988.

b) 17 gxf5 exd2 18 ♕xd2 ♘c5 19 ♕d1 ♖xf5 20 ♗g4 ♖f4 21 ♖e1 ♕xe1+ 22 ♕xe1 ♖xg4+ 23 ♗g3 ♘g5 24 ♕e2 h5 25 ♘b5 ♖e4 26 ♕c2 h4 27 ♘xc7 hxg3 28 ♘xa8 gxf2+

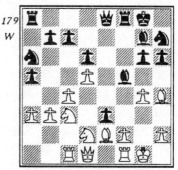

29 ♔f1? (The correct outcome to Black's highly imaginative attack would be a perpetual check after 29 ♔xf2! ♗d4+ 30 ♔g3! ♗e5+ 31 ♔f2 ♗d4+) 29 ... ♖g4!-+ (_ ... ♗d4) 30 ♖d1 ♘ce4 31 ♔e2 ♖g1 32 ♖f1 ♘c3 0-1 Bykhovsky - Belov, Pula 1988.

15 ♗h5 ♕c8

Kasparov has mobilised his pawns, but at the same time he has permitted Yusupov's next move which wins material by force.

16 ♗e7 ♖e8

There are many instances in the King's Indian where Black gives up material in order to remove White's queen's bishop and thereby seize control of the dark squares. But Kasparov wants the light-squared bishop instead. It is strikingly reminiscent of Fischer's celebrated ... ♘h5 in the third game of his match with Spassky, which also seemed to break all the rules.

17 ♗xe8   ♕xe8
18 ♗h4   e4 *(180)*

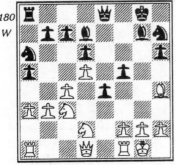

180
W

19 ♕c2

19 ♖c1 gets hit by ♘c5 - d3 but may be White's best, e.g. 20 ♖c2 ♘f8 21 ♘e2 ♘g6 22 ♗g3 ♘d3 23 f3 (23 f4 h5 24 h3 h4 25 ♗h2 c5 26 a4 ♕e7 27 ♔h1 ♗h6 28 ♘b1 ♔h7 29 ♖d2 ♘b4 30 ♗g1 ½-½ Brunner - Hickl, Bern Zt. 1990) 23 ... e3 (23 ... h5 and now in Hoffmann - Grunberg, Lippstadter 1991, the players helpfully agreed a draw) 24 ♘b1 ♘b2 25 ♖xb2 ♗xb2 26 ♖e1 h5 27 h3 ♕f7 28 f4 h4 29 ♗h2 ♗g7 30 ♕d3∞ Naumkin - Kuzmin, Moscow 1989.

19 ...   ♕h5
20 ♗g3   ♖e8

To bolster e4 and answer f3 breaks with ... e4 - e3.

21 ♗f4?

In view of what follows, this must be the wrong plan. White's best move may be 21 ♖ad1, a suggestion of the American GM Patrick Wolff. The idea is

to unravel the knights with ♘db1 and ♘e2 to cover f4. One continuation now is 21 ... ♘c5 22 ♘db1 (not 22 f3 ♗xc3 and ... e4 - e3) 22 ... ♘g5 23 ♘e2 ♘d3 24 ♘f4 ♘xf4 25 ♗xf4 ♗e5 26 ♗xe5 dxe5 and now White must break up the phalanx with 27 f4 but after 27 ... exf3 28 gxf3 ♘xf3+ 29 ♔h1 ♔h8 Black has more than enough compensation.

Another try is 21 f4, halting ... f4 and covering the e5- and g5-squares. The problem is that White's rooks are further immobilized while the black knights are free to dance all over the board. For example, 21 f4 ♘f6 22 ♖ae1 ♘c5 23 ♘e2 ♘d3 with nasty thoughts of ... ♘g4 - e3.

21 ...   ♕g4
22 g3   ♘g5
23 ♔h1

If 23 ♗xg5 hxg5 24 f3 then 24 ... ♕h3 25 fxe4 f4! is strong as White cannot take on f4 because the c3-knight hangs.

23 ...   ♘f3
24 ♖ac1 *(181)*
24 ...   ♘c5
25 ♘xf3   ♕xf3+
26 ♔g1   ♘d3

Kasparov has whipped up a ferocious counter-attack for his material - so ferocious, in fact, that Yusupov feels impelled to return the

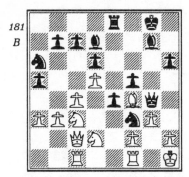

181
B

material he has won. After White's following move Kasparov could simply have played 27 ... ♘xc1 with at least equal prospects.

27 ♕d2   ♗d4

Kasparov has the chance to recoup his material but boldly spurns this in the interests of stoking up his attack, but the black offensive is ultimately quashed after a couple of time trouble blunders wreck his attacking formation.

28 ♖c2   ♔h7
29 h3   ♖g8
30 ♔h2   ♕h5

Kasparov should have considered 30 ... ♘xf4 31 ♕xf4 ♕d3 32 ♕c1 f4 33 g4 ♗xg4 34 hxg4 ♖xg4 with a winning attack, or 32 ♖fc1 e3 and ... ♗e5. Incidentally, the kamikaze 30 ... ♖xg3 fails to 31 ♗xg3 f4 32 ♕e2!

31 ♘d1   ♘e5

31 ... ♘xf4 32 gxf4 (32 ♕xf4 ♗e5 and ... e3!) 32 ... ♕g6 33 f3 ♕g3+ wins. But Kasparov had only one

minute left to reach the time control at move 40.

32 f3

To answer 32 ... ♘xf3+ with 33 ♖xf3 ♕xd4.

32 ...   ♘d3
33 ♘e3   ♘xf4
34 gxf4 *(182)*

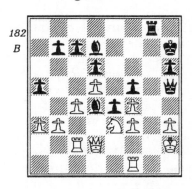

182
B

34 ...   ♗b6??

For the last time missing a clear win. He must play 34 ... ♕h4! Now 35 ♕xd4 fails to 35 ... ♖g3 36 ♔h1 ♖xh3+ mating. The extra tempo enables Yusupov to cover h4. Suddenly the black attack has been neutralised and White's material advantage is the decisive factor. A tragedy for Kasparov, who had conducted the attack with such brilliant *élan*.

35 ♕f2   ♕g6
36 ♖e2   ♗c5
37 fxe4   fxe4
38 f5   ♕h5
39 ♖d2   ♖g5
40 ♕f4   ♕e8
41 ♘g4   1-0

11) Classical others

In this chapter we examine early deviations in the Classical System. These lines are ideal for players of either colour who are reluctant to enter into the minefield of the main lines. Although perhaps not theoretically challenging, they provide fertile territory for creating unusual situations where the players are thrown on their own resources.

Game 20 examines 6 ... ♗g4 and in games 21 and 22 we consider the moves 6 h3 and 5 ♘ge2. These lines wander in and out of fashion, but have the advantage of being quite threatening against stereotyped replies.

Game 20
Speelman - Fuller
Commonwealth Ch.
Hong Kong 1984

1	d4	♘f6
2	c4	g6
3	♘c3	♗g7
4	e4	d6
5	♘f3	0-0

6	♗e2	♗g4 *(183)*

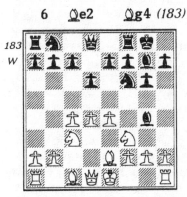

It looks slightly strange to offer the exchange of the light squared bishop, which is often Black's best piece in the King's Indian, but the intention is to play ... ♘fd7 and pressurise the d4-square. White must be careful not to play too automatically in response.

7 ♗e3

7 0-0 ♘fd7 is an alternative *(184)*:

a) 8 ♘e1 ♗xe2 9 ♘xe2 e5 10 d5 a5 11 ♘d3 ♘a6 12 ♘c3 f5 13 ♕e2 ♕h4 (White's play has been rather insipid and now Black provokes the weakening g3, after which he has no problems) 14 g3 ♕h3 15 f3 ♖f7 16 ♗d2 ♖af8

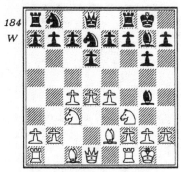

17 ♕g2 ♕h5= Nikcevic – Akopian, Niksic 1991.

b) 8 ♗e3 ♘c6 (This is taking provocation too far. Black's knight ends up horribly offside) 9 d5 ♗xf3 10 ♗xf3 ♘a5 11 ♗e2 b6 12 ♖c1 e5 13 dxe6 fxe6 14 f4 ♔h8 15 b3 ♘b7 16 ♗d3 c6 17 ♗b1 ♕e7 18 ♕d2± I Sokolov – Krause, Brocco 1989.

7 ... ♘fd7 *(185)*

Black continues methodically with his plan, but 7 ... ♘c6 also merits attention. The resultant positions are similar to those from the ♗e3 variations of the Pirc/Modern Defence: 8 d5 ♗xf3 9 ♗xf3 ♘e5 10 ♗e2 c6 11 0-0 ♕a5 12 ♖c1 (White has a space advantage, but Black has chances to snipe from the wings in genuine hypermodern fashion. An alternative method of trying to keep Black under control is with queenside play, a highly successful example of which was D Gurevich – Bonin, New York

Open 1990: 12 ♕b3 ♖fb8 13 a4 ♘ed7 14 ♕a3 ♕d8 15 a5 cxd5 16 cxd5 a6 17 f3 ♖c8 18 ♖fc1 b6 19 axb6 ♘xb6 20 ♘a2 ♘fd7 21 ♘b4 ♘e5 22 ♕a5 ♘ec4 23 ♗xc4 ♖xc4 24 ♘c6 ♖xc1+ 25 ♖xc1 1-0) 12 ... ♖fc8 13 f4 ♘ed7 14 ♔h1 a6 15 g4!? (Encouraging enormous complications) 15 ... cxd5 16 g5 ♘xe4 17 ♘xd5 ♖e8 18 ♗f3 e6∞ Kozul – Damljanovic, Sarajevo 1990.

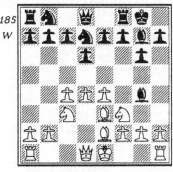

8 ♘g1

There are other ways to handle the white position:

a) 8 d5!? to cut Black's knight out of c6. Hort – Hug, Malta Ol. 1980 continued 8 ... ♘a6 9 ♘d4 ♗xe2 10 ♕xe2 ♘ac5 11 h4!? (11 0-0 would leave White with a slight, but tangible, edge but not 11 b4 as Black can hit back with 11 ... ♘a6 12 a3 c5!) 11 ... ♘f6 12 f3 ♕d7 13 g4 h5 14 g5 ♘h7 15 0-0-0 ♘a4 16 ♘xa4 ♕xa4 with a double-edged position as Black can counter White's central push of e4 – e5 with the queenside breaks ... c7 - c6 and ... b7 - b5.

b) 8 h3!?, intending a speedy thrust of the h-pawn, is an aggressive continuation which can easily catch Black unawares. The game Keene - Fuller, Sydney 1979 is an excellent example, and we follow this in full; 8 ... ♗xf3 9 ♗xf3 ♘c6 (9 ... e5 also failed to help the black cause in Keene - Avner, Orebro 1966: 10 d5 f5 11 h4 ♘f6 12 ♕c2 f4 13 ♗d2 c5?! {*Black's position is already dangerous, but this ill-advised advance deprives him of any possibility of counterplay, which might have come from the break ... c6 or by playing a knight to c5*} 14 g3! fxg3 15 fxg3 a6 16 ♕d3 ♘bd7 17 g4 b5 18 h5 bxc4 19 ♕e2! {*There is no rush to recapture on c4. The pawn temporarily blocks Black's own countermeasures*} 19 ... ♖f7 20 hxg6 hxg6 21 g5 ♘h7 22 ♗g4 ♘df8 23 ♕xc4 and White won easily) 10 ♘e2 *(186)*
(It is important to protect the d4 square against ... e5 and ... ♘d4, which would be played even if it involved a pawn sacrifice) 10 ... e5 (10 ... e6 as in Keene - Reefschlager, Hannover 1976 also fails to furnish sufficient counterplay) 11 d5 ♘e7 12 h4! (A thematic advance) 12

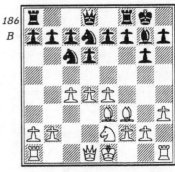

186
B

... f5 13 h5 (Now 13 ... ♘f6 is possible, as is 13 ... fxe4 14 ♗xe4 ♘f6. But in the former case 14 ♘c3 is good, while in the latter 15 ♘g3 is clearly better for White. Alternatively, if 13 ... fxe4 14 ♗xe4 ♘f5 then 15 ♕d3 is strong. It is important for White, in all of these lines, to maintain a resolute piece blockade on the e4-square. This blockade stifles Black's king's bishop and provides a springboard for White's kingside attack) 13 ... f4 14 ♗d2 ♘f6 (If 14 ... g5 15 ♗g4! at once) 15 hxg6 hxg6 (It looks aesthetic to recapture with the pawn, but 15 ... ♘xg6 is more resilient and gives Black more space in which to manoeuvre) 16 g3! *(187)*
(The fatal rupture. White's king's bishop is fighting to reach the h3 - c8 diagonal, after which Black's resistance will be broken) 16 ... g5 17 gxf4 gxf4 (17 ... exf4 18 ♘d4! gives White the

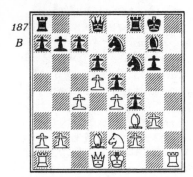

crushing threat of ♘e6.
Black has no time for tactics down the long dark-
squared diagonal) 18 ♘c3
(Threatening ♗g4. Black
tries to stop this, but his
solution only exacerbates
matters) 18 ... ♕d7 19 ♗g2!
(This wins. Black has no
light-squared defence to
♗h3) 19 ... c6 20 ♗h3 ♕c7 21
♗e6+ ♖f7 22 ♕f3 b5 23 cxb5
cxd5 24 exd5 ♖e8 25 ♕g2
♘c8 26 ♘e4 ♘xe4 27 ♕xe4
♕b7 28 ♕g6 ♖xe6 29 ♕h7+
♔f8 30 dxe6 ♖f6 31 0-0-0
♘e7 32 ♖dg1 ♘f5 33 ♕h8+
1-0.

c) 8 h4!? is a fairly blunt
declaration of intent which
provoked Black into over-
reacting in Kishnev - Hug,
Gelsenkirchen 1991: 8 ... c5
9 d5 b5?! 10 cxb5 a6 11 ♕d2
axb5 12 ♗xb5 ♗xf3 13 gxf3
♕a5 14 ♗h6 ♘e5 15 ♖h3 and
Black had little to show
for his pawn investment.

    8   **...**   **♗xe2**
    9   **♘gxe2**   **e5**

9 ... c5 appears to be

weaker. After 10 0-0 Black
has two choices *(188)*:

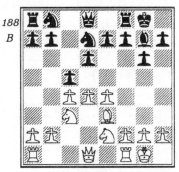

a) 10 ... cxd4 leads to a
Maroczy Bind structure,
e.g. 11 ♘xd4 ♘c6 12 ♖c1 a6
13 ♘b3 ♖c8 14 ♕e2 ♘ce5 15
♘d2 f5 (Weakening, but it
generates reasonable counterplay for Black) 16 exf5
gxf5 17 ♘d5 ♘g6 18 ♗g5
♖f7±/= Thorsteins - Bra-
ga, Thessaloniki Ol. 1988.

b) 10 ... ♘c6 11 d5 ♘a5 12
b3 and Black has problems
making the thematic ... b7 -
b5 break, e.g. 12 ... a6 13 ♖b1
♕b8 14 a4 e5 15 ♕d3 and
White can open the queen-
side with b3 - b4. If Black
fails to try the b5-break,
then White can gain space
on the kingside with f4.

    10   **d5**

Speelman diverges from
Kasparov's treatment ag-
ainst Vukic from Banja
Luka 1979. There, the future
World Champion played 10
0-0 a5 11 ♕d2 ♘c6 12 f3
exd4 13 ♘xd4 ♘c5 14 ♖ad1
and now 14 ... ♘xd4 15 ♗xd4

♗xd4 16 ♕xd4 f6 would have left White with a territorial advantage but perhaps only a slight plus.

Speelman prefers to immediately defuse the central tension.

10 ... f5 (189)

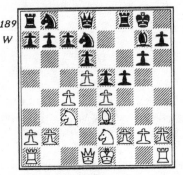

189
W

11 exf5

This appears to be a strong move. Previous theory gives 11 f3 ♗h6 as equal, but although Black has activated his dark-squared bishop, by playing ♗f2, White may still be better if he holds the e4-square and advances on the queenside.

Capturing the bishop (after 11 f3 ♗h6) is incorrect: 12 ♗xh6 ♕h4+ 13 ♘g3 ♕xh6 14 0-0 f4 15 ♘h1 ♘f6 16 b4 ♘a6 17 ♘b5 g5 18 ♘f2 ♕g7 19 a3 h5 20 h3 ♕d7 21 ♖c1 ♖f7∓ van Wely - Timmerman, Dieren 1988. Black's kingside build-up proved to be the most relevant factor in the position.

11 ... gxf5

12 f4 ♕e7

The immediate 12 ... exf4 seems more annoying. If White captures with the bishop 13 ♗xf4 then 13 ... ♕h4+ and if 14 g3 then 14 ... ♕h3 stops from from castling. White's best is to play 13 ♘xf4 and to answer 13 ... ♖e8 with 14 ♕d2 and the threat of ♘e6 allows White the necessary time to escape from the e-file.

13 0-0 exf4

A better plan might be 13 ... e4 which, although giving up the d4-square without gaining the crucial e5 outpost in compensation, leaves Black possibilities of ... ♘c5 - d3.

14 ♗d4!

Eliminating Black's king's bishop.

14 ... ♗xd4+

If 14 ... ♘e5 then 15 ♘xf4 seems strong, e.g. 15 ... ♘xc4 16 ♗xg7 ♕xg7 17 ♘e6 ♕f6 18 ♘xf8 ♘e3 19 ♕d3 ♘xf1 20 ♘e6 and White wins. It is important to notice how e6 is weakened by the early commitment and eventual exchange of the light-squared bishops.

15 ♕xd4 ♕e3+ (190)

Black decides to force the exchange of queens and so lessen the force of White's attack before he can bring up more artillery.

16 ♕xe3 fxe3

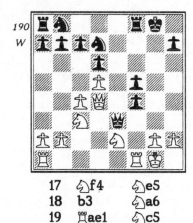

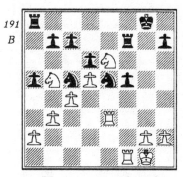

17	♘f4	♘e5
18	b3	♘a6
19	♖ae1	♘c5

An interesting position. The strong points on e5 and c5 appear to balance White's knight entrenched at f4 and eyeing e6. However, White stands better as f5 is potentially weak and Speelman has a weak square (e6) to aim at deep in the heart of the black position.

20	♖xe3	♖f7
21	♘b5	a5

After this Black is lost. He had a chance to make things difficult for his opponent with 21 ... ♘e4! answering 22 ♘e6 with 22 ... c6 and 22 ♘bd4 with 22 ... ♘g4 and if 23 ♖e2 ♘c3 24 ♖c2 ♘e4, and White has problems constructively avoiding a repetition.

22 ♘e6! *(191)*

White now builds up a winning advantage with some neat tactical possibilities.

22	...	♘xe6
23	dxe6	♖g7

If 23 ... ♖e7 24 ♖xf5 and ♖e6 is not possible because of the knight fork.

24	c5	♘g4
25	♖e2	♖e7

To prevent 26 e7. 25 ... ♘e5 loses the d-pawn whilst 25 ... ♖e8 allows 26 cxd6 cxd6 27 ♘xd6 ♖8e7 28 ♘xf5.

26 ♘xc7

26 ♖xf5 also wins but the text is extremely efficient and leads to a very picturesque finish.

26	...	♖xc7
27	cxd6	♖c5
28	d7	♖e5
29	e7	1-0

Game 21
Kavalek – Kasparov
Bugojno 1982

1	c4	g6
2	♘c3	♗g7
3	d4	♘f6
4	e4	d6
5	♘f3	0-0

6 h3 *(192)*

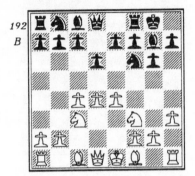

Larsen used to be quite keen on 6 ♗e3, with the intention of playing the endgame after 6 ... e5 7 dxe5 dxe5 8 ♕xd8 ♖xd8 9 ♘d5, but this method of play has fallen out of favour. Black should not be disturbed by it, e.g. 9 ... ♖d7 10 ♘xf6+ ♗xf6 11 c5 ♘c6 12 ♗b5 ♖d8 13 ♗xc6 bxc6 14 ♘d2 ♖b8 15 0-0-0 ♗e6= Rivas - Lukin, Leningrad 1984.

6 ... e5

6 ... c5 is another way for Black to attack the white centre. 7 d5 e6 8 ♗d3 reaches a position which often arises when White plays an early ♗d3. Some possiblities:

a) 8 ... ♘a6 and now:

a1) 9 0-0 e5 (Obviously losing a tempo, but the position is blocked and so this is not a vital consideration. Also, the white set-up of ♘f3 and ♗d3 is not ideal) 10 a3 h6 11 ♖b1 ♘h7 12 ♘h2 f5 13 f4 exf4 14 ♗xf4 g5 15 ♗d2 f4∞ Khalifman - Damljanovic, Bled 1991.

a2) 9 ♗g5 h6 10 ♗e3 ♘c7 11 ♕d2 exd5 12 cxd5 ♔h7 13 a4 b6?! (This manoeuvre, which is rather slow, is rarely a good idea in Benoni structure positions. More to the point is 13 ... a6, planning a quick ... ♖b8 and ... b5) 14 0-0 ♗a6 15 ♗f4 ♗xd3 16 ♕xd3 ♘h5 17 ♗h2 f5 18 ♖fe1± Bareev - Damljanovic, Novi Sad Ol. 1990.

b) 8 ... exd5 9 exd5 (9 cxd5 transposes into the Modern Benoni) 9 ... ♖e8+ 10 ♗e3 with the further possibilities *(193)*:

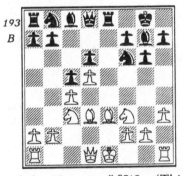

b1) 10 ... ♗f5!? (This looks like a beginner's move, but the coming ... ♘e4 will soon straighten out Black's structure. Nevertheless, the long-term weakening of the kingside may be more relevant) 11 ♗xf5 gxf5 12 0-0 ♘e4 13 ♘xe4 fxe4 14 ♘d2 ♘d7 15

♔g4± Hubner - Shirov, Manila Izt. 1990.

b2) 10 ... ♘h5 11 0-0 ♘d7 12 g4 ♘hf6 13 ♘b5 h5 14 ♘xd6 ♖xe3 15 fxe3 ♕c7 16 g5 ♕xd6 17 gxf6 ♕g3+ 18 ♔h1 ♕xh3+ 19 ♘h2∞ Shirov - Cramling, Ter Apel 1991.

b3) 10 ... ♗h6 is well met by 11 0-0! ♗xe3 12 fxe3 ♖xe3?! 13 ♕d2 and White generates an enormous attack.

7   d5

7 dxe5 dxe5 8 ♕xd8 ♖xd8 is okay if White's ambitions stretch no further than a draw, but should not cause Black problems. A couple of recent examples should suffice:

a) 9 ♗g5 ♘bd7 10 0-0-0 ♖f8 11 ♗e3 b6 12 ♘d5 ♘xd5 13 cxd5 ♗b7 14 ♗b5 ♘f6 15 ♘d2 c6! (A neat tactic completely freeing Black's game) 16 dxc6 ♗xc6 17 ♗xc6 ♖ac8 18 ♔b1 ♖xc6 19 ♖c1 ♖fc8 20 a4 ♗f8 21 ♖xc6 ♖xc6 22 ♖c1= Piket - Nijboer, Dutch Ch. 1990.

b) 9 ♘d5 ♘a6 10 ♗g5 ♖d6 11 ♗xf6 ♗xf6 12 b4 c6 13 ♘xf6+ ♖xf6 14 a3 c5 15 b5 ♘c7 (The black e-pawn is not loose due to ... ♖e6) 16 ♗e2 ♖e6 17 0-0-0 ♖e8 18 a4 f6 19 a5 ♗e6= Larsen - Hellers, Esbjerg 1988.

7   ...   ♘a6

The alternative deployment of the knight with 7 ... ♘bd7 is also playable. We now follow the game Piket - Nunn, Wijk aan Zee 1990: 8 ♗e3 ♘c5 9 ♘d2 a5 10 g4 (Very double-edged. A more restrained approach is 10 a3 ♘e8 11 b4 axb4 12 axb4 ♖xa1 13 ♕xa1 ♘a6 14 ♕a3 f5 15 ♘b3 b6 16 ♗e2 ♖f7 17 ♘b5 ♘f6 18 exf5 gxf5 19 ♘a7 ♗b7 20 ♘c6 ♕f8 21 0-0∞ Kaidanov - Watson, Budapest 1989) 10 ... ♘e8 11 ♕c2 f5 (Piket has himself been on the black side of this variation. In Larsen - Piket, Lugano 1989, the continuation was 11 ... ♔h8 12 ♗e2 f5. It looks more natural to play 11 ... f5 immediately) 12 gxf5 gxf5 13 ♖g1 f4 14 ♗xc5 dxc5 15 ♘f3 ♔h8 16 0-0-0 ♖a6 *(194)*

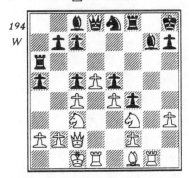

(An imaginative way to air-lift the rook to the zone of real action. It might appear that it was White who enjoyed more prospects on the king's wing but in fact his h-pawn is weak and Nunn exploits the fact to create useful squares for his pieces) 17 ♘b5 ♕e7 18 ♕c3 ♖h6 19 h4 (If 19 ♕xa5 then Black has the cunning device 19 ... ♖a6, switching back to the original flank, followed by ... ♖xa2) 19 ... b6 20 ♗d3 ♗f6 21 ♗c2 ♘d6 22 ♘a7 ♗d7 (Of course, the white h-pawn is immune to capture since the black pawn on e5 would hang) 23 ♖g2 ♖g8 24 ♖xg8+ ♔xg8 25 a3 ♖g6 (Preparing a powerful penetration with White's f- and h-pawns as targets) 26 ♖h1 ♖g2 27 ♕e1 ♕g7 28 ♗d3 ♕g4 *(195)* (The prelude to the forthcoming queen sacrifice which won the brilliancy prize. White had evidently been relying on the next move to fend off the black attack but Nunn had seen further)

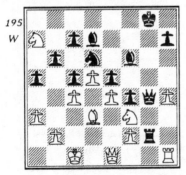

195
W

29 ♗f1 ♕xf3 30 ♗xg2 ♕xg2 31 ♖g1 f3 32 ♘b5 ♘xb5 33 ♖xg2+ fxg2 34 cxb5 (The best defence is 34 ♕g1 when Black could of course simply play 34 ... ♘d4 with

three minor pieces for the queen. More incisive, however, would be 34 ... ♗h3 35 cxb5 a4 followed by manoeuvring the black bishop to the a4-square and an advance of the black king to capture White's h-pawn when Black's two connected passed pawns will ultimately triumph) 34 ... ♗xb5 35 ♕g1 ♗f1 36 ♕h2 ♗xh4 37 ♕xh4 g1♕ 38 ♕d8+ ♔g7 39 ♕xc7+ ♔h6 40 ♕xb6+ ♔h5 41 b4 ♗d3+ 42 ♔d2 ♕xf2+ 0-1.

8	♗e3	♘h5
9	♘h2	♕e8
10	♗e2 *(196)*	

196
B

10 ...   ♘f4

10 ... f5 11 exf5 ♘f4 12 0-0 (12 ♗xf4 exf4 13 fxg6 ♕xg6 gives Black clear counterplay for the pawn sacrifice. e.g. 14 ♔f1 ♘c5 15 ♖c1 {*This gets White into difficulties; 15 ♘f3 ♗d7∞ is better*} 15 ... ♗f5 16 ♘f3 ♗f6 17 ♔g1 ♔h8 18 ♔h2 ♖g8 19 ♖g1 ♕h6∓ Chernin - J Polgar. New Delhi 1990) 12 ... ♗xf5

13 ♖e1 ♕f7 *(197)*

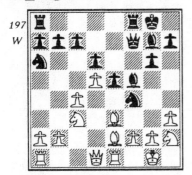

14 ♘f1 (14 a3 ♘c5 15 ♗xc5
dxc5 16 ♗f3 e4 17 ♘xe4
♗xb2 18 ♖b1 ♕g7 19 ♕d2
♗e5 20 ♖xb7 ♗xe4 21 ♖xe4
♘xh3+ 22 ♔h1 ♗f4 23 ♕b2
♕xb2 24 ♖xb2 ♘g5 25 ♖ee2
♗d6= Ibragimov – Kruppa,
Kherson 1991) 14 ... ♗xh3
(This, in combination with
Black's eighteenth move,
constitutes a remarkably
speculative sacrifice to rip
away the protection around
White's king. Nevertheless,
Kasparov criticised this
gambit, and advocated
instead the continuation 14
... ♘b4 15 ♘g3 ♘c2 16 ♗xf4
♘xf1 17 ♘xf5 gxf5 18 ♗d2
♘xg2 19 ♔xg2 ♔h8 which
he assesses as unclear) 15
gxh3 ♘xh3+ 16 ♔g2 ♘xf2 17
♕b1 e4 18 ♘g3 ♕d7 19 ♗xf2
♖xf2+ 20 ♔xf2 ♕h3 21 ♕xe4
♘c5 22 ♕e7 (Here Black
could play 22 ... ♗d4+ 23
♔f3 ♖f8+ which would
force White to give up the
queen) 22 ... ♗e5 23 ♖g1
♖f8+ (White could still

sacrifice the queen for the
black rook but he also has
the option of running to
safety with his king. He
chooses the latter) 24 ♔e1
♗xg3+ 25 ♔d2 ♖f7 and after
further adventures a draw
resulted, C Hansen – Ka-
sparov, Danish TV 1990.

11 ♗f3   f5 *(198)*

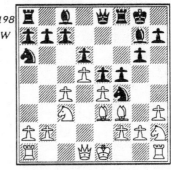

12 h4

White decides that he
cannot stomach the continued presence of the knight
on f4, and is prepared to
take risks in order to dis-
charge it.

A more conservative app-
roach is 12 0-0 b6 (12 ... ♘c5
13 ♕c2 a5 14 ♖ad1 b6 15 ♖fe1
♕f7∞ Guseinov – Kuzmin,
USSR 1991) and now:

a) 13 ♖e1 ♕f7 14 a3 ♘c5 15
♗xc5 bxc5 16 b4 cxb4 17
axb4 a6 18 ♕c2 ♘h5 19 b5±
Anastasian – Kuzmin, Bla-
goveshchensk 1988. Black's
play is rather passive in
this game.

b) 13 h4!? ♘c5 14 ♗xc5
bxc5 15 g3 ♘h3+ (This gives

rise to an interesting situation: the black knight is trapped on h3, but also generates serious pressure against the white kingside. However, the more telling feature of the position may be the white control over the e4-square) 16 ♔g2 h5 17 ♖h1 fxe4 18 ♘xe4 ♗f5 19 ♕e2 ♕d7 20 ♖hf1 ♖f7 21 ♘c3± Korchnoi - Romanishin, Tilburg 1985

12 ... ♕e7

12 ... c6?! seems to be a rather optimistic pawn sacrifice. Black certainly did not get much in the following example: 13 dxc6 bxc6 14 ♕xd6 ♖f6 15 ♕d1 ♗e6 16 ♗xf4 exf4 17 ♕e2 ♕f7 18 b3 ♕c7 19 0-0 ♖ff8 20 ♖ac1 ♖ae8 21 ♖fd1±/± Fauland - Timoshenko, Moscow GMA 1989.

13 g3 ♘b4!!

A typical Kasparov bolt from the blue.

14 ♕b3

14 0-0 was relatively best, to which Kasparov would have responded 14 ... g5, after which he evaluates the position favourably for Black.

14 ... ♘fd3+
15 ♔e2 f4
16 ♗d2 *(199)*

16 ... fxg3?!

Kasparov criticises this and prefers 16 ... ♘xf2! 17 ♔xf2 ♘d3+ 18 ♔g2 (18 ♔e2

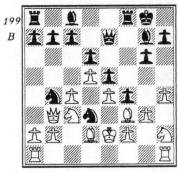

♘c5 19 ♕c2 fxg3 20 ♘f1 ♕f6) 18 ... fxg3 19 ♔xg3 ♖f4! when all of Black's pieces co-operate in the attack. He further gives the following analysis to prove the point: 20 ♘g4 h5! 21 ♘e3 (21 ♘f2 ♖xf3+ 22 ♔xf3 ♕f6+ 23 ♔e2 ♘xf2 mating) 21 ... ♗f6! 22 ♘g2 ♗xh4+ 23 ♖xh4 ♕g5+ or 20 ♗xf4 exf4+ 21 ♔g2 ♕xh4 22 ♖hf1 ♘h3+ 23 ♔h1 ♗xf1 24 ♖xf1 ♘f2+ 25 ♖xf2 ♕xf2 26 ♕xb7 ♖f8 and the black initiative should prove decisive.

17 fxg3 ♖xf3

In spite of this bombardment White should still be able to hang on for a draw with best play.

18 ♘xf3 ♗g4
19 ♖af1 ♖f8 *(200)*

A critical position where, although superficially life seem to be going splendidly for Black, a closer examination reveals that his knights have become somewhat bogged down in the opponent's camp.

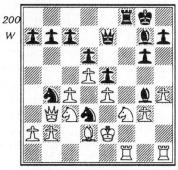

200
W

20 ♘d1?

Kavalek misses his only chance. 20 ♗e3! just holds as Black has nothing better than 20 ... ♘h6 (To weaken the f2-square) 21 ♗xh6 ♗xf3+ 22 ♖xf3 ♖xf3 23 ♔xf3 ♕f6+ 24 ♔g2 ♕f2+ 25 ♔h3 ♕f3 26 ♔h2! and a draw is the best Black can achieve.

20	...	♕f7!
21	♗e3	♗xf3+
22	♔d2	

Of course not 22 ♖xf3 ♕xf3+ and 23 ... ♕xh1.

22	...	♕d7
23	♖hg1	♕h3
24	a3	♗xe4
25	♖xf8+	♗xf8
26	axb4	♕h2+
27	♔c3	♘c1
	0-1	

28 ♗xc1 ♕xg1 is devastating.

Game 22
Keene - Blees
Amstelveen 1985

| 1 | d4 | ♘f6 |
| 2 | c4 | g6 |

| 3 | ♘c3 | ♗g7 |
| 4 | e4 | d6 *(201)* |

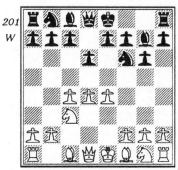

201
W

5 ♘ge2

5 ♗d3 is often used as a transpositional device to reach lines of the Saemisch or the Modern Benoni. Examples of its independent existence are 5 ... 0-0 6 ♘ge2 and now:

a) 6 ... ♘bd7 (Remarkably, this move is not mentioned in *ECO*) 7 ♗c2 a6 8 a4 e5 9 d5 a5 10 h3 ♘c5 11 ♗e3 ♘fd7 12 0-0 ♘a6 13 ♘a2 ♘dc5 14 ♕d2 ♗d7 15 ♕xa5 ♘xe4 (The position is highly unclear) 16 ♕e1 ♘f6 17 b4 ♘h5 18 f3 f5 19 ♖b1 b6 20 ♘ac3 ♗f6 21 ♕d2 ♗h4 22 f4 ♗f6 ½-½ Seirawan - Ivanchuk, Reykjavik 1991.

b) 6 ... c5 7 d5 e6 8 0-0 exd5 9 exd5 ♘g4 10 ♗c2 (10 h3 ♘e5 11 ♘g3 ♘bd7 12 f4 ♘xd3 13 ♕xd3 a6 14 a4 = Plachetka - Abramovic, Champigny sur Magne 1984) 10 ... ♕h4 11 ♗f4 ♘e5 12 b3 ♘a6 13 ♖c1 f5 14 ♕d2 ♕e7 15 ♖ce1 ♗d7 16 ♗g5 ♗f6 17

♗xf6 ♕xf6∞/= Olafsson - Kuzmin, Moscow Open 1989.

c) 6 ... e5 7 d5 ♘h5 (7 ... c6 8 ♘g3 ♘a6 9 0-0 ♗d7 10 h3 ♘c5 11 ♗e3 cxd5 12 cxd5= Kveinys – Kupreichik, Rimavska Sobota 1990) 8 0-0 f5 9 exf5 gxf5 10 f4 ♘d7 11 ♖b1 exf4 12 ♘xf4 ♘xf4 13 ♗xf4 ♘e5= Byrne – Weinstein USA Ch. 1960/61.

d) 6 ... ♘c6 7 0-0 ♘d7 8 ♗e3 e5 9 d5 ♘d4 10 ♗xd4 exd4 11 ♘b5 ♘e5 12 ♘bxd4 c5 13 dxc6 bxc6 14 ♖c1 ♗a6 with sufficient play for the pawn.

    5   ...   0-0
    6   ♘g3   ♘c6

A provocative sortie. Another possibility is 6 ... e5 7 d5 *(202)* but it doesn't really throw down any serious challenge and White should be slightly better. Some examples:

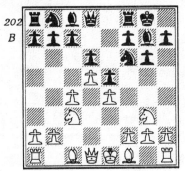

202
B

a) 7 ... c6 8 ♗e2 (8 h4 ♕b6 9 ♗e2 ♘a6, Keene – Lauri, Malta 1985 and now the amazingly unclear line

10 ♗e3!? ♕xb2 11 ♘a4 ♕a3 12 ♗c1 ♕b4+ 13 ♗d2 ♕a3 14 ♘f5! gxf5 15 ♖h3 ♕xh3 16 gxh3 ♘xe4 gives Black has compensation for the queen) 8 ... cxd5 (Black can delay the exchange but this is not going to alter the basic features of the position, e.g. 8 ... a6 9 ♗g5 h6 10 ♗e3 cxd5 11 cxd5 ♘bd7 12 0-0 b5 13 a3 ♘b6 14 b3 ♘fd7 15 ♕c2 ♗b7± Novikov – S Ivanov, Tuzla 1989. Black has misplayed the position and is left without a constructive plan - there is no way to take the initiative on the queenside, and ... f5 is going to be very difficult to achieve) 9 cxd5:

a1) 9 ... ♘a6 10 0-0 ♘c7 11 a4 a6 12 ♖b1 ♘d7 13 ♗f4 ♘e5 14 ♕d2 h5 15 f3 Novikov – Gufeld, Tbilisi 1988. This Benoni-type position is dynamically equal.

a2) 9 ... ♘bd7 10 ♗e3 a6 11 a4 h5 12 ♘f1 ♘c5 13 ♘d2 ♘g4 14 ♗xc5 dxc5 15 ♘c4 b6 16 a5 b5 17 ♘b6 ♖a7 18 d6 ♘f6 19 ♕d3 ♗e6 20 0-0 ♕b8 21 f4 exf4 22 e5 ♘d7 23 ♘xd7 ♖xd7 24 ♕e4 ♗f5 25 ♕c6 ♕c8 26 ♕xc8 ♖xc8 27 ♘d5 ♗xe5 28 ♘e7+ ♖xe7 29 dxe7 ♗xb2 30 ♖ae1 0-1 Rodriguez – Vogt, Thessaloniki Ol. 1988

b) 7 ... a5 8 ♗e2 ♘a6 9 h4! *(203)* (This advance of the h-

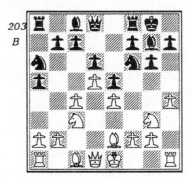

203
B

pawn is a trademark of the ♘ge2 systems. White hopes to weaken Black's kingside structure in order to make counterplay on that wing more difficult to achieve) 9 ... c6 10 h5 cxd5 11 cxd5 ♘c5 12 ♗g5 a4 13 ♕d2 ♕a5 14 f3 ♗d7 15 ♔f2 b5 16 b4 axb3 17 axb3 ♕b6 18 ♗e3 b4 19 ♘a4 ♗xa4 20 bxa4 ♗h6 21 ♖hb1∞ Novikov – J Polgar, Oberena 1991.

c) 7 ... ♘bd7 8 ♗e2 a5 9 h4 h5 10 ♗g5 ♘c5 11 ♗xh5 gxh5 12 ♘xh5 with compensation for the material.

7	d5	♘e5
8	♗e2	c6
9	f4	♘ed7
10	♗e3	h5

Considerably more combative than 10 ... cxd5 11 exd5 a5 12 0-0 ♘c5 13 f5 ♗d7 14 ♕d2, Keene – Jassem, Dubai 1984. Black is completely passive and can only watch as White prepares to advance.

11 h3

Alternatively, 11 ♗f3 ♘b6!? 12 b3 ♘fxd5 (An adventurous plan, but Black's last move would not make much sense unless he plays this) 13 ♘xd5 cxd5 14 exd5 ♗xa1 15 ♕xa1 f5 16 ♘e2∞ Nabill – Khait, Moscow 1991. As is nearly always the case with such combinations, Black has acquired an extra exchange, but has paid a heavy price with the exposure of the dark squares on the kingside - a weakness from which he will suffer for the rest of the middlegame.

11 ... ♘c5 (204)

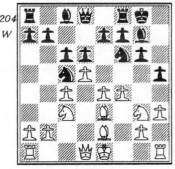

204
W

12 ♗f3

Inviting complications. The sensible course is 12 ♗xc5 dxc5 13 e5 with a solid plus for White.

12	...	♕b6
13	♖b1	

Avoiding the hideous trap 13 ♕d2? ♕xb2! 14 ♕xb2 ♘d3+.

13	...	♕b4
14	e5	dxe5
15	a3	♕a5

15 ... ♛xc4? 16 ♗e2 wins a piece.

16	fxe5	♘fd7
17	0-0	♘xe5
18	♗xh5	

The justification of White's play. If 18 ... gxh5 19 ♘xh5 and White's forces pour into the kingside attack while Black's queen is cut off on the far extremity of the board. Note that White could not play b4 on move 17 or 18 since ... ♛xa3 attacks the knight on c3. Remarkably, the white bishop now remains *en prise* on h5 for a further 12 moves.

18	...	♘xc4

More resistance was offered by 18 ... ♘cd3, cutting out the fork possibility of b4.

19	♗d4 *(205)*	

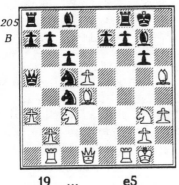

19	...	e5
20	b4	

Now this works.

20	...	♛xa3

The only chance was 20 ... exd4 21 bxa5 dxc3 though 22 ♗xg6! fxg6 23 ♖xf8+ ♗xf8 24 ♕c2 favours White.

21	♗xc5	♛xc3
22	♘e4	

What follows is slaughter.

22	...	♛a3
23	♖a1	♛b2
24	♖f2 *(206)*	

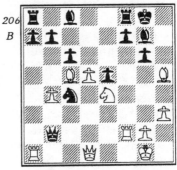

Finally forcing the win of a piece.

24	...	♘e3
25	♗xe3	♛xb4
26	♖a4	♛e7

Or 26 ... ♛b5 27 ♘c3.

27	♗c5	♛d8
28	♗xf8	♗xf8
29	dxc6	♛b6
30	♗xg6	

At last.

30	...	fxg6
31	♛d5+	♚h8
32	♘f6	1-0

12) Saemisch Panno

The Saemisch, named after Fritz Saemisch, a German grandmaster who once defeated Capablanca, came to prominence in the 1920s. It is the most directly vigorous attack at White's disposal against the King's Indian Defence and at the same time it can also be used as a purely positional weapon. Thus White's pawn at f3 can be regarded either as the anchor for a general kingside pawn storm with g4, h4 and h5, usually combined with queenside castling, or as a means of strengthening White's centre prior to a positional struggle in which White will attempt to use his big centre to constrict Black's game.

In the Saemisch Panno, Black maintains the option between the traditional Panno-style counter-attack on the queenside by ... a6 and ... ♖b8 or a more direct thrust in the centre with ... e5. White, in turn, has alternative strategies at his disposal; he can go vigorously for a kingside attack, castling long and advancing the h-pawn early; or he can choose a more sedate positional line based on maintaining his strong pawn centre.

Play in the Saemisch Panno is complex, and further practical tests are required to establish the best procedure for both sides.

Game 23
Kasparov – Spassky
Bugojno 1983

1	d4	♘f6
2	c4	g6
3	♘c3	♗g7
4	e4	d6
5	f3	♘c6
6	♗e3	a6

The King's Indian is a most unusual choice for Spassky, whose style tends to the classical in the opening, but doubtless the former World Champion wanted to revive memories of his win at Tilburg 1981 against Kasparov with this defence.

      7 ♘ge2   ♖b8
      8 ♕d2   0-0
      9 h4 *(207)*

      9 ...   b5!?

9 ... h5 is examined in the next game. Other possibilities are:

a) 9 ... e5 appears, on recent evidence, to be okay for Black. After 10 d5 ♘a5 11 ♘g3 we have the following:

a1) 11 ... c6?? is a completely unsound sacrifice, e.g. 12 b4 cxd5 13 cxd5 ♘c6 14 dxc6 bxc6 15 ♖b1+- Tataev – Zimmerman, Moscow 1991.

a2) 11 ... c5 12 ♖b1 (This is illogical. White should probably bite the bullet and play 12 h5, rather than the hesitant text) 12 ... b6 (12 ... h5 13 b4 cxb4 14 ♘a4 b5 15 cxb5 axb5 16 ♖xb4 ♗a6 17 ♘b2 ♘d7 18 a4 ♘c4 occurred in Chevallier – Dufrenoy, French League 1991. Black has tremendous counterplay here. If 14 ♖xb4 ♘d7!

△ ... ♘c5 and ... ♗f6. White is hampered by weak dark squares and exposed h4-pawn) 13 ♗e2 h5 14 b3 ♗d7 15 a4 ♘h7 16 ♗f2 ♗f6 17 ♘f1 ♗g7 18 b4 ♘b7 19 b5 axb5 20 axb5 Portisch – Nijboer, Wijk aan Zee 1990. This is a sticky position where White isn't really going anywhere.

b) 9 ... ♖e8 is too slow. The following material all looks good for White:

b1) 10 h5 b5 11 hxg6 (11 g4 b4 12 ♘d5 e5 13 hxg6 fxg6 14 ♗h6 ♗h8 15 ♗g5 exd4 16 0-0-0± Christiansen – J Watson, USA 1984) 11 ... hxg6 12 0-0-0 e5 13 d5 ♘a5 14 ♘g3 b4 15 ♘b1 c6 16 ♗h6 ♗h8 17 b3 cxd5 18 cxd5 ♘b7 19 ♗c4 ♘c5 20 ♗g5 ♗g7 21 ♗h6 ♗h8 22 ♖h2 a5 23 ♖dh1 a4 24 ♗g5 ♗g7 25 ♗h6 ♗h8 26 ♘f5 ♗xf5 27 exf5 axb3 28 axb3 ♕c8 29 ♔b2 e4 30 fxg6 fxg6 31 ♗e3 ♘h5+ 32 ♗d4 ♘d3+ 33 ♔c2 ♗xd4 34 ♕g5 ♘df4 35 ♖xh5 ♘xh5 36 ♕xg6+ ♘g7 37 fxe4 ♖f8 38 ♕xd6 ♖f2+ 39 ♔d3 ♗c5 40 ♕g6 ♕e8 41 d6+ 1-0 Elsness – Wibe, Gjovik 1991.

b2) 10 ♗h6 ♗h8 11 h5 e5 12 d5 ♘d4 13 hxg6 fxg6 14 ♗e3 c5 15 dxc6 ♘xc6 16 ♘d5 ♗e6 17 ♗b6 ♕d7 18 0-0-0 ♖bc8 19 ♔b1 ♕f7 20 ♕h6 ♘d7 21 ♗e3 ♖b8 22 ♘ec3 ♖ec8 23 ♗g5 b6 24 ♘e3 ♘d4 25 ♘cd5 ♗xd5 26 ♘xd5 ♘c6 27 c5 ♘xc5 28 ♗c4 ♘e6 29

♘e7+ ♘xe7 30 ♗xe6 ♕xe6 31
♕xh7+ ♔f8 32 ♗xe7+ ♔e8 33
♖xd6 ♕xe7 34 ♕g8+ ♕f8 35
♕e6+ 1-0 Murey - W Watson, Montpellier 1985.

10 h5 *(208)*

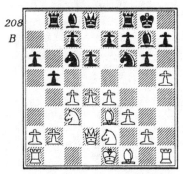

10 ... bxc4

a) 10 ... ♖e8?! transposes to 9 ... ♖e8 10 h5 b5. A good rule of thumb for the Saemisch is that ... ♖e8 is too slow when White is trying to deliver mate with h4 and h5. The waste of time involved in the rook move is too much of a luxury.

b) 10 ... ♘a5 11 ♘g3! e5 12 hxg6 fxg6 13 dxe5 dxe5 14 cxb5 axb5 15 ♘xb5 c6 16 ♘d6 ♗e6 17 ♖d1 ♗xa2 18 b4± Petursson - Brendel, Reykjavik Open 1990.

c) 10 ... e5 11 d5 ♘a5 12 ♘g3 bxc4 (12 ... c6 13 cxb5 cxd5 14 exd5 axb5 15 b4 ♘c4 16 ♗xc4 bxc4 17 ♖b1 ♗f5 18 ♘xf5 gxf5 19 h6± Razuvaev - Hracek, Stary Smokovec 1990) 13 0-0-0 ♘d7 14 hxg6 fxg6 15 ♘b1 ♕b5? (15 ... ♘b7±/±) 16 b4

cxb3 17 ♗xb5 c5, Timman - Kasparov, Bugojno 1982, and now 18 ♗e2!! is winning for White.

11 g4!? *(209)*

New at the time. 11 hxg6 fxg6 12 ♘f4 e6 13 ♗xc4 d5 (13 ... ♕e8!?∞) 14 ♗b3 ♖xb3 15 axb3 dxe4 16 0-0-0 exf3 17 gxf3 ♘e7!, Weih - Spassky, Bundesliga 1983, leads to wild, uncharted territory.

Another possibility is (11 hxg6 fxg6 12 ♘f4) 12 ... ♘a5 13 0-0-0 e6 14 g4 c6 15 g5 ♘h5 16 ♘xh5 gxh5 17 f4± Murey - Kljako, Cannes Open 1989.

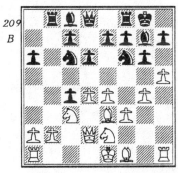

11 ... ♗xg4!?

Spassky, now a highly conservative player, reverts to a *sturm und drang* sacrifice, reminiscent of his youth.

If 11 ... ♘b4 12 ♘g3 ♘d3+ 13 ♗xd3 cxd3 14 g5 ♘d7 15 ♕h2±, or alternatively 11 ... ♖e8 12 0-0-0±.

12 fxg4 ♘xg4 *(210)*
13 0-0-0

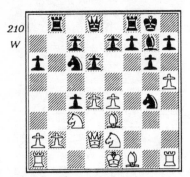

Not 13 hxg6? ♘xe3! 14 gxf7+ ♖xf7 15 ♕xe3 ♖xb2 16 0-0-0 ♕b8! with the attack, while 13 ♗g5 h6! 14 ♗h3 (14 ♗h4? g5 15 ♗g3 ♘b4!∓) 14 ... ♘b4! 15 ♘c1 hxg5 16 ♗xg4 f5 is unclear.

Instead, a complete mess arose from 13 ... ♘b4 14 ♘f4 ♗xd4 15 ♗xc4 ♗f2+ 16 ♔f1 ♘c2 17 ♘d1 ♘ce3+ 18 ♘xe3 ♘xe3+ 19 ♔xf2 ♘xc4 20 ♕c3 ♘e5 21 ♖ag1 c6 22 ♔f1 Hort - Miles, London 1983.

Lasker once said of Alekhine that he was like a child who would prefer to see the pieces dropped straight from the box randomly onto the board, such was his love of wild chaotic positions. This extract, which is virtually impossible to assess reminds us of that.

13 ... ♘xe3

13 ... e5 14 hxg6 (14 d5? ♘d4 15 ♘xd4? 15 ... exd4 16 ♗xd4 ♗h6-+; 15 hxg6 ♘f5!-+; 15 ♘g1!∞) 14 ... fxg6 15 ♗h3

(15 ♗g5!±) 15 ... ♘xe3 16 ♗e6+ ♔h8 17 ♕xe3±.

14 ♕xe3 e6

14 ... e5 15 d5 ♘d4 16 ♘xd4 exd4 17 ♖xd4 ♗xd4 18 ♕xd4±

15 hxg6 *(211)*

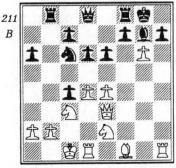

15 ... hxg6

Kasparov first thought that 15 ... fxg6 could be met by 16 ♕h3 and that in the variation 16 ... ♕g5+ 17 ♔b1 ♖xb2+ 18 ♔xb2 ♖b8+ 19 ♔a1 ♘b4 White extricated himself advantageously by 20 a3, but White must be content with a draw as 20 ... ♘c2+ 21 ♔a2 ♕a5 puts pressure on the king's position, e.g. 22 ♘d5!? (22 ♘b1 ♘b4+ =) 22 ... exd5 23 ♕c3 ♕a4!∞.

Therefore the theoretical verdict on this super-sharp line is that 15 ... fxg6 is level. The rest of this game is thematic and fascinating, but not theoretically accurate.

16 ♖d2?

16 ♘g1!±.

16 ... ♖e8?

16 ... ♕f6!∞.

17 ♘g1! d5

If 17 ... e5 18 d5 ♘d4 19 ♘h3!? planning ♖g2, ♘g5 with attack.

18 ♘f3 a5

19 e5?!

Better was 19 ♖dh2!, e.g. 19 ... e5 20 ♖h7! exd4 21 ♖xg7+ ♔xg7 22 ♕h6+ ♔f6 23 ♘xd5+ winning.

19 ... ♘e7? *(212)*

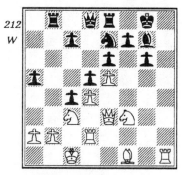

20 ♗h3?

20 ♘a4! eliminates Black's counterplay.

20 ... c5

21 dxc5?!

21 ♖dh2 cxd4 22 ♘xd4 ♕b6∞.

21 ... ♕c7

22 ♕f4 ♘c6!

22 ... ♕xc5? 23 ♘g5!+-.

23 ♖e1 d4!

24 ♖xd4

24 ♘xd4? ♘xe5∓.

24 ... ♘xd4 *(213)*

25 ♘xd4!

If 25 ♕xd4 ♕b7 26 ♕f2 (26 ♘e4 ♖ed8 27 ♕c3 ♖d3 wins for Black) 26 ... ♗h6+ 27 ♔b1 ♖ed8 28 ♖e2 ♕b4! 29

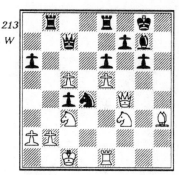

♕e1 ♕xc3!!-+.

25 ... ♕xc5

26 ♘f3 ♖ed8?

Time pressure. Better first 26 ... ♕b6! and on 27 ♖e2 ♖ed8.

27 ♘g5! ♕e7

If 27 ... ♖d7 28 ♘xe6! fxe6 29 ♕h2 ♗h8 30 ♕h6!+-.

28 ♕h4 ♖d3 *(214)*

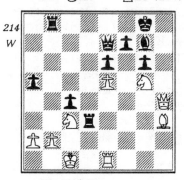

29 ♕h7+

29 ♘ce4! and after 29 ... c3 30 ♖f1!, which should win, e.g. 30 ... ♕b4 31 ♘f6+ ♔f8 32 ♘gh7+ ♔e7 33 ♘d5+ +-, or 30 ... ♖b6 31 ♕h7+ ♔f8 32 ♘xf7!

29 ... ♔f8

30 ♘xe6+ fxe6

31 ♖f1+ ♔e8

32	♕g8+	♘f8
33	♕xg6+	♔d8 *(215)*

0-1 (time)

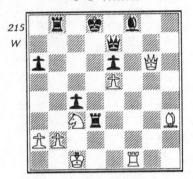

The position is no longer good for White, e.g. 34 ♗xe6 when White could survive after 34 ... ♖b6? 35 ♕g8! ♖xc3+ 36 ♔b1! ♖xb2+! 37 ♔xb2 ♕a3+ 38 ♔b1 ♖f3, but should lose to 34 ... ♕b4! 35 ♘a4 ♗e7! 36 ♕g8+ ♔c7 37 ♕h7 ♖bd8! An incredibly dramatic and complicated clash between the leading representatives of their generations.

Game 24
Qi Jing Xuan - Blackstock
China 1981

1	d4	♘f6
2	c4	g6
3	♘c3	♗g7
4	e4	d6
5	f3	♘c6
6	♘ge2	a6
7	♗e3	0-0
8	h4	h5
9	♕d2	♖b8
10	0-0-0	

The alternatives in this sharp position are:

a) 10 ♘c1 is a solid way for White to continue which has scored well in practice whether Black opts for the unorthodox plan of ... ♘e8 and ... f5 or the standard ... e5:

a1) 10 ... ♘e8 11 ♘b3 f5 12 0-0-0 ♘f6 13 exf5 (13 ♗e2±) 13 ... ♗xf5 *(216)*

(This is an interesting and unusual plan as both sides have sacrificed time) 14 ♗e2 (14 ♗h6 e5 15 ♗xg7 ♔xg7 16 dxe5 dxe5 17 ♕e3 ♕e7 18 ♗d3 ♗xd3 19 ♖xd3 ♖bd8 20 ♖hd1 ♖xd3 21 ♖xd3 e4 22 ♘xe4 ♘xe4 23 ♕xe4 ♕xe4 24 fxe4 ♘e5 25 ♖d5 ♖f1+ 26 ♔c2 ♘xc4 27 ♖d7+ ♔f6 28 ♖xc7 ♘e3+ 29 ♔d3 ♘xg2 30 ♘d2 ♖h1 31 ♖xb7 ♘xh4 32 ♖b6+ ♔e5 33 ♖xa6 ♖h3+ 34 ♔e2 g5 35 ♖h6 ♖h2+ 36 ♔d3 ♖h3+ 37 ♔e2 g4 38 ♖xh5+ ♔f4 39 ♘f1 g3 40 ♘xg3 ♔xg3 ½-½ Bykhovsky - Smirin, Beijing 1991) 14 ... b5 15 ♗h6 bxc4 16 ♗xc4+ d5 17

♗d3 ♖xb3 18 ♗xg7 ♔xg7 19 axb3 ♘xd4 20 ♕e3 ♘xb3+ 21 ♔c2 ♗xd3+ 22 ♖xd3 c5 23 ♖e1 ♖f7 24 ♕e5 ♘d4+ 25 ♔b1 ♘c6 26 ♕e6 ♘b4 27 ♖dd1 ♕a5 28 ♖e5 c4 29 ♖g5 ♘d3 30 ♘xd5 ♕a4 31 ♖d2 ♘xb2 32 ♔xb2 ♕b3+ 33 ♔c1 c3 34 ♖c2 ♕c4 35 ♖xc3 1-0. Novikov - Smirin, USSR Ch. 1990.

a2) 10 ... e5 11 d5 ♘d4 12 ♘b3 (12 ♘b3 c5 13 dxc6 bxc6 14 ♘xd4 exd4 15 ♗xd4 ♗e6 16 ♖c1 ♕a5 17 b3 occurred in Gheorghiu - Schaffner, Bern Open 1991 and Bischoff - Sznapik, Biel 1991. Black has insufficient compensation) 13 axb3 c5 *(217)*

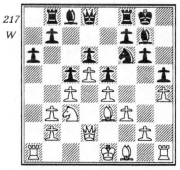

217
W

14 ♗e2 ♗d7 15 ♘d1 ♕b6 16 ♘f2 ♕xb3 17 ♘d3 ♖fc8 18 0-0 ♗e8 19 ♖a3 ♕b6 20 b4 ♘d7 21 bxc5 dxc5 22 ♗h6 ♗h8 23 f4 (White has excellent compensation for the pawn) 23 ... ♕d6 24 f5 b5 25 ♘f2 bxc4 26 ♗xc4 ♖b6 27 ♘h3 ♘f6 28 fxg6 fxg6 29 ♘g5 ♗b5 30 ♗xb5 ♖xb5 31 ♘e6 ♖b7 32 ♕g5

♔h7 33 ♖g3 ♘g4 34 ♗f8 1-0 Christiansen - Nunn, Bundesliga 1988.

b) 10 ♘d5 b5 11 cxb5 *(218)* is a typically unusual approach introduced into top-level tournament chess by the fertile brain of Yakov Murey:

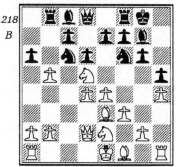

218
B

11 ... ♖xb5 12 ♘ef4 ♖b8 13 ♖c1 ♗d7 14 ♘xf6+ ♗xf6 15 ♘d5 ♗g7 16 ♗g5 ♖e8 17 ♖c4 ♕c8 18 b3 ♕b7 19 g4 ♗e6 20 gxh5 ♗xd5 21 exd5 ♘d8 22 ♕a5 e6 23 ♖xc7 ♕xd5 24 ♕xd5 exd5+ 25 ♔d1 ♘e6 26 ♖d7 ♖b4 27 ♗d2 ♖xd4 28 hxg6 fxg6 29 ♖g1 ♘f4 30 ♗xa6 ♗h6 31 ♖g4 ♖e3 32 ♖xd6 ♖xf3 33 ♖dxg6+ ♔h7 34 ♔c1 ♖xd2 35 ♖xh6+ ♔xh6 36 ♔xd2 d4 37 a4 ♔h5 38 ♖xf4 ♖xf4 39 a5 ♖xh4 40 ♗e2+ ♔g5 41 a6 ♖h7 42 b4 d3 43 ♗xd3 ♖h2+ 44 ♗e2 1-0 Murey - Nunn, London 1983. Black may do better with 11 ... axb5 12 ♘xf6+ ♗xf6 13 ♖c1 ♗d7 14 g4 hxg4 15 h5 e5 Nikolic - Cvorovic, Yugoslav Ch. 1991.

10 ... b5 *(219)*

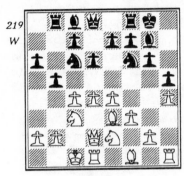

11 ♘f4!?

An unusual move which tries to exploit the fact that Black has moves the h-pawn from h7.

Other possibilities in this sharp position:

a) 11 ♗h6 is dealt with in a later game, Mestel - Gufeld.

b) 11 ♘d5 (This is identical to the later game, Lautier - Piket, except that Black has the move ... ♖e8 instead of ... ♖b8. This is an indication of how fiendishly difficult the transpositional subtleties are in the Saemisch Panno and that the slightest nuance in the order in which Black plays one of his three key moves, ... a6, ... ♖b8 and ... ♖e8 may make a world of difference to the assessment of the position) 11 ... bxc4 12 g4 (12 ♗h6 ♘xd5 13 exd5 ♘b4 14 ♘c3 c6 15 g4 ♕a5 16 ♗xc4 cxd5 17 ♗b3 ♗e6 18 ♗xg7 ♔xg7 19 ♔b1

♖h8 20 ♖dg1 ♘c6 21 ♗a4 ♘a7 22 ♖h2 ♖b4 23 ♗b3 ♘c6 24 ♘e2 ♕b6 25 gxh5 ♗f5+ 26 ♔a1 ♖xb3 27 axb3 ♘b4 28 ♘c3 ♘c2+ 29 ♔a2 ♖b8 0-1 Petursson - Nunn, Lucerne Ol. 1982) 12 ... ♘xd5 13 exd5 ♘b4 14 ♘c3 c6 15 ♗xc4 cxd5 16 ♗b3 ♕b6 17 ♖hg1 ♗e6 18 gxh5 ♗f5 19 ♖g5 ♗h6 20 ♖dg1 ♗xg5 21 ♖xg5 e6 22 hxg6 fxg6 23 h5 ♖b7 24 ♕g2 ♖g7 25 h6 ♖b7 26 ♖xf5 exf5 27 ♕xg6+ ♔h8 28 ♕g2 f4 29 ♗g1 ♖g8 0-1 Kuligowski - Nunn, Wijk aan Zee 1983.

11 ... e5

Apart from this immediate central advance, Black can also consider:

a) 11 ... ♗d7 12 cxb5 axb5 13 ♘xb5 e5 14 dxe5 ♘xe5 15 ♘c3 ♕c8 16 b3 ♖e8 17 ♘d3 ♘c6 18 ♘f4 ♘e5 19 ♘d3 ♘c6 20 ♘f4 ½-½ Timman - Nunn, Tilburg 1982 but Ree later improved against Nunn at Wijk aan Zee 1983 with 12 g4! ♘xd4 13 ♗xd4 e5 14 ♗xe5 dxe5 15 g5 b4 16 ♘cd5 ♘xd5 17 ♘xd5 ♗e6 18 ♕e3±.

b) 11 ... bxc4 12 ♗xc4 e5 (This was originally recommend by me {*RK, Modern Chess Theory 1981*} and tried out by John Nunn against Vaganian: 13 dxe5 (13 ♘xg6 exd4 14 ♗xd4 ♖b4!) 13 ... ♘xe5 14 ♗b3 ♕e8 15 ♔b1 a5 16 ♕c2 ♗d7 17 ♗d4 ♔h7 18 ♘d3 (18 ♘h3∞ Nunn) 18 ... ♘c6 19 ♗xf6

♗xf6 20 ♘d5 ♗g7 21 ♗a4 ♘e5 22 ♗xd7 ♕xd7 23 ♖d2 ♖b7 24 ♘e3 ♘xd3 25 ♕xd3 ♖fb8 26 ♘c4 ♖b4 27 ♖c1 ♕e7 28 g3 a4 29 ♖cc2 a3 30 ♘xa3 ♕e5 31 ♘c4 ♕xg3 32 ♕f1 ♕xh4 33 a3 ♖b3 34 ♔a2 ♕f6 35 f4 ♕e6 36 ♕e2 f5 37 exf5 ♕xf5 38 ♕e7 ♖3b7 39 ♖f2 ♔g8 40 ♕e2 ♕d5 41 ♔b1 ♕f5 42 ♔a2 ♖b5 43 ♕e7 ♗f8 44 ♕e3 ♕f7 45 ♕d3 ♖d5 46 ♕f1 ♖f5 47 ♖f3 ♗g7 48 ♖cf2 ♖f8 49 b3 g5 50 ♘e3 ♖xf4 51 ♖xf4 gxf4 52 ♘g2 f3 53 ♘h4 ♕d5 54 ♕c4 ♕xc4 55 bxc4 ♖f4 56 ♘xf3 ♖xc4 57 ♘g5 ♖g4 58 ♘e6 h4 59 ♘xc7 h3 0-1 Vaganian - Nunn, Skelleftea World Cup 1989.

c) 11 ... b4 12 ♘cd5 is possible when the exchange of the black knight on f6 will ease White's plan of pushing through with g4. Meanwhile, Black has lost the chance of opening lines on the queenside against White's king.

| 11 | ... | e5 |
| 12 | dxe5 | ♘xe5 *(220)* |

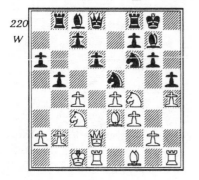

13 c5!

White cannot risk capturing the pawn on b5, e.g. 13 cxb5 axb5 14 ♘xb5 ♗a6 when Black's rook, bishop and knight are co-ordinated to attack b2, and the extra pawn is certainly not worth this.

13	...	b4
14	♘cd5	♘xd5
15	♘xd5	♗e6
16	♔b1	♕d7

White has strengthened his position and left Black with a number of weak points to defend. Black could improve on the text with 16 ... c6 17 ♘b6 (17 ♘xb4? ♕a5) 17 ... d5 18 exd5 cxd5 19 ♗d4 when the situation is not so clear.

| 17 | ♗e2 | ♕a4 |

This does not help Black's cause. Better is 17 ... f5, which would at least help to confuse the situation.

| 18 | b3 | ♕a5 |

If 18 ... ♕a3 19 ♕c2 with the threat of ♗c1.

19 ♕c2

Aparently just defending the c5-pawn, but White's real intention is to exchange queens and achieve a very favourable ending, where Black has numerous vulnerable pawns.

| 19 | ... | ♖fe8 |

Black was afraid of f4 followed by ♘e7+ and ♘c6,

trapping Black's queen.

20	cxd6	cxd6
21	♕c7	♕xc7
22	♘xc7	♖e7
23	♘xa6	♖a8
24	♖xd6	f5
25	♗g5	♖ee8
26	♘c7	♗xb3
27	♘xa8	♗xa2+
28	♔xa2	♖xa8+
29	♖a6	1-0

Game 25
Beliavsky - Kasparov
Linares 1990

1	d4	♘f6
2	c4	g6
3	♘c3	♗g7
4	e4	d6
5	f3	0-0
6	♗e3	♘c6
7	♕d2	

With the white queen on d1 the manoeuvre ♘ge2 - c1 - b3 is too slow, viz. 7 ♘ge2 ♖b8 8 ♘c1 e5 9 ♘b3 exd4 10 ♘xd4 ♘h5! 11 ♗e2 ♘f4!∓ Ree - Keene, Caorle 1972.

7	...	a6
8	♘ge2	♖b8

8 ... ♗d7 9 ♘c1 ♖e8 10 ♘b3 ♕b8 11 ♗e2 b5 12 cxb5 axb5 13 ♗xb5 ♘a5 14 ♘xa5 ♗xb5 15 b4 c5 16 ♖b1, Quinteros - Planinc, Amsterdam 1973, 16 ... cxb4 17 ♖xb4 ♖xa5 18 a4 ♖c8∞.

9 ♘c1 (221)

This is the main alternative to the aggressive 9 h4. Other ways to play more conservatively are:

a) 9 a3 ♗d7 10 b4 b5 11 cxb5 axb5 12 d5 ♘e5 13 ♘d4 c6⊼.

b) 9 ♖b1 b5 10 cxb5 axb5 11 b4 e5 12 d5 ♘e7 13 g4 c6 with chances for both sides according to Kasparov.

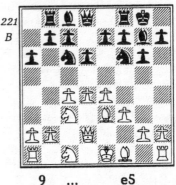

221
B

9	...	e5

There is a very interesting black plan here of recent provenance which looks time consuming but is justified by the fact that White wastes three moves to get his king's knight to b3. It is certainly worth considering: 9 ... ♘e8!? 10 ♘b3 f5 11 ♗e2 ♘f6 12 0-0 e5 13 d5 f4 14 ♗f2 ♘e7 15 c5 g5 16 ♘a4 g4 17 cxd6 cxd6 18 ♕a5 ♕e8 19 ♕c7 gxf3 20 ♗xf3 ♗g4 21 ♕xd6 ♗xf3 22 gxf3 ♘xe4 23 ♕e6+ ♔h8 24 fxe4 ♖f6 25 ♕h3 ♕g6+ 26 ♕g2 ♕h5 27 ♗g3 fxg3 28 hxg3 ♖g6 29 ♖f3 ♖g8 30 ♘c3 ♗h6 31 ♔f2 ♘c8 32 ♖h1 ♕g5 33 ♕h3 ♘d6 34 ♕h4 ♖c8 35 ♕xg5 ♗xg5 36 ♔e2 b5 37 ♔d3 ♘c4 38 ♖h2 ♔g8

39 ♘d1 ♖g7 40 ♖c2 ♖gc7 41
♘f2 a5 42 ♖f5 h6 43 ♘h3
♗e7 44 ♘d2 ♘xd2 45 ♖xc7
♖xc7 46 ♔xd2 ♗b4+ 47 ♔d3
♖g7 48 ♖f3 ♗e1 49 ♘f2
♗xf2 50 ♖xf2 ♖xg3+ 51 ♔e2
a4 52 ♖f5 ♖g2+ 53 ♔e3 ♖xb2
54 ♖xe5 ♖xa2 55 d6 ♖a3+ 56
♔d4 ♖a1 57 ♖xb5 a3 58 ♔e5
a2 59 ♖a5 ♔f7 60 ♖a7+ ♔f8
61 ♔e6 ♖e1 62 d7 ♖xe4+ 63
♔d5 1-0 Beliavsky - Smirin,
USSR Ch. 1990. The plan of
... ♘e8 and ... f5 is a Smirin
patent - see also the notes
to Qi - Blackstock.

10   ♘b3

The alternative is 10 d5
♘d4 and now *(222)*:

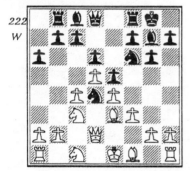

222
W

a) 11 ♘b3 ♘xb3 12 axb3 c5
13 b4 cxb4 14 ♘a4 b5 15
cxb5 axb5 16 ♕xb4 ♘e8 17
♘c3 ♗h6 18 ♗xh6 ♕h4+ with
adequate counterplay for
Black, Gheorghiu - Sich, Baden Baden 1987. White
should probably play on
the other side of the board
with 13 g4 h5 14 h3 ♘h7 15
0-0-0 h4 16 g5∞.

b) 11 ♘1e2 c5 12 dxc6 and

now:

b1) 12 ... ♘xc6! 13 ♖d1 ♗e6
14 ♘d5 b5 15 cxb5 axb5 16
♘xf6+ ♗xf6 Zsu Polgar -
Gufeld, Wellington 1988.
Black has adequate coun-
terplay.

b2) Also possible is 12 ...
bxc6 13 ♘xd4 exd4 14 ♗xd4
♕a5 15 ♖c1 ♗e6 16 ♗e2 ♖fd8
17 0-0 ♕b4 Wiedenkeller -
Gavric, Banja Luka 1987.

The attentive reader will
notice that these variations
are extraordinarily similar
to those in Qi - Blackstock.
The difference here is that
Black doesn't have the
weakness on h4 to work
with.

10   ...   exd4
11   ♘xd4 *(223)*

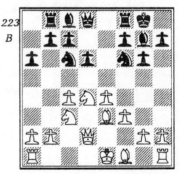

223
B

11   ...   ♘e5

The alternative here is 11
... ♘xd4 12 ♗xd4 and:

a) 12 ... c6 13 ♗e2 b5 14
0-0 ♗e6 15 b3 is considered
in 'b22' below.

b) 12 ... ♗e6 13 ♗e2:

b1) An interesting gambit
is 13 ... c5 14 ♗e3 b5 15 cxb5

axb5 16 ♘xb5 d5 17 ♗xc5
dxe4 18 ♗xf8 ♕xf8 19 ♕d6
exf3 20 ♕xf8+ ♔xf8 21 gxf3
♘d5 22 ♔f2 ♘f4 23 a4 ♗xb2
24 ♖ab1 ♗f6 25 h4 ♖e8 26
♗f1 ♖c8 27 ♔e3 ♘d5+ 28
♔d2 ♖d8 29 ♔e1 ♖a8 30 ♗h3
♗xh4+ 31 ♔f1 ♗xh3+ 32
♖xh3 ♖xa4 33 ♘d6 h5 34
♖h2 ♗e7 35 ♖d2 ♘e3+ 36
♔e2 ♗xd6 37 ♖xd6 ♘f5 38
♖d7 ♖f4 39 ♖bb7 ♘d4+ ½-½
Brenninkmeijer - Bosboom,
Dutch Ch. 1988.

b2) 13 ... c6 *(224)* and
now:

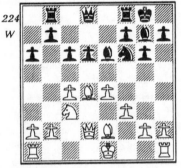

b21) 14 a4 d5 15 cxd5 cxd5
16 e5 ♘d7 17 f4 f6 18 exf6
♘xf6 19 ♖d1 ♕d7 20 0-0±
Beliavsky - Nunn, Reykjavik
1988.

b22) 14 0-0 b5 15 b3 bxc4
16 bxc4 ♕a5 (16 ... c5 17 ♗e3
♘d7 18 ♖ab1± Petursson -
Timoshenko, Moscow GMA
1989) 17 ♖ac1 ♖fd8 18 ♔h1
c5 19 ♗e3 ♕a3 20 ♖c2 ♘d7
21 f4= Hjartarson - Nunn,
Rotterdam 1989.

12 ♖d1

This doesn't allow Black

the possibility of ... c5 and
is therefore more accurate
than 12 ♗e2 c5 13 ♘c2 ♗e6
14 ♘a3 ♘c6 15 0-0 ♘d7 16
f4 ♘d4 17 ♗d3 b5∞ Beliav-
sky - Hjartarson, Reykjavik
1991.

It is interesting to note
that following their en-
counters against Nunn, Beliavsky stayed true to the
white side, but Hjartarson
was converted to the black
cause.

12 ... c6 *(225)*
Not 12 ... c5? 13 ♘b3.

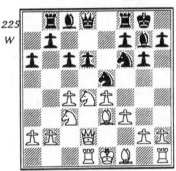

13 ♗e2 b5
14 cxb5

White's most consistent
course - all alternatives are
inferior: 14 b3?! ♕a5 15 0-0
b4 16 ♘b1 c5; 14 f4? b4! 15
fxe5 bxc3 16 ♕c2 ♘g4!; and
14 0-0?! c5 15 ♘b3 b4 16 ♘b1
♗e6 17 ♖c1 ♕c7.

14 ... axb5
15 b4

White should avoid 15
0-0 b4 16 ♘b1 d5∓ but has
two other choices here
which are worth considera-

tion:

a) 15 a3!? b4?! 16 axb4 🖢xb4 17 f4 c5 18 fxe5 cxd4 19 exf6 dxe3 20 👑xd6.

b) 15 b3!?

15 ... c5

Black has to play actively to stay in the game. Passive options to avoid are:

a) 15 ... 🖢d7?! 16 🖢c2 🖢e8 17 0-0 👑e7 18 🖢fe1 f5 19 f4 🖢g4 20 🖢xg4 fxg4 21 e5! Webb – Kondali, Corr 1983.

b) 15 ... 👑c7 16 0-0 🖢d7 17 🖢c1.

16 🖢c2

This is doubtless best if only because Beliavsky repeated it in a later game. Others:

a) 16 bxc5!? b4 17 🖢b1 dxc5 18 🖢b3 👑xd2+ 19 🖢1xd2=

b) 16 🖢b3!? sets a trap, but Black does not ned to fall into it, namely 16 ... cxb4 17 🖢xb5 🖢xe4? 18 fxe4 🖢xb5 19 🖢xb5 🖢f3+ 20 gxf3 🖢c3 21 0-0++-.

16 ... cxb4

17 🖢xb4 (*226*)

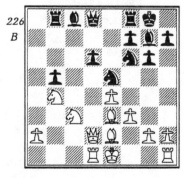

17 ... 🖢e6

Although this move bears the approval of the World Champion, one player was brash enough to seek to improve on it, and his efforts were rewarded with success: 17 ... 👑a5 18 🖢b1 🖢c4 19 🖢xc4 bxc4 20 👑xd6 🖢g4 21 🖢d2 🖢e5 22 👑d5 👑a7 23 fxg4 🖢xc3 24 👑g5 🖢xd2+ 25 👑xd2 🖢e8 26 👑f4 c3 27 🖢e2 👑d4 0-1 Xu Jun – Belotti, Novi Sad Ol 1990. Nevertheless, by replying to 17 ... 👑a5 with 18 🖢cd5 🖢e6 19 0-0 🖢xd5 20 🖢xd5 👑xd2 21 🖢xf6+ 🖢xf6 22 🖢xd2 White maintains an edge.

18 0-0

Risky for White is 18 🖢xb5?! 👑a5.

18 ... 👑a5

18 ... 🖢c4 19 🖢xc4 🖢xc4 20 🖢c6 loses material.

19 👑xd6

19 🖢cd5!?

19 ... 🖢c4

19 ... 🖢fd8? 20 🖢b6! is clearly better for White.

20 🖢xc4 bxc4

Not 20 ... 🖢xc4? 21 🖢c6 👑xc3 22 🖢d4 👑c2 23 🖢xf6 🖢xf1 24 🖢e7+ 🖢h8 25 👑e5+-.

21 🖢c6 👑xc3

22 🖢d4 🖢xe4!

23 🖢xc3 🖢xd6

24 🖢xg7 🖢xg7

25 🖢xb8 🖢f5

26 🖢d7 (*227*)

26 ... 🖢c8

It is barely credible that

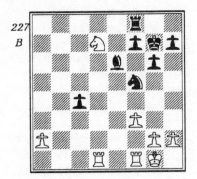

227
B

this position should be the starting point for a whole game. Nevertheless, this is true and it turns out that 26 ... ♖a8 is a prefectly adequate alternative: 27 ♘c5 ♖xa2 28 ♖f2 ♖a7 29 ♘xe6+ fxe6 30 ♖e2 ♔f6 31 ♖e4 ♖a6 32 ♖de1 ♖c6 33 ♔f2 c3 34 ♖c1 ♘e7 35 h4 ♘d5 36 g4 h6 37 f4 c2 38 ♔e1 h5 39 gxh5 gxh5 40 ♔d2 ♔f5 41 ♖e5+ ♔xf4 42 ♖xh5 ♘e3 43 ♖h8 ♖d6+ 44 ♔e2 ♖d1 45 ♖xc2 ♘xc2 46 ♔xd1 ♘e3+ 47 ♔d2 ♘f5 48 ♔d3 ♔g4 ½-½ Beliavsky - Loginov, USSR Team Ch. 1991.

27 ♘b6   ♖c6
28 ♖b1?!

Alternatively, 28 ♘a4! c3! 29 ♖d3 c2 30 ♖c3 ♖a6 31 ♘c5 ♖xa2 32 ♖c1 ♘d4= Kasparov.

28 ...   c3
29 ♖b4   ♗xa2
30 ♖c1   h5!=
31 ♔f2   c2
32 ♔e2   ♗e6
33 ♔d2   ♖d6+
34 ♔xc2?!

34 ♔e2 was equal.

34 ...   ♘e3+
35 ♔b2   ♘xg2
36 ♘c4 (228)

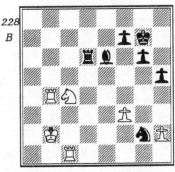

228
B

36 ...   ♖d3?

If Black wanted to keep winning chances alive he had to move his rook to a square which prevents the white knight entering play on e5, thus 36 ... ♖d5! 37 ♘b6 ♖d2+ 38 ♖c2 ♖xc2+ 39 ♔xc2 ♘e1+ 40 ♔d1 ♘xf3.

37 ♘e5   ♖e3
38 ♖e4   ♔f6
39 ♖xe3   ♘xe3
40 ♘d3   ♗d5
41 ♘e1   ½-½

Game 26
Lautier - Piket
Cannes 1990

1   d4   ♘f6
2   c4   g6
3   ♘c3   ♗g7
4   e4   d6
5   f3   0-0
6   ♗e3   ♘c6 (229)
7   ♘ge2

7 ♕d2 will clearly often

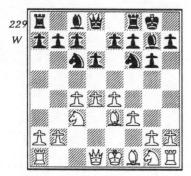

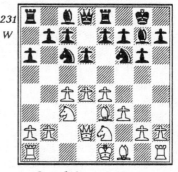

... a6 makes more sense than 7 ... ♖b8.

7	...	a6
8	♕d2	♖e8?! *(231)*

8 ... ♗d7 is much too slow for Black, e.g. 9 h4 h5 10 0-0-0 b5 11 ♗h6 ♔h7 12 ♗g5 bxc4 13 g4± Miles – Jadoul, Brussels 1986.

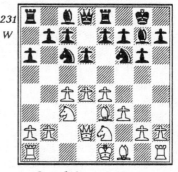

transpose following a quick ♘ge2, but it can also lead to independent play, e.g.

a) 7 ... ♖b8!? 8 0-0-0 0-0 9 h4 h5 10 ♗h6 ♗xh6 11 ♕xh6 e5 12 ♘ge2 b5 13 g4 bxc4 14 ♘g3 ♗xg4 15 ♗xc4∞ Lerner – W Watson, Moscow 1985.

b) 7 ... a6! 8 0-0-0!? b5! *(230)*

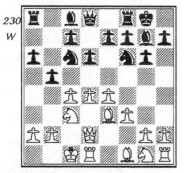

9 cxb5 axb5 10 ♗xb5 ♘a5 11 ♔b1 ♗a6 12 ♗xa6 ♖xa6 13 ♕d3 ♕a8 14 ♘ge2 ♖b8 15 ♗c1 e6 16 h4 d5 17 h5 ♘c4∓ Petursson – Gufeld, Hastings 1986/87. Black has a fantastic position.

As a response to 7 ♕d2, 7

9 h4

White has two other standard possibilities:

a) 9 ♘c1 e5 10 d5 ♘d4 11 ♘1e2 c5 12 dxc6 ♘xc6 13 ♘d5 b5 14 ♗b6 ♕d7 15 ♘c7 ♖b8 16 ♘xe8 ♕xe8 17 ♗e3 bxc4⚌ Beliavsky – Kasparov, Moscow 1981.

b) 9 0-0-0 b5 10 g4 ♖b8 11 h4 h5 12 ♘d5 e5 13 ♗g5 ♘xd4 14 ♘xd4 exd4 15 gxh5 c6 16 h6 ♗h8 17 h7+ ♔xh7 18 h5 *(232)*

18 ... cxd5 19 hxg6+ ♔g8 20 ♖xh8+ ♔xh8 21 ♕h2+ ♔g8 22 g7 ♘h7 23 ♗xd8 ♖xd8 24 ♗d3 ♔xg7 25 ♖g1+ ♔f8 26 ♕xh7 bxc4 27 ♖g8+ ♔e7 28 ♕h4+ 1-0 Puri – Larsen, Chicago Open 1989. This is a very brilliant and convin-

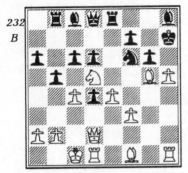

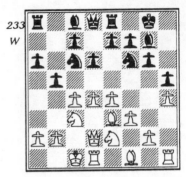

cing game. The plan of prefacing h4 with g4 makes 8 ... ♖e8 look like a waste of time.

9 ... h5

Given that White is lining up ♘d5, this is a further loss of time. 9 ... b5 is a better try, e.g. 10 h5 e5 11 hxg6 fxg6∞/± Dejkalo - Pedzich, Polish Ch. 1990.

10 0-0-0

10 ♘c1 e5 11 d5 ♘d4 12 ♘b3 c5 13 dxc6 bxc6 14 ♘xd4 exd4 15 ♗xd4 d5 16 cxd5 cxd5 17 e5∞ Nikolaev - Borisenko, Voronez 1991. This is an unnecessary deviation, since the text is strong for White.

10 ... b5 *(233)*

The scene has been set. This is one of the most typical variations, highly susceptible to intense openings analysis. Both sides castle on opposite wings and then the attack on the enemy king assumes far greater significance than any material considera-

tions.

11	♘d5	bxc4
12	♘xf6+	♗xf6
13	g4	hxg4
14	h5	g5

14 ... gxf3 would be excessively greedy. For his three pawns White would obtain a tremendous attack after 15 ♘f4 g5 16 ♘d5 following up with moves such as ♗xc4 and ♖dg1.

| 15 | ♗xg5 | e5 |

And here if 15 ... gxf3 White has the simple 16 ♗xf6 exf6 17 ♕h6 and ♖g1+.

16	♗xf6	♕xf6
17	fxg4	exd4
18	g5	♕f3
19	g6!!	*(234)*

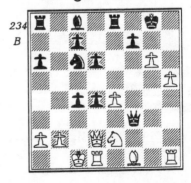

A quite unexpected yet fully correct and brilliant sacrifice to strip away the final vestiges of defence around the denuded black king. If Black snaps at the bait with 19 ... ♕xh1 White continues 20 ♕h6 with the following possibilities: 20 ... ♕f3 21 ♘f4 ♕e3+ 22 ♔b1 fxg6 (If 22 ... ♕xe4+ 23 ♗d3 wins) 23 ♕xg6+ ♔f8 24 ♕f6+ ♔g8 25 ♗xc4+ and wins. Alternatively, 20 ... fxg6 21 ♕xg6+ ♔f8 22 ♕f6+ ♔g8 23 ♘g3 ♕h2 24 bxc4+ ♗e6 and now either 25 ♗xe6+ or even 25 h6 and White triumphs.

| 19 | ... | fxg6 |
| 20 | ♘xd4 | |

The white rook on h1 is indirectly defended because of ♗xc4+.

20	...	♘xd4
21	♕xd4	♖xe4
22	♕d5+	♔g7
23	h6+	♔h7
24	♗g2	*(235)*

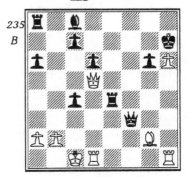

A further gambit in a game which is repiete with

brilliant points. Black cannot play 24 ... ♕xg2 since 25 ♕f7+ would force checkmate. The peculiar configuration of forces on the long diagonal means that White now wins material.

| 24 | ... | ♕f4+ |
| 25 | ♔b1 | c6 |

A necessary diversion so that Black can play ... ♗f5 without succumbing to the deadly ♕f7+.

26	♕xc6	♗f5
27	♔a1	♖a7
28	♖hf1	♕e5
29	♗xe4	♗xe4
30	♕xd6	♕xd6
31	♖xd6	♔xh6
32	♖c1	*(236)*

This ensures a win in the endgame. For example 32 ... ♖c7 33 ♖d4 ♗d3 34 ♖xd3 or 32 ... ♗xd3 33 b3!

32	...	♗f3
33	♖xc4	♔h5
34	♖f6	♖e7
35	b4	♗b7
36	♖f8	g5
37	♖h8+	♔g6
38	♖g8+	♔f6

39	♖c5	♖e4
40	♖b8	♖e7
41	♖f8+	♔g7
42	♖ff5	♖e1+
43	♔b2	♖e2+
44	♔b3	♖e3+
45	♔a4	♗f3
46	♖xg5+	♔f6
47	♖cf5+	♔e6
48	♖xf3	♖xf3
49	♖g6+	1-0

The conclusion to be drawn here is that Black may not have time for the luxury of 8 ... ♖e8 when White can simply play 0-0-0 and h4/g4. Black has got to get on with ... a6 and ... ♖b8 against this plan.

Game 27
Ostermeyer - Keene
Rotterdam 1984

1	d4	♘f6
2	c4	d6
3	♘c3	g6
4	e4	♗g7
5	f3	0-0
6	♗e3	♘c6
7	♘ge2	a6

7 ... ♖b8 8 ♕d2 ♖e8 (Black plays here in similar style to the main game, but this version should be worse for him as after the eventual opening of the f-file, his rook is misplaced) 9 ♖b1 a6 10 b4 b5 11 cxb5 axb5 12 d5 ♘e5 13 ♘d4 ♗d7 14 ♘cxb5 e6 15 dxe6 fxe6 16 ♗e2, Polugaevsky -

Gufeld, USSR Ch. 1975, 16 ... ♘xf3+! 17 gxf3 e5 18 0-0 exd4 19 ♘xd4∞. 19 ... d5?±, 19 ... ♖a8∞.

8 a3

Others are:

a) 8 ♖b1 b5 9 cxb5 axb5 10 d5 ♘e5 11 ♘d4 e6 12 dxe6 fxe6 13 ♘dxb5 ♘h5∞ Boleslavsky.

b) 8 d5 ♘e5 9 ♘g3 c6 10 a4 cxd5 11 cxd5 e6 12 ♗e2 exd5 13 exd5 ♖e8 14 ♕d2 ♕e7 15 ♔f2 h5 16 ♖he1 h4 17 ♘f1 ♘h5 18 ♔g1 h3 19 g4 ♘f6 20 ♗d4 ♕f8 21 ♘g3 ♘h7 22 g5 f6 23 f4 ♘g4 24 ♘ce4 ♗d7 25 gxf6 ♘gxf6 26 ♗f3 ♘xe4 27 ♖xe4 ♖xe4 28 ♗xe4 ♗xd4+ 29 ♕xd4 ♕xf4 30 ♖f1 ♕g4 31 ♕b6 ♘g5 32 ♗xg6 ♘f3+ 33 ♔h1 ♘d2 34 ♗f7+ ♔h7 35 ♗h5 ♕g5 36 ♖f7+ ♔g8 37 ♕g1 ♖c8 38 ♘e2 ♕xg1+ 39 ♔xg1 ♗e8 40 ♖f5 ♗xh5 41 ♖xh5 ♖c2 ½-½ Seirawan - Nunn, Brussels 1988. This game was always about equal.

c) 8 ♘c1 e5 9 d5 ♘d4 10 ♘b3 ♘xb3 11 ♕xb3 c5 12 dxc6 bxc6 13 0-0-0 ♕e7 14 ♕b6 (14 c5 is clearly worth consideration as a possible improvement on Timman's play, e.g. 14 ... d5 15 exd5 ♘xd5 16 ♘xd5 cxd5 17 ♕xd5 ♗e6 18 ♕e4 ♖ab8 19 ♖d2 ♖fd8 20 ♖xd8+ ♕xd8 21 ♗e2 ♕a5 22 ♗c4 ♗f5 23 ♕d5 e4 24 ♕xf7+ ♔h8 25 ♗b3 exf3 26 gxf3 ♕b5 27 ♖d1 ♕e2 28

♗d2 ♕xf3 {*If 28 ... ♕d3 29 ♕xg7+ ♔xg7 30 ♕c3+ △ ♖xd3. White stands well despite being the exchange behind*} 29 ♖e1 ♕c6 30 ♗c3 ♗xc3 31 bxc3 ♗e4 32 ♖xe4 1-0 van der Sterren - Cifuentes, Wijk aan Zee 1991) 14 ... ♗b7 15 g4 ♖ab8 (15 ... ♖fb8!∞) 16 h4 ♖fc8 17 h5 ♘d5 *(237)*

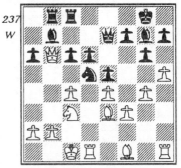

237
W

18 exd5 cxd5 19 ♖xd5 (19 cxd5±) 19 ... ♗xd5 20 ♘xd5 ♕e6 21 ♕a7 ♖a8 22 ♕b7 ♖ab8 23 ♕a7 ♖a8 24 ♕b7 ½-½ Timman - Kasparov, Moscow 1981.

8   ...   ♗d7

Also possible is 8 ... e5 9 d5 ♘e7 10 c5 ♘e8 11 ♕d2 f5 12 0-0-0 dxc5 13 ♗xc5 ♘d6 14 ♔b1 b6 15 ♗g1 ♗d7 16 ♘c1 ♕e8 17 ♗d3 ♕b8 18 ♗c2 a5 19 a4 ♕e8 20 ♕e2 ♔h8 21 h3 ♕f7 22 ♗h2 ♖ae8∞/= Agdestein - Nunn, Naestved 1985.

9   b4   b5
10 cxb5   axb5
11 d5

Of course not 11 ♘xb5

♘xb4 12 ♘xc7 ♗a4.

11   ...   ♘a7!? *(238)*

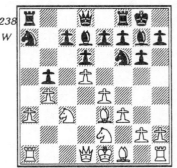

238
W

An unorthodox move. Normally, Black would play 11 ... ♘e5.

12 ♘d4   e6
13 dxe6

13 ♘dxb5 ♘xb5 14 ♘xb5 exd5 15 cxd5 ♖e8 with a terrible attack.

13   ...   fxe6
14 ♖c1

Or 14 ♘dxb5 ♘xb5 15 ♘xb5 ♘xe4 16 fxe4 ♖xf1+ 17 ♖xf1 ♕h4+.

14   ...   ♘h5
15 ♕d2   ♗e5
16 ♘ce2   c6

Defending b5 and thus preparing the manoeuvre ... ♘c8 - b6 - c4. If immediately 16 ... ♘c8! it is difficult to see a clear reply to 17 ♗g5.

17 g4   ♘f6
18 g5   ♘h5
19 f4

German players appear to be heavily influenced by their great chess teacher, Dr. Siegbert Tarrasch. It was Tarrasch who conducted a theoretical dispute with Nimzowitsch over the relative value of the initiative plus domination of space (even with weaknesses) as against a cramped position without weakness, but with counter-attacking potential. Nimzowitsch, of course, supported the latter view, and when I (RK) have played against a German, it seems that the ghost of Dr. Tarrasch descends and persuades them to push forward with their pawns over the entire board. The present game is a good case in point.

| | 19 | ... | ♗g7 |
| | 20 | ♕a2 | ♔h8 *(239)* |

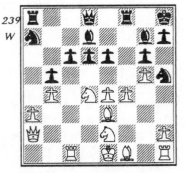

239
W

Black could have won a pawn with 20 ... ♗xd4, but the dark-squared bishop is so valuable, that to give it up for anything less than a rook does not come into question.

| | 21 | ♘xe6 | ♗xe6 |

| | 22 | ♕xe6 | ♘c8! |

A mysterious retreat, leaving a second pawn en prise. The move seemed to have a mesmeric effect on White who had probably only been expecting 22 ... ♖e8 23 ♕b3 ♖xe4 24 ♗g2 ♖e7 25 0-0.

| | 23 | ♖xc6 | ♖xa3 |
| | 24 | ♔f2 | ♖e8 |

24 ... ♖xe3 25 ♔xe3 ♘xf4 only leads to perpetual check.

| | 25 | ♕g4 | ♘e7 |

The rest is easy for Black as White's overextended structure collapses into ruins.

	26	♖c2	♘d5
	27	exd5	♖axe3
	28	♘g3	♕b6
	29	♔g2	♕d4
	30	♖g1	♘xg3
	31	hxg3	♕e4+
		0-1	

Game 28
Mestel - Gufeld
Hastings 1986

	1	c4	g6
	2	e4	♗g7
	3	d4	d6
	4	♘c3	♘f6
	5	f3	0-0
	6	♗g5	♘c6

6 ... c5 7 d5 e6 8 ♕d2 exd5 9 cxd5 transposes to a Modern Benoni Defence.

| | 7 | ♘ge2 | a6 |
| | 8 | ♕d2 | ♖b8 |

9 h4 h5 *(240)*

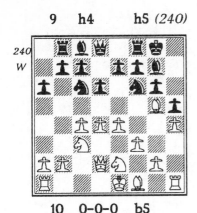

10 0-0-0 b5
11 ♗h6

11 ♕e3 ♘a5 12 ♘f4 ♘h7
(Black loses time, but it is
worthwhile to exchange
the useful queen's bishop)
13 e5 ♘xg5 14 hxg5 c5 15
dxc5 ♗xe5 16 ♘fd5 ♖e8
(Rather too risky. The simple 16 ... ♗e6 guarantees
Black an easy life. Gufeld
runs an enormous risk in
the pursuit of a fascinating
idea) 17 g4 hxg4 18 cxd6
exd6 19 f4? (Much stronger
is the immediate 19 ♘e4,
but the text also appears
to be devastating) 19 ... ♗g7
20 ♘e4 ♗c6 21 ♘ef6+ ♔f8
22 ♘h7+ ♔g8 23 ♘df6+ *(241)*
(Black appears to be in a
vice but turns the tables
with a brilliant queen sacrifice, which wins easily)
23 ... ♕xf6 24 ♘xf6+ ♗xf6
25 ♕a3 ♗g7 26 ♖h2 ♘xc4 27
♗xc4 bxc4 28 ♕g3 ♗f3 29
♖xd6 c3 30 ♖f6 cxb2+ 31
♖xb2 ♖ad8 32 f5 ♖d1+ 33
♔c2 ♖c8+ 34 ♔b3 ♖d3+ 35

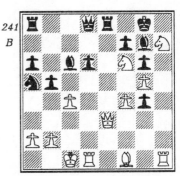

♔b4 ♘f8+ 0-1 Kotronias
- Gufeld, Athens 1985.

11 ... e5

11 ... bxc4 worked out
badly for Black in Salov -
Khalifman, USSR Ch. 1987:
12 g4 ♘b4 13 ♘g3 c5 14
♗xg7 ♔xg7 15 d5 ♖h8 16
♗xc4 ♗d7 17 g5 ♘h7 18 a3
♕c7 19 f4 ♖hc8 20 f5 ♕b6 21
♖hf1 a5 22 ♖f2 ♘a6 23 ♖df1
♖f8 24 f6+ exf6 25 gxf6+
♔h8 26 e5 1-0.

12 ♗xg7 ♔xg7

It is a key point that in
this position Black invites
the exchange on g7 rather
than luring White's queen
to h6 with ... ♗xh6. On h6
the queen is dangerously
close to the black king and
might do some real damage.

13 dxe5 dxe5!

Mestel had actually been
on the black side of this
position once himself. He
had played 13 ... ♘xe5 *(242)*
and suffered catastrophic
defeat:
14 cxb5 axb5 15 ♘f4 b4 16
♘cd5 ♘xd5 17 ♘xd5 c5 18

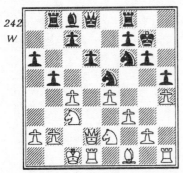

242
W

f4 ♘c6 19 f5 ♘e5 20 g4
♘xg4 21 ♗e2 ♘f2 22 f6+
♔h7 23 ♗xh5 ♘xh1 24 ♖xh1
♖e8 25 ♕g5 ♖e5 26 ♘e7 ♕g8
27 ♗d1 ♔h8 28 ♕h6+ 1-0.
Rivas - Mestel, Marbella
1982. Not unnaturally, Mestel wanted to repeat this
but Gufeld comes up with
an important improvement.

14 ♕g5?!

Better is 14 ♕e3 ♕e7 15
♘d5 ♘xd5 16 cxd5 ♘a5 17
♔b1 ♘c4 18 ♕c3∞ Rapp -
Krug, Bundesliga 1989.

14	...	♕e7
15	♘d5	♘xd5
16	exd5	f6
17	♕d2	♖d8
18	g4	bxc4 (243)

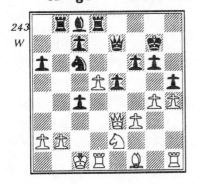

243
W

19 ♘c3

After 19 gxh5 Gufeld pro-
poses the following remarkable variation: 19 ... ♘b4
20 ♘c3 ♗f5 21 ♗xc4 (Not 21
hxg6? ♖xd5! intending ...
♘a2) 21 ... ♕c5 22 ♕e2 ♗d3!!
23 ♗xd3 ♘xa2+ 24 ♔c2
♖xb2+ 25 ♔xb2 ♕xc3+ 26
♔xa2 ♖b8 27 ♕d2 ♕b3+ 28
♔a1 ♕a3+ 29 ♕a2 ♕c3+-+.

19	...	hxg4
20	♗xc4	

Gufeld gives 20 h5 g5 21
♕c2 ♘d4 22 ♕g6+ ♔f8 23 d6
cxd6 24 h6 ♗f5 25 h7 ♗xg6
26 h8/♕+ ♔f7 27 ♗xc4+ d5
28 ♗xd5+ ♖xd5 29 ♕xb8
♘e2+ 30 ♘xe2 ♕c5+ mating.

20	...	♘d4
21	fxg4	♗xg4
22	♖df1	♖b4 (244)

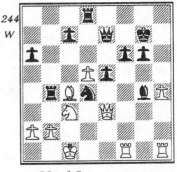

244
W

23 h5

A clear admission of de-
feat, but otherwise ... ♖db8.

23	...	♖xc4
24	hxg6	♖xc3+
25	♕xc3	♘e2+
26	♔c2	♘xc3
27	♖h7+	♔xg6
	0-1	

13) Saemisch Orthodox

For many years the lines of the Saemisch Orthodox were more or less shunned by theory in favour of the Saemisch Panno. White was thought to get a tremendous space advantage and that was that. Gligoric, in particular, suffered a lot of discouraging reverses with this line as Black against players such as Portisch and Petrosian.

Recently, however, Kasparov has shown that virtually every line of the Orthodox Saemisch is perfectly valid for Black. Indeed, 6 ... e5 may be Black's best bet as Kasparov has shown in the games Karpov - Kasparov, Reggio Emilia 1992 and Timman - Kasparov, Linares 1992. In recommending which of these the reader should play we should point out that although in the former Black's chances are theoretically adequate his queenside does come under a lot of pressure. In the second line, represented by Timman - Kasparov Black's position is solid, yet aggressive and with the players invariably castling on opposite wings it leads to the kind of carniverous slugfest which a red-blooded King's Indian devotee should normally relish.

Game 29
Ivanchuk - Zapata
Novi Sad Ol 1990

1	d4	♘f6
2	c4	g6
3	♘c3	♗g7
4	e4	0-0
5	♗e3	d6
6	f3	e5
7	♘ge2	*(245)*

This is a relatively unusual move. White maintains the option of castling queenside or central play while simultaneously avoiding the well charted paths of 7 d5, considered in the following games.

7 ... c6

This is the standard move. Also seen are:

a) 7 ... ♘bd7 8 ♕d2 a6

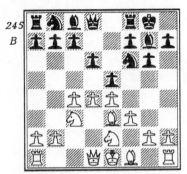

9 d5 h5 (9 ... ♘h5!? 10 g4 ♘f4 11 ♘xf4 exf4 12 ♗xf4 ♘e5 13 ♗e2 f5 14 ♗g5 doesn't give Black enough for the pawn) 10 ♘c1 ♘h7 11 ♘b3 f5 12 exf5 gxf5∞ Kurz-Paehtz, Bundesliga 1990.

b) 7 ... ♘c6 is just plain weak, e.g. 8 d5 ♘e7 9 c5 ♘e8 10 ♕d2 f5 11 0-0-0 ♘f6 12 h3 a6 13 g4 f4 14 ♗f2 g5 15 ♔b1 ♔f7 16 h4 h6 17 ♘c1 ♗d7 18 ♘d3 ♖g8 19 ♖c1± Lev - Frick, Bern Zonal Zt. 1990.

8   ♕d2 (246)

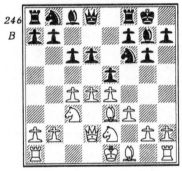

8   ...   ♘bd7

a) 8 ... a6 weakens Black's queenside: 9 dxe5 dxe5 10 ♕xd8 ♖xd8 11 ♘a4 ♘bd7 12

0-0-0 b5 13 ♘b6± Schlosser - Werner, Bundesliga 1990.

b) 8 ... exd4 9 ♘xd4 ♖e8 (9 ... d5 10 cxd5 cxd5 11 e5 ♘e8 12 f4±) 10 ♗e2 d5 11 exd5 cxd5 12 0-0 takes us back to a position which is analysed in depth in the chapter on 7 ♗e3, and may be Black's best course. An interesting alternative for White is 10 0-0-0 here.

9   0-0-0

White can also play the immediate 9 d5, aiming to recapture on d5 with pieces to leave the d-pawn exposed: 9 ... cxd5 10 ♘xd5 ♘xd5 11 ♕xd5 ♘b6 12 ♕b5 ♗h6 13 ♗f2 ♗e6 14 ♘c3 (247)

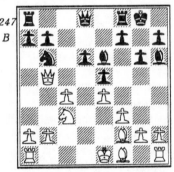

14 ... ♕c7 15 b3 ♘d7 16 ♕b4 a6 17 ♖d1 ♖fc8 18 ♘d5 ♗xd5 19 ♖xd5 b5 20 a4 bxa4 21 ♕xd6 ♕b7 22 bxa4 ♗f8 23 ♕xd7 ♕b4+ 24 ♖d2 ♖d8 25 ♕xd8 ♖xd8 26 ♗e3 ♗c5 27 ♗g5 ♖d6 28 ♔e2 ♖xd2+ 0-1 Deep Thought - Wahls, Hannover 1991.

9   ...   a6 (248)

9 ... ♕a5 appears less

promising as the queen is exposed on a5: 10 ♔b1! b5 11 cxb5 (11 ♘c1 is also good for White) 11 ... cxb5 12 ♘d5 ♕xd2 13 ♘e7+ ♔h8 14 ♖xd2 ♗b7 15 ♘c3 a6 16 ♗e2 b4 17 ♘a4 ♖fe8 18 dxe5 ♘xe4 19 exd6 ♘xd2+ 20 ♗xd2 ♗c6 21 ♗d1 ♗b5 22 ♗xb4 a5 23 ♗a3 ♗e5 24 ♗b3 ♖a6 25 ♖d1 ♔g7 26 ♘d5 ♗xd6 27 ♘ac3 ♗xa3 28 ♘xb5 ♖e2 29 ♘xa3 ♖a7 30 ♘b5 ♖b7 31 ♘d6 ♖b8 32 ♘f4 ♖e7 33 ♗xf7 ♘c5 34 ♗c4 ♘a4 35 ♗b5 ♘c5 36 a4 1-0 Murey - Gallagher, London (Haringey) 1988. It is important for White to play 11 cxb5 before ♘d5 because if 11 ♘d5 ♘xd5 12 ♕xa5 ♘xe3, followed by ... ♘xc4, and Black has interesting compensation for the sacrificed queen.

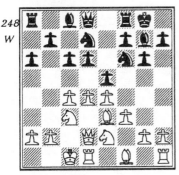

10 ♔b1

This good prophylactic move, which improves White's king's position and allows the knight to drop back to c1, is by far the best. It avoids unnecessary

adventures such as:

a) 10 h4 b5 11 h5 ♕a5 12 ♗h6 ♗xh6 (12 ... b4 13 ♘b1 ♕xa2 14 ♘g3 exd4 15 ♘f5?! *{Beliavsky gives 15 ♗xg7 ♔xg7 16 ♕xd4 as winning for White, whilst 15 ... ♘c5 fails to 16 ♕h6}* 15 ... ♘c5∞ Murey - Apicella, Paris 1991) 13 ♕xh6 b4 14 ♘b1 ♕xa2 15 ♘g3 ♘b6? 16 c5 ♘c4 17 ♖d2± Beliavsky - Timman, Linares 1991.

b) 10 g4 b5 11 c5 ♕a5 12 cxd6 ♘e8 13 dxe5 b4 14 f4 bxc3 15 ♕xc3 ♕xc3+ Lev - Dannevig, Gausdal 1991.

10 ... b5
11 ♘c1 *(249)*

This is a very subtle move that prevents Black from playing his queen to a5 with any degree of ease.

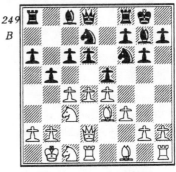

11 ... ♗b7

Black doesn't have an easy route to equality in this position. For example:

a) 11 ... ♕e7 12 dxe5 dxe5 13 ♕d6 ♕xd6 14 ♖xd6 ♗b7 15 ♗e2±. White has a favourable endgame.

b) 11 ... bxc4 12 dxe5
♘xe5 13 ♕xd6 ♕xd6 14 ♖xd6
♗e6 15 ♗e2± Wiedenkeller –
Mortensen, Pohja 1985.

12 dxe5   dxe5

12 ... ♘xe5 13 ♕xd6 bxc4
14 ♕xe5 ♘d5 15 ♕xg7+ ♔xg7
16 exd5 cxd5 17 ♗xc4 dxc4
18 ♖xd8 ♖axd8 19 ♖d1 f6 20
♘1e2 ♖xd1+ 21 ♘xd1 g5 22
♗d4 ♔g6 23 ♘e3 ♖e8 24
♔c2 ♗c8 25 ♘g3 ♗e6 26 ♘e4
f5 27 ♘d6 ♖e7 28 g3 h6 29
♔c3 ♖c7 30 ♗e5 ♖d7 31 f4
1–0 Granda – Barbero, Buenos Aires 1991.

13 ♘b3   ♕c7
14 ♖c1   ♕b8 *(250)*

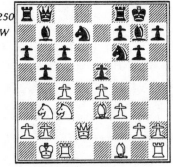

15 ♕f2!

This is a particularly fine
move by Ivanchuk. The re-
mainder of this game is a
thematic exploitation of
Black's dark square wea-
knesses.

15	...	♖e8
16	g3	♘f8
17	♗e2	♘e6
18	♖hd1	♗f8
19	a3	♖d8
20	♖xd8	♕xd8

21	♘a5	♕e7
22	f4	♘d8
23	f5	♘d7
24	c5	♗c8
25	g4	♘b8
26	♖f1	♗d7
27	h4	♗e8 *(251)*

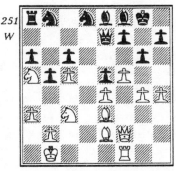

Black is being strangled
on both sides of the board.

28	♗d1	♘b7
29	♘xb7	♕xb7
30	♗b3	♕e7
31	fxg6	hxg6
32	♗g5	♕d7
33	♖d1	1–0

Ivanchuk's play in this
game casts some doubt on
Black's system and we re-
commend that Black should
take the option to trans-
pose into the Gligoric system by playing 8 ... exd4.

Game 30
Karpov – Kasparov
World Championship (21)
Lyons 1990

1	d4	♘f6
2	c4	g6
3	♘c3	♗g7

4	e4	d6
5	f3	0-0
6	♗e3	e5
7	d5	*(252)*

Here White resolves the tension in the centre at the first opportunity.

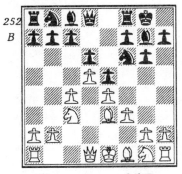

7 ... ♘h5

This was the original way to play the Saemisch for Black. He liberates his f-pawn, prepares to play ... ♘f4 in the future and keeps open all sorts of queenside breaks based on ... c6 or ... a6 and ... b5. It may well be in fact that this is Black's best line.

Kasparov's most recent preference, 7 ... c6 is dealt with in the next game. Less convincing is the strategy of switching to a severely locked Benoni situation:

a) 7 ... c5 8 g4! and:

a1) 8 ... h5 9 h3 ♘e8 (9 ... ♘h7? 10 gxh5 ♕h4+ 11 ♗f2 ♕xh5 12 ♘b5+–) 10 ♕d2 ♘d7 11 ♗d3 a6 12 ♘ge2 ♘df6 13 ♗g5 ♕c7 14 ♗h4 ♔h7 15 0-0-0 ♖h8 16 ♖df1 ♔g8 17 ♘g3 b5 18 ♗g5 bxc4 19 ♗xc4 ♖b8 20 gxh5 ♘xh5 21 ♘xh5 ♖xh5 22 h4 ♖b4 23 ♗e2 ♖h7 24 ♖fg1 ♔f8 25 h5 gxh5 26 ♖g2 f6 27 ♗e3 h4 28 f4 h3 29 f5 ♖d4 30 ♕e1 ♖xe4 31 ♘xe4 ♗xf5 32 ♖g4 ♕f7 33 ♘c3 ♗xg4 34 ♗xg4 f5 35 ♗xh3 f4 36 ♗e6 ♖xh1 37 ♕xh1 ♕g6 38 ♗f2 ♘f6 39 ♗h4 ♗h6 40 ♗xf6 f3+ 41 ♔d1 ♕xf6 42 ♕h3 1-0 Chernin - Uhlmann, Dortmund 1991.

a2) 8 ... ♘e8 9 h4 ♗f6 (The immediate 9 ... f5 is well met by 10 exf5 gxf5 11 gxf5 ♗xf5 12 ♗d3±) 10 ♗f2 a6 11 ♕d2 ♘d7 12 0-0-0 ♖b8 13 ♗e3 ♗e7 14 ♗h6 ♘g7 15 ♗d3 f6 16 ♕c2 ♖f7 17 ♘ge2 ♘f8 18 ♘g3 ♗d7 19 ♖dg1 ♗e8 20 ♗e3 ♗d7 21 ♕g2 ♗c8 22 ♘f5 gxf5 23 gxf5 ♘d7 24 h5 ♔h8 25 h6 ♘xf5 26 exf5 b5 27 ♕h2 bxc4 28 ♕h5 ♕e8 29 ♖g7 ♖f8 30 ♕g4 ♖g8 31 ♖g1 ♗b7 32 ♗e4 ♘b6 33 ♖g2 ♘a8 34 ♕h3 ♖f8 35 ♖2g3 ♘c7 36 ♕g2 ♖f7 37 a4 ♕f8 38 ♖3g4 ♗a8 39 ♕h1 ♘e8 40 ♖xf7 ♕xf7 41 ♗d2 ♗f8 42 ♗e3 ♘c7 43 f4 ♖e8 44 fxe5 ♖xe5 45 ♗f4 ♖xe4 46 ♕xe4 ♗xd5 47 ♘xd5 ♕xd5 48 ♕xd5 ♘xd5 49 ♗d2 ♘b6 50 a5 ♘d7 51 ♖xc4 ♘e5 52 ♖c3 c4 53 ♖g3 d5 54 b3 d4 55 bxc4 ♘xc4 56 ♖b3 ♗d6 57 ♖b7 d3 58 ♖a7 ♔g8 59 ♖xa6 1-0 van der Sterren - Uhlmann, Ter Apel 1990.

b) 7 ... ♘e8 8 ♕d2 *(253)*

and:

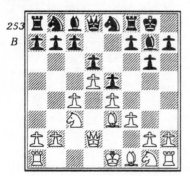

253
B

b1) 8 ... c5 9 dxc6 ♘xc6 10 0-0-0 ♗e6 11 ♔b1 ♖c8 12 ♘d5 ♘d4 13 ♖c1± Jolles - Calvo, Torcy Open 1991.

b2) 8 ... f5 9 exf5 gxf5 10 0-0-0 ♘a6 11 ♗d3 ♘c5 12 ♗c2 ♕h4 13 f4 ♘e4 14 ♘xe4 fxe4 15 ♘e2 ♗g4 16 fxe5 ♗xe5 17 h3± Timman - Diez del Corral, Lucerne Ol. 1982.

8 ♕d2 f5

8 ... ♕h4+ is an important alternative:

a) 9 g3 and now Black has the choice of retreating the queen, or sacrificing it.

a1) 9 ... ♕e7 10 0-0-0 f5 11 exf5 gxf5 12 ♘h3 (12 ♗d3 a5 13 ♘ge2 ♘a6 14 f4 ♗d7 15 fxe5 dxe5 16 ♖hf1 a4 17 ♗h6 ♘c5 18 ♗c2 ♖a6 19 ♗xg7 ♘xg7 20 ♕e3 ♕d6 21 ♔b1 ♖b6 22 a3 ♖e8 23 ♘c1 ♖a6 24 ♘d3 b6 25 ♘b5 ♗xb5 26 cxb5 ♖a5 27 ♘xc5 bxc5 28 g4 ♖b8 29 gxf5 ♖axb5 30 f6 ♖xb2+ 31 ♔c1 ♕b6 32 ♗xh7+ ♔h8 33 fxg7+ ♔xh7 34 g8♕+ ♖xg8 35 ♕h3+ ♔g7 36 ♖g1+ ♔f8 37 ♖xg8+ 1-0 Vyzma-

navin - Akopian, Lvov Zt. 1990) 12 ... ♘a6 13 ♖g1 ♘f6 14 ♘f2 ♔h8 15 ♗e2 (This is very instructive. White intends g4 and the position is already ±) 15 ... ♗d7 16 ♗g5 ♘c5 17 g4 e4 18 fxe4 fxe4 19 ♗e3 ♘a4 20 g5 ♘xc3 21 bxc3 ♘g8 22 ♘g4 c5 23 dxc6 ♗xc6 24 h4 d5 25 cxd5 ♗xd5 26 ♕xd5 ♖ac8 27 ♕d6 ♖xc3+ 28 ♔b1 ♕f7 29 ♗d4 1-0 Karpov - Kasparov, World Ch. (23) Lyons 1990.

a2) 9 ... ♘xg3 10 ♕f2 ♘xf1 11 ♕xh4 ♘xe3 12 ♔e2 ♘xc4 13 ♖c1 ♘a6 *(254)* and now:

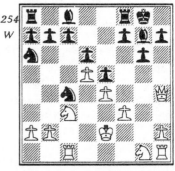

254
W

a21) 14 ♘d1 ♘b6 15 ♘e3 ♗d7 16 ♘h3 f6 17 ♘f2 ♘c8 18 ♖c3 (Possibly better is 18 ♘d3 c5 19 ♕g3 ♗h6 20 h4, as in Levitt - A Martin, Glasgow 1989) 18 ... ♘e7 19 ♖hc1 ♖ac8 20 ♖b3 ♖b8 21 ♘d3 ♖f7 22 ♕e1 ♘c8 23 ♕a5 ♘b6 24 ♖xc7 f5 25 ♖c2 fxe4 26 fxe4 ♖bf8 27 ♖xb6, Kasparov - Seirawan, Barcelona World Cup 1989. Black held on to draw, but White was clearly better in this game.

a22) 14 ♘h3 ♗d7 15 b3 ♘b6 16 ♖hg1 f6 17 f4 exf4 18 ♘xf4 ♖ae8 19 ♘xg6 hxg6 20 ♖xg6 ♖f7 21 ♖cg1 ♘c5 22 ♔d1 f5 23 ♖h6 ♔f8 24 ♖h7 ♘xe4 25 ♘xe4 ♖xe4 26 ♕d8+ ♖e8 27 ♕g5 ♘xd5 28 ♖xg7 ♘f6 29 ♕g6 1-0 van der Sterren - Berg, Kerteminde 1991.

b) 9 ♗f2 *(255)*:

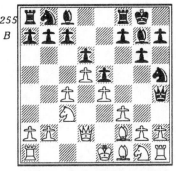

255
B

b1) 9 ... ♕e7 10 0-0-0 f5 11 ♔b1 ♘d7 12 ♘ge2 ♘df6 13 exf5 gxf5 14 ♘c1 ♗d7 15 h3 ♖ae8∞ Fedorowicz - Remlinger, St Martin Open 1991.

b2) 9 ... ♕f4 10 g4 (Another method of avoiding repetition is 10 ♕c2 ♕g5 11 c5 f5 12 cxd6 cxd6 13 ♘b5 fxe4 14 fxe4 ♘a6 15 ♘f3 ♕f4 16 ♘xd6 ♗g4 17 ♗e2 ♕f6 18 ♘c4 ♘f4 19 ♘e3 ♘b4∞ Knaak - Djurhuus, Novi Sad Ol. 1990) 10 ... ♕xd2+ 11 ♔xd2 ♘f4 12 ♘ge2 c6 13 ♗e3 f5 14 gxf5 gxf5 15 ♖g1 ♘xe2 16 ♗xe2 f4 17 ♗f2 ♘a6 18 ♖ad1 ♗h3 19 ♗f1 ♗xf1 20 ♖gxf1 ♗f6 21 a3 ♔f7 22 b4± Christiansen - Grefe,

San Francisco 1991.

In spite of one or two isolated achievements the plan based on 8 ... ♕h4+ seems to be unrelievedly gloomy for Black. The sacrificial lines appear to be unsound while retreating the queen leaves White with gains in time and space.

9 0-0-0 *(256)*

White can also manoeuvre his king's knight into the action as he is not yet obliged to commit his king: 9 ♘ge2 ♘d7 10 ♘c1 ♘df6 11 ♘d3 fxe4 12 ♘xe4 ♘xe4 13 fxe4 c5 14 ♘f2 ♗d7 15 g3 ♕f6 16 ♕e2 a6 17 ♗h3± Ljubojevic - Piket, Tilburg 1989.

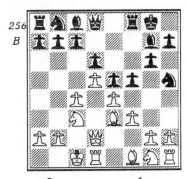

256
B

9 ... a6

Kasparov introduces a new, and not entirely favourable plan in this game. More typical choices are:

a) 9 ... f4 10 ♗f2 ♗f6 (Black's plan is to trade the dark-squared bishops which White strenuously avoids) 11 ♕e1 ♗e7 12 g4 ♘g7 13 h4 ♘d7 14 ♘ge2 h6 15 ♔b1 c5 16 a3 a6 17 ♘c1 ♘e8 18 ♗d3 Ivanchuk – M Gurevich, Linares 1991. This position is ± but Black quickly made it ± by unsoundly sacrificing with 18 ... b5 19 cxb5 when Black could neither regain his pawn nor open adequate lines for a queenside offensive.

b) 9 ... ♘d7 10 ♗d3 *(257)*

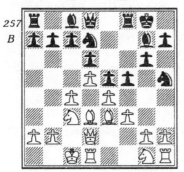

10 ... ♘c5 (This is Kasparov's latest word in the variation and is preferable to the alternatives which commit Black too much: 10 ... ♘df6 11 exf5 {*11 ♘ge2 fxe4 12 ♘xe4 ♘xe4 13 ♗xe4 ♗f5 14 ♘c3 ♘f6 15 ♗xf5 gxf5 16 h3 ♕d7 17 g4± van der Sterren – Martin del Campo, Thessaloniki Ol. 1988*} 11 ... gxf5 12 ♘ge2 ♔h8 13 ♗g5 ♕e8 14 ♖he1 ♗d7 15 ♘d4 ♕c8 16 ♘c2 a6 17 ♔b1 ♖b8 18 c5 dxc5 19 ♖xe5 b5 20 ♗h6 c4 21 ♗xg7+ ♘xg7 22 ♗f1 b4 23 ♘e2 c3

24 ♕d4 c6 25 dxc6 ♗xc6 26 b3 ♕c7 27 ♕d6 ♕xd6 28 ♖xd6 ♗b5 29 ♔c1 f4 30 ♘cd4 ♘fe8 31 ♘xb5 axb5 32 ♖d4 ♘c7 33 ♖xb4 ♘ge6 34 ♘xc3 ♖a8 35 ♗xb5 ♖g8 36 ♗f1 ♖gd8 37 ♖be4 ♖d6 38 ♗c4 ♘d4 39 ♖xf4 1-0 Kir Georgiev – Uhlmann, Dortmund 1991) 11 ♗c2 a6 12 ♘ge2 b5 13 b4 ♘d7 14 cxb5 axb5 15 ♘xb5 ♖xa2 16 ♘ec3 ♖a8 17 ♔b2 ♘df6 18 ♘a7 fxe4 19 ♘c6 ♕d7 20 g4 ♘f4 21 g5 *(258)*

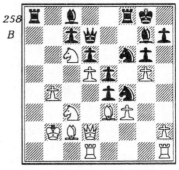

♘6xd5 22 ♘xd5 ♘d3+ 23 ♗xd3 exd3 24 ♘ce7+ ♔h8 25 ♘xc8 e4+ 0-1 Timman – Kasparov, Linares 1992. Yet another virtuoso performance from the World Champion.

10   ♗d3   c5 *(259)*
11   dxc6!

11 ♘ge2 allows Black to stir up trouble with 11 ... b5 12 exf5 gxf5 13 g4 e4∞ Zsinka – Degenhardt, Frankfurt 1990.

11   ...   ♘xc6
12   ♘d5   ♗e6

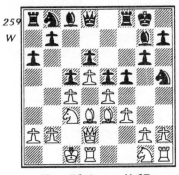

259
W

13	♗b6	♕d7
14	♘e2	♖ac8
15	♔b1	♕f7
16	♖he1	♔h8 (260)

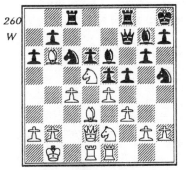

260
W

17 ♗c2

17 ♗g1 ♘f6 18 ♘b6 ♖cd8
19 ♘g3 ♘d7 20 ♘d5 ♘c5 21
♗c2 b5= Brenninkmeijer -
Wahls, Groningen 1990.
White has wasted too much
time to keep any plus.

17 ... ♘f6

Karpov has a slight edge
which will not run away
(control of d5). His next
move is a symptom of in-
decision, not an offer to
repeat. Kasparov correctly
recognises this, and does
not repeat himself.

18	♗d3	♘d7
19	♗g1	♘c5
20	♘b6	♖cd8
21	♘c3	♘d4
22	♘cd5	♗xd5
23	♘xd5	fxe4
24	fxe4	b5
25	♖f1	♕d7
26	cxb5	axb5
27	♖xf8+	♖xf8
28	h3	♕d8
29	♗xd4	exd4
30	♕e2	♕h4
31	♖f1	♖e8
32	♖f4	♕g5
33	a3	h5
34	♔a2	b4

With both players very
short of time and in a highly complex position, Kasparov sacrifices a pawn to
lunge for White's throat.
But this may be over-
reaching.

35	axb4	♖a8+
36	♔b1	♘b3
37	♔c2	♘a1+
38	♔b1	♘b3
39	♕f2	♕d8 (261)

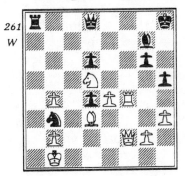

261
W

With one move to go
before the time control,

and just one minute in which to play it, Karpov implements an attractive invasion of the black camp. Lengthy post-game analysis indicated that instead the forcing line 40 ♗c4 ♖a1+ 41 ♔c2 ♘c1 42 ♖f7 ♕e8 43 ♖xg7 ♕xe4+ 44 ♔d2 ♔xg7 45 ♕f6+ ♔h6 46 ♕f4+ ♕xf4 47 ♘xf4 d3 48 ♘xd3 ♘xd3 49 ♗xd3 would have offered White the best winning prospects. Paradoxically, in the endgame which has resulted from this variation, White's duo of passed b-pawns would be more valuable than Black's extra exchange. The reason is that they can be handily supported by the mobile white king. Nevertheless, it is difficult to think of anyone who, with one minute left, would have passed over the exceedingly natural move which Karpov now plays.

40 ♖f7   ♕e8

In this position Karpov had to seal his 41st move, over which he spent 28 minutes. The most immediately critical line is 41 ♘e7 ♖a1+ 42 ♔c2 ♘c1 43 ♘xg6+ ♔h7 44 ♔d2! when Black cannot capture the knight 44 ... ♔xg6 45 ♕f5+ ♔h6 46 g4 and thus must content himself with 44 ... ♘b3+ and a draw by repetition.

Although 41 ♘e7 looks dangerous for Black (and the immediate 41 ♖xg7 is also worth consideration) the counter-attack given above puts the onus on White to prove equality. Karpov's sealed move turns out to be much the best of the moves available.

41 b5!

A dual purpose advance. Clearly, the closer White's passed pawn approaches the eighth rank, the more dangerous it becomes, but this pawn thrust also has the virtue of closing the attacking diagonal of the black queen towards White's king.

41 ...   ♖a1+
42 ♔c2   ♘c5 (262)

262
W

The threats are becoming serious, including 43 ... ♖c1+ 44 ♔xc1 ♘xd3+. White, therefore, decides that the time has come to carry out the sacrifice of the exchange which has been in the air for so long.

43	Rxg7	Kxg7
44	Qxd4+	Qe5

Black must seek his salvation in the endgame.

45	Qxe5+	dxe5
46	b6	Rg1

Only by this counterattack against White's kingside pawns can Black hope to achieve enough counterplay to hold the draw.

47	Ne3	Re1
48	Nc4	

A better chance is 48 b4.

48	...	Rg1
49	Ne3	Re1
50	Nc4	Rg1
51	b4	Rxg2+
52	Kc3	Na4+
53	Kb3	Nxb6
54	Nxb6	Rg3
55	Kc3	Rxh3 *(263)*

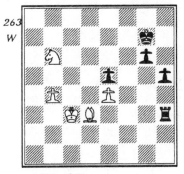

263
W

56 b5

Here 56 Nd7 is a superior try. It is surprising that Karpov, knowing the sealed move, which was obviously opaque to Kasparov, should have failed to make the most of his chances in the adjourned session of play.

56	...	h4
57	Nc4	Rxd3+

Completing a remarkable defensive sequence which permits Black to draw.

58	Kxd3	h3
59	b6	h2
60	b7	h1(Q)
61	b8(Q)	Qf1+
62	Kc3	Qc1+
63	Kb3	Qd1+
64	Ka2	Qa4+
65	Na3	Qxe4 *(264)*

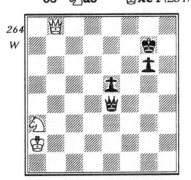

264
W

This is a dead draw, but Karpov flogged a very dead horse until move 86 before acquiescing in the inevitable.

66	Qc7+	Kh6
67	Nc4	Qd5
68	Kb2	e4
69	Qf4+	Kg7
70	Kc3	Qd3+
71	Kb4	Qd4
72	Qh4	Kf7
73	Kb5	Qd5+
74	Kb4	Qd4
75	Qh7+	Qg7
76	Qh1	Qd4
77	Qh4	Kg8

78	♕f4	♔g7
79	♕c1	♔f6
80	♔b5	♕d5+
81	♔b4	♕d4
82	♔b5	♕d5+
83	♔b6	♕d4+
84	♔c6	♔e6
85	♘e3	♕a4+
86	♔b6	♕b4+

½-½

A superbly typical and instructive fighting game.

Game 31
Timman - Kasparov
Paris (Immopar) 1991

1	d4	♘f6
2	c4	g6
3	♘c3	♗g7
4	e4	d6
5	f3	0-0
6	♗e3	e5
7	d5	c6 *(265)*

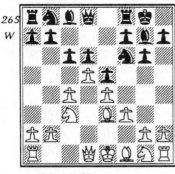

265
W

8　♗d3

The main alternative is 8 ♕d2 cxd5 9 cxd5 and now:

a) 9 ... a6 10 ♗d3 ♘e8 (10 ... ♘h5 11 ♘ge2 f5 12 exf5 gxf5 13 0-0 ♕e8 14 ♔h1 ♘d7, and now 15 g4?, van der

Sterren - Vogt, Budapest Open 1988, is very strange. 15 ♖ac1 is better - compare with Petrosian - Gligoric, note to move 13) 11 0-0-0 (The game continuation is fine for Black. Correct and logical would be 11 ♘ge2 ⌐ 0-0) 11 ... f5 12 ♔b1 ♘d7 13 ♘ge2 b5 14 ♘c1 ♘c5 15 ♗c2= Suetin - Agnos, London (Lloyds Bank) 1990.

b) 9 ... ♘a6 10 ♗d3 (10 ♗b5!? has the reputation of being a super-subtle refinement, but this is hard to understand! Play ends up being little different to the main lines, so long as Black avoids the exchange of light-squared bishops with ... ♗d7) 10 ... ♘h5 11 ♘ge2 f5 12 exf5 gxf5 13 0-0 ♔h8 14 ♔h1 ♘c7 15 ♗c4 ♗d7 16 a4 ♘e8 17 ♗g5 ♘ef6= Ree - Visser, Amsterdam 1989) 10 ... ♘e8 11 ♘ge2 ♗d7 12 0-0 ♘c5 13 ♗b5 f5 14 b4 ♘a6 15 exf5 gxf5 16 ♖ab1 ♘f6 17 ♔h1 ♘c7 18 ♗c4 ♔h8= Gulko - Ermenkov, Amsterdam 1988.

c) 9 ... ♘e8 10 0-0-0 (10 g4 f5 11 gxf5 gxf5 12 0-0-0±) 10 ... f5 11 ♗d3 ♘a6 12 ♘ge2 ♘c5 13 ♗c2 a5 14 exf5 gxf5 15 h3 b5 16 ♘xb5 a4 17 ♘ec3 ♗d7 18 ♘a3 (18 ♘xd6 would be much too dangerous) 18 ... ♕b6 19 g4 ♖b8 Gheorghiu - Kozul, Graz Open 1987. Black has excellent counterplay for the pawn.

d) 9 ... ♘h5 10 ♗d3 ♘f4 11 0-0-0 ♘xd3+ 12 ♕xd3 f5 13 ♘ge2 a6 14 ♔b1 b5 15 a3 ♘d7 16 ♘c1 ♘c5, Zsu Polgar – Liberzon, Haifa 1989. Black has an excellent position. If White was always so obliging, everyone would play the King's Indian!

e) 9 ... ♘bd7 10 ♘ge2 a6 11 g4 h5! 12 h3 (12 gxh5 ♘xh5∓; 12 g5 ♘h7 13 h4 f6 14 gxf6 ♖xf6 △ ... ♖f4 with compensation for the exchange – Gligoric; 12 ♗g5 hxg4 13 fxg4 ♘c5 {*13 ... ♕b6 is better*} 14 ♘g3 ♗xg4 15 b4⩲⩱ Botvinnik – Tal, World Ch. (10), Moscow 1960) 12 ... ♘h7 13 0-0-0 h4=. Black plans ... ♗f6 – g5.

8 ... cxd5

We shall consider Black's alternatives here in the next game.

9 cxd5 *(266)*

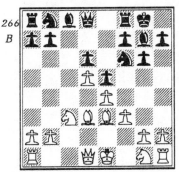

9 ... ♘h5

Others are:

a) 9 ... ♘e8 10 ♕d2! (10 ♘ge2? ♗h6!∓ △ 11 ♗xh6 ♕h4+ Miralles – Summermatter, Bern 1991, is a standard tactical resource with which Black activates the King's Indian bishop) 10 ... f5 11 exf5 gxf5 12 ♘ge2 ♘d7 *(267)* and now:

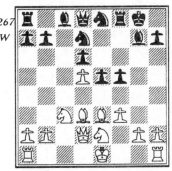

a1) 13 0-0 ♔h8 14 ♔h1 a6 15 ♖ac1 b5 16 ♗g5 ♘f6 17 ♗h6 ♗g7 18 ♗xg7+ ♘xg7 19 f4± Christiansen – Kozul. Biel 1991.

a2) 13 0-0-0 (This is a dubious plan. Black should always be okay if White castles long in this variation) 13 ... a6 14 h3 b5 15 ♔b1 ♘b6 16 ♖c1 ♔h8 17 g4 b4∞ Zsu Polgar – Mortensen, Vejstrup 1989.

10 ♘ge2 f5
11 exf5 gxf5
12 0-0 ♘d7 *(268)*
13 ♖c1

Also possible is 13 ♕d2 and now:

a) 13 ... ♘df6 14 ♔h1 ♔h8 15 ♗g5 ♗d7 16 ♕c2 ♕c8 17 ♖ac1± Portisch – Gligoric. Milan 1975.

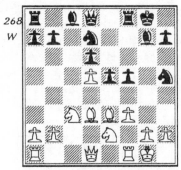

b) 13 ... ♘c5! 14 ♗c2 a5 15 f4 e4=. White should now play 16 ♘d4 instead of 16 ♘a4 ♘xa4 17 ♗xa4 ♘f6 18 h3 ♗d7 19 ♗c2 a4 20 b4 ♗b5 21 ♖fd1 ♗c4 22 ♘c3 b5 23 ♔h1 ♖c8 24 ♖g1 ♘g4 25 ♖ad1 ♗xc3 26 ♕xc3 ♗d3 27 ♗c5 ♕h4 0-1 Paehtz - Uhlmann, East German Ch. 1982.

13 ... ♘c5 *(269)*

Black has not had a happy time with the alternative 13 ... a6 14 ♔h1 and:

a) 14 ... ♘df6 15 ♗g5 ♕e8 16 ♕c2 ♔h8 17 ♗xf5 ♗xf5 18 ♕xf5 ♘xd5 19 ♕d3 ♘hf4 20 ♘xf4 ♘xc3 21 bxc3 exf4 22 ♕xd6 ♕f7 23 ♖fe1 ♖ac8 24 ♖e7 ♕xa2 25 ♗xf4 ♖cd8 26 ♕c7 ♕a4 27 ♗d6 ♗f6 28 ♖e6 ♖d7 29 ♕c5 ♖ff7 30 ♕f5 ♔g7 31 c4 ♕b3 32 ♕g4+ 1-0 Popov - Krogius, USSR 1976.

b) 14 ... ♔h8 15 ♕d2 b5 16 ♗xf5 ♖xf5 17 g4 ♘df6 18 gxf5 ♗xf5 19 ♗h6 ♗xh6 20 ♕xh6 ♗g6 21 ♖g1± Timman - Thipsay, Thessaloniki Ol. 1984.

14 ♗c4

This looks strange. In the game Knaak - Reyes, Novi Sad Ol. 1990, White did well with 14 ♗b1 a5 15 f4 keeping his bishop trained against the black kingside.

The game continued: 15 ... b6 16 fxe5 dxe5 17 d6± As is nearly always the case in this variation, whenever White plays f4 Black has to react ... e4 as in Paehtz - Uhlmann.

In our main game, Timman soon retracts his bishop and replaces it on the b1 - h7 diagonal. Timman's idea is to stop Black securing his knight with ... a5, since then 15 ♗xc5 dxc5 16 d6+ is clearly better for White who will follow up with ♘b5.

14 ... a6

Black prevents the afore-mentioned variation, but in doing so White gains time to drive Black's knight back with tempo.

15 b4 ♘d7

16 a4 ♛e8 *(270)*

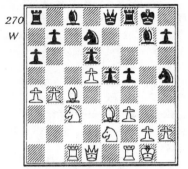

270
W

As usual, when he has nothing better to do Kasparov simply ferries as many pieces as possible towards the direction of his opponent's king. Playing against Kasparov must be like watching somebody continually loading a very large gun. One's hope must be that it goes off in his face before he succeeds in aiming it and pulling the trigger.

However, the plan of ... ♛e8 - g6 is not the most effective way of lining up the black queen against the white king. A couple of months later Kasparov had the same position against Karpov (Reggio Emilia 1992) and the World Champion found the considerably more effective 16 ... ♛h4 17 f4 ♚h8 18 ♕d2 ♖g8 19 g3 ♗h6 20 ♖f2 ♛h3 21 ♖g2 ♞hf6 22 ♚h1 ♞g4 when Black had the initiative. This is also an interesting

case in which Black did not need to react to f4 with ... e4 since his queen's knight had already been driven back to d7 and was ready to re-emerge on e5 should White capture on that square.

17	♚h1	♞df6
18	b5	♛g6
19	♗d3	e4
20	♗c2	♗d7
21	bxa6	bxa6
22	♖b1	♖ae8

This turns out to be a mistake with 22 ... ♖ac8 being the preferred option.

| 23 | ♛d2 | ♚h8 |
| 24 | ♖b6 | |

Black will now lose pawns but he has distinct attacking chances against White's king.

24	...	♖g8
25	♖g1	♛f7
26	♖xa6	

White reaps his harvest too soon. 26 ♗d4! would have pre-empted Black's cunning combination.

26	...	f4
27	♗d4	♞g3+
28	♞xg3	fxg3
29	♛f4	*(271)*

After a complex middlegame Kasparov now goes seriously wrong. He had to play 29 ... ♛h5. If then 30 h3 ♗xh3 wins for Black or 30 h4 ♞g4 31 ♗xg7+ ♖xg7 32 ♛xg3 e3 33 fxg4 ♖xg4 and again Black wins by

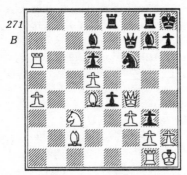

exposing the white king. Finally 30 ♕xg3 ♘xd5 31 ♖xd6 ♗xd4 32 ♖xd5 ♕h6 33 ♕d6 exf3 34 ♕xh6 fxg2+ 35 ♖xg2 ♖e1+ with mate to follow. Having missed this opportunity Black's position goes downhill.

29	...	gxh2
30	♖f1	exf3
31	♕xf3	♖ef8
32	♖xd6	♗g4 *(272)*

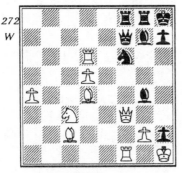

33   ♖xf6

Inviting complications which keep Black in the game. Simplest and best is 33 ♕d3 powering up with queen and bishop against black's pawn on h7.

33	...	♗xf3

34   ♖xf7   ♗xg2+

The last chance was 34 ... ♖xf7, though after 35 ♗xg7+ ♖gxg7 36 ♖xf3 ♖xf3 37 gxf3 ♖g1+ 38 ♔xh2 ♖c1 39 ♗e4 ♖xc3 40 d6 ♖c1 41 d7 ♖d1 42 a5 ♔g7 43 a6 ♔f7 44 a7 Black is hopelessly placed in the endgame. The text, however, loses at once

35   ♔xh2   1-0

Game 32
Gulko - Kasparov
Linares 1990

1	d4	♘f6
2	c4	g6
3	♘c3	♗g7
4	e4	d6
5	f3	0-0
6	♗e3	c6
7	♗d3	e5

7 ... a6 leads to the Byrne Variation which is hardly seen at all these days. Black aims to expand on the queenside, but this plan is rather slow. Nevertheless, Kasparov tried it out in the most recent World Championship match: 8 ♘ge2 b5 9 0-0 ♘bd7 10 ♖c1 e5 11 a3 exd4 12 ♘xd4 ♗b7 13 cxb5 cxb5 14 ♖e1± Karpov - Kasparov, World Ch. (1), New York 1990.

8	d5 *(273)*	
8	...	b5

Kasparov likes to play this pawn sacrifice, though

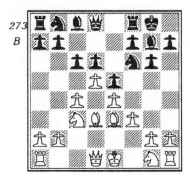

273
B

its consequences are by no means clear. The less ambitious continuation, 8 ... cxd5 is examined in the previous game.

A further possibility is 8 ... a6 when practice has seen: 9 ♘ge2 ♘bd7 (9 ... b5 10 b3 b4 11 ♘a4 ♘fd7 12 0-0 a5 13 ♕d2 ♘a6 14 ♖ad1 ♘dc5 15 ♘xc5 ♘xc5 16 dxc6± Razuvaev - Ehlvest, Moscow TV 1987) 10 0-0 c5 11 ♕c2 ♔h8 12 a4 a5 13 ♗g5 h6 14 ♗h4 ♘b8 15 ♕d2 b6 16 ♗f2 ♘a6 17 ♖ae1±/± Renet - I Sokolov, Haifa 1989.

9   cxb5 *(274)*

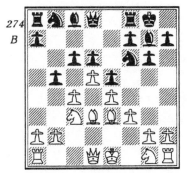

274
B

Boldly taking what few men have taken before.

Others are:

a) 9 ♘ge2 is best met by 9 ... b4!, forcing the white knight out of play, e.g. 10 ♘a4 c5 11 0-0 ♘h5 12 a3 ♘a6 13 ♕d2 f5 14 exf5 gxf5 15 f4 e4= Lautier - Gallagher, French Team Ch 1989. Alternatively, 9 ... bxc4 10 ♗xc4 will always leave White with an edge, e.g. 10 ... c5 11 ♕d2 ♘fd7 12 g4 ♘b6 13 ♗d3 ♗a6 14 ♘g3 ♗xd3 15 ♕xd3 ♘8d7 16 h4 ♖c8 17 h5± Tarjan - Plachetka, Odessa 1976.

b) 9 a3 *(275)* and now:

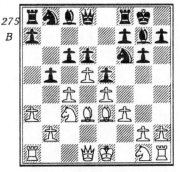

275
B

b1) 9 ... cxd5 (White now loses a tempo on the variation 8 ... cxd5 9 cxd5 as later he will play a3 - a4) 10 cxd5 a6 11 ♘ge2 ♘e8 12 0-0 ♘d7 13 ♔h1 ♔h8 14 b4 f5 15 exf5 gxf5 16 a4 bxa4 17 ♖xa4 ♖b8 18 ♕c2 ♘b6 19 ♖a5 ♕c7 20 ♕a2 ♘d7 21 ♖c1 ♕d8 22 b5 e4 Ivanchuk - Piket, Tilburg 1989. Black has good counterplay.

b2) 9 ... bxc4 10 ♗xc4 c5 11 ♘ge2 (Or even 11 b4!? -

Ivanchuk) 11 ... ♘bd7 12 b4 ♘h5 13 0-0 ♘f4 14 ♔h1 ♖b8 15 ♖b1 ♘b6 16 ♗b5 cxb4 17 ♖xb4±/± Razuvaev - Uhlmann, Dortmund 1991.

c) 9 ♕d2 bxc4 10 ♗xc4 c5 (10 ... ♗b7 11 ♘ge2 cxd5 12 ♘xd5 ♘bd7 13 ♘ec3± Ward - Kotronias, Stockholm 1988) 11 ♘ge2 ♘bd7 12 0-0 ♖b8 13 ♖ab1 ♘e8 14 a3 ♘b6 15 ♗d3 c4 16 ♗c2 ♗d7 17 f4± Petrosian - Kochiev, USSR 1976.

9 ♕d2 is an interesting idea since if 9 ... b4 10 ♘ce2! c5 11 g4 and all White's forces are concentrated on the kingside, while Black is very slow on the queenside.

| 9 | ... | cxd5 |
| 10 | exd5 | e4 *(276)* |

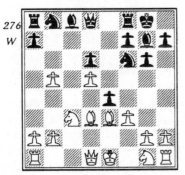

Kasparov's novelty which he introduced at Reykjavik 1988. If instead 10 ... ♗b7, White gains an advantage as follows, according to analysis by the Yugoslav, Barlov: 11 ♘ge2 ♘bd7 (11 ... ♘xd5 12 ♘xd5 ♗xd5 13 ♘c3

♗b7 14 ♗e4) 12 0-0 ♘b6 13 ♗g5 ♘bxd5 14 ♘xd5 ♗xd5 15 ♘c3 ♕b6+ 16 ♔h1 ♗b7 17 ♗xf6 ♗xf6 18 ♗e4 with central control. The point of Black's 10th move here is to wrench open the dark-squared diagonal for his king's bishop, while the white king is still stuck in the centre.

In the main game, Kasparov's gambit looks insufficient for Black, but a recent attempt to rehabilitate it is with 10 ... ♘bd7(!), which generated tremendous counterplay for Black in the following two examples: 11 ♗c2 (Koeksma is a fast learner, e.g. 11 ♘ge2 ♘b6 12 ♗g5 h6 13 ♗h4 ♗b7 14 0-0 ♕d7 15 ♗e4 ♘e8 16 ♗f2 f5 17 ♗c2 ♘f6 18 a4 ♔h7 19 ♗b3 ♖ac8 20 a5 ♘c4 21 ♗xc4 ♖xc4 22 ♗xa7 ♗a6 23 ♗f2 ♗xb5 24 ♕b3 ♗a6 25 ♕b6 ♕c8 26 ♖fd1 e4 27 ♘d4 e3 28 ♗xe3 ♖xc3 29 bxc3 ♘xd5 30 ♕xd6 ♘xe3 31 ♕e6 ♘xd1 32 ♕xc8 ♖xc8 33 ♖xd1 0-1 Jolles - Hoeksema, Groningen Open 1990) 11 ... ♘b6 12 ♗b3 e4 13 f4 a6 14 bxa6 ♗xa6 15 ♘h3 ♘c4 16 ♗xc4 ♗xc4 17 ♘f2 ♕a5 18 ♕d2 ♘xd5 19 ♘xd5 ♕xd2+ 20 ♗xd2 ♗xd5 21 ♘d1 ♗xa2 0-1 Hoeksema - Uhlmann, Dieren Open 1990.

11 ♘xe4
Much the best way of

accepting the offer. The alternatives are somewhat depressing for White and Black always seems to emerge with a healthy initiative, e.g. 11 fxe4 ♘g4 12 ♕d2 (12 ♗f4 ♕b6 13 ♕d2 f5) 12 ... f5 13 ♘f3 ♘xe3 (perhaps 13 ... ♗xc3 14 bxc3 fxe4 15 ♗xe4 ♖e8 16 0-0 ♖xe4 17 ♗d4 is also playable, though now White has the attack in return for sacrificed material) 14 ♕xe3 f4 15 ♕f2 ♘d7 16 0-0 ♘e5 17 ♘xe5 ♗xe5. This is a typical case in the King's Indian where Black gives up a pawn or pawns to dominate the dark squares. It must be observed that such long-range sacrifices nearly always turn out well for Black.

The second possibility for White is 11 ♗xe4 ♘xe4 12 fxe4 ♕h4+ 13 ♔d2 (if 13 g3 ♗xc3+ 14 bxc3 ♕xe4 15 ♕f3 ♗f5 16 g4 ♕xg4 17 ♕xg4 ♗xg4) 13 ... ♘d7 14 ♘f3 ♕g4 with compensation for the sacrificed pawns.

11	...	♘xd5
12	♗g5 *(277)*	
12	...	♕b6

Against Timman, Reykjavik World Cup 1988, Kasparov had played 12 ... ♕a5+ 13 ♕d2 ♕xd2+ 14 ♗xd2 ♗xb2 15 ♖b1 ♗g7 and ultimately won. Presumably he feared

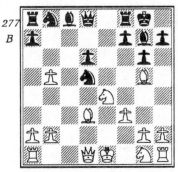

277
B

here some improvement – maybe 15 ♖d1 which ultimately led to White's advantage in Razuvaev – Lautier, Paris Open 1989. Worth quoting here are some relevant words from Jon Speelman about openings novelties in chess. They are quite pertinent to the debate, which we see here, raging around Kasparov's attempts to make his gambit 8 ... b5 work.

"Until about 25 years ago, news used to travel very slowly in the chess world. A man with an opening novelty might be able to use it two or three times in the course of a year before it became 'public knowledge'. Since then there has been a gradual acceleration, partly due to better technology and partly due to a better informed and more demanding chess public. Today a professional like myself can expect to see the bulletin of a major tournament within a few days of the end – if not in instalments by fax during the event."

(Jon Speelman in *The Sunday Correspondent*).

13 ♕d2 ♘d7
14 ♗c4 ♘5f6
15 ♘xf6+ *(278)*

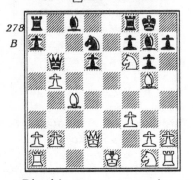

Black's next move is an unnatural way to recapture. In the first instance it encourages exchanges when Black is material down, while secondly, Black voluntarily offers the exchange of his king's bishop, conventionally his most potent unit in the King's Indian. The sole virtue of Black's next move is that it somewhat undermines White's grip on the central dark squares. As we shall see, though, when Black seeks to take advantage of this, later in the game, his efforts are exposed as illusory. The natural and strong recapture is 15 ... ♘xf6, for example 16 ♗e3

♖e8 17 ♔f2 ♖xe3 18 ♕xe3 ♘g4+ 19 fxg4 ♗d4, exploiting the latent force of Black's King's Indian bishop to skewer the white queen. Alternatives are 16 ♘e2 ♖e8 17 ♗h4 d5! 18 ♗f2 ♕e6 19 ♗d3 ♘e4! or 18 ♗d3 ♗b7 19 ♗f2 d4 followed by ... ♘d5 and ... ♘e3. This last variation was pointed out by Kasparov after the game at Linares and goes a long way towards justifying Black's choice of opening variation.

15 ... ♗xf6
16 ♗xf6 ♘xf6
17 ♘e2 ♖e8
18 0-0-0 d5
19 ♗d3

There is a complicated and probably stronger alternative here in 19 ♗b3 ♖xe2 20 ♕xe2 ♗f5 21 ♖d2 ♖c8+ 22 ♗c2 d4 23 g4.

19 ... a6

Hoping to open up some lines against White's king, and at last admitting that he will be unable to re-establish material equilibrium ever by capturing the White pawn on b5.

20 bxa6 d4

In *Europe Echecs*, Barlov looks at 20 ... ♗xa6 21 ♗xa6 ♕xa6 22 ♘c3 ♖ec8 23 ♔b1 ♖c4, but claims that White beats off the attack after 24 a3.

21 ♔b1 ♖e3 *(279)*
The threat to capture on

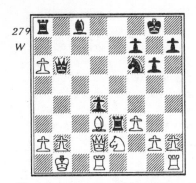

d3 is too transparent. Moreover, on e3 the rook is over-exposed. As so often against Gulko, Kasparov is carried away by the exuberance of his own attacking schemes, when the simple 21 ... ♗xa6 22 ♗xa6 ♕xa6, and White must retreat with 23 ♘c1, would still keep him in contention.

22 ♗c4   ♗xa6
23 ♗xa6

By exchanging dark-squared bishops, Black has gained control of e3, but it was not hard to repulse him. If now 23 ... ♕xa6 24 ♘c1 ♖d8 25 ♕xe3 and the two rooks win easily against Black's queen.

23 ...   ♖xa6
24 ♘xd4   ♖e8

Their clock times were now Gulko thirty and Kasparov twelve minutes left to reach move 40. If 24 ... ♖ea3 25 ♘c2! ♖xc2 26 ♕d8+ ♕xd8 27 ♖xd8+ ♔g7 28 ♘a3 wins. Gulko now played the excellent knight

retreat ...

25 ♘e2

By redirecting to c3 White establishes full control.

25 ...   ♖b8
26 ♘c3   ♕b4
27 ♖he1   ♖d6
28 ♕c2

Of course not 28 ♕xd6?? ♕xb2 mate!

28 ...   ♖db6
29 ♖e2   ♕f4
30 h3 *(280)*

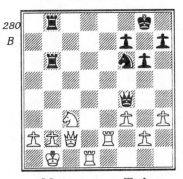

30 ...   ♖c6

After 30 ... ♖xb2+ 31 ♕xb2 ♖xb2+ 32 ♖xb2 Black does not have much chance in the endgame, but it might still have been superior to what he now plays.

31 ♕d2   ♕f5+

If 31 ... ♕xd2 32 ♖exd2! ♖xc3 33 ♖d8+! ♖xd8 34 ♖xd8+ ♔g7 and the pawn is unpinned, so 35 bxc3! follows and White wins.

32 ♔a1   ♖b7
33 ♕h6   ♖c8
34 ♖ed2   ♕a5

35	♕e3	♔g7
36	g4	

"One of the secrets of winning is not to try too hard. Gulko slowly improves his position awaiting favourable opportunities to exchange pieces." (words of wisdom from Jon Speelman in *The Sunday Correspondent*).

36	...	♖e8
37	♕d4	♖d7
38	♕f2	♖c7
39	♖d3	♖a8 *(281)*

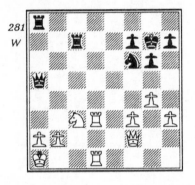

281
W

The rest is a long slow death agony for Kasparov, as Gulko gradually but inexorably gathers together all the disparate threads of his position. Ultimately in such situations, the player with the big material advantage who survives the attack, always gets the attack himself, and then it is time to resign.

40	♕d2	h6
41	♖d6	♖c4
42	♖d4	♖ac8
43	♔b1	♕e5
44	f4	♕e6
45	♕e2	♖xd4
46	♖xd4	♕b6
47	♕d2	♕a6
48	♕d3	♕c6
49	a3	♕g2
50	♖d6	♖b8
51	♕e2	♕h1+

If 51 ... ♕xh3 52 ♕e5 ♕h4 53 g5! etc.

52	♔a2	♖e8
53	♕d3	♖e1
54	♕d4	1-0

14) Saemisch others

In this section we concentrate on the gambit 6 ... c5. Black gives away a pawn, apparently for nothing, but practice has shown that if White takes the pawn he must face such a wave of dark square counterplay that he cannot hope objectively for any advantage. Paradoxically, as in the extract Christiansen - Polgar White fares better when he declines the bait.

Other sixth move alternatives for Black such as 6 ... a6, 6 ... b6 and 6 ... ♘bd7, although they have on occasion led to resounding victories for the second player are frankly speaking inferior. Correct White treatment, as given here, invariably leaves the black camp drained of inner vitality.

**Game 33
Karpov - J Polgar
Monaco 1992**

1	c4	g6
2	d4	♗g7
3	♘c3	♘f6
4	e4	d6
5	f3	0-0

It is possible to attack White's centre by playing c5 at once but after 5 ... c5 6 dxc5 dxc5 7 ♕xd8+ ♔xd8 8 ♗e3 Black's position has no dynamism, and, as even the great Bobby Fischer once had to admit, Black can generate no winning chances from this barren wilderness. Indeed, it is Black who has to defend carefully because of the misplaced position of his king.

| 6 | ♗e3 | c5 *(282)* |

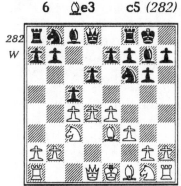

*282
W*

Interestingly, this thrust makes more sense as a pawn sacrifice since, in order to accept it White has to activate Black's king's rook which plays an important part in proceedings.

Others are:

a) 6 ... a6 7 ♘d3 c5 8 dxc5 dxc5 9 e5 ♘fd7 10 f4 ♘c6 11 ♘f3 f6, Piasetski – Eslon, Alicante 1977, 12 exf6±. Compare this with Christiansen – J Polgar, note to White's 8th below, and here White effectively enjoys an extra tempo. However, less convincing is 9 ♗xc5 ♘c6 10 ♘ge2 (10 ♗e3! ♘d7 11 f4∞) 10 ... ♘d7 11 ♗f2 ♘de5∞ Beliavsky–Kasparov, Candidates Quarter-Final (8) 1983.

b) The convoluted 6 ... ♘bd7 was tried in the well-known game Beliavsky – Nunn, Wijk aan Zee 1985. After 7 ♕d2 c5 8 d5 ♘e5 9 h3?! ♘h5! 10 ♗f2 f5! 11 exf5 ♖xf5 12 g4 ♖xf3! 13 gxh5 ♕f8 14 ♘e4 ♗h6, the English grandmaster went on to win brilliantly and the game was subsequently voted the best of the year by the *Informator* panel. However, later in the tournament Timman improved on White's play with 9 ♗g5(!) and after 9 ... a6 10 f4 ♘ed7 11 ♘f3 b5 12 cxb5 axb5 13 ♗xb5, Black was a pawn down for not much compensation, but managed

to draw, Timman – Nunn, Wijk aan Zee 1985.

The English grandmaster and King's Indian guru, William Watson later attempted to revive the line for Black with 9 ... e6, but after 10 f4 ♘eg4 11 dxe6 ♗xe6 12 ♘f3 b5 13 cxb5 d5 14 e5 d4 15 exf6 ♘xf6 16 ♗xf6 ♕xf6 17 ♘e4 ♕e7 18 ♔f2, Plaskett – Watson, British Ch. 1990, Black's piece sacrifice was looking rather speculative.

c) 6 ... b6 *(283)* is another attempt to sidestep the main lines which is not much seen these days. A couple of recent examples:

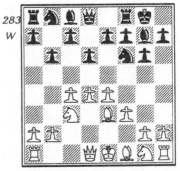

283
W

c1) 7 ♕d2 c5 8 ♘ge2 ♘c6 9 d5 ♘e5 10 ♘g3 e6 (10 ... h5 11 ♗e2 h4 12 ♘f1 a6 13 ♗h6∞ Shirov) 11 ♗e2 exd5 12 cxd5 a6 13 a4 ♘h5 14 ♘xh5 gxh5 15 ♗h6 ♕h4+ 16 g3 ♕f6 17 ♗xg7 ♕xg7 18 f4 ♘g4 19 h3 ♘f6 20 0-0-0 ♖e8 21 ♗f3 b5 22 ♖de1 ♘d7 23 e5 dxe5 24 d6 ♖b8 25 axb5 axb5 26 ♗c6 c4 27 ♕e3 ♖e6 28 ♘e4 c3 29

f5 cxb2+ 30 ♔b1 ♖e8 31 g4
f6 32 ♖hg1 ♔h8 33 gxh5 ♕f7
34 h6 ♗b7 35 ♖g7 ♕c4 36
♕g3 ♖g8 37 ♗xb7 ♕a4 38
♘c3 ♕a1+ 39 ♔c2 b4 40 ♗d5
1-0 Ivanchuk - Hellers, Biel
1989.

c2) 7 ♗d3 *(284)* (This
move is the reason that the
variation with 6 ... b6 has
gone out of fashion)

c21) 7 ... c5?? 8 e5! △
♗e4+-.

c22) 7 ... ♘fd7 8 ♘ge2 c5
9 ♗c2 a6 10 0-0 ♘c6 11 ♕d2
♖b8 12 a4 e5 13 dxe5 dxe5 14
♘d5 ♘d4 15 b4± Brennink-
meijer - Damljanovic, Wijk
aan Zee 1990.

c23) 7 ... ♗b7 8 ♘ge2 c5 9
d5 e6 10 ♗g5± Gheorghiu -
Stein, Moscow 1967. After
this game Black's 7th was
never seen again as the b7-
bishop is facing a granite
wall.

c24) 7 ... a6 8 ♘ge2 c5 9
e5 ♘e8 10 ♗e4 ♖a7 11 dxc5
bxc5 12 ♗xc5 ♖d7 13 ♗e3±
Biyiasis - Torre, Manila Izt.
1976.

7   **dxc5**

7 ♘ge2 ♘c6 8 ♕d2 b6 9
d5 ♘e5 10 ♘g3 transposes
into Ivanchuk - Hellers above.

7   ...   **dxc5**
8 **♕xd8**

White also has an inter-
esting way of declining the
sacrifice which has been
successful in practice: 8 e5
♘fd7 9 f4 f6 10 exf6 exf6
(If 10 ... ♖xf6!? 11 ♗xc5 ♕a5
12 ♗f2 ♖d6 13 ♕c1 ♘c5 14
♘f3 ♖e6+∓ Gavrikov - Shi-
rov, Biel 1991. However, 11
♘f3!±) and now *(285)*:

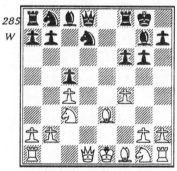

a) 11 ♗e2 ♘c6 12 ♘f3 ♖e8
13 ♗f2 ♘b6 (13 ... f5 14 0-0±
Gelfand) 14 ♕xd8 ♘xd8 15
♗xc5 ♘xc4 16 0-0-0 ♗e6 17
♘d4 ♗f7 18 ♘db5 ♖c8 Por-
tisch - Gelfand, Linares
1990. A very complicated
position but Black's re-
sources should be ade-
quate.

b) 11 ♘f3 ♕e8 12 ♕d2 ♘b6
13 ♗e2 ♘a6 14 ♖d1 ♗f5 15
♔f2! (This is an improve-
ment over 15 0-0 ♕e7 16

♘h4 ♗c2∞ Christiansen - Nunn, Vienna 1991, because there are now no tactics for Black) 15 ... ♕f7 16 b3 ♖fe8 17 ♖hf1 ♗f8 18 ♘h4± Christiansen - J Polgar, Vienna 1991. White plans an eventual f5 when Black's position would become uncomfortable.

8 ... ♖xd8
9 ♗xc5 ♘c6 *(286)*

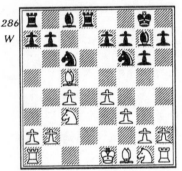

286
W

10 ♘d5

A natural move, though 10 ♗a3 has recently proved more popular if less effective:

a) 10 ... a5 and now:

a1) 11 ♘d5 ♘xd5 12 cxd5 ♘b4 13 0-0-0 (13 ♖d1?! e6 14 ♗c4 exd5 15 exd5 ♘c2+ 16 ♔f2 ♘xa3 17 bxa3 ♗d7∓ Timoshenko - Khalifman, USSR 1987) 13 ... e6 14 ♗c4 exd5 15 ♗xb4 axb4 16 ♖xd5 ♗e6⩲ Beliavsky - Nunn, Amsterdam OHRA 1990.

a2) 11 ♗c5 is a strange idea, e.g. 11 ... ♘d7 12 ♗e3 a4 13 0-0-0 a3 Knaak - Wojtkiewicz, Stara Zagora

Zt. 1990. Black has compensation and eventually won.

a3) 11 ♖d1 ♗e6 12 ♘d5 ♗xd5 13 cxd5 ♘b4 14 ♗b5 ♘c2+ 15 ♔f2 ♘xa3 16 bxa3 e6 was played in both Knaak - Piket, Novi Sad Ol. 1990 and van der Sterren - Shirov, Kerteminde 1991. Again Black has perfectly adequate compensation for the pawn.

b) 10 ... e6!? is the latest nuance in this line. This was played in Ivanchuk - Gelfand, Reggio Emilia 1991/92, when Black equalised after 11 ♘ge2 b6 12 ♘a4 ♗h6 13 ♖d1 ♗a6 14 ♘ec3 ♘d4 15 ♗d3 ♘h5.

10 ... ♘d7 *(287)*

If 10 ... ♘xd5 (In his original notes, Karpov claimed this move was forced which is clearly not the case) 11 cxd5 ♗xb2 12 ♖b1 (If 12 ♖d1 ♗c3+ followed by ... b6 causes trouble) 12 ... ♗c3+ 13 ♔f2 b6 (Not good, but as Karpov points out 13 ... ♗d4+ 14 ♗xd4 ♘xd4 15 ♔e3 e5 16 f4 f6 17 fxe5 fxe5 18 ♘f3 ♘xf3 19 gxf3 is winning) 14 ♗a3 ♘e5 15 ♗xe7, Karpov - Barle, Ljubljana/ Portoroz 1975. Black has no compensation for the pawn.

11 ♗xe7

If 11 ♘xe7+ ♘xe7 12 ♗xe7 ♗xb2 13 ♗xd8 (Or 13 ♖b1 ♗c3+ 14 ♔f2 ♗d4+ 15 ♔g3 ♖e8 16 ♗g5 ♘f6 17 ♘h3 ♘h5

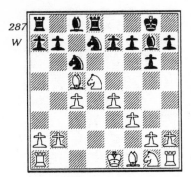

½-½ Timman - Sax, Zagreb 1985) 13 ... ♗xa1 and White's development is too retarded and his pawns too scattered to be able to speak of any advantage, e.g. 14 ♗e7 ♘e5 15 f4 ♘c6 16 ♗d6 ♗e6⯁ Rodriguez - Chekhov, Algarve 1975.

11 ♗a3, refusing the bait on e7, is an alternative, e.g. 11 ... e6 12 ♘c7 ♖b8 13 0-0-0 13 ... b6 (13 ... a6 14 f4 ♗f8 15 ♗xf8 ♔xf8 16 ♘f3 ♔e7 17 ♖e1 ♘a7 18 b4∞ Petursson - Mortensen, Espoo Zt. 1989) 14 ♘b5 ♗a6 15 ♘e2 ♘de5 16 ♘ec3 ♗h6+ 17 ♔c2 ♖xd1 18 ♘xd1 ♖d8⯁ Ward - Hassapis, British Ch. 1990.

The capture with the bishop on move 11 exchanges a useful piece but has the virtue of maintaining the White structure intact and of retaining the useful knight on the dominating d5-square.

11	...	♘xe7
12	♘xe7+	♔f8
13	♘d5	♗xb2

14 ♖b1 ♗a3

This is a curious bishop retreat, especially considering that Black has done okay after the more natural 14 ... ♗g7 *(288)*, e.g.

a) 15 ♘e2 ♘c5 16 ♘c1 ♗e6 17 ♘d3 ♖ac8 18 ♗e2 ♘a4 19 ♘3f4 g5 20 ♘h5 ♗c3+ 21 ♔f1 ♗d4⯁ Gheorghiu - Gelfand, Palma de Mallorca GMA 1989.

b) 15 g4 b6 16 g5 ♗b7 17 h4 ♖ac8 18 f4 ♘c5 19 e5 ♗xd5 20 cxd5 ♖xd5 21 ♖h2 ♖d4∓ Levitt - W Watson, London (Watson, Farley & Williams) 1990.

c) 15 ♘h3 ♘c5 16 ♘f2 (Black has his usual compensation but now chose incorrectly to play to get it back rather than maintaining the pressure) 16 ... f5 (16 ... b6) 17 ♗e2 ♗d4 18 ♖d1 ♗xf2+ 19 ♔xf2 fxe4 20 ♘c7± Karpov - Gallati, Zurich Simultaneous 1988. Presumably, Karpov would also have chosen 15 ♘h3 against Judit if she had played 14 ...

♗g7 instead of 14 ... ♗a3.

15	♘h3	b6
16	♗e2	♘e5
17	♘f2	♗b7
18	f4	♘c6 *(289)*

19 h4

Partly to generate counterplay by advancing the pawn and partly to develop his rook via h3.

19	...	♘d4
20	♖h3	♖ac8
21	h5	

Black clearly has superb positional compensation for the sacrificed pawn in terms of superior coordination. White obviously cannot play 21 ♖xa3 on account of 21 ... ♘c2+. Even after the text Black has adequate counterplay.

21	...	♗xd5
22	cxd5 *(290)*	
22	...	♖c2

At this point the fifteen-year-old Hungarian teenage girl prodigy overplays her hand. If 22 ... ♘xe2 23 ♖xa3 (23 ♔xe2 ♖c2+) 23 ... ♘xf4 24 hxg6 hxg6 25 g3 is ann-

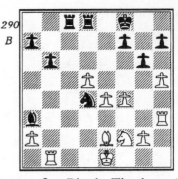

oying for Black. The best is 22 ... ♗b4+ 23 ♔f1 (Not 23 ♖xb4 ♘c2+) 23 ... ♘xe2 24 ♔xe2 (24 ♖xb4 ♘xf4) 24 ... ♖c2+ 25 ♔f1 ♗c5 seems fine. After the text her pieces get into something of a tangle and Karpov does what he is best at doing. namely consolidation.

23	♗d3	♖xa2
24	♗c4	♖c2
25	♖xa3	♖xc4
26	♖xa7	

Suddenly White has the advantage again. Karpov is still a pawn up, he has a rook on the seventh rank. Black's b-pawn is weak. White's centre is secure (the knight on f2 is a brilliant defender) and even White's h-pawn has something to say in the future.

26	...	b5
27	h6	b4
28	♘g4	♘c2+
29	♔d2	♘a3
30	♖f1	

Karpov has seen that he does not need to defend his

e-pawn.

| 30 | ... | ♖xe4 |
| 31 | ♘f6 (291) | |

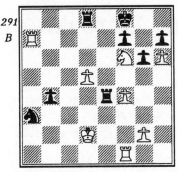

This is decisive since Black can no longer defend the pawn on h7, after which White's h6-pawn becomes a mighty force.

| 31 | ... | ♖d4+ |

32	♔e3	♘c2+
33	♔f3	♖d3+
34	♔e2	♖3xd5

Vainly hoping that White will be distracted by the meagre booty of 35 ♘xd5 but first Karpov introduces an important *intermezzo*.

| 35 | ♘xh7+ | |

The rook on d5 cannot run away.

35	...	♔g8
36	♘f6+	♔h8
37	♘xd5	♖xd5
38	♖xf7	b3
39	♖b7	♘d4+
40	♔f2	♘b5
41	♖a1	♖d2+
42	♔g3	♖a2
43	♖d1	1-0

15) Four Pawns and Averbakh

In this chapter we look at two lines which have been common in former years but are no longer so popular.

The Four Pawns Attack, attempting to dominate the centre from an early stage, was considered the refutation of the King's Indian Defence in the 1920s, until the correct methods for Black to attack the pawn centre were unearthed. Nowadays, it is regarded as a speculative attacking line, perhaps most effective as a surprise weapon.

The Averbakh system, named in honour of the Russian grandmaster who invented it, Yuri Averbakh, is designed to give White a permanent strategic grip and stifle Black's tactical aspirations. In common with the Four Pawns Attack, it is has remained part of the arsenal of a few grandmasters, but is nowadays, from a theoretical standpoint at least, something of a sideline.

Game 34
Christiansen – Kasparov
Moscow Interzonal 1982

1	d4	♘f6
2	c4	g6
3	♘c3	♗g7
4	e4	d6
5	f4	0-0
6	♘f3	*(292)*

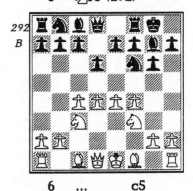

292
B

| 6 | ... | c5 |

Others:

a) 6 ... ♗g4 7 ♗e3 ♘fd7 8 h3 ♗xf3 9 ♕xf3 e5 10 dxe5 dxe5 11 f5 ♘c6 12 0-0-0 ♘d4 13 ♕f2 c6 14 g4 ♕a5 15 g5 ♖fd8 16 h4 ♘c5 17 ♔b1 b5 18 cxb5 cxb5 19 ♗g2 ♘a4 20 f6 ♗f8 21 ♘d5 b4 22 ♘e7+ ♔xe7 23 fxe7 ♖db8 24 ♗xd4 exd4 25 ♖hf1 f5 26 gxf6 ♔f7 27 ♕xd4 1-0 Glek – Damljano-

	Conover	Jones			
1.	d4	Nf6	33.	R4	Nb4
2.	c4	g6	34.	Ng3	Nd7
3.	Nc3	Bg7	35.	h5	Ne7
4.	e4	d6	36.	g5	Bd4
5.	Be2	O-O	37.	f5	Ne5
6.	Bg5	c5	38.	Kg2	Bf2
7.	d5	a6	39.	Bf4	Na6
8.	a4	Qa5	40.	Ne4	gb
9.	Bd2	e6	41.	Nf6	gb
10.	Nf3	ed	42.	Ng8	Kb
11.	ed	Qc7	43.	Nkb	Kf6
12.	O-O	Bg4	44.	g6	Nc7
13.	h3	Bf3	45.	Bg5	Bc5
14.	Rf3	Nbd7	46.	Ned7	Na6

1st 6 moves same as Jones

	Conover	Schmidt
7.	d5	R6
8.	B×3	×6
9.	g3	×d
10.	×d	Na6
11.	N×f3	R×8
12.	O-O	K×7
13.	B×d3	Lg7
14.	×4	Nc7
15.	R×b3	×5
16.	Ra×1	Na6
17.	Bb-1	Nb-4
18.	B×4×7	B×7
19.	×d1	R×1
20.		

B×B
Bd7
Bd8
Q×7
B×7
N×5
B×5
+?
+?
+?
+?

---

22. R×R2
23. N×R2
24. Q×3
25. Ng4
26. Q×7
27. Nd4
28. N×5
29. g5
30. R4
31. R5
32. Bd2
33. g5 Ng5
34. N×7
35. N×8
36. (1–0)

15. Bxa?   Rxa8
16. Rax1   Re1
17. Re1   Ne5
18. Be2   Re8
19. Bf3   Ned7
20. Bf3   Re1
21. Be1   Qb6
22. Bd2   Qd8
23. g3   Qb6
24. Kg2   a5
25. Qd3   Ne8
26. g4   Qe7
27. g4   Qe4
28. Be4   Nc7
29. Re3   Kf8
30. Ne2   Nab
31. Nf3   Nf6
32. Bb1   Kx8

47. Nf3
48. Nd8   Kg7
49. Ne6   Bc1
50. Kg3   Ng7
51. Kh3   Ne8
52. Nf8
53. Nd7

(1-0)

vic, Belgrade 1988. A very instructive game, where White was always better.

b) 6 ... ♘a6!?, demonstrating contempt for White's expansionist ideology, is the latest try *(293)*:

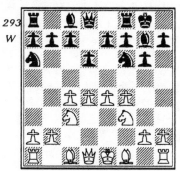

7 ♗e2 (7 e5 is obviously a critical test: 7 ... ♘e8 {7 ... ♘d7!?} 8 c5!? dxe5 9 fxe5 ♗g4 10 ♗e3 c6 11 ♗c4 ♘ec7 12 0-0 b5 13 ♗b3 ♘b4 14 ♕d2 ♘bd5 15 ♗h6 ♕d7 16 ♖ae1 a5 ½-½, although this position is ±/±, Dittmar - Kochiev, Gausdal 1991) 7 ... e5 8 fxe5 (Feeble is 8 dxe5 dxe5 9 ♕xd8 ♖xd8 10 ♘xe5 ♘c5 11 ♗f3 ♘fd7 12 ♘xd7 ♗xc3+ 13 bxc3 ♗xd7 14 0-0 ♗c6 15 ♗e3 ♘xe4 16 ♗xe4 ♗xe4= Vera - Bass, Barcelona 1990) 8 ... dxe5 9 d5 and now:

b1) 9 ... c6?! doesn't look right, e.g. 10 ♗g5 ♕b6 11 ♕b3 ♕a5 12 ♘d2 h6 13 ♗h4 g5 14 ♗f2 ♗g4 15 ♕d1 ♗xe2 16 ♕xe2± Maksimenko - Martynov, USSR Teams 1991.

b2) 9 ... ♘c5 10 ♗g5 h6 11

♗xf6 ♕xf6 12 b4 ♘d7 13 c5 a5 14 a3 axb4 15 axb4 ♖xa1 16 ♕xa1 ♕f4 17 g3 ♕e3 18 ♕b2 ♘xc5 19 bxc5 ♗h3 20 ♕b4 ♖a8 21 ♘d1 ♖a1 22 ♕b2 ♖c1 23 ♘d2 ♗g4 24 ♕b5 c6= Hausner - Khalifman, Bundesliga 1990/91.

7   d5

7 dxc5 is another try for White which has the benefit of obliging Black to waste time recovering the pawn: 7 ... ♕a5 8 ♗d3 ♕xc5 9 ♕e2 ♘c6 10 ♗e3 ♕h5 (10 ... ♕a5 11 0-0 ♗g4 12 ♖ac1 ♘d7 is a safer route to equality) 11 h3 ♗g4 12 0-0 ♗xf3 13 ♖xf3 ♘d7 14 ♕d2 ♕a5 15 ♖c1 ♘c5 16 ♗b1 a6 17 ♖f2 ♘a4 18 ♘d1± Braga - Reyes, Toledo 1991.

7   ...   e6

When White has extended himself somewhat with f4, the Benko Gambit approach is always going to be a possibility, e.g. 7 ... b5 8 cxb5 a6 9 a4 (9 bxa6 allows good counterplay, e.g. 9 ... ♕a5 10 ♗d2 {10 ... ♘bd7 11 ♕c2 ♗xa6 12 ♘b5 ♕b6 13 a4 c4 14 ♗xc4 ♘g4∓ Herzog - Dzindzichashvili, St. Martin 1991} 10 ... ♗xa6 11 ♗e2 ♕b4 12 e5 dxe5 13 fxe5 ♘g4 14 ♗xa6 ♘xa6∓ Kozul - Kochiev, Palma 1989) 9 ... e6 10 dxe6 ♗xe6 11 ♗e2 axb5 12 ♗xb5 ♘a6 13 0-0 ♘c7 14 ♗d3 ♕b8 15 e5 dxe5 16 ♘xe5± S Ivanov - Kupreichik, Leningrad 1989.

8 dxe6

8 ♗e2 is considered in the next game.

8 ... fxe6 *(294)*

9 ♗d3

9 ♗e2 may give White more chances to develop the initiative, e.g. 9 ... ♘c6 10 0-0 a6 11 ♔h1 ♕c7 12 ♖b1 ♗d7 13 a3 ♖ad8 14 ♕d3 ♗c8 15 b4± Kouatly - Nijboer, Wijk aan Zee 1988.

9 ... ♘c6
10 0-0 ♘d4

This move turns out highly successfully, but there has been a curious reluctance to repeat it. Others:

a) 10 ... a6 11 ♕e1 (11 ♔h1 led to a promising attack for White in Bykhovsky - Ginsburg, New York 1990: 11 ... ♘d4 12 e5 ♘h5 13 ♘xd4 cxd4 14 ♘e4 dxe5 15 fxe5 ♗xe5 16 ♗g5 ♖xf1+ 17 ♕xf1 ♕c7 18 ♕f2 ♗d7 19 ♖f1 ♗c6 20 ♗h6±) 11 ... b5 12 cxb5 axb5 13 ♗xb5 ♘d4 14 ♘xd4 cxd4 15 ♘d1 ♕b6 16 ♗d3 ♗a6

17 ♖f3 ♗xd3 18 ♖xd3 ♖fc8∞ Danner - Kindermann, Prague 1988.

b) 10 ... ♘h5 led to a powerful performance by Black in Maximenko - Velimirovic, Vrnjacka Banja 1991: 11 ♘g5 e5 12 fxe5 ♘xe5 13 ♗e2 ♘f6 14 ♘b5 h6 15 ♘f3 ♘xf3+ 16 ♗xf3 ♗e6 17 ♘xd6 ♘g4∓ 18 ♗xg4 ♗d4+ 19 ♕xd4 ♖xf1+ 20 ♔xf1 cxd4 21 ♗xe6+ ♔h7 22 e5 ♕e7 23 ♗d5 ♕xe5 24 ♘e4 ♖f8+ 25 ♔g1 b5 26 ♗d2 bxc4 27 ♗c6 ♕e6 28 ♗b7 ♕b6 0-1.

11 ♘g5 e5
12 f5 h6 *(295)*

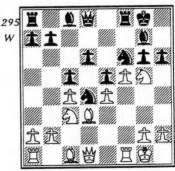

13 ♘h3

The piece sacrifice 13 fxg6 hxg5 14 ♗xg5 was worth a look, although after 14 ... ♗e6 15 ♘d5 ♗xd5 16 exd5 the pawn sacrifice 16 ... e4! 17 ♗e4 ♕e7 allows Black to activate his forces.

13 ... gxf5
14 exf5 b5!

This flanking blow is all the more powerul for having been delayed.

15	♗e3	bxc4
16	♗xc4+	♔h8
17	♗xd4	cxd4
18	♘d5	

Black has a clear positional advantage, but the play remains complex. Kasparov continues in determined fashion.

18	...	♗a6!

Giving up the bishop pair in the interests of liberating his central pawns. Christiansen prefers an exchange sacrifice to gain tactical chances on the kingside.

19	♘xf6	♗xc4
20	♘h5	♗xf1
21	♕g4	♕d7
22	♖xf1	d3
23	♕f3	d2! *(296)*

This pawn proves to be a bone in White's throat for the remainder of the game, preventing him from developing the kingside initiative.

24	g4	♖ac8
25	♕d3	♕a4
26	♘f2	♕d4

27	♕xd4	exd4

The black pawns look feeble, but persist in causing White problems.

28	♘f4	♖fe8
29	♘e6	♖c1
30	♘d1	♗f6
31	♔f2	♗g5
32	♔e2	♖c5
33	♔d3	♖e5
34	♘xg5	*(297)*

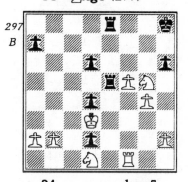

34	...	hxg5

Black still has to be careful, e.g. 34 ... ♖e1? 35 ♘f7+ ♔g8 36 ♖f2 ♖xd1 37 ♘xd6 and White escapes.

35	♖f2	♖e4
36	h3	♖e3+
37	♔xd4	♖8e4+
38	♔d5	♖e2
39	♖f3	♖e1
40	f6	♖f4
	0-1	

Notes based on Kasparov's in *The Test of Time*.

Game 35
Szabo – Timman
Amsterdam 1975

1	c4	g6

2	♘c3	♝g7
3	d4	d6
4	e4	♞f6
5	f4	c5
6	d5	0-0
7	♘f3	e6
8	♗e2	exd5 (298)

298
W

9   cxd5

Others:

a) The highly sharp 9 e5!? is adequately countered by 9 ... dxe5 10 fxe5 ♞e4! 11 cxd5 ♞xc3 12 bxc3 ♝g4!= or 9 ... ♞e4 10 cxd5 ♞xc3 11 bxc3 ♞d7 (11 ... ♝g4=) 12 e6 fxe6 13 dxe6 ♞b6 14 0-0 ♗xe6 15 ♞g5 ♛f6 16 ♛xd6 ♗f5 17 ♛xf6 ♗xf6= Ivanov - Hernandez, St. John 1988.

b) 9 exd5 is a less dynamic recapture. Black has various reasonable responses and can choose according to taste, e.g. 9 ... b5!? (The Benko Gambit idea. After 10 cxb5 a6 Black will obtain good compensation against White's queenside by combining pressure in the open a- and b-files with the activity of his king's

bishop. The move f4 is not very helpful to White in such situations. 9 ... ♞h5 is also perfectly playable for Black, e.g. 10 0-0 ♗xc3 11 bxc3 f5! 12 ♞g5 ♝g7= Gligoric, as is 9 ... ♜e8 10 0-0 ♗f5 11 ♗d3 ♛d7! 12 h3 ♞a6 13 a3 ♞c7 14 g4 {*14 ♛c2?* b5 15 cxb5 ♞fxd5 16 ♞xd5 ♞xd5 17 ♗xf5 gxf5 18 ♜b1 ♜e4 19 ♜d1 ♞b6 20 b4 ♛xb5 21 ♜xd6 c4 22 ♛f2 c3 23 ♛g3 ♛e2 24 ♞e5 c2 0-1 Peng Zhao Qin - J Polgar, Novi Sad Ol. 1990} 14 ... ♗xg4 {*14 ... ♗xd3 15 ♛xd3 b5!?* 16 cxb5 ♜eb8⇄ *Geller*} 15 hxg4 ♛xg4+= Conquest - Mestel, Hastings 1986/87) 10 ♞xb5 ♞e4 11 0-0 a6 12 ♞a3?! (Feeble. White should return the pawn with 12 ♞c3! ♞xc3 13 bxc3 ♗xc3 14 ♜b1) 12 ... ♜a7 13 ♗d3 ♜e7 14 ♞c2 ♜fe8 15 ♜e1 ♞d7 16 ♞e3 ♞df6 17 ♛c2 ♞h5 18 g3 ♗d4! (An original idea! Black is prepared to exchange his king's bishop in order to increase his control of e3) 19 ♞xd4 cxd4 20 ♞g2 ♞g5! (*Une petite combinaison*) 21 ♜xe7 ♞h3+ 22 ♔f1 ♜xe7! (Most players would have recaptured with the queen, but see Tal's 25th) 23 ♗d2 ♞f6 24 ♞h4 ♞g4 25 ♞f3 ♜e3! 26 ♔g2 ♛e7 27 ♜e1 ♞xf4+! 28 gxf4 ♜xe1 29 ♞xe1 ♛h4 30 ♗c1 (He has to defend f2) 30 ... ♛xe1 31 h3

♘h6 32 f5 ♘xf5 33 ♗f4 ♘h4+ 34 ♔h2 ♘f3+ 35 ♔g2 ♗xh3+! 36 ♔xf3 ♛g1 37 ♗xg6 ♛g4+ 38 ♔f2 ♛xf4+ 39 ♔g1 hxg6 0-1 Thorbergsson – Tal, Reykjavik 1964.

Returning to the position after 9 cxd5 *(299)*:

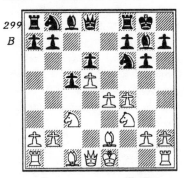

299
B

9 ... ♖e8

Black has alternative ways to play here:

a) 9 ... b5 10 e5! dxe5 11 fxe5 ♘g4 12 ♗g5!±. This line was quite popular in the late 1970s, but is not seen at all these days.

b) 9 ... ♗g4 is a very safe move for Black, e.g. 10 0-0 ♘bd7 11 h3 ♗xf3 12 ♗xf3 ♖e8 13 ♖e1 ♖c8 14 ♗e3 b5= Noguieras – Kasparov, Barcelona World Cup 1989.

10 e5

A very sharp line. White tries to swamp Black with his centre pawns.

10 0-0!? is a speculative gambit, which was successful in Kouatly – Arnason, Innsbruck 1977: 10 ... ♘xe4 11 ♘xe4 ♖xe4 12 ♗d3 ♖e8 13

f5 ♘d7 14 ♘g5 ♛f6 15 fxg6 ♛d4+ 16 ♔h1 fxg6 17 ♖f4 ♛xd3 18 ♛xd3 ♖e1+ 19 ♖f1 ♘e5 20 ♖xe1 ♘xd3 21 ♖e8+ ♗f8 22 ♘e6 ♗xe6 23 ♖xa8 ♗xd5 24 ♗h6 1-0.

10 ... dxe5
11 fxe5 ♘g4
12 ♗g5 f6

Or 12 ... ♛b6 13 0-0 ♗f5 14 d6 ♛xb2 15 ♘d5 ♘xe5 16 ♘e7+ ♖xe7 17 dxe7 ♘bc6 18 ♔h1 ♘xf3 △ ... ♛xa1= (Filip).

13 exf6 ♗xf6
14 ♛d2 ♗f5! *(300)*

The games Forintos – Ghitescu and Forintos – Enklaar, Wijk aan Zee 1974, had continued respectively with 14 ... ♗xg5 and 14 ... ♘e5. In neither case did Black equalise.

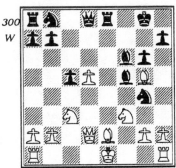

300
W

15 0-0 ♗xg5
16 ♛xg5 ♘d7

In Peev – Janosevic, Nis 1972, Black lost a tempo by playing at once 16 ... ♘e3 which was met by 17 ♛h6!. Now White has to waste a move with his h-pawn to

force the desired attacking
formation.

17 h3   ♘e3
18 ♕h6

White prepares to give
up material to get to grips
with Black's king.

18 ...   ♘xf1
19 ♘g5   ♕e7
20 d6   ♕e3+

After a wild opening
Black decides to play for a
win. he could instead have
drawn with 20 ... ♕g7 21
♗c4+ ♔h8 22 ♘f7+ etc. That
is the drawback of such
lines as the Four Pawns
Attack. They look hyper-
aggressive but can fizzle
out to equality against
accurate defence.

21 ♔xf1   ♘f8
22 ♖d1   ♖e5
23 d7   ♖d8
24 ♗c4+   ♗e6 *(301)*

301
W

All seems well, but
Szabo springs a horrid surprise.

25 ♘xe6!!

If now 25 ♘xe6 ♕xh6 26
♘xd8+ ♔g7 27 ♘e6+ ♘xe6

28 ♗xe6 and the d-pawn
queen. Or 25 ♘xe6 ♘xe6 26
♕xe3 ♖xe3 27 ♘d5 wins.

25 ...   ♖f5+
26 ♘f4+   ♔h8
27 ♘cd5   ♕e4
28 ♗e2   ♘e6
29 ♗f3   ♕c4+
30 ♔g1   ♘xf4
31 ♘e3

The end of a remarkable
combination. Black cannot
protect all of his pieces.
Meanwhile, White's d-pawn
remains posed as a terrible
threat.

31 ...   ♕e6
32 ♘xf5   ♕xf5
33 ♖e1   ♘e6
34 ♗g4   1-0

Game 36
Bareev - Kasparov
Linares 1992

1 d4   ♘f6
2 c4   g6
3 ♘c3   ♗g7
4 e4   d6
5 ♗e2   0-0
6 ♗g5 *(302)*

A novelty, lent respec-
tability by the strength of
the white player was 6 g4!?
a6 7 g5 ♘h5 8 ♗e3 b5 9
♗xh5 gxh5 10 ♕xh5 ♘c6 11
♘ge2 ♘b4 12 ♔d2 c5∞ Ba-
reev - Djuric, Bled 1991.

6 ...   ♘a6

This development of the
queen's knight, increasingly
frequent in all variations of

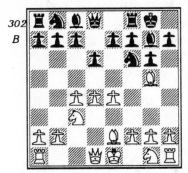

♔g2 ♘g8 24 ♗c2 ♘gf6 25 f4
♘e8 26 ♗d3 ♘c7 27 ♘e4
♗d4 28 ♘g3 ♘e8 29 a4 ♗b2
30 h4 Petursson – Velimi-
rovic, Novi Sad Ol. 1990.
This is a perfect example
of the kind of thing that
Black should avoid. White
is always slightly better,
and Black's position is
prospectless) 8 ♗f4 (8 ♗e3
e6 9 h3 exd5 10 exd5 ♗f5 {10
... ♖e8 is better} 11 g4 ♗c8
12 ♕d2 b5 13 ♗xh6 b4 14
♗xg7 ♔xg7 15 ♘d1 ♘e4 16
♕f4 and Black has insufficient compensation, Hort –
J Polgar, Munich 1991) and
now (303):

the King's Indian, gives
Black maximum flexibility.
He retains the option of
striking at White's centre
either by ... c5 or ... e5.

a) 6 ... c6 led to the following highly impressive
game by Bareev, one of the
very few world class cham-
pions of the Averbakh: 7
♕d2 ♘bd7 8 f3 a6 9 ♘h3 b5
10 ♘f2 bxc4 11 ♗xc4 d5 12
♗e2 dxe4 13 fxe4± e5 14 d5
cxd5 15 exd5 ♘b6 16 d6 ♗b7
17 0-0 h6 18 ♗xh6 ♗xh6 19
♕xh6 ♕xd6 20 ♘h3 ♘bd5 21
♘g5 ♘f4 22 ♗f3 ♗xf3 23
♖xf3 ♕d2 24 ♖g3 ♖fc8 25
♖f1 ♖xc3 26 bxc3 ♖c8 27
♔h1 ♖xc3 28 ♘e6!! ♘6h5 29
♕f8+ ♔h7 30 ♘g5+ 1-0 Ba-
reev – Kupreichik, Podolsk
1990.

b) 6 ... c5 7 d5 h6 (7 ...
♕a5 8 ♗d2 ♖e8 9 ♘f3 e6 10
0-0 exd5 11 exd5 ♗g4 12 h3
♗xf3 13 ♗xf3 ♘bd7 14 ♕c2
a6 15 ♖ae1 ♖xe1 16 ♖xe1 ♖e8
17 ♖xe8+ ♘xe8 18 b3 ♕d8 19
♗d1 ♕e7 20 ♕e4 ♔f8 21
♕xe7+ ♔xe7 22 g4 ♘ef6 23

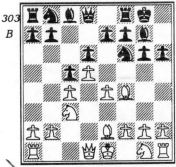

b1) 8 ... e6 9 dxe6 ♗xe6 10
♕d2 ♔h7 (10 ... ♕b6! 11 ♗xh6
♗xh6 12 ♕xh6 ♕xb2 13 ♖c1
♘c6 14 h4∞) 11 ♗xd6 ♖e8 12
e5 (12 ♘f3 ♘c6 13 0-0 ♗g4
14 ♖ad1 ♘xe4 15 ♘xe4 ♖xe4
16 ♗xc5 ♗xf3 17 ♗xf3 ♕xd2
18 ♖xd2 ♖xc4 19 ♗e3 ♖b4 20
b3 a5 21 ♖c1 a4 22 ♗d5±
Gelfand – Akopian, USSR
1990) 12 ... ♘fd7 13 f4 f6 14
h4 fxe5 15 h5 ♘c6 16 0-0-0

♘d4 17 ♗d3 ♔g8 18 ♘f3 ♗g4 19 hxg6 ♖e6 20 fxe5 ♗xf3 21 gxf3 ♘xf3 22 ♔g2 Bareev - Akopian, Moscow 1990. White always looked better here and he went on to win in 42 moves.

b2) 8 ... ♖e8 9 ♕d2 ♔h7 10 0-0-0?! (This works out badly after Black's response) 10 ... b5! 11 f3 ♕a5 12 cxb5 a6 13 b6 ♘bd7 14 b7 ♗xb7 15 g4 ♖eb8 16 h4 ♗c8‡ 17 ♕c2 ♖xb2!! 18 ♔xb2 ♖b8+ 19 ♔c1 ♕a3+ 20 ♔d2 ♖b2 21 ♖b1 ♘xe4+ 22 ♘xe4 ♖xc2+ 23 ♔xc2 f5 24 gxf5 gxf5 25 ♗d3 c4 26 ♘g5+ hxg5 27 ♗xf5+ ♔g8 28 ♗d2 ♕xa2+ 29 ♔c1 ♘c5 0-1 Petursson - Wojtkiewicz, Vienna 1990. This was a fine game by Black.

c) 6 ... h6 7 ♗e3 *(304)*:

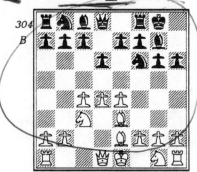

c1) 7 ... e5 8 d5 c6 (8 ... ♘bd7 9 h4 {9 g4 ♘c5 10 f3 c6 11 ♘h3 cxd5 12 cxd5 a5 13 ♘f2 ♗d7 14 a4∞ Keene - Gligoric, Hastings 1971/72} 9 ... h5 10 ♗g5 a5 11 g4? hxg4 12 ♗xg4 ♘c5 13 ♘f3 c6

14 ♕d2 ♕b6 15 ♖b1 ♕b4 16 b3 a4 17 ♘ge2 axb3 18 axb3 cxd5 19 cxd5 ♗g4-+ Griffiths - Keene, Birmingham 1971. White should have tried 15 0-0-0) 9 ♕d2 (9 h4 cxd5 10 cxd5 ♘bd7 {10 ... b5!?∞} 11 h5 g5 12 f3 a6 13 g4 b5 14 a4 with a distinct advantage to White, Petrosian - Schweber, Stockholm Izt. 1962) 9 ... h5:

c11) 10 f3 cxd5 (10 ... a6 11 h4 cxd5 12 cxd5 b5 13 ♘h3 ♗xh3 14 ♖xh3 ♘bd7 15 a4±/± b4 16 ♘d1 ♕a5 17 ♘f2 ♘c5 18 ♗d1 ♘fd7 19 g4 f5 20 gxf5 gxf5 21 exf5 ♖xf5 22 ♗c2 ♖f7 23 ♔e2 ♘f6 24 ♖g3 e4 25 ♖ag1 exf3+ 26 ♔f1 ♖aa7 27 ♘d4 ♕d8 28 ♕h6 ♕e7 29 ♖xf3 ♘cd7 30 ♗xa7 ♘e5 31 ♖xg7+ ♖xg7 32 ♖xf6 1-0 Bareev - Uhlmann, Dortmund 1990) 11 cxd5 ♗d7 12 ♗d3 ♘a6 13 ♘ge2 ♘c5 14 ♗c2 a5 15 a4 ♘e8 16 0-0 ♘c7 17 ♖a3± Petursson - Gallagher, Brocco Open 1990. This game is like a Saemisch Variation where Black has failed to organise effective counterplay.

c12) 10 h3 cxd5 11 cxd5 ♘a6 12 ♘f3 ♘c5 13 ♘g5 ♗d7 14 b4 ♘a4 15 ♘xa4 ♗xa4 16 b5 a6 17 b6 ♗b5 18 ♖c1 ♖c8= Hort - Uhlmann, Novi Sad Ol. 1990.

c2) 7 ... c5 8 dxc5 ♕a5 9 ♕d2 (9 ♗d2=) 9 ... dxc5 10 ♗xh6 ♖d8 11 ♕e3 ♗xh6 12

Variation b2 pg 235 instead -

♕xh6 ♘xe4 13 ♖c1 ♘c6 14
♘f3 ♘d4 15 h4 ♘xe2 16 ♘g5
♘f6 17 ♔xe2 ♗f5 18 f3 ♕b4
19 b3 ♕a3 20 ♔f2 ♖d2+ 21
♔g3 ♖xg2+!! *(305)*

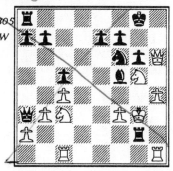

305
W

22 ♔xg2 ♕b2+ 23 ♔g3 ♘h5+
24 ♕xh5 gxh5 25 ♘d5 ♔f8
26 ♖cd1 e6 27 ♘f4 ♔e7 28
♖h2 ♕e5 29 ♖hd2 ♕c7 30
♘xf7 ♖g8+ 31 ♘g5 ♖xg5+ 32
hxg5 h4+ 33 ♔f2 ♕xf4 34
♖d7+ ♔e8 35 ♖d8+ ♔f7 36
♖1d7+ ♔g6 37 ♖g8+ ♔h5 38
♖dg7 ♕d2+ 39 ♔g1 ♕e1+ 0-1
Seirawan - Timman, Tilburg
1990) 8 ... dxe5 9 dxe5
♕xd1+ 10 ♖xd1 ♘g4 11 ♗xc5
♘xe5 12 ♘d5 ♘bc6 13 ♘f3
♗e6 14 b3 ♖fd8 15 0-0 ♖d7
16 ♘f4 ♗f5 17 ♘xe5 ♗xe5=
Petursson - Piket, Wijk aan
Zee 1990.

c3) 7 ... ♘bd7 8 ♕d2 c5
9 d5 ♕a5 10 f3 ♔h7 11 ♘h3
a6 12 ♘f2 b5 13 cxb5 ♘b6 14
0-0 ♘fd7 15 ♘fd1 ♘e5 16 b3
axb5 17 ♗xb5 f5 18 ♖c1 g5∞
Yakovich - Bologan, Gaus-
dal 1991.

7 h4

An extraordinary looking

move but it soon trans-
poses to more familiar situations. Others are:

a) 7 ♘f3 h6 8 ♗f4 e5 9
dxe5 ♘h5 10 ♗e3 dxe5 11
♕c1 ♔h7 12 0-0 (12 c5 f5 13
♗xa6 and now in Seirawan -
Spraggett, Manila Izt. 1990,
the players decided to take
the day off) 12 ... c6 13 c5
♕e7 14 ♘d2 ♘f4 15 ♗xa6
bxa6 16 ♘c4 ♕e6 17 ♗xf4
exf4 18 ♘d6 ♗e5 19 ♖d1 f3∞
Uhlmann - Nunn, Dortmund
1991.

b) 7 ♕d2 e5 8 d5 *(306)* and
now:

This one

NO

306
B

4/23/94 !!

b1) 8 ... c6 9 ♗d3 (9 ♗d1
cxd5 10 cxd5 b5 11 a3 ♘c5 12
f3 a5 13 ♗xb5 ♗a6 14 a4 ♖b8
15 ♘e2 ♗xb5 16 axb5 ♖xb5
17 ♖a2 ♕b6 18 ♘c3 ♖b4 19
♗e3± Petursson - Wojt-
kiewicz, Bad Wörishofen
1991) 9 ... ♘c5 10 ♗c2 ♕b6 11
♖b1 ♕b4 12 ♘ge2 a5 13 a3
♕xc4 14 ♗xf6 ♗xf6 15 b4
axb4 16 axb4 cxd5 17 bxc5
d4 18 ♘d5 ♗d8 19 ♗b3+-
Petursson - Nunn, Reykjavik
1990. Black does not have

13.Bb6!!

enough compensation for the sacrificed piece.

b2) 8 ... ♕e8 9 ♘d1 ♘c5 10 ♗c2 a5 11 ♘ge2 ♘h5 12 ♘b5 ♕d7 13 0-0-0 b6 14 f3 a4 15 g4 ♘f4 16 ♘xf4 exf4 17 ♗xf4 ♗a6∞ Seirawan - Piket, Wijk aan Zee 1991.

c) 7 f4 *(307)* and:

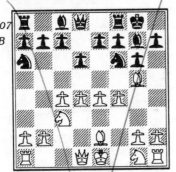

307
B

c1) 7 ... c6 led to very interesting play by both sides in Seirawan – Gelfand, Tilburg 1990: 8 ♘f3 ♘c7 9 d5 ♘h5 10 f5 gxf5 11 exf5 ♘f6 12 dxc6 bxc6 13 g4 ♖b8 14 ♕d2 ♘a6∞.

c2) 7 ... c5 8 d5 ♕a5 9 ♕d2 e6 10 dxe6 ♗xe6 11 ♘f3 ♗g4 12 0-0 ♘c7 13 f5± Tukmakov - Barbero, Wijk aan Zee 1991.

c3) 7 ... ♕e8 8 ♕d2 (8 ♘f3 e5 9 fxe5 dxe5 10 d5 h6 11 ♗xf6 ♗xf6 12 a3 ♕e7 13 0-0 ♖d8∞ Mohr - Miles, Bad Wörishofen 1990. Both sides have chances here) 8 ... e5!? (This is a promising try for Black to deal with White's aggressive seventh move) 9 fxe5 dxe5 10 d5 ♘c5 11 ♕e3

♘a4 12 ♘b5 ♕e7 13 0-0-0 a6 14 d6 cxd6 15 ♘xd6 ♕c7 16 ♔b1 ♘c5 17 ♗xf6 ♗xf6 18 ♘xc8 ♖fxc8∓ Tukmakov – Mortensen, Reykjavik 1990.

| 7 | ... | h6 |
| 8 | ♗e3 | e5 |

Also possible is 8 ... c5 9 d5 h5 followed by ... e6 to undermine the white centre.

9	d5	♘c5
10	♕c2	c6
11	h5	g5
12	f3	a5
13	g4	♗d7
14	♘h3	a4 *(308)*

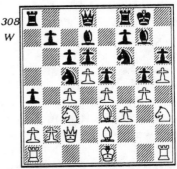

308
W

White has established exactly the kind of grip with a massive V of pawns stretching from the h-file to the d-file, which brought Petrosian victory in his similar game against Schweber. The main difference here is that Kasparov has considerably advanced his play on the queenside.

15	♕d2	cxd5
16	cxd5	♕a5
17	♘b1 *(309)*	

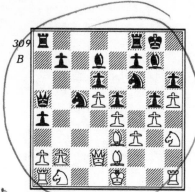

309
B

A typical strategic device. White offers the exchange of queens to reduce Black's attacking chances and if Black declines with some such move as 17 ... ♕c7 then 18 ♘a3 will stymie Black's operations on the queen's wing. Instead of falling for this Kasparov sacrifices a piece to confuse the issue.

17	...	♘fxe4
18	fxe4	♘xe4
19	♕xa5	♖xa5
20	♘c3	♘g3

It is more important to eliminate White's light-squared bishop, the chief guardian of the remnants of White's kingside pawn chain, than to snatch at an extra pawn with ... ♘xc3 and ... ♖xc5.

21	♖g1	♘xe2
22	♔xe2	e4

The remarkable thing about this game is that Black's initiative persists even after the trade of queens. If now 23 ♘xe4

then 23 ... a3 is extremely annoying for White.

23	♖ac1	f5
24	gxf5	♖xf5
25	♘f2	(310)

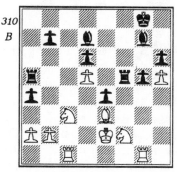

310
B

At long last removing this piece from the concealed radius of action of Black's queen's bishop lurking on d7.

25	...	♗e8
26	♖h1	♗b5+

It may seem odd for Black to surrender one of his bishops but after the virtually obligatory exchange the black rooks become ideally poised to mop up White's remaining pawns.

27	♘xb5	♖xb5
28	♖c8+	♔h7
29	♖d1	♖xb2+
30	♖d2	a3
31	♖c7	♖xd5
32	♘xe4	♔g8
33	♖cc2	(311)

Here White overplays his hand somewhat. Of course White must never capture on b2 which would give

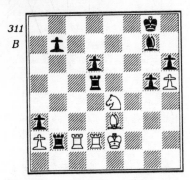

311
B

Black a most dangerous passed pawn, e.g. 33 ... ♖xb2 34 axb2 ♖xb7 35 ♖a5 but at this moment White could steer for a draw, which would indeed have been the logical outcome of the game with 33 ♖c8+ ♔f7 34 ♖c7+ when Black's king cannot escape the checks. In striving for more than this Bareev permits Black's initiative to flare up anew.

33	...	b5
34	♖xd5	♖xc2+
35	♖d2	♖b2
36	♔d3	d5
37	♘c5	

Black swiftly turns his attention to White's weak pawn on the h-file.

37	...	♖b4
38	♘e6	♖h4
39	♘xg7	♔xg7
40	♗d4+	♔g8

41	♗e5	♔f7
42	♖e2	♖xh5
43	♔d4	♔e6
44	♗b8+	♔f5
45	♖e3	♖h1
46	♖f3+	*(312)*

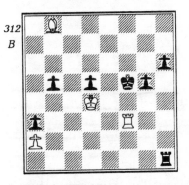

312
B

It turns out in any case that the balance of the position has not been seriously disturbed. True, if he took time of to play 46 ♖xa3 then Black's kingside pawns could become dangerous but by giving this timely check, White forces a draw.

| 46 | ... | ♔g4 |
| 47 | ♖g3+ | ♔f5 |

Black could play for a win with 47 ... ♔h4 but it would not be wise since the king would block the march of his own passed pawns on that square.

| 48 | ♖f3+ | ½–½ |

16) g3 system - Classical

The Classical Variation with Black playing ... ♘bd7 and ... e5, represents the most straightforward way of organising counterplay against White's fianchetto development. This was, in fact, the method elaborated by the Soviet pioneers of the King's Indian Defence, Boleslavsky and Bronstein, in their games from the late 1940s and early 1950s.

Black's strategic plan is to exert pressure against the d4-point in the hope that White will be forced to advance d5, thus exposing the centre to the flanking blow ... f5. Failing this, Black will exchange in the centre with ... exd4, basing future operations on a concerted attack against White's e-pawn (involving such moves as ... ♘c5, ... ♖e8 and possibly ... c6 followed by ... d5, liquidating White's central bind formation). Black will combine this with a queenside advance (... a5 - a4 and ... ♛a5 or ... ♛b6) intending to weaken White along the a1 - h8 diagonal.

An entirely new idea for Black after exchanging on d4 has been to play the unlikely looking ... ♗d7 followed by ... ♛c8. Instead of augmenting Black's pressure on the dark squares, which was formerly the strategic norm, Black lines up his attack against the white h-pawn which invariably has gone to h3. Whether White responds with ♔h2 or g4 to this manoeuvre, Black invariably gains excellent counterplay by means of the thrust ... h5.

Game 37
Timman - Kasparov
Tilburg 1991

1	d4	♘f6
2	c4	g6
3	♘f3	♗g7
4	g3	0-0
5	♗g2	d6
6	0-0	♘bd7 (313)
7	♘c3	

The alternative is 7 ♛c2

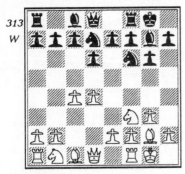

e5 8 ☐d1:

a) 8 ... ☐e8!? and now:

a1) 9 ♘c3 c6 10 e4 ♕c7! 11 b3?! b5 12 cxb5 cxb5 13 ♗a3 ♗b7 14 ☐ac1 ♕b6 15 dxe5 dxe5 16 ♕d2 a5 and Black has the initiative, Piket – C Hansen, Hamburg 1991. This is a clever idea – it is difficult for White to avoid the pin on the c-file after ... ♕c7 and ... b5, without wasting a tempo.

a2) 9 h3 c6 10 dxe5 dxe5 11 e4 ♕c7 12 c5 b6 13 b4 bxc5 14 bxc5 ♗f8! (Diverges from above and should be equal) 15 ♗e3 ♕a5 16 ☐c1 ♗a6 17 ♘bd2 ☐ab8 18 a3 ♘h5 19 ♘c4 ♗xc4 20 ♕xc4 ♘g7 21 ♘g5 ♘e6 22 ♘xe6 ☐xe6 23 h4 ☐ee8 24 ♗h3 ☐b7 25 h5 ♘f6 26 hxg6 hxg6 27 ♕c2 ½-½ Greenfeld – Smirin, Tel Aviv 1991.

a3) 9 dxe5 dxe5 10 e4 c6 11 h3 ♕c7 12 c5 b6 13 b4 bxc5 14 bxc5 ♘h5 15 ♗e3 ♘f8 16 ♘bd2 ♗a6 17 ♘c4± Salov – Lautier, Wijk aan Zee 1991.

b) 8 ... ♕e7 9 ♘c3 c6 10 e4 exd4 11 ♘xd4 ☐e8 12 b3 ♘c5 13 f3 (13 ♗b2 a5 14 ☐d2 h5 15 ♘a4 ♘xa4 16 bxa4 ♘d7 17 ♘b3 ♗xb2 18 ♕xb2 ♘b6= Salov – Hjartarson, Amsterdam 1991) 13 ... ♘fd7 14 ☐b1 ♘e5 15 ♘ce2 a5 16 a3 h5 17 h4 ♗d7 18 ♗e3 a4 19 b4 ♘e6= Salov – Kasparov, Linares 1991.

c) 8 ... exd4 9 ♘xd4 ☐e8 10 ♘c3 a6 11 b3 ☐b8 12 ♗b2 ♘e5 13 ☐d2 h5 14 ☐f1 (Maybe 14 h4. As played, Black is fine) 14 ... h4 15 ♘d5 ♘fd7 16 e4 hxg3 17 hxg3 ♘g4 18 ☐e1 c6 19 ♘e3 ♘de5 20 ♘xg4 ♗xg4 21 f4 ♘d7 22 ♘f3 ♘f6 23 e5 ♗f5 24 ♕d1 ♘e4 25 ☐d4 ♘xg3 26 ☐xd6 ♕b6+ 27 ♕d4 ♕a5 28 ♔f2 ♘h5 29 ♘h4 ♗g4 30 c5 Piket – van Wely, Dutch Ch. 1991.

7   ...   e5 *(314)*

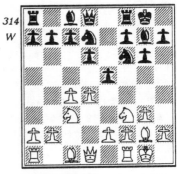

8   ♕c2

We do not like this move and consider the follow-up to be passive. Occupation of the centre by 8 e4 or 8 h3 is more natural, transposing to the lines considered in the next game.

Alternatively:

a) 8 dxe5 dxe5 9 ♕c2 c6 10 h3 ♕e7 11 ♗e3 ♘h5 12 ♖ad1 f5∓ Hamdouchi – C Hansen, Novi Sad Ol. 1990.

b) 8 b3 ♖e8 9 e4 exd4 10 ♘xd4 a6 11 h3 ♖b8 12 ♖e1 c5 13 ♘c2 b5 14 ♕xd6 ♖b6 15 ♕d1 b4 16 ♘a4 ♖be6∞ Csom – Bellon Lopez, Ter Apel 1991.

8 ... c6

8 ... ♖e8 led to one of the most remarkable games of recent years, Ivanchuk – Yusupov, Candidates' Quarter-Final Play-off 1991: 9 ♖d1 c6 10 b3 ♕e7 11 ♗a3 e4 12 ♘g5 e3 13 f4 (13 f3! Korchnoi) 13 ... ♘f8 14 b4 ♗f5 15 ♕b3 h6 16 ♘f3 ♘g4 17 b5 g5 18 bxc6 bxc6 19 ♘e5 gxf4 20 ♘xc6 ♕g5 21 ♗xd6 ♘g6 22 ♘d5 ♕h5 23 h4 *(315)*

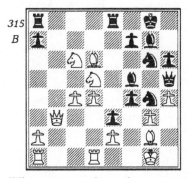

315
B

(The scene has been set. Ivanchuk has marched through the centre and virtually annihilated Black's queen's wing. Meanwhile. Yusupov has massed his forces for an onslaught against the white king. He now makes his first piece sacrifice to blast his way into greater proximity to the white monarch) 23 ... ♘xh4 24 gxh4 ♕xh4 25 ♘de7+ (It is hard to see that 25 ♘ce7+ is a superior way of accepting Black's sacrifice of a second piece. The point is that it is important for White to keep a knight on d5 where it has at least some defensive contact with the white king) 25 ... ♔h8 26 ♘xf5 ♕h2+ 27 ♔f1 ♖e6 28 ♕b7 ♖g6 (Oblivious to material sacrifice the black rook hurls itself into the attack) 29 ♕xa8+ ♔h7 (If White now plays 30 ♘xg7 Black has the diabolical sacrifice 30 ... ♕h1+ 31 ♗xh1 ♘h2+ 32 ♔e1 ♖g1 checkmate *(316)*.

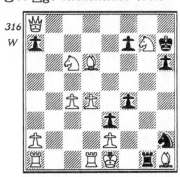

316
W

This fantastic variation. ending in checkmate with a huge disparity of material.

deserves an analysis diagram. This is what qualifies this game as the most brilliant of 1991) 30 ♕g8+ (The only way to delay checkmate) 30 ... ♔xg8 31 ♘ce7+ ♔h7 32 ♘xg6 fxg6 33 ♘xg7 ♘f2 (With the deadly threat of 34 ... ♘h3 35 ♗xh3 ♕h1 mate) 34 ♗xf4 ♕xf4 35 ♘e6 ♕h2 36 ♖db1 ♘h3 37 ♖b7+ ♔h8 38 ♖b8+ ♕xb8 39 ♗xh3 ♕g3 0-1.

9	♖d1	♕e7
10	b3	exd4
11	♘xd4	♖e8

Black stores up energy in the all important e-file.

12	♗b2	♘c5
13	e3	a5
14	a3	h5 *(317)*

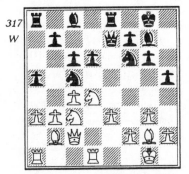

317
W

With his centre secure, Black can launch into an adventure on the wing, one which has the added benefit of drawing White's king into the firing line.

15	b4	♘ce4
16	b5	♗d7
17	♖ac1	h4
18	a4	

White is obsessed with wing manoeuvres which can lead nowhere. It was high time to eliminate Black's threatening central knight by means of 18 ♘xe4.

18	...	hxg3
19	hxg3	♘xf2! *(318)*

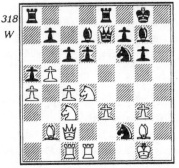

318
W

Apparently a bolt from a blue sky but the sacrifice is not that surprising to any student of centralisation.

20	♕xf2	♘g4
21	♕f3	♘xe3
22	♖e1	

Timman has in mind an ingenious counter-attack. In any case his hand is forced since both 22 ♖d2 and 22 ♖d3 fail to 22 ... ♘xc4.

22	...	♗xd4
23	♘d5	

This looks alarming. If Black were forced to play 23 ... cxd5 then 24 ♗xd4 would actually win for White. Nevertheless, the World Champion had foreseen this eventuality and decides the game with a sacrifice of his queen.

Watch now as the terrifying power of the black rooks is unleashed against White's king in the open avenue of the central e-file.

23	...	♘g4+
24	♗xd4	♕xe1+
25	♖xe1	♖xe1+
26	♗f1	cxd5
27	♕xd5	♖ae8
28	♗f2	♗e6
29	♕xb7	*(319)*

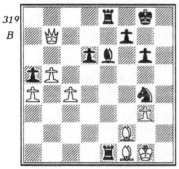

319
B

Timman is granted a brief respite to harvest a few innocuous pawns but in the long run his king is helpless against the combined onslaught of Black's forces.

29	...	♖c1
30	♕c6	♖c8
31	♕e4	♖8xc4
32	♕a8+	♔h7
33	b6	♖b4
34	♕xa5	♖bb1
35	♔g2	

White's passed pawns cannot advance and Black has a pleasant choice of methods of execution, either by 35 ... ♖xf1 or the move

played.

35	...	♖c2
	0-1	

Game 38
Yusupov - Kasparov
Linares 1990

1	♘f3	♘f6
2	c4	g6
3	g3	♗g7
4	♗g2	0-0
5	d4	d6
6	0-0	♘bd7
7	♘c3	e5
8	h3	*(320)*

8 e4 usually amounts only to a transposition of moves.

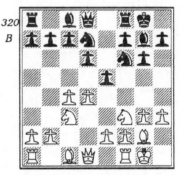

320
B

8	...	c6

Black has a couple of promising alternatives here:
a) 8 ... ♖e8 9 dxe5 dxe5 10 ♗e3 ♕e7 11 ♘d2 ♖d8 12 ♕b3 c6 13 ♖ad1 ♘f8 14 ♕a4 ♘e6 15 b4 ♘d4∓ Kurajica-Damljanovic, Yugoslav Ch 1991. As is usually the case when White has supinely played dxe5, and Black has been able to sink a knight on d4.

Black stands better.

b) 8 ... exd4 9 ♘xd4 ♖e8 10 e4 (10 b3 ♘c5 11 ♗b2 ♘d7 12 ♕c2 ♕c8 13 h4 ♗h3 14 ♖ad1 ♗xg2 15 ♔xg2 c6 16 ♘f3 ♕c7 17 b4=/± P Nikolic - Bischoff, Munich 1990) 10 ... ♘c5 11 ♖e1 ♗d7! 12 ♖b1 ♕c8 13 g4 h5 14 f3 c6 15 ♗f4 hxg4 16 hxg4 ♘e6 17 ♗e3 (17 ♘xe6 ♗xe6 18 ♕e2 ♘d7 19 ♖bd1 ♘e5 ½-½ Yusupov - Spasov, Novi Sad Ol. 1990) 17 ... ♕d8 18 ♘de2 ♕e7 19 ♕d2 ♖ed8 20 ♖bd1 ♗e8 21 ♘f4 ♘d7 22 ♘xe6 ♕xe6 23 b3 ♘e5 24 ♘e2 ♕e7 25 ♘f4 ♕f6 26 ♕f2 a5 27 ♘h3 ♕e7 28 ♕g3 a4 29 f4 axb3 30 axb3= P Nikolic - Gelfand, Moscow GMA 1990. This ... ♗d7 plus ... ♕c8 idea is a truly superb resource. It looks like the correct treatment for Black and it maintains the balance. As soon as White has had to play h3/f3 and g4 his chances of being better are pretty small.

In general, White's centre is too unwieldy. The bishop on g2 doesn't give it enough support, while the pawn on h3 is a target.

9 e4   ♕b6

a) 9 ... ♖e8 10 ♖e1 a5 11 ♕c2 exd4 12 ♘xd4 ♘c5 13 ♗f4! ♘fd7 14 ♘b3± Keene - Ciocaltea, European Team Ch. Bath 1973.

b) 9 ... ♕a5 10 ♖e1 exd4 11 ♘xd4 ♖e8 12 ♖b1 ♘e5 13 ♗f1 ♗e6 14 b4 ♕b6 15 ♗e3 ♕d8 16 ♘xe6 ♖xe6 17 f4 ♘ed7 18 ♕c2 ♕c7 19 ♗f2 ♖ae8, Yrjola - Mestel, Reykjavik 1990. Black has an active position in exchange for White's bishop pair.

10 c5

A fascinating attempt to try to break up Black's pawn centre, the purpose of which is to forestall Black's normal pressure against White's pawn centre.

Alternatives are:

a) 10 d5 used to be almost a main line of the King's Indian, but is not seen these days. After 10 .. ♘c5, two possibilities are:

a1) 11 ♘e1 cxd5 12 cxd5 ♗d7 13 ♘d3 ♘xd3 14 ♕xd3 ♖fc8 with adequate play. Botvinnik - Tal, World Ch. (6), Moscow 1960.

a2) 11 ♖e1 ♗d7 12 ♖b1 a5! 13 ♗f1 ♕c7 14 a4? (Better is 14 b3 △ a3, b4∞) 14 ... ♘a6 15 ♗e3 c5 16 ♔h2 ♖ae8 17 ♖c1 ♘b4-+ O'Kelly - Kavalek, Caracas 1970.

b) 10 ♖e1 exd4 11 ♘xd4 *(321)*:

b1) 11 ... ♘e8 12 ♘f3 ♘e5 13 ♘xe5 dxe5 14 ♕a4 (14 ♗e3 ♕xb2 15 ♕b3 ♕xb3 16 axb3 ♘c7 17 ♗xa7 ♘a6 18 ♗b6 ♗e6 19 ♖ed1 ♖fe8 20 ♘a4 ♗f8 21 h4 ♗e7 22 ♔h2 ♗d8 23 ♗e3 ♗c7 24 ♗h3 f5 25

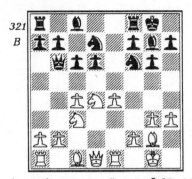

321
B

♘c5 ♘xc5 26 ♗xc5 ♔f7 27
♗g2 ♖ec8 28 ♗f3 ♗d8 29
♔g2 ♗e7 30 ♗b6 ½-½ Kir
Georgiev - Lautier, Novi
Sad Ol. 1990. This game was
played after the Karpov
game - Lautier obviously
still regards this line as
playable) 14 ... a5 15 a3 ♘c7
16 ♗e3 ♕xb2 17 ♖ec1 b5 18
♕d1 bxc4 19 ♗c5 ♘e6 20
♘a4 ♕b3 21 ♗xf8 ♗xf8 22
♗f1 ♘d4 23 ♖xc4 ♕xd1 24
♖xd1 ♗e6 25 ♖c3 ♖d8 26
♔g2 ♖b8 27 ♘c5 ♖b2 28 ♗d3
♗a2 29 ♘a4 ♖b3 30 ♖a1±
Karpov - Lautier, Biel 1990.

b2) 11 ... ♖e8 12 ♘a4 ♕a5
13 ♗f4 ♘e5 14 ♗f1 c5 15 ♗d2
♕d8 16 ♘f3 ♘c6 17 ♘c3 ♗e6
18 ♗f4 ♕b6 19 ♗xd6 ♖ed8 20
♘a4 ♕a5 21 ♘xc5 ♖xd6 22
♕xd6 ♘e8 23 ♘xb7 ♕b6 24
♕d2 ♕xb7 25 e5 ♖b8 26 b3
♗f8 27 ♕f4 ♗c5 28 ♗g2 ♕b6
29 ♘g5 ♘d4 30 ♖ad1± Stu-
rua - Nunn, London (Lloyds
Bank) 1990. This treatment
looks bad for Black.

10 ... dxc5
11 dxe5 ♘e8

12 ♘a4 ♕a6
Black also has a good
alternative:

12 ... ♕b5 13 ♕c2 ♘c7 14
♗e3 ♘e6 15 ♖fd1 c4 16 ♗f1
♘xe5 17 ♘xe5 ♕xe5 18 ♕xc4
♘g5 19 ♗xg5 ♕xg5 20 ♕c5
♕xc5 21 ♘xc5 b6 22 ♘d3
c5= Yusupov - Dolmatov,
Wijk aan Zee C 1991.

*From now on we follow
Yusupov's notes from New
In Chess.*

After 12 ... ♕c7 White can
hardly hope for an advan-
tage in the case of 13 ♗f4
♘e5 14 ♘c5 ♘xf3+ 15 ♕xf3
♕c7 16 ♘d3 ♘d6. However,
he has the interesting possibility 13 e6!?

13 ♗f4 (322)

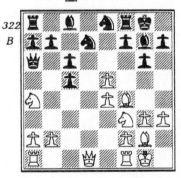

322
B

I could not clearly de-
termine the best move in
this position - the text
move or 13 ♗g5!? (13 ♕c2 is
an interesting alternative).
The critical position arises
after 13 ♗g5 b5 14 ♘c3 ♘c7
15 ♗e7 ♖e8 16 ♗d6. During
the game I did not want to
waste time by bringing the

bishop to d6, as the e5-pawn could also be defended immediately. Still, the bishop is more active on d6 and Black's queenside is slightly weakened by the move b5.

13 ...   ♘c7
14 ♕c2   ♘e6
15 ♖fd1   ♖e8!

15 ... b5 (This looks premature) 16 ♘c3 c4 17 ♖d6 ♕b7 18 ♖ad1 ♘dc5 19 ♗f1 ♕c7 20 b3 b4 21 ♘a4 ♘xa4 22 bxa4 c3 23 ♗c4, Adianto – Wojtkiewicz, New York Open 1991. White's pieces are too active.

16 ♖d6

This arrangement seemed perfectly natural to me. But here the difference between the World Champion and a mediocre top grandmaster (Yusupov's own phrase!) becomes evident. One of Kasparov's greatest abilities is accurate and subtle play during the transition from the opening into the middlegame. His next two moves demonstrate that he has got to the heart of the position, solving all his opening problems. Perhaps White has to confine himself to the modest 16 ♘c3!? intending 17 ♘e2.

16 ...   ♕a5
17 ♖ad1

Now 17 ♘c3 can be met by 17 ... c4 and the chronic

weakness of e5 becomes evident.

17 ...   ♘b6!
18 ♘xb6

If 18 ♘c3, then Black obtains the initiative on the queenside by playing 18 ... ♘c4 19 ♖6d3 b5.

18 ...   axb6
19 a3   ♕a4 (323)

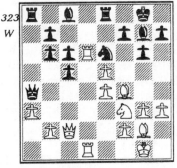

20 ♕e2

I wanted to play 20 ♕d2?! but I could not find compensation after the simple 20 ... ♕xe4. True, White can win the black queen with 21 ♘d4, but after 21 ... ♕xd4 22 ♖xd4 cxd4 (Or perhaps 22 ... ♘xd4!?) Black is much better.

20 ...   b5
21 ♕e3?

While Black carries out his strategic plan, prepared by his 16th and 17th moves, with implacable consistency - a queenside pawn attack - White is wasting his time. 21 h4 was considerably stronger, trying to complicate the game on the kingside. White's mistake leaves the initiative entirely to Kasparov.

21	...	b4
22	axb4	♛xb4
23	♖6d2	♖a2
24	♖b1	c4
25	♖c2	b5
26	♗h6	

The only positional try White has been able to prepare for during the last eight moves. This was not possible on the previous move because of the blow ... c4 - c3.

| 26 | ... | ♛c5 *(324)* |

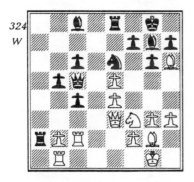

324
W

27 ♛c1?

Of course, the endgame after 27 ♛xc5 ♘xc5 28 ♗xg7 ♔xg7 29 ♘d4 is in Black's favour, but this was obviously the lesser evil. Black should not exchange pawns because after 29 ... ♖xe5 30 ♘xc6 ♖e6 31 ♘d4 ♖b6 White has the terrible blow 32 b4! Superior is 29 ... ♗d7 30 f4 ♘d3 31 ♗f1 c5 32 ♘e2 with a slightly

better position for Black.

27	...	♘d4
28	♗xg7	♔xg7
29	♘xd4	♛xd4
30	b3	

White has a strategically lost position and his only chance is to confuse the game in his opponent's time trouble. Probably Black has more than one way to convert his advantage into a win. Kasparov conducts the game quite logically.

30	...	♖xc2
31	♛xc2	c3
32	♖d1	♛c5
33	b4	

The only possibility to put up resistance.

33	...	♛xb4
34	♖d3	c5
35	♖xc3	c4
36	f4	♛c5+
37	♔h2	

This is just searching for practical chances. The game can hardly be saved by 37 ♛f2 ♛xf2 38 ♔xf2 ♗e6 39 ♖c1 ♖d8 either.

| 37 | ... | ♛d4 |
| 38 | ♖f3 | b4 *(325)* |

At this moment I could not believe my luck; did Kasparov, who still had several minutes on his clock commit such a simple blunder? Had he just played 38 ... ♖d8 then, probably, he would have won easily with technical

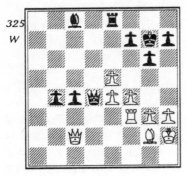

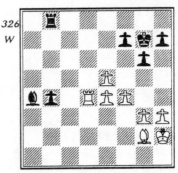

means.

39 ♕a4

Here the World Champion thought for a while, and gradually it became clear to me that today I would not even be lucky.

39 ... c3!!

An amazingly beautiful way to win. Considerably worse was 39 ... b3??, with the same idea, in view of the primitive 40 ♖xb3.

40 ♖xc3

The thing is that after 40 ♕xe8 ♕d7!! 41 ♕xd7 ♗xd7 the pawns are unstoppable.

40 ... ♗d7
41 ♖c4 ♗xa4

Kasparov had assessed this accurately, though it is not obligatory. Of course, Black also wins after 41 ... ♕xc4 42 ♕xd7 ♖e6.

42 ♖xd4 ♖b8 *(326)*
43 ♗f1?!

White continues the same line of defence - looking for practical chances. It was better to change course by 43 ♗f3! and if 43

... b3 (43 ... ♗c2?! 44 ♘d1 b3 45 g4), then 44 ♘e2 b2 45 ♘d3 b1♕ 46 ♗xb1 ♖b2+ 47 ♔g1 ♖xb1+ 48 ♔f2 and Black still has to overcome some technical difficulties.

43 ... ♗c2
44 ♘c4

44 ♘d3 b3 45 ♗xc2 bxc2 46 ♖c4 loses because of 46 ... ♖b2.

44 ... b3
45 ♘xb3

If 45 ♖d7 b2 46 ♗xf7 then 46 ... ♖d8, indicated by Kasparov, is the simplest solution.

45 ... ♖xb3
46 g4 ♖e3
47 f5 gxf5

Avoiding another trap: 47 ... ♖xe4? 48 f6+ ♔h6 49 ♖xe4 ♗xe4 50 e6 ♗d5 (50 ... fxe6?? 51 g5) 51 e7 ♗c6 52 h4 g5 53 h5 with a draw.

48 exf5 ♖xe5
49 ♖d2 ♗a4
50 ♔g3 ♖e3+
51 ♔h4 ♗b5
52 ♖d5 *(327)*
52 ... ♗d3

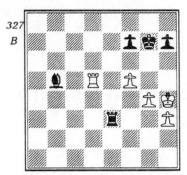

327
B

My last chance was 52 ...
♗f1? 53 f6+! with drawing
chances.

53	♖c5	h6
54	♖c3	♖f3
55	♖b3	♗e2
56	♖b2	♗f1
57	♖h2	♔f6
58	♖h1	♔e5
59	♖h2	f6
60	♖h1	♔e4

61	♖h2	♔f4
62	♖h1	♗g2
63	♖h2	♖g3
	0-1	

Notes based on those by
Yusupov in *New In Chess*.

This game shows, I (RK)
think, why the g3 lines are
so out of fashion. When I
used to play them as White
I always did well, but I had
a feeling that White, after
either d5 (or ... exd4 by
Black at some moment).
simply had too much ex-
posed territory to defend.
I am very impressed by the
... ♗d7 and ... ♕c8 man-
oeuvre, for example, in Yusupov - Spasov and Nikolic
- Gelfand, which seems to
underscore this motif.

17) g3 system - Yugoslav/Panno

The strategic basis of the Yugoslav is the substitution of ... c5 for ... e5, intending to increase the scope of Black's fianchettoed king's bishop along the a1 - h8 diagonal, combining this with an advance in the b-file against White's queen's wing. This system was worked out by Yugoslav analysts and numbers Gligoric among its most enthusiastic practitioners.

The chief drawback of the Yugoslav as a winning attempt for Black is the Exchange variation, which leaves Black with a shade the worse of the draw.

The Panno Variation gives rise to a wealth of complex strategic problems. Manoeuvres unfold over the whole board - on the queenside, kingside and in the centre.

It is clear that the old main lines of the Panno, in which White seals up the centre with d5, according to the latest practice give Black enormous scope for tactical counterplay. Therefore attention is focusing, from White's point of view, on less well charted 8th-moves such as 8 ♗g5 which we see in Kasparov - Nunn. Another system which is worth watching out for is 8 b3 ♖b8 9 ♗b2 b5 10 cxb5 axb5 11 ♖c1 which contains considerably more venom than might at first sight appear.

Game 39
Timman - Kasparov
Tilburg 1981

1	d4	♘f6
2	c4	g6
3	g3	♗g7
4	♗g2	0-0
5	♘f3	d6

5 ... c5 6 ♘c3 cxd4 7 ♘xd4 ♘c6 8 0-0 transposes to the English Opening, which is not dealt with in this volume.

| 6 | 0-0 | c5 |

Kasparov used to favour the dynamic King's Indian Defence in his early youth, subsequently found it too risky, and switched to the Grunfeld. But now he has come back to the King's Indian again, as is amply testified by games in this book.

7 ♘c3   ♘c6
8 d5

White maintains a modest edge with 8 dxc5 but Timman is out for bigger game.

8 ...   ♘a5
9 ♘d2   a6

9 ... e5 is a good move here, probably better than 9 ... a6. The point is that this position is normally reached via the move order 1 d4 ♘f6 2 c4 g6 3 g3 ♗g7 4 ♗g2 0-0 5 ♘f3 d6 6 0-0 ♘c6 7 ♘c3 a6 8 d5 ♘a5 9 ♘d2 c5 when a later ... e5 is usually met by dxe6. Some material after 9 ... e5 *(328)*:

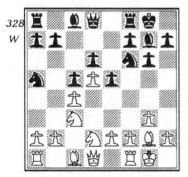

a) 10 a3 b6 11 b4 ♘b7 12 ♗b2 ♘g4 13 h3 ♘h6 14 e3 f5 15 f4 ♘f7 16 ♔h2= Vaganian – Gligoric, Baden 1980.

b) 10 e4 ♘g4 11 h3 ♘h6 12 b3 a6 (12 ... f5 13 exf5 gxf5

14 ♗b2 ♘d7 15 ♕c2 b6 16 ♘e2 ♕c7 17 f4 ♖ae8 18 ♖ae1 ♘b7 19 ♘c1 ♗c8 20 ♗c3 exf4 21 gxf4± Vaganian – Spassky, Tilburg 1983) 13 ♗b2 ♖b8 14 ♘e2 b5 15 ♗c3 f6 16 ♔h2?! f5! and Black has an ideal position due to the blocked centre, Jukic – Velimirovic, Yugoslavia 1988.

10 ♕c2   ♖b8

10 ... e5 11 e4 ♘g4 12 b3 f5 13 exf5 gxf5 14 h3 ♘h6 15 ♗b2 ♖b8 16 f4 b5∞ Birnboim – Pein, Tel Aviv 1987. This is similar to Jukic – Velimirovic but here 11 a3 ⌐ ♖b1 and b4 is worth considering since Black has already played ... a6 and thus the b6-square is weaker than in Vaganian – Gligoric.

11 b3   b5
12 ♗b2 *(329)*

An interesting alternative is 12 ♖b1 ♗d7 13 ♗b2 bxc4 14 bxc4 ♖b4 15 ♘ce4 ♘xe4 16 ♗xe4 ♕a4 17 ♕c1 ♗xb2 18 ♖xb2 ♕b6 19 ♖b1 ♖xb1 20 ♕xb1 ♖b8 21 ♕d3 ♕d8 22 ♕c3± Kasparov – I Gurevich, New York Simultaneous 1988.

12 ...   bxc4

A premature exchange. Kasparov was later to promulgate the improved move order: 12 ... ♗h6! 13 f4 (13 ♘cb1 is silly, since ♗c3 can always be met by ... b4!) 13 ... bxc4 14 bxc4 e5 which transposes to a line

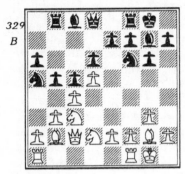

considered later under the move order 12 ... bxc4 13 bxc4 ♗h6 14 f4 e5.

Others:

a) 12 ... e5 13 ♖ae1! (13 ♘d1? ♘g4 14 e4 f5 15 exf5 ♗xf5 16 ♘e4 bxc4 17 bxc4 ♗h6 18 ♕e2 ♖b4 19 ♗c3 ♖a4 20 ♘b2 ♖a3 21 ♕e1 ♗g7 22 ♕d2 ♘f6 23 ♘xd6 ♕xd6 24 ♗xa5 ♘e4 25 ♕e1 ♘g5 26 ♗c3 ♗h3 27 f3 ♕d7 0-1 Cvitan - Purtov, Budapest Open 1990) 13 ... ♘h5 14 ♘d1 f5 15 f4± Wojtkiewicz - J Polgar, Haifa 1989.

b) 12 ... ♗d7 13 cxb5? (This never works for White. 13 ♖ae1 is one rational alternative, with the standard plan of ♘d1) 13 ... axb5 14 ♘d1 e6 15 dxe6 fxe6 16 e4 ♘c6 17 a3 e5 18 ♘e3 ♘d4∓ Ristic - Ivanovic, Yugoslav Ch. 1991.

13 bxc4 *(330)*

13 ... ♗h6

13 ... e5 14 ♖ab1 ♗h6 15 f4 exf4 16 ♘ce4 (16 gxf4! The remainder of this game serves as a good cautionary tale) 16 ... ♖xb2∓ 17 ♖xb2

♘g4 18 gxf4 ♗g7 19 ♖bb1 ♗d4+ 20 ♔h1 ♘xh2 21 ♘f3 ♘xf3 22 exf3 0-1 Stankovac - Milanovic, Belgrade 1989.

14 ♘cb1!

A very solid move, defending his knight on d2 and preparing to harass the Black knight on a5 with ♗c3. It makes good sense now that Black no longer has ... b4 at his disposal. The alternative is 14 f4 e5 and now:

a) 15 dxe6 ♗xe6 (15 ... fxe6!?) 16 ♘d5 ♖xb2 (16 ... ♗xd5 17 cxd5 ♘g4 {17 ... ♖xb2!? 18 ♕xb2 ♗g7∞} 18 ♘b3 f5 19 h3 ♘f6 20 ♘d2 ♘h5 21 ♔h2 ♖e8 22 e4 ♖xb2 23 ♕xb2 ♗g7 24 ♕c2 ♗xa1 25 ♖xa1 ♕f6 26 ♕a4 ♖e7 27 ♕xa5 ♕xa1 28 ♕d8+ ♔f7 29 ♘c4 ♕f6 30 ♘xd6+ 1-0 Stohl - Kindermann, Dortmund 1991) 17 ♕xb2 ♗g7 *(331)*:

a1) 18 ♕c1!? (This looks terrible for White, but works out okay here) 18 ... ♘g4 19 ♖b1 ♗xd5 20 ♗xd5 ♘e3 21 ♖e1 ♖e8 22 ♘f3 ♗f6

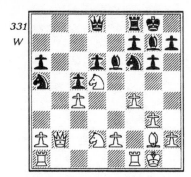

331
W

23 ♔h1 ♔f8 24 ♕a3 ♘c2 25 ♕d3 ♘xe1 26 ♘xe1 ♕c7 27 ♘c2 ♖b8 28 ♘e3 ♖xb1+ 29 ♕xb1 ♗d4 30 ♘f1± C Hansen - Ernst, Lugano Open 1987.

a2) 18 ♕a3 ♘xc4 19 ♘xc4 ♘xd5 20 ♖ac1 ♘b4 21 ♔h1 d5∞ Hübner - Nunn, Wijk aan Zee 1982.

b) 15 ♖ae1 exf4 16 gxf4 ♘h5 17 e3 ♗g7 18 ♘d1 ♗f5 19 ♗e4 ♗xb2 20 ♘xb2 ♖xb2!! 21 ♕xb2 ♘xc4 22 ♘xc4 ♗xe4 ("unclear/better for Black" according to Kasparov's analysis in *BCO*).

c) 15 ♖ab1 is possibly an improvement here, e.g. 15 ... exf4 16 gxf4 ♘h5 17 e3 ♖e8 18 ♘ce4 ♗f5 19 ♗c3 ♖xb1 20 ♖xb1 ♗xe4 21 ♗xe4 ♗g7 22 ♗xg7 ♔xg7 23 ♕c3+ ♔g8 24 ♗f3 ♘f6 25 e4 ♘d7 26 ♗g2 g5 27 ♗h3 ♘f8 28 ♕g3 h6 29 ♗f5 ♕f6 30 fxg5± Horvath - Kindermann, Hungarian Team Ch. 1991.

14 ... e5
Seeking central counterplay, but Black's coming

idea could perhaps be implemented in improved form by 14 ... ♗d7 15 ♗c3 ♕c7 16 ♘a3 ♖b4!?

15 ♗c3 ♗d7
16 ♘a3 ♖b4
Looks surprising, but offering his queen's rook for White's queen's bishop is the only way to generate counterplay, viz. 16 ... ♗g7 17 ♖ab1 ♕c7 18 e4 h5 19 f4 ♖b4 20 ♕d3 ♘b7 21 ♘c2 ♖xb1 22 ♖xb1 h4 23 fxe5 dxe5 24 ♘f3 hxg3 25 ♗xe5 gxh2+ 26 ♗xh2 ♕c8 27 ♘e3 ♘g4 28 ♘xg4 ♗xg4 29 ♘e5 ♘a5 30 ♖f1± Zaid - Kasparov, USSR 1977.

17 ♗xb4 cxb4
18 ♘ab1 *(332)*

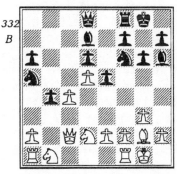

332
B

All this is, in fact, well-known opening theory. This may seem astonishing, but modern 'opening' investigation extends deep into what might be legitimately termed the middlegame. Black's next move improves on Petrosian - Toran, Bamberg 1968; 18

... ♕b6? 19 ♘b3 ♘b7 20 ♘1d2 ♖c8 21 a3!+-.

18 ...   ♕c7!

Putting pressure on White's c4-pawn.

19 e3

Blocking the path of Black's king's bishop. Alternatively, 19 c5 ♕xc5 20 ♕b2 ♘g4 21 ♘e4 ♕b6 22 ♗f3 ♗g7 23 ♘bd2 ♘h6 24 ♖ab1 f5 25 ♕xb4 ♕xb4 26 ♖xb4 fxe4 27 ♘xe4 ♘f5 28 ♖c1 ♘d4 29 ♔g2 ♗b5 30 ♖c7 Kurajica - Filipovic, Banja Luka 1983 is very unclear. 20 ... ♘g4 is possibly not the best in any case; 20 ... ♖c8!?

19 ...   ♗f5

During the game Timman feared the cavalier attack 19 ... ♘g4!? threatening 20 ... ♘xe3 21 fxe3 ♗xe3+ and 22 ... ♗d4. The only reply is the cautious 20 ♖e1! which was overlooked in the understandably tumultuous post mortem, but which appears to consolidate White's position. A practical example is 19 ... ♘g4 20 ♖e1 f5 21 h3 ♘f6 22 ♘b3 ♕xc4 23 ♕xc4 ♘xc4 24 a3 bxa3 25 ♘xa3 ♘b6 26 ♘c2 ♗b5 27 ♘b4 e4 28 ♘xa6 ♘fxd5 29 ♗f1 ♗xf1 30 ♖xf1 Tischer - Carstens, Bundesliga 1984, which was always better for White, but Black held the draw.

20 ♘e4   ♗xe4

21 ♗xe4 *(333)*

21 ...   ♘b7?!

An amazing decision, renouncing material in order to create a blockade. Nevertheless, the simple 21 ... ♘xe4 22 ♕xe4 ♕xc4 is preferable, in as much as 23 ♕xc4 ♘xc4 24 ♖c1 permits 24 ... ♘xe3 25 fxe3 ♗xe3+.

A variation on this theme is 21 ... ♘xe4 22 ♕xe4 f5 23 ♕c2 ♕xc4 24 ♖c1 ♕xd5 25 ♘d2 f4 26 ♘f1 fxe3 27 ♘xe3 ♕f3 28 ♖e1 ♘c6∞ D'Andrea - Lotti, Correspondence 1985.

22 ♘d2   ♘c5

23 ♗g2   ♖b8

24 ♖fb1   a5

Kasparov shows no interest in defensive grovelling after 24 ... ♕b6 25 ♖xb4 ♕xb4 26 ♖b1 ♕xb1+ 27 ♘xb1 ♖b4, as suggested by Ulf Andersson.

25 a3   e4

26 axb4   axb4

27 ♗h3

To prevent ... ♘fd7 supporting the knight on

c5. White is gradually gaining the upper hand.

27	...	♗g7
28	♖a2	h5
29	♘b3	♘d3
30	♖d1	

White threatens just 31 ♖xd3, wiping out Black's counterplay.

| 30 | ... | ♘e5 |
| 31 | c5! | *(334)* |

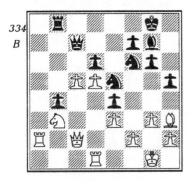

334
B

Black's blockade is broken and he is definitely losing.

31	...	♘d3
32	cxd6	♕xd6
33	♗f1	♘e5

In serious time pressure, Kasparov's final moves give a disjointed impression.

34	♖a6	♕d7
35	♖xf6!	♗xf6
36	♕xe4	♖c8
37	♕xb4	h4
38	♕f4	♔g7
39	gxh4	♕d6
40	♘d2	1-0

Black lost on time. 40 ... ♕xd5 41 ♘e4 ♕xd1 42 ♕xf6+ wins easily.

Game 40
Salov - Speelman
Reykjavik World Cup 1991

1	d4	d6
2	♘f3	g6
3	g3	♗g7
4	♗g2	♘f6
5	0-0	0-0
6	c4	c5
7	♘c3	

7 d5 can be met in various ways:

a) 7 ... b5 transposing to a Benko Gambit is a possibility that White must reckon with.

b) 7 ... ♘a6 8 ♘c3 ♘c7 9 a4 ♖b8 and now:

b1) 10 ♗f4 a6 11 a5 b5 12 axb6 ♖xb6 13 b3 e6 14 dxe6 ♘xe6 ♘a4 ♘xf4! 16 ♘xb6 ♕xb6 (16 ... ♘xe2+ 17 ♕xe6 ♕xb6 18 ♘d2 ♖e8 19 ♕d1 ♗g4 20 ♗f3 h5± Marovic - Janosevic, Skopje 1970) 17 gxf4 ♘h5 18 ♖a2 ♘xf4=/∞ Donner - Matanovic, Utrecht 1962.

b2) 10 e4 a6 11 a5 b5 12 axb6 ♖xb6 13 ♖a3! and now instead of 13 ... e6? 14 dxe6 ♗xe6 15 ♕d3 ♘g4 16 ♘a4 ♖b4 17 b3 ♕e7 18 ♗f4± Korchnoi - Visier, Palma 1968, Korchnoi recommends 13 ... ♗g4.

c) 7 ... e6 giving White the option of transposing to the Modern Benoni with 8 ♘c3 or accepting the challenge with 8 dxe6!?, which seems to be very good for White, e.g. 8 ... ♗xe6 9 ♘g5 ♗xc4 10 ♗xb7 ♘bd7 11 ♘a3! (An important move. If White has reached this position having played ♘c3 instead of 0-0, then Black's sacrificial play is quite promising, whereas here it is simply dubious) 11 ... ♖b8 12 ♘xc4 ♖xb7 13 ♘xd6 ♖b4 14 ♕c2± Korchnoi - Velimirovic, USSR v Yugoslavia 1966.

The variations after 7 d5 used to be very popular, but these days are hardly ever seen.

7 ... ♘c6 *(335)*

7 ... cxd4 8 ♘xd4 again transposes to the English Opening.

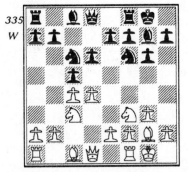

After 7 ... ♘a6 White's best is 8 d5! transposing to note 'b' at White's last move. Alternatively, 8 b3?! d5! 9 cxd5 ♘xd5 10 ♗b2 ♘xc3 11 ♗xc3 ♘c7 12 ♕d3 ♗f5 13 e4 cxd4 14 ♗xd4 ♗g4= Mortensen - Wang Zili, Thessaloniki Ol. 1988

is a very interesting way to equalise.

8 dxc5

8 e3 is insipid, e.g. 8 ... ♗f5 9 d5 ♘a5 10 ♕e2 ♘e4 11 ♘d1 ♗d7 12 ♘d2 ♘xd2. Hausner - Landenbergue. Prague 1989. Black has no problems.

8 ... dxc5 *(336)*

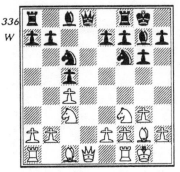

9 ♗f4

Or 9 ♗e3!? and now:

a) 9 ... ♗e6:

a1) 10 ♗xc5!? ♕a5 11 ♗a3 ♗xc4 (11 ... ♖fd8= *ECO*) 12 ♘d4 ♘xd4 13 ♕xd4 ♖ac8 14 ♕f4 ♘h5 (14 ... g5? 15 ♕e3± Spassky - Tal USSR Ch. 1961) 15 ♕e3 ♗xc3 16 ♕xc3 ♕xc3 17 bxc3 ♗xe2 (17 ... ♖c7 - Tal) 18 ♖fe1 ♗a6 19 ♗xe7 ♖fe8 20 ♗b4 ♘f6 21 a4 ♘d7 22 f4±/± Yrjola - Maki. Helsinki 1991. This is a very interesting reference. Boleslavsky gives the position after 19 ... ♖fe8 as equal but, as the game continuation shows, White maintains a nagging plus.

a2) 10 ♕a4 ♕a5 (If 10 ...

♘d4 11 ♖ad1 ♗d7 12 ♕a3 ♘c2
13 ♕xc5 b6 14 ♕g5 h6 15 ♕f4
g5 16 ♕e5 ♖c8 17 ♘d5 ♘xd5
18 ♕xd5 ♗e6 19 ♕b7 ♕c7 20
♕xc7 ♖xc7 21 b3 ½-½ Grig-
orian - Kasparov, USSR 1981)
11 ♕xa5 ♘xa5 12 ♗xc5 ♘xc4
13 b3 ♘d7 14 ♗d4 ♘d6 15
♖ac1 ♖ac8 16 ♗xg7 ♔xg7 17
♘d4 a5 18 f4 ♘c5 19 h3
♖fd8 20 g4= Mikhalchishin
- Tringov, Banja Vrucica
1990.

b) 9 ... ♕a5 10 ♕b3! led
to an impressive demon-
stration by White in Szil-
agyi - Piket, European Cup
1987: 10 ... ♘g4 11 ♗f4 ♗xc3
12 bxc3 ♘f6 13 ♖fd1 ♗d7 14
♖xd7 ♘xd7 15 ♕xb7 ♖ac8 16
♕xd7±.

9 ... ♗d7!?

9 ... ♗e6 10 ♘e5 ♘a5 is
given by *ECO* as leading to
equality, the main reference
being 11 ♘d3 ♘h5 12 ♘xc5
♘xf4 13 gxf4 ♗xc4 14 ♖c1
♕c7 15 ♘xb7 ♕xf4 16 e3 ♕e5
17 ♘xa5 ♕xa5 18 ♗xa8 ♗xf1
19 ♕d5 ♕xd5 20 ♘xd5 ♖xa8
21 ♔xf1 ♗b2 22 ♘xe7+ ♔f8
23 ♖c8+= Tal - Kasparov,
Moscow TV 1987.

10 ♘e5 ♘xe5
11 ♗xe5 ♕c8
12 ♕b3

A critical alternative is 12
♘d5 ♘xd5 13 ♗xg7 *(337)*:

a) 13 ... ♘e3 with comp-
lications favourable to-
White, e.g. 14 ♕b3! ♔xg7
(14 ... ♘xf1!? 15 ♗xf8 ♘d2 16

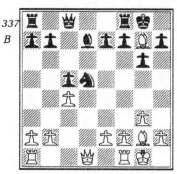

337
B

♕c3 ♕xf8 17 ♕xd2 ♕c8±; 14
... ♘xg2?! 15 ♗xf8 ♔xf8 16
♖fd1 ♗h3±) 15 ♗xb7 ♕c7 16
fxe3 ♖ab8 17 ♕c3+±.

b) 13 ... ♔xg7 14 cxd5 ♗h3
15 ♖c1 ♗xg2 16 ♔xg2 b6 17
b4 ♕a6±/∞.

12 ... ♗c6
13 ♘d5

13 ♗xc6 ♕xc6 14 ♘d5
♖ae8=.

13 ... ♘xd5
14 ♗xg7

14 cxd5 ♗xe5 15 dxc6
bxc6 leads to dead equality.

14 ... ♘f4!
15 ♗xf8

This position was agreed
drawn in Gorelov - Muratov,
Moscow 1988!

15 ... ♘xe2+
16 ♔h1 ♘d4
17 ♕e3 ♗xg2+
18 ♔xg2 ♕c6+
19 f3 ♖xf8
20 ♖f2 ♘f5 *(338)*

Black has good compen-
sation for the exchange
with a superbly centralised
knight and safe king. Other
moves which Black can con-

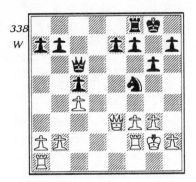

sider are:

a) 20 ... e6 when White can try 21 b4!?

b) 20 ... b6 21 b4!? (21 ♕xe7 ♖e8 22 ♕g5 ♘xf3 23 ♕d5 ♕xd5 24 cxd5 ♘d4) 21 ... ♘f5 22 ♕e4 ♕f6!

21 ♕a3 ♖d8
22 ♖e1 e6
23 ♕xa7

Not 23 g4? ♘d4 24 ♕xa7? ♘xf3!

23 ... b6
24 ♕a3

White can take two rooks for the queen with 24 g4!? ♖a8 25 ♕xa8+ ♕xa8 26 gxf5 gxf5 27 b3 but after 27 ... ♕d8 Black should be okay.

24 ... ♖a8
25 ♕c3 ♖xa2
26 ♕f6

26 b3! was best, when Black should play 26 ... ♖a7 27 ♖a1 ♖xa1 28 ♕xa1 ♘d4.

26 ... ♕d6?!

26 ... ♕d7! was stronger. If then 27 b3 ♖a7 28 ♖a1? ♘e3+ 29 ♔g1 (29 ♔h3?? e5+) 29 ... ♕d3 is good for Black, while 28 g4 ♕d4 transposes

back to the game.

27 b3 ♖a7
28 g4

White misses a chance here: 28 ♖a1! ♘e3+ 29 ♔h3 (29 ♔g1?? e5!) 29 ... ♖xa1 30 ♕xa1 ♕f8?! (30 ... ♕d3!? 31 ♕a8+ ♔g7 32 ♕e4 and White has good chances since the Black king is not very safe) 31 ♕f6 (Not 31 g4? ♕h6+ 32 ♔g3 g5) and White stands well.

28 ... ♕d4
29 ♕xd4 ½–½

Notes based on those by Jon Speelman in *Maxwell Macmillan Chess*.

Game 41
Kasparov – Nunn
TV Exhibition Blitz Game,
London 1987

1	d4	♘f6
2	c4	g6
3	g3	♗g7
4	♗g2	0-0
5	♘f3	d6
6	0-0	♘c6
7	♘c3	a6 (339)

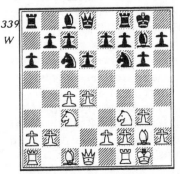

The Panno Variation, invented by the Argentine grandmaster Oscar Panno in the mid 1950s to exploit the absence of White's king's bishop from the f1 - a6 diagonal.

8 ♗g5

White has numerous alternatives here:

a) 8 ♗d2 and now:

a1) 8 ... ♗d7 9 b3 ♖b8 10 ♖c1 b5 11 d5 ♘a5 12 ♘xb5 ♘xc4 13 bxc4 axb5 14 ♘d4 ♘xd5 15 cxd5 ♗xd4 16 ♗h6 ♗g7 17 ♗xg7 ♔xg7 18 ♕d4+ f6 19 ♕a7 ♖a8 20 ♕b7 ♔f7 21 ♖xc7 ♖b8 22 ♕a7 ♖a8 23 ♕b7 ♖b8 ½-½ McNab - Nunn, Dubai Ol. 1986. Although quite sharp and interesting, this game was equal all the time. The bishop on d2 is directed against the knight on a5.

a2) 8 ... ♖b8 9 ♖c1 e6 10 b3 ♖e8 11 h3 ♗d7 12 ♗g5 h6 13 ♗e3 b5 14 d5 ♘e7 15 dxe6 ♗xe6 16 ♘d4 ♗d7 17 ♘d5± P Nikolic - C Hansen, Wijk aan Zee 1988.

b) 8 b3 ♖b8 *(340)*:

b1) 9 a4 is dubious because it weakens the b4-square, e.g. 9 ... e5 10 d5 ♘b4 11 a5 c5 12 e4 ♘e8 13 ♘a2 ♘xa2 14 ♖xa2 f5, Lobron - Kindermann, Hamburg 1991. This is an easy position for Black to play.

b2) 9 e3 b5 10 ♕e2 bxc4 11 ♕xc4 ♘b4 12 ♕e2 a5 13 ♖d1

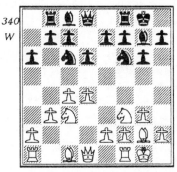

♗a6 14 ♕d2 c5 15 ♗a3 ♘d7 16 ♖ac1 (Black has fulfilled the basic strategy of the Panno, but here makes a mess of it with his next move. 16 ... ♖c8 is =/∓) 16 ... cxd4? 17 ♘xd4±/± Cvitan - Loncar, Pula 1990.

b3) 9 ♘d5 is not theoretically dangerous. The following material tends to equality: 9 ... ♘e4 (9 ... ♗g4 10 ♗b2 e6 11 ♘e3 ♗xf3 12 ♗xf3 d5 13 ♕d3 ♘e7 14 b4 c6 15 a4 ♘f5 16 ♘xf5 gxf5 17 cxd5 cxd5= Kantsler - Kuzmin, Podolsk 1989) 10 ♗b2 f5 11 ♕c1 (11 ♕c2 e6 12 ♘e3 ♕e7 13 ♖ad1 ♗d7 14 d5 ♘d8 15 dxe6 ♘xe6 16 ♘d5 ♕f7 17 ♘d4 ♖be8 18 e3 ♗c8 19 ♘e2 ♗xb2 20 ♕xb2 ♘f6 21 ♘xf6+ ♕xf6 22 ♕xf6 ♖xf6 ½-½ Davies - Byrne, London {*Watson, Farley & Williams*} 1991. This game was always equal) 11 ... ♗d7 12 ♖d1 e6 13 ♘f4 ♘e7 14 ♘d2 ♘f6 15 c5 g5 16 ♘d3 ♗c6 17 ♘c4 ♗xg2 18 ♔xg2 h6 19 a4 d5 20 ♘ce5 ♘d7 21 b4 ♘xe5 22 dxe5 f4

23 b5 ½-½ Ribli – Zapata, Novi Sad Ol. 1990.

b4) 9 ♘b2 b5 10 cxb5 axb5 11 ♖c1 b4 (11 ... ♘b4!? 12 e4 *{12 a3 ♘bd5 13 ♘xd5 ♘xd5 14 e4 is the critical variation}* 12 ... ♘d7 13 ♖e1?! c5 14 ♘d5? *{A mistake, after which White's position is riddled with weaknesses}* 14 ... ♘xd5 15 exd5 c4 16 ♕e2 ♘b6 17 ♕xe7 ♕xe7 18 ♖xe7 ♘xd5 19 ♖e2 ♘h6∓ Crouch – Hebden, Ramsgate 1983) 12 ♘a4 ♘a7 13 ♕c2 c6 14 e4 ♗a6 15 ♖fe1 ♗b5 16 e5 ♘d5 17 h4 ♕a5 18 h5± Razuvaev – Zsu Polgar, Dortmund 1985.

c) 8 h3 ♖b8 (8 ... ♗d7 9 ♗g5 h6 10 ♗e3 ♖b8 11 ♘d5 b5 12 ♘xf6+ exf6± Lautier – Shirov, Manila 1990; 8 ... e5 9 d5 ♘e7 10 e4 ♘e8 11 ♘e1 b5 12 cxb5 axb5 13 ♘d3 ♖b8 14 a3 f5 15 exf5 gxf5 16 f4 e4 17 ♘b4 ♘f6 18 ♗e3 ♕e8 19 ♕e2 ♗d7 20 ♔h2 h5∓ Burger – Zsu Polgar, New York Open 1987) and now *(341)*:

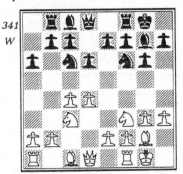

c1) 9 ♗g5 b5 10 cxb5 axb5:

c11) 11 ♗xf6 ♗xf6 12 ♖c1 ♗d7 13 e3 ♗g7 14 ♘e2 ♘a5 15 b3 c6 16 ♕c2 b4 17 ♖fd1 ♕b6 18 h4 ♗c8 19 ♕d2 ♖d8 20 h5± Fedorowicz – Gunawan, Lugano 1988.

c12) 11 d5 b4 (11 ... ♘a5 12 b4 ♘c4 13 ♘d4 ♗d7 14 e3 ♕c8 15 ♕e2 h6 16 ♗xf6 ♗xf6 17 a4 ♗xh3 18 ♘cxb5 ♗xg2 19 ♔xg2± Agdestein – C Hansen, Wijk aan Zee 1988) 12 ♗xf6 exf6 13 dxc6 bxc3 14 bxc3 f5 15 ♕d2 ♗a6 16 ♖fb1± Stohl – Sznapik, Stara Zagora Zt. 1990.

c2) 9 ♗e3 b5 (9 ... ♗d7 10 b3 b5 11 cxb5 axb5 12 d5 ♘a5 13 ♖c1 b4 14 ♘b1 ♕c8 15 ♔h2 ♕b7 16 ♘g5∞ Gutman – Zapata, Wijk aan Zee 1987) 10 ♘d2 *(342)*:

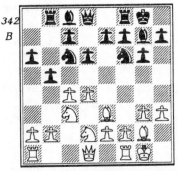

c21) 10 ... ♗b7 11 cxb5 axb5 12 ♘xb5 ♘a5 13 ♕a4 ♗xg2 14 ♔xg2 ♕d7 15 ♘c3 ♕xa4 16 ♘xa4 ♘d5∞ Greenfeld – Nunn, Biel 1986.

c22) 10 ... ♗d7 11 ♖c1 ♘a5 12 cxb5 axb5 13 b4 ♘c4 14 ♘xc4 bxc4 15 b5 d5 16 a4 c6 17 ♗f4 ♖b7 18 ♖b1 ♕a5=

Lagunov - Yusupov, USSR 1989.

c23) 10 ... ♞a5 11 cxb5 axb5 12 b4 ♞c4 13 ♞xc4 bxc4 14 b5 d5 15 a4 ♗f5 16 a5 ♕d7 17 h4 ♗g4 18 ♗f4 e5 19 dxe5 d4∞ Hjartarson - Ernst, Gausdal Zt. 1987.

c3) 9 e4 b5 (9 ... ♞d7 10 ♗g5 h6 11 ♗e3 ♞a5 12 b3 b5 13 cxb5 axb5 14 ♕d2 ♔h7 15 ♖fd1 e6±/± Piket - Nijboer, Dutch Ch. 1991) 10 e5 (10 cxb5 axb5 11 ♖e1 b4 {11 ... ♞d7 12 ♗g5 b4 13 ♞e2± Keene - Kestler, Dortmund 1973, but 11 ... e6! is strong and okay for Black} 12 ♞a4 ♖e8 13 b3 e5 14 dxe5 ♞xe5 15 ♞xe5 ♖xe5 16 ♗b2 ♖e8 17 e5 dxe5 18 ♗xe5 ♞d7 19 ♗xg7 ♖xe1+ 20 ♕xe1 ♔xg7 21 ♖c1 ♕f6 22 ♖xc7 ♞e5 23 ♕e3 ♗f5 24 f4 ♞d3 25 g4 ♕d6 26 ♖c4 ♖c8 27 ♖d4 ♖c1+ 28 ♔h2 ♖e1 29 ♕xd3 1-0 Damljanovic - Peelen, Wijk aan Zee B 1990) and now (343):

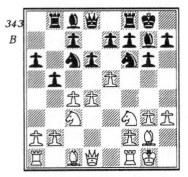

343
B

c31) 10 ... ♞d7 11 e6 fxe6 12 d5 bxc4 (12 ... exd5 13

cxd5 ♞a5 14 ♞d4 ♞e5 15 b4 {Better is 15 ♞ce2 ♗d7 16 ♞f4±} 15 ... ♞ac4 16 f4 ♞f7 {16 ... c5!? 17 dxc6 ♞xc6 18 ♞xc6 ♕b6+ is also possible} 17 ♞c6 ♕e8 18 ♞xb8 ♗f5 19 ♖f3 ♕xb8 20 g4 ♕b6+, Hübner - Nunn, South Africa 1981. Black has compensation for the exchange but it is not clear that it is adequate) 13 dxc6 ♞c5 14 ♞g5 h6 15 ♞ge4 ♞d3 16 ♕g4 ♕e8 17 ♞d2 d5 18 ♞xc4 ♖b4 19 ♞xd5 exd5 20 ♗xd5+ e6 21 ♗g2 ♞e5 22 ♞d6 (22 ♞xe5!? ♖xg4 23 ♞xg4 h5 24 ♞e3∞) 22 ... ♞xg4 23 ♞xe8 ♖xe8 24 hxg4 e5 25 a3 ♖b6 26 ♗e4 ♗xg4 27 ♗xg6 ♖f8 28 ♗e4 ♗f3 29 ♖e1 ♗xe4 30 ♖xe4 ½-½ Manor - Hebden, London 1987.

c32) 10 ... dxe5 11 dxe5 ♕xd1 12 ♖xd1 ♞d7 13 e6 fxe6 14 cxb5 axb5 15 ♗f4 (15 ♞g5 ♞d4) 15 ... b4 (This line is unpleasant for Black. Another continuation is 15 ... ♞de5 16 ♞e1 ♞b4 17 a3 ♞a6 18 ♖ac1 ♞c4 19 ♞d3 ♗b7 20 ♗xb7 ♖xb7 21 ♖c2 ♖d8 22 ♔f1 ♗xc3 23 ♖xc3 e5 24 ♗c1 e4 25 b3 ♞e5 26 ♞b2 ♖xd1+ 27 ♞xd1 ♞d3 28 ♗g5 b4 29 axb4 ♞axb4 30 ♖c4= Vaganian - Sax, Lucerne 1985) 16 ♞a4 ♞b6 17 ♞xb6 ♖xb6 18 ♗xc7 ♖b7 19 ♗f4 ♗xb2 20 ♖ab1 ♗c3 21 ♞g5 ♖b6 22 ♞e4 ♗d4 23 ♖bc1± Goldin - Gruenberg, Moscow GMA

1989.

d) 8 d5 ♞a5 9 ♞d2 c5 transposes to the earlier game, Timman - Kasparov, Tilburg 1981.

A very unexplored situation. It is not clear what Black's best reply is.

8 ... ♗d7

Alternatively, 8 ... ♖b8 9 ♖c1 and:

a) 9 ... b5 10 d5 ♞e5 11 ♞xe5 dxe5 12 cxb5 axb5 13 ♕d2 ♗b7 14 ♖fd1 ♕d7 15 ♗xf6 exf6 16 ♞e4 ♗a8 17 ♕a5 ♖fe8 18 ♞c5 ♕d6 19 ♞a6 ♖b7 20 ♖c6 ♕d8 21 d6 ♖a7 1-0 Nogueiras - Medina, Mexico City 1991.

b) 9 ... ♗g4 10 d5 ♗xf3 11 exf3 ♞e5 12 ♕e2 ♖e8 13 ♖fe1 c5 14 dxc6 ♞xc6 15 ♖cd1 h6 16 ♗c1 ♞d7 17 f4±/± Kasparov - van der Wiel, Brussels Blitz 1987.

9	♖c1	b5
10	d5	♞a5
11	b3	c5
12	dxc6	♞xc6
13	♞d5	bxc4
14	♗xf6	exf6 *(345)*

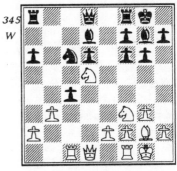

The damage inflicted on the black pawn structure ensures that White will exert complete domination over the key square d5.

15	♖xc4	♖e8
16	♕d2	f5
17	♖fc1	♖c8
18	e3	♞e5

After White's next move Nunn should have seized the opportunity to alleviate the pressure against his position by interpolating the exchange of knights on f3, with check.

19	♖xc8	♗xc8
20	♞d4	♗b7
21	♞e2	♕b8
22	♞ef4	♞d7
23	♖c7	♞c5
24	b4	♞e4 *(346)*

Now Kasparov obtains decisive strategic pressure by securing absolute control of the open c-file. This will be utilised as the springboard to complete the invasion of Black's fortress.

| 25 | ♕c2 | ♗xd5 |

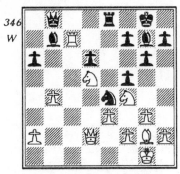

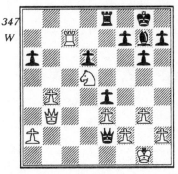

26 ♘xd5   ♛b5

Kasparov's coming move sets up a concealed battery against Black's most vulnerable point, the f7-pawn.

27 ♛b3   ♛e2
28 ♗xe4   fxe4 *(347)*

As so often, Kasparov, having established an overwhelming strategic advantage, finishes off the game with a crisp display of tactics. It should be noted that White could not win without the exchange of black's knight on e4, since at some stage he has to deal with the black threat to play ... ♛f2+.

29 ♘f6+   1-0

After 29 ... ♗xf6 30 ♛xf7+ checkmate is forced.

18) g3 system - Others

The move 7 ... ♗f5, which forms the subject of our main game in this chapter, is known as the Lesser Simagin Variation. Black's strategic plan is similar to that of Panno's Variation, but he hopes to profit from his omission of ... a6 and the insertion of the developing move ... ♗f5. In some lines, Black can generate excellent counterplay by blending queenside activity with some such manoeouvre as ... ♕d7 followed by ... ♗h3. The defect of Black's idea is that the bishop is often exposed to attack and time must be consumed to redeploy it.

This chapter also covers lines where Black remains flexible with ... c6, combined with moves such as ... ♗f5, ... ♗g4 or ... ♕a5. As Black has not been committed to any fixed pawn structure, there are opportunities to follow-up with ... c5, ... e5, ... d5 or even to ignore the central pawns and play ... a5. Hence the variation appeals to players with a liking for strategic complexity and adaptability and has been employed sporadically by Larsen and Smyslov.

Game 42
Yusupov – Gulko
Reykjavik 1990

1	d4	♘f6
2	c4	g6
3	♘f3	♗g7
4	g3	0-0
5	♗g2	d6
6	0-0	*(348)*

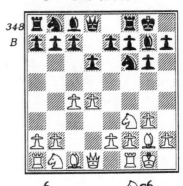

348
B

6	...	♘c6

a) 6 ... c6 7 ♘c3 (7 b3 led to equality in the following two examples: 7 ... ♕a5 {7 ... a6 8 ♗b2 b5 9 ♘bd2 ♘bd7

10 ♕c2 ♖e8 11 ♖fd1 ♗b7 12 ♖ac1 ♕c7 13 a4 bxa4 14 bxa4 c5 15 d5 e5 16 e4 ♖eb8 17 ♗c3 a5 18 ♖b1 ♗a6 19 ♘f1 ♖b4 20 ♗xb4 axb4 21 ♘b3 ♖e8 22 a5 ♘h6 23 ♖a1 ♘h5 24 ♘bd2 ♖f8 25 ♗h3 ♘b8 26 ♘f1 ♘g7 27 ♘e3 ♗xe3 28 fxe3 ♕e7 29 ♖f1 ♘e8 30 ♖f2 ½-½ *Ribli - Gulko, Munich 1990*} 8 ♗b2 ♕h5 9 ♘bd2 d5 10 ♖e1 ♗h3 11 e4 ♗xg2 12 ♔xg2 dxe4 13 ♘xe4 ♘bd7 14 ♘xf6+ ♗xf6 15 ♘e5 ♕xd1 16 ♖axd1 ♖ad8 17 ♘g4 ♖fe8 18 ♘xf6+ ♘xf6 19 d5 ♔f8 20 dxc6 bxc6 21 ♗xf6 exf6 22 ♖xe8+ ♖xe8 23 ♖d7 a5 24 ♖a7 ♖e5 25 ♖a6 ♖c5 26 g4 g5 27 h3 ♔e7 28 ♔g3 f5 29 gxf5 h5 30 ♖a7+ ½-½ Adorjan - Barlov, Novi Sad Ol. 1990) and now *(349)*:

349
B

a1) 7 ... ♗f5 and now:

a11) 8 ♘e1 ♕d7 9 e4 ♗h3 10 ♘d3 (10 f3 ♗xg2 11 ♔xg2 ♘a6 12 ♗e3 ♖fc8 13 ♘d3 e8 14 ♕e2 c5 15 d5 c7 16 ♘f2 ♖cb8 17 a4 ♘b4 18 ♘g4 ♖f8 19 ♗h6 ♗xh6 20 ♘xh6+ ♔g7 21 ♕d2 e6 22 dxe6 ♕xe6 23

♘g4 f6 24 h4 ♖ad8 25 h5 f5 26 exf5 ♕xf5 27 hxg6 ♕xg6 28 ♘e4 e6 29 ♖h1 ♖xf3 30 ♕h6+ 1-0 Yusupov - Speelman, Linares 1991. An unclear game until the end) 10 ... ♗xg2 11 ♔xg2 b5 12 cxb5 cxb5 13 f3 ♕b7 14 ♕b3 a6 15 d5 ♘bd7 16 a4 ♖fb8 17 axb5 axb5 18 ♗e3 ♘e8 19 ♘e2 ♘e5 20 ♘xe5 dxe5 21 ♖xa8 ♖xa8 22 ♖c1 ♘d6 23 ♖c6 ♗f6 24 ♘c3 ♖c8 25 ♖xc8+ ♕xc8 26 ♕b4 ♕c4 27 ♕xc4 ♘xc4 28 ♗c1 b4 29 ♘a4 e6 30 dxe6± King - Speelman, British Ch. 1990. Black looked okay here but seemed to overpress.

a12) 8 ♘h4 ♗e6 9 d5 cxd5 (9 ... ♗d7 10 ♗e3 ♘a6 11 ♘f3 ♕a5 12 a3 ♖fc8 13 h3 ♕d8 14 ♘d4 e5 15 dxe6 fxe6 16 ♗g5 h6 17 ♗e3 e5 18 ♘f3 ♕f8 19 c5 e4 20 ♘h4 g5 21 ♘g6 ♕f7 22 cxd6 ♕xg6 23 ♕b3+ ♘d5 24 ♘xd5 cxd5 25 ♕xd5+ ♕f7 26 ♕xb7 ♘c5 27 ♗xc5 ♖ab8 28 ♕xa7 ♖a8 29 ♕b7 ♖ab8 ½-½ Frias - Speelman, New York {*Watson, Farley & Williams*} 1990) 10 cxd5 ♗d7 11 e4 ♘a6 12 h3 ♘c5 13 ♗e3 ♕a5 14 ♗d4 ♘a4 15 ♘xa4 ♗xa4 16 b3 ♗b5 17 ♖e1 ♖fe8 18 ♘f3 ♕a3 19 ♕d2 a5 20 ♗b2 ♕b4 21 ♗c3 ♕c5 22 ♖ac1 ♕b6 23 a4 ♗d7 24 e5 dxe5 25 ♘xe5 ♕xb3 26 ♘xd7 ♘xd7 27 ♗xg7 ♔xg7 28 ♕d4+ ♘f6 29 ♖b1 ♕a3 30 ♖xb7 0-1 Wojtkiewicz -

Mortensen, Reykjavik Open 1990. These lines look okay for Black - the knight on h4 is misplaced.

a2) 7 ... a6 8 e4 ♘fd7 9 ♗e3 b5 10 ♘d2 ♗b7 (10 ... e5 11 d5 b4 12 ♘a4 c5 13 f4 exf4 14 gxf4 ♘f6 15 h3 ♘bd7 16 e5 dxe5 17 fxe5 ♘xe5 18 ♗xc5 ♘h5 19 ♗xf8 ♔xf8 20 ♘f3 ♗d7 21 ♘xe5 ♗xe5 22 d6 ♕h4 23 ♕d5 ♗d4+ 24 ♔h1 ♔g7 25 ♖xf7+ ♔h6 26 ♖f3 ♖f8 27 ♖af1 ♖xf3 28 ♖xf3 ♗xa4 29 d7 1-0 Damljanovic - Kr Georgiev, Novi Sad Ol. 1990) 11 ♕c2 e5 12 d5 b4 13 ♘a4 a5 14 c5 cxd5 15 exd5 ♘xc5 16 ♘xc5 dxc5 17 ♗xc5 ♖e8 18 ♘c4 ♘d7 19 ♗e3 ♖c8 20 ♖fd1 e4 21 ♕b3 ♘c5 22 ♗xc5 ½-½ Stohl - Kr Georgiev, Stara Zagora Zt. 1990

a3) 7 ... ♕a5 8 e4 *(350)*:

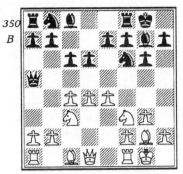

a31) 8 ... ♗g4 9 h3 ♗xf3 10 ♗xf3 ♘fd7 11 ♗e3 a6 12 ♖c1 c5 13 dxc5 dxc5 14 ♕d5 ♕c7 15 ♖fd1 ♖a7 16 ♗g2 b6 17 f4 e5 18 ♕d2 ♘c6 19 f5 ♘d4∞ Kindermann - Maus, Ham-

burg 1991.

a32) 8 ... e5 9 d5 cxd5 10 ♘xd5 ♘xd5 11 cxd5 ♘d7 12 ♗d2 ♕b6 13 b4 ♘f6 14 ♕e2 ♗d7 15 a4 ♖fc8 16 ♖fb1± Agdestein - Damljanovic, Manila 1990.

b) 6 ... c5 7 dxc5 dxc5 8 ♘e5 ♘a6 9 ♘c3 ♖b8 10 ♘d3 ♘h5 11 ♘b5 ♗e6 12 ♕b3 ♕b6 13 ♗e3 f5 14 ♖ad1 ♗f7 15 ♕c2 ♕a5 16 a3 e5 17 ♘xc5 ♘xc5 18 ♗xc5 ♖fc8 19 b4 ♕a6 20 ♘d6 b6 21 b5 1-0 Ehlvest - Byrne, New York Open 1991. Compare with the Yugoslav variation.

7　♘c3

7 d5 ♘a5 8 ♘bd2 c5 9 ♘e1 a6 (9 ... e5 10 e4 ♘e8 11 b3 f5 12 exf5 ♗xf5 13 ♘e4 h6 14 h4 a6 15 ♕e2 ♖b8± Kochiev - Gudmundsson, Gausdal 1991) 10 ♖b1 ♗f5 11 e4 ♗g4 12 f3 ♗d7 13 ♘d3 b5 14 b3 ♖b8 15 ♗b2 e5 16 ♗c3 ♘h5 17 f4 exf4 18 ♗xg7 ♔xg7 19 gxf4 bxc4 20 bxc4 ♖xb1 21 ♕xb1 ♕f6± Piket - Nijboer, Amsterdam OHRA 1990.

7　...　♗f5 *(351)*

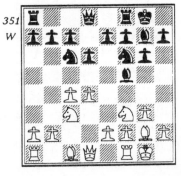

A provocative sortie which is not often played, although it is something of a speciality of the young Dutch GM, Jeroen Piket. Black positively invites White to gain space and time by attacking the bishop but hopes that in the process White will overreach himself. More traditional choices are 7 ... e5 8 d5 ♘e7 9 e4 or 7 ... a6, the famous Panno variation, considered earlier.

a) 7 ... ♗g4 8 h3 (8 d5 ♘a5 9 ♘d2 c5 10 ♕c2 a6 11 h3 ♗d7 12 b3 b5 13 ♗b2 ♖b8 14 ♘d1 e5 15 ♔h2 ♘h5 16 e3 f5 17 f4 e4= Wojtkiewicz – Cabrilo, New York Open 1990. The white pawn on h3 may be an extra tempo, but it doesn't necessarily represent a bonus for White) 8 ... ♗xf3 9 ♗xf3 ♘d7 10 e3 e5 11 d5 ♘e7 12 e4 f5 13 h4 ♘f6 14 h5 ♖f7 15 ♗g5 ♕d7±/± Blagojevic – Cabrilo, Pula 1990.

b) 7 ... e5 8 d5 (8 dxe5 is well documented as equal. The example here does not upset this judgement: 8 ... ♘xe5 9 ♘xe5 dxe5 10 ♕xd8 ♖xd8 11 ♗g5 ♖d4 12 b3 c6 13 ♘a4 ♗g4 14 ♖fe1 h6 15 ♗e3 ♖dd8 16 h3 ♗e6 17 ♘c5 ♗c8 18 ♖ad1 ♖e8 19 ♖d6 ♘h7 20 ♖ed1 ♗f6 21 ♘e4 ♗e7 22 ♖6d3 ♘g5 23 ♘d6 ♗xd6 24 ♖xd6 ♘xh3+ 25 ♗xh3 ♗xh3

26 ♗xh6 ♗e6 27 ♗g5 ♔g7 28 f3 ♖h8 29 g4 ♖ae8 30 ♔g2 and Black stands well and went on to win, Ribli – J Polgar, Vienna 1991) 8 ... ♘e7 (352)

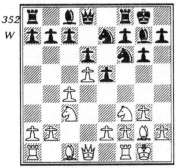

9 ♘e1 (9 e4 ♘e8 10 b4 f5 11 ♘g5 h6 12 ♘e6 ♗xe6 13 dxe6 c6 14 ♕b3 ♕c8 15 c5 ♖f6 16 cxd6 ♘xd6 17 b5∞ Ribli – Hook, Novi Sad Ol. 1990: 9 c5 ♘e8 10 cxd6 cxd6 11 ♕b3 h6 12 e4 f5 13 exf5 gxf5 14 ♘d2 ♘g6 15 ♘c4 ♖f7 16 a4 ♗f8 17 ♗d2 ♘g7 18 ♗xh6 f4, Vaganian – Stein, USSR Ch. 1970. Black has excellent counterplay for the pawn) 9 ... a5 10 ♘d3 ♘e8 11 e4 c5 12 ♕e2 f5 13 f4 exf4 14 ♘xf4 ♘c7 15 ♗d2 fxe4 16 ♗xe4± Werner – Spiriev. Budapest 1991.

8 d5

White accepts the challenge and starts to chase the black minor pieces. Alternatively:

a) 8 ♘e1 ♕c8 9 e4 ♗h3 10 ♘c2 ♗xg2 11 ♔xg2 e5 12 d5 ♘e7 13 ♘e1, Korchnoi – Portisch, Brussels 1986, when White's grip on the light squares gives him some advantage. 13 ♕e2 is less convincing. The knight is not good on c2, e.g. 13 ... ♘d7 14 f3 a5 15 ♗g5 ♖e8 16 ♗e3 b6 17 b3 f5 18 a3 ♔h8 19 b4 ♘g8 20 ♖ab1 axb4 21 axb4 ♘gf6 22 ♕d3 ♖f8 23 ♗g1 ♘h5∞ Salov – Piket, Wijk aan Zee 1991.

b) 8 h3 ♘e4 9 ♘d5 ♗d7 10 ♗e3 e6 11 ♘f4± f5 (Too early) 12 d5 e5 13 dxc6 exf4 14 cxb7 fxe3 15 ♕d5+, Tukmakov – Piket, Amsterdam OHRA 1990.

c) 8 b3 ♘e4 9 ♗b2 ♘xc3 10 ♗xc3 ♗e4 11 ♕d2 d5 12 ♖fd1± Schroll – Kindermann, Vienna 1991, is a safe and solid way to play.

8 ... ♘a5 *(353)*

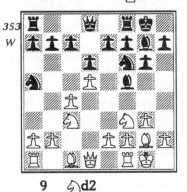

9 ♘d2

A more aggressive alternative is 9 ♘d4 ♗d7 10 b3 c5 11 dxc6 bxc6 12 ♖b1 ♖c8 13 ♗b2 ♕b6 14 e3 ♗g4 15 ♕d2 e5 16 ♘de2 ♘b7 17 h3± Udovcic – Vladimirov, Leningrad 1967; or (9 ♘d4 ♗d7) 10 ♕d3?! c5 11 dxc6 ♘xc6 12 ♘xc6 bxc6 13 h3 ♖b8 14 ♖b1 ♕c8 15 ♔h2= Miralles – Piket, Lyon Zt. 1990.

9 ... c6

The most natural move. More convoluted is 9 ... ♘e8 10 e4 ♗d7 11 ♖b1 c6 12 dxc6 ♘xc6± Stohl – Hellers, Amsterdam OHRA 1990.

10 e4

The superficially attractive 10 b4, trapping black's knight on the edge, fails to the tactical riposte 10 ... ♘xd5 11 cxd5 ♗xc3 or 11 ♘xd5 cxd5 with an attack against both a1 and c4. A perfectly good line for White is 10 dxc6 bxc6 11 e4 ♗g4 12 ♕c2 ♖c8 13 b4 ♘b7 14 h3 ♗e6 15 ♗b2 d5 16 ♖fd1± Marovic – Westerinen, Beverwijk 1966.

10 ... ♗g4
11 ♕c2

Another possibility 11 f3 ♗d7 12 ♔h1 ♖c8 13 ♕e2 with a balanced position.

11 ... cxd5
12 cxd5 ♖c8
13 ♖e1 b5 *(354)*

It would seem that the opening phase has been successful for Black, who has now seized the initiative on the queen's wing. Nevertheless, the black position still exhibits the defect that his minor pieces

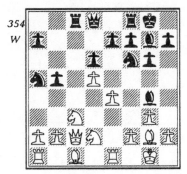

are somewhat scattered and out on a limb. Black would like to play ... ♘d7 but, as yet, this is impossible since 14 h3 wins a piece.

14 a3   e6
15 ♕d3

Avoiding Black's trap, namely 15 h3 exd5 16 hxg4 d4, regaining the piece.

15 ...   exd5

Otherwise his bishop on g4 would be in grave danger in view of the threat of h3.

16 ♘xb5   ♖e8

If 16 ... dxe4 17 ♘xe4 ♗f5 18 ♗g5 ♘c4 19 ♘xa7 ♗xb2 20 ♕xd6 ♗xe4 21 ♘xc8+-.

17 h3   ♗f5
18 g4 *(355)*

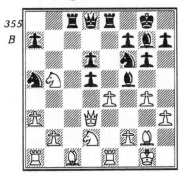

Boldly forcing Black to surrender his light squared bishop. If Black refuses then White anticipates 18 ... dxe4 19 ♕xd6 ♗e6 20 ♕xd8 ♖exd8 21 ♘xa7 ♖b8 22 ♘xe4 ♘xe4 23 ♗xe4 ♗xb2 24 ♗xb2 ♖xb2 25 a4 and White maintains his extra pawn.

18 ...   ♗xe4
19 ♘xe4   ♘xe4
20 ♘xa7   ♖b8
21 ♗e3   ♗xb2
22 ♖ab1   ♖b3

And not 22 ... ♘c3 23 ♖xb2 ♖xb2 24 ♕xc3 with a win on material.

23 ♕xd5   ♘c3
24 ♗g5

The beginning of fantastic complications leading to one of the most original positions ever seen in a game between two grandmasters. Gulko now opts to trade his queen for White's rooks, but in doing so misses his chance. 24 ... ♕d7 (Not 24 ... ♘xd5 25 ♗xd8 ♖xd8 26 ♗xd5 ♖b6 27 ♖e7 ♖f8 28 a4 ♔g7 29 g5 when Black is more or less paralysed by White's dominant bishop on d5) would have left Black with good chance to emerge on top.

24 ...   ♘xb1
25 ♗xd8   ♖xe1+
26 ♗f1

Entering a nasty pin but 26 ♔h2 ♗e5+ is fatal.

26 ... ♘c3 *(356)*

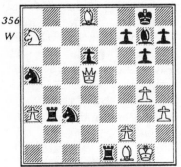

356
W

27 ♕d2

If White wants to win he must avoid 27 ♕xa5 ♘e2+ 28 ♔g2 ♘f4+.

27 ... ♘e2+
28 ♔g2 ♗c3
29 ♕h6 ♘c4

Not the best. Stronger is 29 ... ♖bb1.

30 ♘c6

With the brutal threat of ♘e7+ and ♕f8 mate.

30 ... ♗g7
31 ♘e7+ ♔f8?

A misguided attempt to win. Black should play 31 ... ♔h8 32 ♕g5 h6 when Black wins. The best line for White is 32 ♘xg6+ fxg6 33 ♗f6 ♖b7 34 ♗xe2 ♖xe2 35 ♗xg7+ ♖xg7 36 ♕f4 with the likely result being a draw by perpetual check.

32 ♕xh7 ♘f4+
33 ♔h2 ♔e8
34 ♕g8+ ♗f8

White is now threatened with ... ♖xf1 and 35 ♗xc4 would evidently fail to 35 ... ♖xh3 mate.

35 ♘xg6!! *(357)*

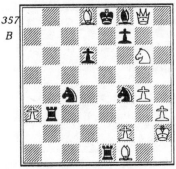

357
B

The brilliant key to the position. After 35 ... ♘xg6 White can play 36 ♗xc4 ♖f3 37 ♗g5 △ ♗b5+.

35 ... fxg6
36 ♕xc4 ♖xf1
37 ♕xf4

White should not play 37 ♕xf1 ♖xh3+ 38 ♔g1 ♗xd8.

37 ... ♖xa3
38 ♗h4 ♖aa1
39 ♕e4+ ♔f7
40 ♕f3+ ♔g8
41 ♕d5+ ♔g7
42 ♕b7+ ♔g8
43 ♗g3 ♖h1+

Gulko defends by giving back the two rooks for White's queen, but the endgame is a win for White, who can more easily create mobile passed pawns. The game concluded 44 ♕xh1 ♖xh1+ 45 ♔xh1 ♔f7 46 ♔g2 ♔f6 47 f4 d5 48 ♗f2 ♗d6 49 ♔f3 ♔e6 50 ♗d4 ♗e7 51 ♔g3 ♗b4 52 h4 ♗e1+ 53 ♔h3 ♗d2 54 ♔g3 ♗e1+ 55 ♗f2 ♗c3 56 ♔f3 ♗g7 57 ♗e1 ♗f8 58 ♗c3 ♗h6 59 f5+ gxf5 60 g5 1-0.